Learning
About
the Law

Second Edition

Learning About the Law

Second Edition

CONSTANTINOS E. SCAROS
Interboro Institute

111 Eighth Avenue, New York, NY 10011
www.aspenpublishers.com

Permissions
Aspen Publishers
111 Eighth Avenue
New York, NY 10011

Printed in the United States of America

1 2 3 4 5 6 7 8 9 0

ISBN 0-7355-5117-0

Library of Congress Cataloging-in-Publication Data

Scaros, Constantinos E.
  Learning about the law/Constantinos E. Scaros.—2nd ed.
      p. cm.
  Includes index.
  ISBN 0-7355-5117-0
  1. Law—United States.   2. Legal assistants—United States—
Handbooks, manuals, etc.   I. Title.

KF387.S297 2005
349.73—dc22

                                                        2004027896

About Aspen Publishers

Aspen Publishers, headquartered in New York City, is a leading information provider for attorneys, business professionals, and law students. Written by preeminent authorities, our products consist of analytical and practical information covering both U.S. and international topics. We publish in the full range of formats, including updated manuals, books, periodicals, CDs, and online products.

Our proprietary content is complemented by 2,500 legal databases, containing over 11 million documents, available through our Loislaw division. Aspen Publishers also offers a wide range of topical legal and business databases linked to Loislaw's primary material. Our mission is to provide accurate, timely, and authoritative content in easily accessible formats, supported by unmatched customer care.

To order any Aspen Publishers title, go to *www.aspenpublishers.com* or call 1-800-638-8437.

To reinstate your manual update service, call 1-800-638-8437.

For more information on Loislaw products, go to *www.loislaw.com* or call 1-800-364-2512.

For Customer Care issues, e-mail *CustomerCare@aspenpublishers.com*; call 1-800-234-1660; or fax 1-800-901-9075.

Aspen Publishers
A Wolters Kluwer Company

Summary of Contents

Contents

8   Criminal Law   157

9   Ethics   199

10 Careers   215

Afterword: Is the Law for You?   225

Appendix A Being a Paralegal   227

Appendix B   The Constitution of the United States   237

Appendix C   The Emancipation Proclamation   257

Appendix D   Court Cases   259

Appendix E   Ethics Codes   345

Preface

This book is intended as valuable reading for anyone interested in learning about the law. Though especially designed for college students, it can and should be read by younger students, older students, paralegals, and anyone else who has a desire to learn about the law.

Chapter 1 introduces the reader to the American legal system, focusing on the three branches of government with particular attention on the judicial system.

Chapter 2 is about legal research. It teaches the reader how to find specific legal authorities and encourages hands-on experience because this is the best way to learn legal research.

Chapter 3 teaches the reader how to brief a case. Two sample cases are provided for the reader to read, analyze, and effectively summarize.

Chapter 4 teaches the very important skill of legal writing. Great emphasis is placed on the importance of good writing for any legal professional.

Chapter 5 introduces the reader to law. The differences between civil and criminal law are outlined, establishing the foundation for subsequent chapters.

Chapters 6, 7, and 8 provide a basic introduction to contracts, torts, and criminal law, respectively. The reader is exposed to many broad elements of these substantive laws, which are at the core of a sound legal education.

Chapter 9 reminds the reader of the ethical obligations of a legal professional. Several hypothetical situations illustrate how a lawyer or paralegal should react to a variety of common dilemmas.

Chapter 10 discusses careers in the law. The chapter emphasizes the range of possibilities within the legal field—virtually everyone can find something that is right for them.

Questions and problems conclude each chapter. They will help the readers review the chapter material, reinforcing their learning about the law.

In the **Afterword**, readers are asked to examine themselves to decide whether the law is an appropriate career choice. While that question may not be completely answered, this portion of the book should elicit some interesting self-analysis.

Appendix A is about being a paralegal. It discusses how broad the title "paralegal" really is, and how greatly the job descriptions and salaries for paralegals vary.

Appendices B through **E** provide examples of the three branches of government at work. First, the **United States Constitution** serves as a valuable starting point because it is the document on which every other law is based.

Next, the **Emancipation Proclamation**, written by President Lincoln, is a historic example of presidential power.

Six **court cases** follow. Their main purpose is to provide the reader with additional exposure to case law and case briefing.

Finally, the **NALA and NFPA codes of ethics** provide valuable models for legal professionals.

For instructors using this book in the classroom, a Teacher's Manual is provided, which should be helpful in answering many questions and as a guide to class preparation.

Acknowledgments

While the list of people who have been positive influences on me is far too numerous to include here, I would like to thank some groups of people.

First of all, all of my loved ones, including family and friends, who have been supportive of this project.

To the wonderful community of Interboro Institute, including administrators, faculty, and staff. Particular thanks to my students, whom I not only teach but from whom I learn.

And, finally, to the folks at Aspen who shared my faith in this project, and who have been very helpful and supportive all the way through.

I gratefully acknowledge the permissions granted to reproduce the following materials:

Figures 1.1 and 1.2: Reprinted with permission of Aspen Publishers.

Figure 2.1: Reprinted with permission from *West's Law Finder*. Reprinted with permission.

Figure 2.2: Reprinted from Shepard's North Eastern Reporter Citations, 2d Series. Reproduced by permission of Shepard's, a subsidiary of The McGraw-Hill companies. Further reproduction of any kind is strictly prohibited.

Figure 3.1: West Group. *Culver v. Culver*, 190 A.D.2d 960. Reprinted with permission.

Figure 9.1: ABA Model Code of Professional Responsibility, Canons 1-9. Copyright ©2004 by the American Bar Association. Reprinted by permission. Copies of ABA Model Code of Professional Responsibility 2004 are available from Service Center, American Bar Association, 321 North Clark Street, Chicago, IL 60610, 1-800-285-2221.

Figure A-1: NALA Code of Ethics and Professional Responsibilities. Courtesy of the National Association of Legal Assistants, Inc.

Figure A-2: NFPA Model Code of Ethics and Professional Responsibility. Courtesy of the National Federation of Paralegal Associations, Inc.

Photo/Cartoon credits: p.3, ©AP Photo/Dennis Cook; p.6, This portrait is from the work *Andrew Johnson: A Study in Courage* by Lloyd Paul Stryker; p.6, ©AP/Wide World Photos; p.6, ©AP/Wide World Photos; p.16, ©Michael Newman/Photo Edit; p.34, p.49, ©PHOTOFEST; ©AP/Photo/Tim Roske; p.69, ©Susan Van Etten; p.101, ©John Neubauer/Photo Edit; p.136, ©AP Photo/Douglas C. Pizac; p.143, ©AP/Wide World Photos; p.173, ©Peter Skinner/Photo Researchers, Inc.; p.184, ©Susan Van Etten; p.211, ©The New Yorker Collection 1989 Henry Martin from cartoonbank.com. All Rights Reserved; p.228, ©PHOTOFEST.

Introduction

Allow me to introduce myself. I am a lawyer, and I also teach law to college students. I wrote this book in order to introduce my teaching approach to the world beyond my classroom door.

First, let me start by telling you some things about the law and lawyers—things that many of my fellow lawyers or professors may not care to admit:

1. The law is a huge collection of simple ideas.
2. These ideas are then intentionally complicated by lawyers and law professors.
3. Accordingly, all "outsiders looking in" to the legal community perceive the law as an extremely difficult concept. It isn't.

Why do those inside the legal community make it so difficult for others to come in? I am certainly not a psychologist, but I have a couple of theories:

Human nature: People who work hard to get somewhere do not want to change the rules for the newcomers. The "insiders" have already paid their dues, so they do not have much sympathy for the next bunch. Also, people generally try to act smarter than they really are, or pretend that whatever knowledge they have attained is more difficult to learn than it really is.

Hazing: The legal community is one big club. Much like fraternities and sororities on college campuses—which torment new "pledges" by making them perform grueling tasks—a legal education appears at times to be nothing more than an initiation process.

Now the good news. I did not write this book in order to speak to you in "legalese" (i.e., legal language, usually not understood by outsiders to the legal community), or to convince you that I am smarter than I really am, or to make you believe that learning the law is some incredibly difficult task that only a genius can master. I wrote this book in order to show you that the best way to learn about the law is to learn the *basics*. I keep such instruction simple. It is important to first master the basics and then worry about the details.

Throughout the book you will encounter many examples and analogies. I have always found that, in both teaching and learning, examples are "the key to life." So here I go with my first analogy: Suppose you know absolutely nothing about auto mechanics, and your friend leads you out to the driveway where you find thousands of individual auto parts. Your friend then tells you, "Okay, now assemble all of these parts together and make a car." You will probably have no idea what to do and will be at best extremely confused.

Now, instead of asking you to assemble a car, imagine that your friend shows you a row of 20 dirty cars, and tells you "Wash and wax all of these." In this case you know that you are in for a great deal of work, but you know *how* to do it. You understand the concept.

In the first scenario, you had a difficult task ahead of you because the idea of assembling the car was completely new to you, and you were confused. But when it comes to washing and waxing, you do not need any special skills. It is not a difficult thing to learn but to do it correctly, you still need to expend time and energy.

Likewise, learning the law is not a difficult and unimaginable task, like assembling a car, but is closer to a big chore that involves simple ideas, like washing and waxing a bunch of cars. But don't panic—the law will not always be as unenjoyable as a row of dirty cars waiting to be washed. The more you study law, the better you will become at mastering the tricks of the trade. Give yourself some time, and it will become as easy as driving your car through an automatic car wash.

Despite my optimism, I do not mean to suggest that learning the law is effortless. It will require some time, energy, and intelligence. However, my book gives you the basics and cuts out the nonsense.

There are many other steps to complete between reading my book and becoming a legal expert. Nonetheless, by the time you have finished this book, you will have mastered the most important part of learning about the law—the basics. And to your surprise, you will find that the experience has been virtually painless!

The American Legal System

1

Chapter Overview

The Legislative Branch
  Term Limits
  State Legislatures
The Executive Branch
  Governors
The Judicial Branch
  State Courts
The System of Checks and Balances
The Supremacy Clause
The Judicial Process
  Jurisdiction
  Basis for Appeal
  Frivolous Lawsuits
The Law in Everyday Life

In beginning our adventure in learning about the law, a great starting point for answering many questions is American history.

The United States operates on a two-tier system of government—**federal** and **state**. What many people often seem to forget is that long before the United States became a political and economic superpower composed of 50 states, it was made up of a handful of independent-minded colonies that were not eager to form one big country. Basically, our government was created by the **United States Constitution**. The Constitution was a compromise that created a federal government and individual state governments. (See Appendix B.)

The Constitution specifically grants certain powers to the federal government. All powers not specifically granted to the federal government, nor contradictory to such powers, are reserved to the states — that is, a state government has the power to create virtually any law that is not specifically granted to the federal government, and is not contradictory to such federal powers or to any right set forth in the Constitution.

Accordingly, we continue to have a federal government working *simultaneously* with 50 individual state governments. Each of these governments, whether federal or state, has its own set of laws. These laws are created by the legislative branch, are carried out by the executive branch, and are enforced by the judicial branch (the courts).

THE LEGISLATIVE BRANCH

Legislative Branch:
The branch of government that creates the law.

Congress:
The U.S. legislative body, composed of the Senate and the House of Representatives.

The **legislative branch** of the United States government is the **Congress.** The Congress is made of two bodies, or "houses": the Senate and the House of Representatives.

The **Senate** is made up of two senators from each state. Each state sends the same number of senators to Congress whether it be a large state like California or a small state like Rhode Island. Accordingly, there are 100 senators in all. Senators serve a term of six years and may be reelected an unlimited number of times.

The **House of Representatives** is made up of 435 persons from the 50 states. Unlike the Senate, each state does not send the same number of representatives to the House. The number depends on each state's population. Representatives serve a term of two years and, like senators, may be reelected an unlimited number of times. Accordingly, there are 535 members of Congress in all.

Term Limits

During the mid-1990s there was a movement throughout the country advocating that members of Congress be subject to term limits. Many people preferred that senators and representatives be permitted to serve for only a specific maximum number of terms.

Supporters of term limits argued that long-time *incumbents* (elected officials already in office) had an advantage over challengers because of their superior financial resources and access to the media. Moreover, they believed that such incumbents would recklessly spend too much money on behalf of their constituents (voters of their state or district) in order to gain reelection.

Those who opposed term limits argued that such a requirement would change the scope of the Constitution, and that term limits already

House of Representatives in Session

existed—in the form of elections. In 1995, the United States Supreme Court declared that imposing congressional term limits would require an amendment to the United States Constitution. Since that time, proponents were unable to gain enough support to pass such an amendment.

State Legislatures

Each state has a congress of its own, commonly known as a **state legislature.** Although the specifics vary from state to state, the legislatures' power and authority are similar to that of the United States Congress.

THE EXECUTIVE BRANCH

The **executive branch** of the federal government is headed by the **President of the United States**, also known as the Chief Executive. The president serves a term of four years and may be reelected only once. Thus, the president may be elected to no more than two terms (a total

Executive Branch: The branch of government that carries out the law.

of eight years). The various administrative government agencies, such as the Federal Bureau of Investigation (FBI), the Central Intelligence Agency (CIA), and the Internal Revenue Service (IRS), are also part of the executive branch. (See Appendix C for an historical example of the exercise of executive power, the Emancipation Proclamation.)

Governors

Like the federal government, each state has an executive branch. The Chief Executive of each state is the **governor.** Every governor is elected to a term of four years, although rules about term limits vary from state to state.

THE JUDICIAL BRANCH

Judicial Branch:
The branch of government that interprets the law.

The **judicial branch** of the federal government includes all of the federal courts (see Figure 1.1). The lowest of these courts are the **district courts**, followed by the **courts of appeals**, and, ultimately, the highest court of our country, the **United States Supreme Court.** The Supreme Court is made up of nine judges, who are called justices. They are appointed by the president, and the appointment must be approved by Congress. The appointments are for life. (See Appendix D for two historically important Supreme Court cases, Brown v. Board of Education (1954) and Roe v. Wade (1973).)

State Courts

Each state has various levels of courts. In some states there are two levels, and in others, three. Generally, a state's highest court is called the Supreme

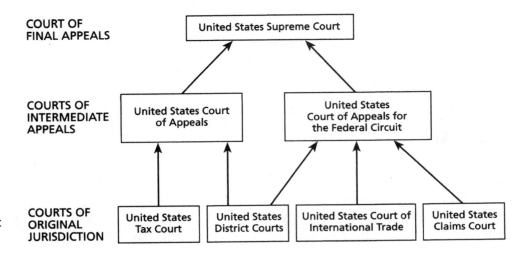

Figure 1.1
The Federal Court System

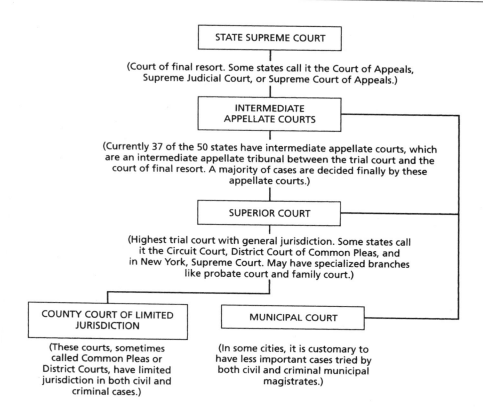

**Figure 1.2
The State Court
System**

Court (see Figure 1.2). But this is not always true. In New York, for example, the Supreme Court is the state's *lowest* court. Later in this chapter we will refer to these "low" courts as trial courts, and to the "high" courts as courts of appeals.

THE SYSTEM OF CHECKS AND BALANCES

In analyzing our three-branch system of government, two questions come to mind: Which branch is the most powerful and influential (1) as established by law and (2) in practical application?

First, let's examine the source of our three-branch system, the United States Constitution. Its authors, collectively known as the Framers, included a system of **checks and balances** in order to prevent any single branch from becoming too powerful. It is this system that allows each branch to "check" on the other two, thus "balancing" the power of government.

For example, as we have already discussed, it is Congress that makes the laws. Proposed laws, known as **bills,** must be approved by the president in order to become actual laws. Moreover, once approved, the Supreme Court may determine whether such laws are consistent with our Constitution. Accordingly, the legislative branch is checked by both the executive and judicial branches.

Bill:
A proposed law to
be brought before a
legislative body.

Next, suppose that the president has taken a particular action. If Congress believes that the act is an unconstitutional abuse of the president's powers, it may call to have the president **impeached.** The president, if convicted, will be removed from office for misconduct.

> ★ **HINT:** Only two presidents have ever been impeached. Do you know who they were? Andrew Johnson and Bill Clinton, our seventeenth and forty-second presidents, respectively. Richard Nixon, our thirty-seventh president, resigned from office but was never impeached.

Moreover, the judicial branch may determine whether a president's conduct is privileged. In 1974, for instance, the United States Supreme Court determined that President Nixon had to turn over tape recordings of certain meetings. Accordingly, the executive branch is checked by both the legislative and judicial branches.

Finally, we can see how the judicial branch is checked by both the legislative and executive branches by looking back at our earlier discussion: A Supreme Court justice, we said, must be appointed by the president, and the appointment must be approved by Congress.

Accordingly, the Constitution provides the system of checks and balances as a method to ensure that no single branch becomes too powerful. But how does this work in practical, day-to-day application? There are many points of view about this question.

Congress makes the laws by which we live. In 1994, for the first time in forty years, the Republican party won control of both houses of Congress.

Andrew Johnson,
Richard Nixon,
Bill Clinton

Why was there so much emphasis placed on this? Because, even though there have been several presidents, both Republican and Democrat, in office during the same forty years, Congress was never controlled by the Republicans during this period. The discussions about the potentially tremendous changes in government that might result is good reason to believe that in many ways Congress may indeed be the most powerful branch of government.

On the other hand, many people argue that nobody is more powerful than the president of the United States. In many ways, the president may be the *single* most powerful and influential public official. The president has broad powers regarding foreign affairs and is the single most recognizable official to the American people. For these reasons, there is a valid argument that the executive branch may indeed be the most powerful.

What about the Supreme Court? Note that presidents, senators, and representatives are all elected for a specific term of years. Supreme Court justices, however, are appointed for *life*. A Supreme Court justice, while appointed to enforce the law, may have a particular judicial philosophy that may change the course of American law. Some justices are **strict constructionists** while others are **loose constructionists**. A strict constructionist generally does not create new law, especially if the issue is not specifically addressed in the Constitution. A loose constructionist, however, may reason that changing times call for changing laws. Confused? Take a look at this example, and it will become clear.

EXAMPLE

• •

Let's take the issue of abortion. There are two prevailing arguments: The "pro-life" argument generally opposes abortion and maintains that a fetus is a human life at any point of development. The "pro-choice" argument emphasizes a woman's right to choose what to do with her own body and suggests that a fetus is not a viable living creature until a certain point in its development.

The pro-life advocates want abortion prohibited, whereas the pro-choice supporters want abortion to remain legal. A strict constructionist will examine the Constitution to determine whether it explicitly or implicitly refers to abortion. If not, then she will probably conclude that the Supreme Court has no authority to support such a law. It would, in her view, be up to the legislature (Congress) to create such a law.

A loose constructionist, however, would consider the changing times, public opinion, and the flexibility of the Constitution. By so interpreting the Constitution, she would create a law regarding abortion even if the legislature is silent on the issue.

Suppose that a president were to appoint, say, three or four Supreme Court justices during a given administration. If these justices were relatively young, they might remain on the Supreme Court for another 30 or 40 years. They would decide the course for America on issues such as abortion, school prayer, or capital punishment for a far longer time period than any president or member of Congress. Accordingly, there is good reason to believe that the judicial branch, in fact, may be the most powerful.

For these reasons, it is apparent that our three-branch system of government is very complex. Each branch has a great deal of power, and there is good reason to believe that any given branch has the *most* power. However, in looking at the big picture, since *all* three branches are very powerful, it is not very likely that any one branch is superior.

THE SUPREMACY CLAUSE

Supremacy Clause:
The U.S.
Constitution's
proclamation of
its superiority over
any state law.

The United States Constitution recognizes that it is "the supreme Law of the Land . . . Laws of any State to the Contrary notwithstanding." This is known as the **supremacy clause**. Thus, the Constitution is superior to any state law. Earlier in this chapter we noted that if a specific power is not designated to the federal government, that power is reserved to the states. How do these two notions compare? Consider the following scenario.

EXAMPLE

Suppose that the state of New Mexico proposed a law requiring all persons who wish to obtain a driver's license to complete ten hours of formal driving instruction. Since such a law is not specifically designated to the federal government, New Mexico (or any other state) has the right to create it. As such a law does not appear to violate the Constitution, it would probably be passed.

Suppose now that there is a federal law requiring each state to perform a specific purification test for its drinking water. Under this law drinking water must be at least 95 percent pure (the term "pure" would further be defined within the actual law). If the state of Tennessee passed its own law requiring that its drinking water be at least 90 percent pure, would this law be permissible under the Constitution? No.

By imposing a *lower* standard, the Tennessee law is actually *in conflict* with the federal law. If, for instance, Tennessee water tested at 92 percent pure, it would satisfy the 90 percent state requirement but not the 95 percent federal requirement.

Suppose, instead, that Tennessee required its drinking water to be 98 percent pure. Would this law be constitutional (permitted under the Constitution)? Yes. Although the standards would still be *different*, they would not be *conflicting*. If Tennessee water tested as 98 percent, 99 percent, or 100 percent pure, it would satisfy *both* the Tennessee law *and* the federal law.

But what if the water tested only 96 percent pure? It would not satisfy the Tennessee law and would not be available for drinking. Would it conflict with the federal law? No. The federal law is only concerned that drinking water be at least 95 percent pure. If a particular state chooses to apply even *stricter* standards, this is not a conflict. Understand?

Having established this basic overview of our two-tier (federal and state), three-branch (legislative, executive, and judicial) system of government, let us now briefly consider the judicial (court) process.

THE JUDICIAL PROCESS

As we discussed earlier, the highest court in our country is the United States Supreme Court. Accordingly, it is the highest court in the land to hear an appeal. Before we actually discuss that court, let's first take a closer look at the judicial process.

The court system is a tool, a vehicle, by which to obtain justice. It is not the *only* vehicle but can often be the most effective one. A lawsuit is a battle, and, as in any other real-life battle, it often proves best to avoid confrontation if possible.

For instance, when people differ in opinion, they usually do not argue. There is even less of a chance that they will physically attack one another. They usually settle their difference in some less drastic way. Similarly, when two parties have a legal dispute, it is rare that they will go through an entire trial to settle their differences. In fact, the overwhelming majority of legal disputes never make it to trial. People usually *settle* their cases long before that. When you think about it, this result makes sense.

EXAMPLE

Suppose that Angelo walked one afternoon into Benson's grocery store. Benson had just finished mopping the floor and had placed a small "Wet Floor" sign at the front of each aisle. Angelo did not notice the sign and proceeded to walk on the freshly mopped floor.

When he realized that the floor was wet, Angelo did not retreat but instead walked more slowly. Nevertheless, Angelo slipped and fell. Luckily, he was not hurt but he did rip his suit pants.

Angelo was very upset because he was wearing one of his finer suits. He took the pants to a tailor, who advised Angelo that he would be better off buying another pair. It cost Angelo $200 to buy a new pair of pants to match his jacket.

Plaintiff:
A person who brings a lawsuit.

Defendant:
A person against whom a lawsuit is brought.

Angelo feels that Benson was at fault and wants to sue him for the value of the pants, $200. If Angelo sues Benson, Angelo will be the **plaintiff** (the person who brings the lawsuit) and Benson will be the **defendant** (the person against whom the lawsuit is brought).

Angelo argues that Benson's sign was too small, and that Benson should not have been mopping the store during business hours. Benson, however, believes that he was not at fault. Benson contends that his store is very busy and often needs mopping during the day. Moreover, Benson feels that since he put a warning sign at every aisle and since Angelo noticed the floor was wet but continued walking on it anyway, Angelo was at fault.

Keep in mind that the amount of money Angelo and Benson are arguing over is $200. In order to fully pursue justice through the judicial system, Angelo will have to sue Benson. This will involve court filing fees, hiring and paying a lawyer, and taking time off from work to attend the trial. Benson, in turn, will also need to make the same investment of time and money. Will all of this effort be worth $200? Probably not.

The dispute will probably be settled out of court. For instance, Benson may offer to give Angelo $100. Angelo, realizing that both he and Benson may have been partially at fault, may be happy with the $100. Now, if Angelo pursues the matter at trial, he will only gain an extra $100. Will it not be easier to just accept $100 now rather than spend so much time and money to gain $200 later? Of course. Accordingly, it is very likely that Angelo will accept Benson's offer, and the matter will be settled.

Litigation:
The process of a case going to trial in court.

However, not all matters are settled out of court. In Chapter 5, we will examine the process of **litigation** (the process in which a case moves toward trial) in detail. But for now let us concentrate more on the actual role and power of the courts.

Think about some court cases you may have read about, both real and fictional. No doubt, you have seen many cases depicted on television or in the movies.

Jurisdiction

Typically, cases you see on television are **trials**, which is the first (and often only) judicial phase of a lawsuit. When the trial is over, the dispute usually comes to a legal end. At times, however, the losing party may **appeal** the trial court's decision.

Appeal:
The act of requesting that a higher court review the decision of a lower court.

Cases are appealed to higher courts. Both the federal government and the state governments have more than one level of courts. The United States Supreme Court is the highest court in the country, and cases may be appealed there from either federal or state courts. In addition, there are certain courts, both on the federal and state levels, that hear cases based on subject matter (such as bankruptcy, criminal, or family matters).

Jurisdiction is the legal power of the court to adjudicate, or judge, a case. What then are the factors that determine jurisdiction?

Location

One of the factors determining jurisdiction is **location.** For example, if a plaintiff who is a resident Of New York sues a defendant who is also a resident of New York, it would make sense that the case be tried in a New York court, right? Of course. Would it make sense for the case to be tried in, say, Kentucky? Generally no. What does Kentucky, for instance, have to do with this matter? Probably nothing. Accordingly, New York would have jurisdiction over the matter but Kentucky would not.

Subject Matter

Another factor is **subject matter.** For example, suppose Ron and Amy want to adopt a baby. Such adoption may be handled by the family court of a particular state. It would not be handled by the criminal court. The family court would have jurisdiction over the matter, whereas the criminal court would not.

Constitutionality

Let's consider one more factor: **constitutionality.** Suppose that a plaintiff challenges a particular state law as violating freedom of speech — a right generally guaranteed by the United States Constitution. When the constitutional question arises (which may be early or late during the course of the legal battle), the United States Supreme Court (and not the state supreme court) has ultimate jurisdiction over the matter.

Now let's examine some of the reasons why a trial decision may be appealed.

Basis for Appeal

Appellant:
A person who brings an appeal (also known as a "petitioner").

Appellee:
A person against whom an appeal is brought (also known as a "respondent").

The person bringing the appeal (the loser at trial) is known as the **appellant**, and the person against whom the appeal is being brought (the winner at trial) is the **appellee**. Alternatively, the appellant is sometimes referred to as the **petitioner**, and the appellee is sometimes referred to as the **respondent**. The following example will help to better explain this point.

EXAMPLE

Suppose that Rita bumps her head as she enters and then falls in Walter's cab. Rita sues Walter for her injuries, claiming that Walter began driving away before Rita completely settled into her seat. Walter in turn claims that he is not liable because Rita was already sitting down when he began driving. He argues that Rita simply started shifting around too much while the cab was moving. Walter owns the cab, and Rita sues him directly.

In this case Rita is the plaintiff, and Walter is the defendant. Suppose that the jury decides in favor of Rita. If Walter is granted an appeal, he will be the appellant (or petitioner). Rita, in turn, will be the appellee (or respondent). But what if the trial jury rules for Walter? In that case, if Rita brings the appeal, she will be the appellant (petitioner) and Walter will be the appellee (respondent).

Suppose that Rita does indeed lose at trial. Will she automatically be granted an appeal? No. An appeal may be based on a variety of reasons, including improper procedure (such as inadmissible evidence) or misinterpretation of the law, but is not granted automatically.

What if an eyewitness saw Walter start driving the cab before Rita fully settled in her seat? If the judge did not allow the eyewitness to testify, Rita may claim that the judge erred. Accordingly, Rita could be granted an appeal on these grounds as well. Later in the book, we will further examine cases where questions of law are raised on appeal.

Frivolous Lawsuits

Over the past few years there has been increasing public concern that there are too many frivolous (unworthy) lawsuits in the United States. Seemingly anyone will sue another over the most trivial matter. Furthermore, it is feared, there are too many attorneys who need work and thus create lawsuits out of thin air.

On the other hand, many argue that our legal system is designed to use the courts as a vehicle to obtain justice. Accordingly, our laws should not prevent the courts from being accessible to the people. If a lawsuit is without merit, this will be proven in a court of law.

To counter the trend of frivolous lawsuits, some critics propose that if a person brings a lawsuit and loses, he should also pay the other person's legal fees. This proposal is regarded by many as a valuable deterrent against frivolous lawsuits, since people will think twice about bringing trivial disputes to court for fear of paying their opponents' attorney fees.

THE LAW IN EVERYDAY LIFE

Unlike many other countries, in the United States it is we, the people, who are responsible for creating and maintaining our existing laws. We vote for the members of Congress who create and change the law. We vote for the president who carries out the law and who appoints the Supreme Court justices who enforce the law.

The laws are created for our benefit, to protect us. While we are all protected by the law, we are required to obey the law so as not to interfere with anyone else's right to be protected as well. However, whether we choose to utilize these laws is up to us.

If we don't like the way something is, we have a right to try to change it. That's what America is all about. This may be done through the courts or by voting in elections. In any event, the system is in place. Whether or not it works for us often depends on how much of an effort we make to use it.

As a lawyer or paralegal, you will be the "driver" of this "vehicle" known as the law. This means that your clients have faith that this vehicle will work for them and that you will be able to "drive" this vehicle to justice. Accordingly, in the chapters ahead you will learn more about how to successfully use the law to benefit your clients.

Key Terms

appeal	governor	respondent
appellant	House of	Senate
appellee	Representatives	state government
bill	impeachment	state legislature
checks and	judicial branch	strict constructionist
balances	jurisdiction	subject matter
Congress	legislative branch	supremacy clause
constitutionality	litigation	trial
court of appeals	loose constructionist	United States
defendant	petitioner	Constitution
district courts	plaintiff	United States Supreme
executive branch	President of the	Court
federal government	United States	

Review Questions

1. What are the two tiers of our system of government?

2. What are the three branches of our system of government?

3. What is the system of checks and balances?

4. What happens if a state law conflicts with a federal law?

5. What is the difference between a plaintiff and a defendant?

6. Describe the basis for an appeal.

7. Name all of the types of courts in your state.

8. What is the difference between a strict constructionist and a loose constructionist?

9. Explain the supremacy clause and give examples.

10. Who are the nine justices of the United States Supreme Court?

Web Sites

- The federal judiciary home page
  http://www.uscourts.gov/
- The United States Supreme Court home page
  http://www.supremecourtus.gov/opinions/opinions.html
- Map of the federal circuits with links to their cases
  http://www.law.emory.edu/FEDCTS
- Information on specific state courts, available through the National Center for State Courts
  http://www.ncsconline.org/D_KIS/info_court_web_sites.html
- The White House
  http://www.whitehouse.gov/

Legal Research: Finding the Law

2

I f a person on a bus steals a woman's purse, should this person go to jail? If a teenager spray paints your car, should the teenager have to pay the cleaning costs? If a man forces a woman to have sex with him, should he be punished? The answer to all of these questions

"Hands-on" legal research

"wrong"? Because we "say so"? Because it wouldn't be "right" if these people were not held accountable for their actions? While all of these explanations may hold merit, the *legal* reason why these people will be held accountable for their wrongdoing is because their actions are against the law. These people can be held liable only if they have broken the law. Accordingly, the only way we can hold someone liable for breaking the law is to know what the law is.

Imagine a prosecuting attorney presenting his case by stating "But your honor, this person did a *bad* thing. It was *wrong*." Without clear proof that the defendant violated an existing law, the prosecutor's case will generally not be successful.

We live in a free society. We can do anything we want to do as long as we do not violate the law. We are not prohibited from acting until the law directs us; the reverse in fact is true: We can do as we please unless the law prohibits us. Therefore, to punish a person or make that person pay damages for some act he committed, we must first establish that that person has broken the law.

In this chapter you will learn many ways of finding the law. This process is known as **legal research.** Before we begin exploring some of these ways, let me give you a bit of advice.

This chapter will serve as a general introduction to the various sources of law and their uses. It is not a "how-to" manual on legal research. In fact, *legal research is best taught "hands on" rather than through a book or in a classroom lecture.* Legal research is, in a sense, much like driving a car. You can sit in a classroom and learn all of the steps but until you get behind the wheel, you will not become proficient at driving. Similarly, a legal research book will take you through some of the steps, and a legal research professor will lecture about the process. To actually become good at finding the law, however, you must get out there and physically do it.

In any event, before you begin your adventure in legal research, you should be familiar with some broad, basic concepts.

SOURCES OF THE LAW

The law can be found through a variety of **sources.** The most common sources, as defined below, are the most valuable tools in solving a particular legal problem. As you become increasingly familiar with these sources, you will grow more comfortable in getting the best use from each of them.

Common Law

The term "**common law**" generally means the law not created by a lawmaking body but incorporated rather from custom and usage. American common law is generally derived from the behavior of the English and American colonial societies. Generally, much of the common law has been adapted or amended into other forms of law we examine below.

Common Law:
Law incorporated from custom and usage.

Statutory Law

A **statute** is a law created by a national, state, or local legislature. Statutes have often replaced common law notions. At times, a statute is simply a formal acceptance of the common law, while at other times it is a complete derivation.

Statute:
A law created by a legislative body.

Case Law

Case Law:
Law created by the court through a case opinion.

Another valuable research tool (one that we will explore more thoroughly in the next chapter) is **case law.** This is law created by the court and interprets common law, statutory law, or previous case law.

As we will discuss later, case law is an insightful source of law because it explains the law as applied to various factual situations.

The Evolving Relationship Between Statutory Law and Case Law

Which came first, the statute or the case? While the answer to that question often varies, one thing is almost certain: Eventually, a relationship will be created between a case and a statute.

EXAMPLE

Suppose that Kyle goes into a bar, drinks several beers, and then gets into his car to drive home. Tom, a police officer, arrests Kyle for drunk driving. Did Tom rightfully arrest Kyle? We all know that the answer to this question is yes (assuming that Kyle was, in fact, drunk). Our answer is certain because in this day and age we are aware that drinking and driving is against the law. But what if this scenario took place much earlier in the century?

Imagine, for instance, that this incident occurred immediately after the automobile was invented and placed on the market. Suppose it was the very first incident of drinking and driving. In that case, Tom the policeman would not be able to arrest Kyle based on a statute, since such a statute would probably not yet *exist*. But what if Kyle caused an accident in which another person was injured or another person's property was damaged? And what if during these events, the court considered the possibility of drunk driving as an offense?

The court would look at **precedent**—that is, previous cases (or the common law) involving similar situations. Obviously, if at that point cars had been on the roads for only a few days, and this was the first incident of its kind, there would be no other case on the books regarding drunk driving. But it is quite possible that there would be cases involving the operation of a *horse and buggy* while driving drunk. Therefore, the court might draw the following analogy: If liability can be imposed for operating a horse and buggy while intoxicated, a similar liability can be imposed for operating a motor vehicle while intoxicated. Accordingly, drinking and driving would now be illegal as a result of case (court-made) law.

Given the court ruling declaring driving while intoxicated to be illegal, the legislature would probably create a statute formally adopting the court's decision. Therefore, the next time a police officer encountered a drunk person driving a car, the officer could make an arrest based directly on the existing statute.

This example shows the creation of case law based on related past law and statutory law evolving from the case law. Now let's examine a situation where case law evolves from statutory law.

Some statutes are concretely clear; they are not subject to significant interpretation. These statutes are commonly referred to as **"black letter" law** (i.e., plainly evident by the black print of the words). Other statutes, however, are overly vague and subject to a great deal of interpretation. Many statutes are somewhere in the middle—not absolutely concrete but not overly vague. It is these statutes that are often subject to interpretation in court by the two opposing attorneys. Take a look at the following examples of black letter law:

Examples of Black Letter Law

1. The maximum speed limit in this state is 55 miles per hour.
2. A person must be 18 years of age or older in order to vote.
3. A person must be 21 years of age or older in order to drink alcoholic beverages.
4. The maximum sentence for auto theft is 15 years.
5. All business establishments that serve alcoholic beverages must not stay open later than 1 A.M.

These examples are not subject to much interpretation. In each there is a fixed number establishing legality or illegality. In Example 1, a person driving zero to 55 miles per hour is within the law. A person driving 56 miles per hour is breaking the law.

In Example 2, a person is not allowed to vote until her eighteenth birthday. But when that person reaches 18, she may vote throughout the rest of her life.

Similarly, in Example 3, a person may drink alcoholic beverages upon the date of his twenty-first birthday. Anytime before that it is prohibited.

Example 4 clearly establishes 15 years as the maximum sentence for auto theft. Accordingly, if a convicted car thief is sentenced to one, two, five, ten, or 15 years in prison, the sentence is legally permissible. If the person is sentenced to 15 years and one day, the sentence is prohibited by law.

Finally, Example 5 specifically requires that businesses that serve alcoholic beverages must close by 1 A.M. Therefore, it is easy to conclude that closing at midnight, 12:30 A.M., 12:45 A.M., or 1:00 A.M. is legal, whereas closing at 1:01 A.M., or beyond, is illegal.

Now compare these examples of "black letter law" with the following unduly vague examples:

★   ★

Examples of Vague Language

1. A person must not drive too fast.
2. A person who is too young may not vote.
3. A person who is too young may not drink alcoholic beverages.
4. The maximum sentence for auto theft must not be excessively long.
5. Businesses selling alcoholic beverages may not stay open very late at night.

★   ★

What do these laws mean? What is "too fast," "too young," "excessively long," or "very late"? Because these standards are extremely difficult to determine, these statutes would probably be repealed for being too vague.

Now let's look at an example where case law may help remedy vague statutes.

EXAGE

• •

A particular statute states that *persons found guilty of reckless driving shall have their license suspended for three months.* Suppose that Ron was arrested for reckless driving because he was driving 100 miles per hour in a 55-miles-per-hour speed zone.

Ron, like the rest of us, is an individual living in a free society. He can do whatever he pleases as long as he does not violate the law. In this case, the applicable law prohibits reckless driving. The question then is: Was Ron guilty of reckless driving? If Ron's driving was reckless, he will have his license suspended for three months; otherwise, he will not. Accordingly, Ron's lawyer will argue that Ron's driving is not considered "reckless" under the statute, whereas the prosecuting attorney will argue that Ron's driving was indeed reckless.

Again, keep in mind that there is no dispute here as to how fast Ron was driving. The only question is whether driving 100 miles per hour in a 55-miles-per-hour speed zone is considered *reckless* driving. Because the statute does not provide a more definitive explanation of "reckless," the next option is to study case law to interpret the statute.

Ron's attorney would be fortunate to find cases that determine that "Reckless driving cannot be established by speeding alone" or "A person driving *110* miles per hour in a 55-miles-per-hour zone can be convicted of speeding but *not* reckless driving."

The prosecuting attorney would best be served by cases that state "When a defendant drives more than 30 miles over the speed limit, this automatically constitutes reckless driving," or "Reckless driving can be established by driving at excessive speeds, which usually means 85 miles per hour or more."

> ★ **HINT:** Since both sides need to find cases that best support their position, there will be an intense "research battle," each side wanting to create a better legal arsenal for its argument.

What if the statute did not identify the standard as reckless driving but instead stated *Persons who drive extremely fast will have their license suspended for three months*. In this instance, how can we determine what "extremely fast" means?

Suppose that Ron's attorney argues that the statute is unduly vague. If the court agrees, the statute will be struck down as being unconstitutional. In that case, the legislature may decide to amend the statute. For example, the new statute may state *Persons who exceed the speed limit by 30 miles per hour will have their license suspended for three months*.

In this example case law overturned statutory law, and the statute was later amended. Such is the evolving, often circular, relationship between case law and statutory law.

Administrative Law

In the previous chapter, we discussed our American legal system. We spoke about the roles of the various branches of government in creating, administering, and enforcing the law. Recall that the president of the United States is head of, or chief executive of, the executive branch of government.

The executive branch, however, is also composed of administrative agencies, to whom Congress has *delegated* the task (given authority and responsibility) of creating certain laws. These laws, as much a part of our legal system as any others, are known as **administrative laws.**

Accordingly, administrative rules and regulations are often highly useful sources of the law.

Administrative Laws: Laws created by administrative agencies.

FINDING THE LAW

Statutes

United States Code:
A text containing federal statutes.

The federal government, as well as each state and local government, makes its laws available in a series of books usually referred to as "The Code." These books are often bound in hardcover or loose-leaf binders. **The United States Code** is commonly available at most well-stocked law libraries, but the state and local codes are harder to find.

Law schools and some colleges often have useful law libraries where you can expect to find the state and local laws of immediate and neighboring locations. For example, a law library in California will probably contain the federal laws, as well as the state laws and the laws of various nearby municipalities. In addition, the library may contain the laws of neighboring states.

Court Cases

Generally, you will analyze decisions of appeals, rather than of trials, when conducting legal research. Appeals cases deal with interpretation of the law whereas trials often concentrate on specific facts. Accordingly, it is the *law interpretation* found in court cases that is useful in determining the meaning of a particular statute; specific facts will usually not serve much educational purpose.

For example, an issue (of *fact*) at trial would be whether or not a store owner's floor was slippery. Whatever the answer, all it proves is that in *that particular situation*, the floor was slippery.

On appeal, however, it is likely the legal issue will be whether a store owner is liable for a shopper's injury when the shopper falls on a slippery floor. This analysis of the law will be useful for future reference.

In any event, a state will typically have one or two tiers of appeals courts. The federal courts, which have jurisdiction over federal cases (such as those involving federal laws), are comprised of federal district courts, courts of appeals, and the United States Supreme Court, which is the highest court in the United States.

Reporters:
A series of books containing a complete set of published cases from a particular jurisdiction or region of jurisdictions.

State cases appear in each state's **reporters** (a series of bound volumes). Moreover, **regional reporters** include cases of a particular geographic region (e.g., the Pacific Reporters include opinions of various Pacific coast states). These regions are shown in Figure 2.1.

Federal cases appear in the **Federal Supplement**, the **Federal Reporter**, or the **United States Reporter**, depending on the tier. Supreme Court cases, which are cited in the United States Reporter, also appear in the Supreme Court Reporter.

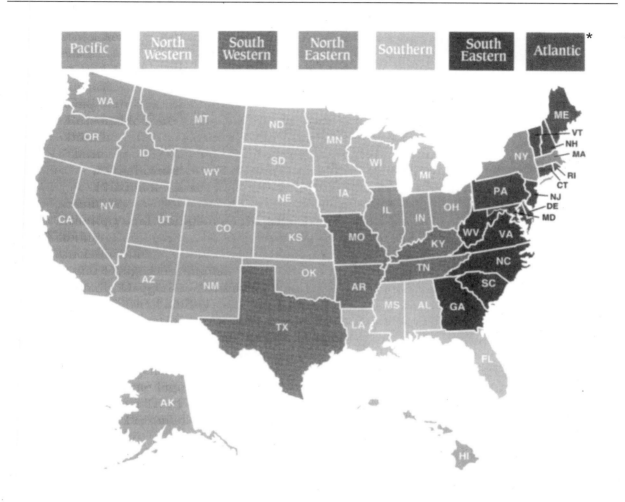

*Editor's Note: The states in each reporting group are as follows:
  Pacific: Alaska, Arizona, California, Colorado, Hawaii, Idaho, Kansas, Montana, Nevada,
    New Mexico, Oklahoma, Oregon, Utah, Washington, and Wyoming.
  North Western: Iowa, Michigan, Minnesota, Nebraska, North Dakota, South Dakota, and Wisconsin.
  South Western: Arkansas, Kentucky, Missouri, Tennessee, and Texas.
  North Eastern: Illinois, Indiana, Massachusetts, New York, and Ohio.
  Southern: Alabama, Florida, Louisiana, and Mississippi.
  South Eastern: Georgia, North Carolina, South Carolina, Virginia, and West Virginia.
  Atlantic: Connecticut, Delaware, Maine, Maryland, New Hampshire, New Jersey, Pennsylvania,
    Rhode Island, Vermont, and District of Columbia.

Figure 2.1
West Reporter System, Showing the States Included in Each Reporter Group

Administrative Laws

Administrative laws may be published directly by each agency and may also be found in the **Code of Federal Regulations (CFR),** which publishes administrative rules and regulations. Daily versions of these laws appear in the Federal Register.

Restatements/Hornbooks/Legal Encyclopedias/Case Digests

While restatements, hornbooks, legal encyclopedias, and case digests vary in form, they are usually texts that explain general or specific principles of law. They may explain a specific state's laws or they may provide a concise anthology of state laws nationwide.

These sources will usually not only describe the law (in varying degrees of detail) but accompany the explanation with citations of court cases from which these explanations are derived.

Specifically, **restatements** and **hornbooks** deal with a particular subject whereas **legal encyclopedias** are (much like general encyclopedias) multivolume sets covering many subjects from A to Z. **Case digests** typically deal with a specific jurisdiction's cases (e.g., California cases), summarizing the law as established by the courts.

These sources are often helpful as a starting point when you know what concept of the law you need to research but are not certain about the details. These books will help you gain a basic understanding of the law and lead you to sources that will be more pertinent to your specific inquiry.

Law Review Articles

Imagine that you have to write a report about Dwight D. Eisenhower. Since Eisenhower was the thirty-fourth president of the United States, it is very easy to find sources discussing his life and times. But what if you had to write a report about John Foster Dulles? Can you identify him? Dulles was secretary of state in the Eisenhower administration. Although there is written information about him, it is probably not as easy to find as information relating to a U.S. president. Wouldn't it be nice if you had a friend who had written a report about Dulles? That's what **law review articles** are: Reports about a particular case, statute, or area of the law, written by law professors, judges, lawyers, law students, or other legal scholars and published by law schools nationwide.

Law review articles are valuable in conducting your research. Suppose, for example, that you need to research the developing law regarding sexual harassment in the workplace. You can certainly find a great number of law review articles dealing with this subject. Accordingly, you have much of the research already done for you.

★ **HINT:** Keep in mind that you should not submit a law review article as your own product because that would be *plagiarism*. You may, however, freely quote from such article as long as you identify it as your source.

Primary vs. Secondary Sources

A **primary source** is firsthand; it is the actual law. A **secondary source** is secondhand; it explains or otherwise describes the primary source (law).

Statutes, cases, and administrative laws and regulations are primary sources, whereas restatements, hornbooks, legal encyclopedias, case digests, and law review articles are secondary sources.

Primary Source:
A firsthand source—the actual law.

Secondary Source:
An authority of law that explains or otherwise describes a primary source.

EXAMPLE

• •

Suppose a particular state statute reads as follows: "An employer may not terminate an employee without sufficient cause." In a subsequent case the judge rules that repeated lateness is sufficient cause for the purposes of termination. Both the statutory language and the case decision are *primary* sources.

Now suppose that someone writes a law review article analyzing employment law in that particular state. The author includes the above statute and case as examples. The law review article is a *secondary* source, which refers to *primary* sources (the statute and the case).

A researcher is much like a detective trying to solve a mystery. Suppose you were assigned to solve a crime. In interviewing various people, you spoke with Rose, who told you that Michael witnessed the crime. Rose then is your secondary source, who will lead you to Michael, your primary source.

Similarly, as a paralegal, you will often begin with secondary sources, which will ultimately lead you to primary sources.

SHEPARDIZING: UPDATING THE LAW

Is abortion legal in the United States? Is it legal to pay an employee less than minimum wage? Are citizens of the United States free to move from one state to another? Are American citizens allowed to be married to more than one person at the same time?

You can probably answer these questions instantly because the correct answers are based on laws that you are very familiar with. Some laws are greatly familiar to everyone and, accordingly, create no need for a great deal of research. However, other laws are not very well known. In fact, most people, including lawyers and paralegals, are not familiar with them unless they conduct research.

EXAMPLE

Suppose that Janet, a nonsmoker, works for a company filled with smokers. In 1990 her state's highest court decided that due to the alleged dangers of secondhand smoke, smoking would be prohibited in the workplace. Suppose that Janet seeks to extinguish smoking in her company and hires your firm to file suit. Imagine that in your research, you encounter a case, decided in 1975, that states that nonsmoker employees do not have a right to a smoke-free environment in the workplace.

What if you rely on this 1975 decision and tell Janet that she does not have a valid claim against her company? Obviously, you will not be doing your job very well, since in 1990, 15 years *after* the case you discovered, the law changed. Under the current law Janet does indeed have a very strong claim against her company. The question, then, is *How do you know if the law that you discover is still "good" (valid)?*

Shepardizing:
The act of updating the law by use of Shepard's citators.

The answer is **shepardizing.** The term, derived from the **Shepard's citators** (the books used for shepardizing), means to update the law. Shepardizing is an easy-to-use system that allows you to determine if the law that you found is still valid. In the above example, for instance, by shepardizing the 1975 case you would have discovered that the 1990 case overturned it, thus changing the law. See Figure 2.2 for an example of a page from a Shepard's citator.

The most important steps you need to know about shepardizing are as follows:

★ ─── ★

1. Make sure you have all of the Shepard's citators you need.
2. Make sure that for every case (or statute) that you seek to shepardize, you look at the Shepard's volumes covering every day from the date when the case was decided (or the statute was enacted) until the present.

★ ─── ★

First, you need to have all of the necessary Shepard's volumes. These can be found in your library. Next, you must look through these volumes from the date the case (or statute) was decided (enacted) until the present.

These volumes will list each case's citation (including volume and page numbers) followed by a list of citations of subsequent cases that mentioned this case. The case may have been "followed" or "discussed"

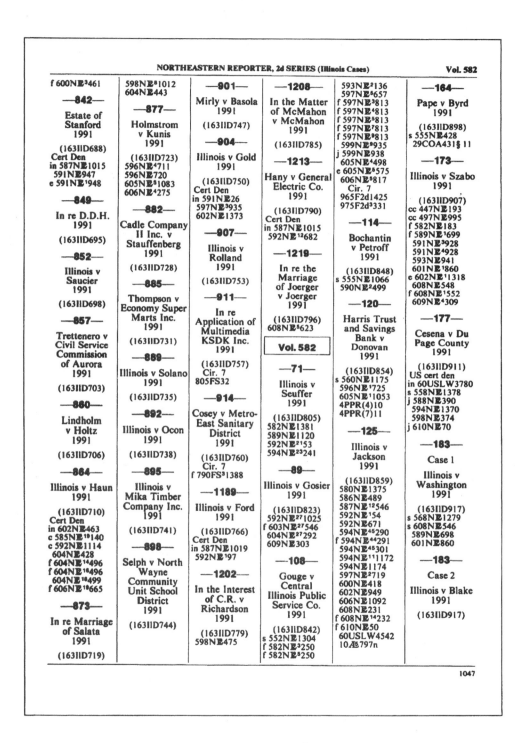

Figure 2.2
Sample Page from Shepard's Citator

or may be the "same case" in a parallel citation (for example, it may be a California case also found in the Pacific Reporter). If the case is "overturned," "distinguished," or "reversed," or there is another treatment that can raise some questions as to the continuing validity of its legal significance, then you should look at these subsequent cases to check for any inconsistency.

Suppose, then, that you are shepardizing the 1975 case in the above example. There are three volumes of Shepard's citators available:

Volume I: Cases from 1800 to 1925
Volume II: Cases from 1926 to 1976
Volume III: Cases from 1977 to the present

Which volumes will you need to look through in order to shepardize your case? Volumes II and III. Why? Because in order to make sure the law represented by the case is completely reviewed, you need to know if it was changed in any way *from the date of its creation until the present*. Volume I is completely unnecessary since it deals with cases that were decided from 1800 to 1925. Since your case was decided in 1975, this volume will not even mention it.

Volume II is necessary because if the case was overturned at any time between 1975 and 1976, this information will be found in this volume.

Similarly, Volume III is vital because if the 1975 case was overturned between 1976 and the present, such information is contained in this volume. In fact, as we mentioned in our example, the case *was* overturned in 1990. Accordingly, this information will be found in Volume III because 1990 falls within the range of years that volume covers.

Consider the following example to help you understand this point.

EXAMPLE

• •

Suppose that a local chapter of the United States Veterans Association was throwing a celebration party commemorating the fiftieth anniversary of D-Day, the famous military victory secured by the United States and the other Allied forces during World War II. The veterans group wanted to contact all of the veterans who fought in that battle, which took place on June 6, 1944.

Suppose, then, that three veterans directories listed all United States veterans since 1800 by the year in which they died. The veterans group used these volumes to discover if a particular veteran died. Any names not on these lists would then be considered for invitation to the party.

Directory I lists veterans who died from 1800 to 1925.
Directory II lists veterans who died from 1925 to 1976.
Directory III lists veterans who died from 1977 to the present.

In searching for veterans who were last seen alive on June 6, 1944, which directories must be searched to determine if any of these people have since died? Volumes II and III.

Directory I only lists veterans who died up until 1925. Accordingly, this would not cover veterans who died afterwards. If a particular veteran died in 1957, 1962, or 1978, for example, this volume would be useless. So which volumes are necessary to establish if a veteran died at any point from June 7, 1944, until the present? Volume II *and* Volume III are needed for a complete review of this information.

If this basic summary of shepardizing confuses you, your reaction is *very typical*. The only way you will become thoroughly familiar with this concept is to go out there and do it — hands on. However, at the very least, you now have a *basic* idea of what shepardizing is all about.

COMPUTERIZED LEGAL RESEARCH

For years the only way to conduct legal research was manually. If you wanted to look up a case, statute, or principle of law, you would have to go to the bookshelf and pull the appropriate book. Given the sweeping revolution of computer technology, most of the legal information you will ever need to research is now available on computer. There are several advantages to computerized legal research:

1. Only the best-stocked law libraries will contain volumes of case reporters from Alaska to Wyoming. Many will contain only the home state reporters and those for large or neighboring states. But with a computer, you have legal information from *all 50 states* at your fingertips.
2. Computerized research gives you quick and easy access to a variety of ways to find what you are looking for.
3. You can completely shepardize a case with the touch of one key.

There are, however, reasons why you should not limit yourself to computerized legal research but should also be thoroughly familiar with manual research:

1. Computerized legal research is often expensive. Accordingly, some law firms and other companies use it sparingly, or may be not at all.
2. If you want to copy your research for future reference, it is usually quicker to copy a book page on a copying machine than to print from the computer terminal. Moreover, the computerized printout

format is not as easy to read as the manual books. If you are copying a small number of pages, it is no major concern. However, if you have close to 100 pages of research, it may be quicker and easier to copy them from a book.

3. Computerized legal services often do not provide cases and statutes that are extremely old. Although it is not highly probable that you will *ever* need to research a case that is over 100 years old, the possibility does exist. Whereas a computerized service may not go back that far, such a case will be printed in a book. (Again, it is very rare for such antiquated cases to be used in modern-day research projects.)

Two common computerized legal research services are **Lexis** and **Westlaw.** They are competing services, and both are quite popular and effective. Given the current technological explosion, they are certainly not the only computerized research tools on the market. Quite often, however, legal professionals continue to refer to computerized legal research generically as "Lexis" or "Westlaw."

> ★ **HINT:** You should practice and become proficient in both manual and computerized research. Being very familiar with both formats will make you increasingly marketable to prospective employers.

FINAL THOUGHTS

Now you have some idea of what legal research is all about. To sum up: In order to provide a convincing legal argument, you must cite (i.e., formally refer to) the law. The law can be found in statutes, cases, restatements, hornbooks, legal encyclopedias, and law review articles. Once you discover your source of law, you must update (shepardize) the law to make sure it is still "good" (i.e., valid). Finally, you can conduct your research manually or by computer.

When doing research, you must remember to be *thorough*. There is no specific amount of research you have to do, just as long as you cover your subject matter thoroughly, and you do your best not do be outdone by your opponent.

Suppose, for example, that you find seven cases supporting your argument. Is that enough? Probably, if your opponent finds *no* cases supporting her argument; probably not, if your opponent finds 30 cases in her favor.

Success means doing better than your competitor, the opposing attorney. A boxer, tennis player, or race car driver will win if their opponents are not as good. There is no set standard of success; the important thing is to be well trained and prepared in order to have a good chance of beating your opponent.

Although many find legal research to be tedious and boring, it's all a matter of how one looks at it. If you are doing something you believe in, research can be challenging and, as a result, entertaining.

Now that you know where to find the law, let's take a look at how to analyze it and at court cases in particular.

Key Terms

administrative law	hornbook	restatement
"black letter" law	law review article	secondary source
case digest	legal encyclopedia	shepardizing
case law	legal research	Shepard's citators
Code of Federal	Lexis	source
Regulations	precedent	statute
(CFR)	primary source	United States Code
common law	recklessness	United States
Federal Reporter	regional reporter	Reporter
Federal Supplement	reporter	Westlaw

Review Questions

1. What are some of the main sources of law?

2. What is common law?

3. Where may case law be found?

4. What is the difference between primary and secondary sources?

5. What is a law review article?

6. What is shepardizing, and why is it important?

7. What are the advantages and disadvantages of computerized legal research?

8. What is black letter law?

9. What is administrative law and where may it be found?

10. Describe how courts may use precedent in making a decision.

Web Sites

- LexisNexis
  http://www.lexisnexis.com/
- Westlaw
  http://www.westlaw.com
- Loislaw
  http://www.loislaw.com/
- The Virtual Chase (free legal research)
  http://www.virtualchase.com/
- Legal Resource Links
  http://www.legalresourcelinks.com/

Briefing a Case

3

Consider this chapter as a three-part lesson, answering the following questions:

1. What is a case brief?
2. Why are case briefs important?
3. How is a case briefed?

WHAT IS A CASE BRIEF?

Case Brief:
A summary of a case opinion.

A **case brief** is a summary of an opinion (i.e., a written case decision issued by the court). Can you recall ever reading a *book* and being asked to write a *book report* about it? Well, a *case brief* is a *report* about the *case*.

As the previous chapter explained, a case begins at the trial level, and, if the losing party's motion to appeal is granted, the case moves up to an appellate court. The cases that you are most likely to brief are appeals; these are the cases in which judges *interpret* the law.

A judge or group of judges will write an opinion. To do a case brief you will read this opinion and write an account that summarizes the opinion's important points.

Case briefs are **objective.** You will write what the judge decided, not whether you agree with the decision or not. You will limit your report to what was written and not add any of your own ideas. There are plenty of other legal documents that provide you an opportunity to be creative and voice your own opinion; a case brief is not one of them.

Panel of Judges

WHY ARE CASE BRIEFS IMPORTANT?

Case briefs are historical. They allow us to look at the past, often for the purpose of determining the present and shaping the future. Consider this example: The U.S. Constitution's First Amendment states that "Congress shall make no law respecting an establishment of religion, or prohibiting the free exercise thereof." We know for certain that this states the supreme law of the land. There is no higher authority than the U.S. Constitution. What we may not be sure of, however, is exactly *what* this law means. In light of the First Amendment, consider the following argument.

EXAMPLE

• •

Suppose that Andrea, Bobbie, Calvin, and David all work at the post office (a federal building). Andrea is Jewish, Bobbie is Muslim, Calvin is Christian, and David does not practice any religion.

In early December the postal workers decide to create a holiday display on a large post office wall. Calvin, who is a talented artist, paints a scene of the birth of Jesus Christ.

David objects to the religious display, contending that the First Amendment states that the government shall neither advance nor inhibit religion. He considers a religious painting on a post office wall to be an unconstitutional government advancement of religion. David argues that the First Amendment was written to keep any type of religious displays off of government property.

Calvin argues that the removal of his painting would amount to an unconstitutional government inhibition of religion. He believes that the First Amendment was written to prevent the government from *imposing* religion on the American people or from preferring one religion over another. Accordingly, Calvin believes that he and other post office employees have the right under the Constitution to decorate the post office with their own religious displays.

Thus, Calvin would support Andrea and Bobbie decorating the post office with their own religious symbols. Moreover, Calvin believes that David has the right to express his view with material that denounces religion.

In short, David believes that the First Amendment means no religious displays on government property. Calvin contends that anyone can place any religious display on government property, as long as everyone else has an equal chance to do the same, and one display is not given priority over another.

Which argument is correct? Recall our earlier conclusion: The Constitution is the supreme law of the land. But the problem is *what* exactly does the First Amendment mean?

Over the past-two centuries the First Amendment has been debated endlessly. There are scores of cases on record that address the answer to the above question. These interpretations of the law serve as valuable tools necessary for building a sound legal argument. How would you answer the question? Whatever your answer, you need the law as your foundation.

In this case, citing the First Amendment may not be enough. You need case law, written by judges who have interpreted the law. Accordingly, reading old cases is very important in determining present case law, which, in turn, will set precedent for the future.

HOW IS A CASE BRIEFED?

As you will continue to discover, a great deal of attention is paid to **format** when drafting legal documents. A case brief, which is a report about a case, is comprised of four basic steps:

★
FACTS:	The facts of a case state what happened.
ISSUE:	The issue is the question brought before the court.
HOLDING:	The holding is what the court has decided, the answer to the initial question.
REASONING:	The reasoning is why the court has decided as it did.
★

Some authorities may recommend other steps, such as cause of action, procedural history, and so on. These steps are not wrong but nevertheless are just a way to "dress up" the brief a little bit. They are icing on the cake. You should concentrate on the four basic steps mentioned above.

Opinion:
The decision by the judge or judges in a court case.

The judge's decision, known as the **opinion,** is a story. When briefing a case, you must read this story carefully and write a report about it. Let's examine each of the four steps in greater detail.

Facts

Facts:
In a case brief, an account of what happened.

The **facts** of a case state what happened. If the example about the postal workers was an actual court case now being briefed, the relevant facts would include Calvin's painting a religious scene and displaying it on the post office wall. It would also be important to discuss David's objection and the language of the First Amendment. Does it matter how old Calvin is? What Andrea is wearing? What Bobbie had for lunch? How many letters David delivered that day? No. None of these facts are relevant.

The opinion is a story as narrated by the judge. Each judge will have a different "storytelling" style. Just as some people get directly to the point while others ramble on and on, judges do the same thing when writing an opinion. (Sometimes the judges instruct their clerks to write the opinion and then simply proofread the final draft. This point about writing style applies in any event.)

Furthermore, some judges, though possessing brilliant legal minds, are horrible writers! Much like a person who is a great driver but has no patience or ability to teach another person how to drive, a judge may know all about the law but have trouble conveying its meaning to others. Also, since each opinion you read may be written by a different judge, there is an even greater chance of disparity in writing style. Some opinions are a breeze — flowing, easy to read. Others are a nightmare. You may have to read through them a couple of times before you figure out what the judge is trying to say.

While narrating the facts of a case, some judges will get right to the point, discussing only the relevant facts. Other judges, however, will spend numerous paragraphs, even pages, addressing the most trivial matters. Accordingly, it is your job to filter out the irrelevant facts and only report those that have bearing on the ultimate issue. You will understand this point better when you master some examples later in this chapter.

Issue

After you have explained to your reader the relevant matters that occurred, you must then discuss what the court is ultimately trying to decide. This is the **issue.** Why are these parties, the plaintiff and defendant, in court? Have they nothing better to do with their time? Are they just wasting their own time and the court's? Are they in court to hear themselves (or their attorneys) speak? Why are they there? *What question are they ultimately disputing?*

Consider the following in order to gain a better understanding of defining an issue.

EXAMPLE
• •

Let's resume our earlier example. Suppose that David sues Calvin (and the U.S. Postal Service) to remove the religious painting from the post office wall. The issue can be determined by first considering why David and Calvin are in court. David is suing Calvin in order to have the painting removed. In order for David to obtain justice, he has to prove that Calvin has done something unlawful. After all, David cannot simply ask the court to remove the painting just because he "feels like it." David can only use the court system as a tool to gain justice if the law has been violated. Therefore, David will use the U.S. Constitution as his source of law, and claim that it is unconstitutional under the First Amendment to display a religious painting on government property.

Calvin, in turn, will argue that the First Amendment permits the freedom of religion, and removing the painting violates his constitutional right. Therefore, the issue will be based on the source of law — the U.S. Constitution. Although there are various ways to phrase the issue, notice that in all of the following examples, the question addresses the constitutional/First Amendment issue.

Examples of Issues: Correct Form

Is it constitutional to display a religious painting on government property? OR

Is it a violation of the First Amendment to display a religious painting inside a U.S. Post Office? OR

Is it permissible under the First Amendment to display a religious painting on government property? OR

Must religious displays be prohibited on government property?

Now compare the above versions with the following:

Examples of Issues: Incorrect Form

Will David win in his lawsuit against Calvin? OR

Must the religious painting be taken down? OR

Will Calvin be allowed to keep the painting on the wall?

Why are these forms incorrect? Because they are too general and do not address the true question of *law*. The first question, "Will David win?" can be asked in virtually *any* situation. It is not enough. You can look at 100,000 cases and always ask, "Will plaintiff win?" or "Will defendant lose?" or vice versa. If you ask such a question and arrive at a yes-no answer, you must still ask why.

Suppose, for instance, that the court decides that the First Amendment prohibits any religious displays on government property. Accordingly, if the question is "Will David win his lawsuit against Calvin?" the answer is yes. However, that question and answer do not even begin to describe what type of case this is. A more specific issue would be "Is it constitutionally permissible to display religious paintings on government property?" The answer would be no, but it would be an answer to a more complete, specific question.

When trying to decide what the issue is, ask yourself: "What is the one question that, when answered, will shed light on everything going on in this situation?" When you determine what that question is, you have found your issue.

Question of Law vs. Question of Fact

Typically, the issue will be a question of *law* rather than a question of *fact*. A question of law is a dispute as to what the law states regarding a particular situation. A question of fact disputes the actual happenings of that situation. Confused? Take a look at this example.

EXAMPLE

Suppose that Smith is murdered, and there is speculation that the murderer lives in the same neighborhood as the victim. In an effort to solve the crime, Officer Jones randomly breaks in and searches apartments in the neighborhood, without a warrant, to find the murder weapon. Jones breaks into Dylan's apartment and discovers the murder weapon, a gun. Dylan argues that he did not murder Smith.

At trial it is proven that the bullets found in Smith's body were fired by Dylan's gun. Accordingly, the jury finds Dylan guilty of Smith's murder. On appeal, Dylan's lawyer argues that the murder weapon should not have been admitted as evidence because it was obtained without a search warrant.

Whether Dylan murdered Smith is a question of fact. It is one person's word against another's and the law is not in dispute. If Dylan did murder Smith, he is guilty; if not, he is innocent. The only question is whether the jury will believe Dylan's version of the story.

Whether Dylan's gun should be admitted as evidence is a question of law. This question will be decided on appeal. And the question will be "Is evidence obtained during a warrantless search of a person's home admissible in court?" Even where there is no question as to the *facts* — whether Dylan killed Smith — the question of *law* remains unanswered.

Briefs Based on Appeals Rather Than Trials

Most of the cases you will brief will be appeals, because they deal with questions of law, rather than trials, which deal primarily with questions of fact. Why would you benefit more by analyzing questions of law than questions of fact? Because a question of fact is only as good as that particular case. But a question of law, once answered, may be applied to future cases.

EXAMPLE

• •

Suppose that Gerald robs a grocery store. He is found guilty at trial and sentenced to 20 years in prison. A question of fact would be, "Did Gerald rob the grocery store?" A question of law, perhaps on appeal, would be, "Is 20 years' imprisonment an excessive sentence for robbing a grocery store?"

The question of fact will not help you in future cases. What if Gerald did, in fact, rob the store—does this mean another defendant, charged with a similar robbery, is guilty, too? Of course not. Or, what if Gerald is innocent—does this mean another defendant is also innocent? No. One question of fact has nothing to do with another.

A question of law, however, may be applied to future situations. Suppose, for instance, that the court decided on appeal that 20 years' imprisonment is not an excessive sentence for robbing a grocery store. This law may be applied to any future case involving a similar crime.

Accordingly, if you brief a question of law, the information may be applied to present and future cases. A question of fact, however, will usually serve no purpose outside the case in which it is raised. The issue, which is probably the most difficult of the four steps of case briefs to master, should state a question that when answered, gives the most complete description of the situation.

★ **HINT:** When briefing a case, there may be more than one issue. However, you should try and narrow the issue down to the most specific form. Take a look at the sample case briefs found later in this chapter.

Holding

Holding:
The court's
decision.

The **holding** is what the court has decided and states the answer to the question. Let us again consider the earlier example about the religious painting in the post office. In that case, the court held that religious displays on government property are impermissible because they violate the First Amendment. Accordingly, if the issue is, "Is it constitutionally permissible to display religious paintings on government property?," the holding is no.

Length of the Holding

Legal educators commonly place greater emphasis on "legalese" than on simple, commonsense instruction. One consequence of this misplaced value is needlessly long case holdings. Notice that the holding in the above case is a one-word answer: no. In fact, the holding will often be nothing more than a yes-no answer.

Holdings longer than a yes-no answer are usually wasteful and often confusing. If, however, you feel the need to "dress up" the holding a bit, you may do so in the following manner.

EXAMPLE

• •

1. Returning to the example of Calvin and David, you may add to your "no" answer by turning the question (issue) into a statement. Accordingly, your holding may read, *No. Religious paintings on government property are constitutionally impermissible. The painting in the post office must be removed.* The last sentence connects the holding to the specific set of facts at hand.

2. Alternatively, you may add to the "no" answer by discussing this decision with respect to a lower court's decision. Recall that the cases you are briefing will most often be appeals, which means that they were originally decided by a lower court. If the current decision is in agreement with the lower court, the lower court's decision is **affirmed.** If the current decision disagrees with the earlier decision, the lower court's decision is **reversed.** Suppose, then, that the lower court in this case had allowed the painting to remain on the post office wall. Since the appellate court has overturned that decision, your holding may read: *No. The lower court's decision is reversed.* Consider, then, these alternate holdings of varying lengths:

ISSUE:	Is it constitutionally permissible to display religious paintings on government property?
HOLDING:	No. OR
	No. Religious paintings on government property are constitutionally impermissible. The painting in the post office must be removed. OR
	No. The lower court's decision is reversed.

In fact, you may use any combination of the above. However, I cannot stress enough the importance of simplicity when dealing with legal documents. For this reason, I see no need for the holding to go beyond the yes-no answer in most cases. If you do indeed feel compelled to add more for whatever reason, you may "dress up" the holding as illustrated above. Do not, however, state the elements of the reasoning in the holding.

Reasoning

Reasoning:
In a case brief, the explanation for the holding.

While the holding identifies *what* the decision is, the **reasoning** explains *why* the court reached that decision. In the above case the reasoning could be written as follows:

> The First Amendment clearly prohibits government involvement in the advancing or inhibiting of religion. In this case, a religious painting was hung on a post office wall. Allowing the painting to remain on the wall effectuates the advancement of religion. Since the First Amendment intended the government to remain completely neutral regarding religion, this painting and all others advancing or inhibiting religion have no place on the walls of government property.

The reasoning need not be exactly the length set forth above. It may be shorter or longer, as long as it accurately captures the reason why the court decided the holding as it did.

The above example about the religious painting was not a real case but one created to assist in explaining the essentials of the briefing process. However, it is quite possible that such a case, or one very similar, did actually exist.

EXAMPLES OF CASE BRIEFING

Look at the following case opinion, taken from an actual court case, and study the sample brief that follows.

Culver v. Culver
594 N.Y.S.2d 68 (App. Div. 1993)

CASEY, Justice.
   Appeal from an order of the Family Court of Warren County (Austin, J.), entered September 23, 1991, which granted petitioners' application, in a proceeding pursuant to Family Court Act article 6, for custody of respondents' children.

At issue on this appeal is whether Family Court erred in granting petitioners' application for custody of their two grandchildren. Respondent Faith Culver (hereinafter respondent), the mother of the two children, had physical custody of the children after she and petitioners' son, who is the children's father, separated in December 1986. Concerned about a lack of stability in the home environment provided for the children by respondent, petitioners sought in October 1990 temporary custody of the children until either of the children's parents developed more stability. Petitioners' son consented to the application, but respondent opposed it. After a fact-finding hearing conducted in late 1990 and early 1991, Family Court granted the petition, resulting in this appeal by respondent.

The Court of Appeals recently reiterated that "[a] biological parent has a right to the care and custody of a child, superior to that of others, unless the parent has abandoned that right or is proven unfit to assume the duties and privileges of parenthood, even though the State perhaps could find 'better' parents" (Matter of Michael B. [Marvin B.], 80 N.Y.2d 299, 309, 590 N.Y.S.2d 60, 604 N.E.2d 122), a principle that has long been recognized in New York (see People ex rel. Kropp v. Shepsky, 305 N.Y. 465, 468, 113 N.E.2d 801). Family Court found that respondent was not unfit, but that "extraordinary circumstances" justified the change in custody from the children's mother to their paternal grandparents. In Matter of Bennett v. Jeffreys, 40 N.Y.2d 277, the Court of Appeals explained that "intervention by the State in the right and responsibility of a natural parent to custody of her or his child is warranted if there is first a judicial finding of surrender, abandonment, unfitness, persistent neglect, unfortunate or involuntary extended disruption of custody, or *other equivalent but rare extraordinary circumstance which would drastically affect the welfare of the child*" (id., at 549, 387 N.Y.S.2d 821, 356 N.E.2d 277 [emphasis supplied]). "So long as the parental rights have not been forfeited by gross misconduct . . . or other behavior evincing utter indifference and irresponsibility . . . the natural parent may not be supplanted . . ." (Matter of Male Infant L., 61 N.Y.2d 420, 427, 474 N.Y.S.2d 447, 462 N.E.2d 1165 [citations omitted]).

The "extraordinary circumstances" found by Family Court are based upon the following findings: (1) respondent's "lack of an established household of her own and her numerous changes of residence, most of which had unsuitable accommodations for the children," (2) the existence of a "psychological bond of the children to petitioners," (3) the parental attention and love given to the children by respondent has been "sporadic," and (4) "the profound insecurity of the children's lives with respondent and the resulting deleterious effect upon them." Based upon our review of the record on appeal, we find no evidence to support the findings of insecurity and the deleterious effect upon the children. Noticeably absent is any expert testimony regarding the physical, mental or emotional health of the children.

Assuming that the evidence is sufficient to support the other three findings by Family Court, we are of the view that those findings are insufficient to constitute the requisite extraordinary circumstances. The first and third findings have a direct bearing on respondent's fitness as a parent, but Family Court expressly refused to find her unfit. We conclude that the first and third findings are irrelevant and impermissible considerations unless they are sufficient to establish respondent's persistent neglect or unfitness (see Matter of Male Infant L., supra, at 430, 474 N.Y.S.2d 447, 462 N.E.2d 1165). At most, respondent and her family moved eight times in six years and many of the moves were prompted at least in part by the financial problems associated with being a single parent who was receiving little or no child support from the children's father, petitioners' son. The evidence does not support the finding that most of the residences were inadequate. Assuming that there is sufficient evidence to support the finding that the parental attention and love given to the children by respondent was sporadic, this finding does not establish the persistent neglect necessary to rise to the level of an extraordinary circumstance (cf. Matter of Bisignano v. Walz, 164 A.D.2d 317, 319, 563 N.Y.S.2d 938). We conclude that the first and third findings relied upon by Family Court, considered alone or cumulatively, are insufficient to establish the type of gross misconduct or other behavior, evincing utter indifference and irresponsibility necessary to supplant the natural parent (see Matter of Male Infant L., supra, 61 N.Y.2d at 427, 474 N.Y.S.2d 447, 462 N.E.2d 1165). Finally, we are of the view that the claimed psychological bond between the children and their grandparents has no bearing on respondent's rights as a natural parent in the absence of unfitness, abandonment, persistent neglect or other gross misconduct or grievous cause (see Matter of Dehar v. Dehar, 134 A.D.2d 656, 657, 521 N.Y.S.2d 335). Respondent is entitled to the custody of her children (see Matter of Abaire v. Himmelburger, 163 A.D.2d 626, 558 N.Y.S.2d 678). We find it unnecessary to address the parties' remaining contentions.

ORDERED that the order is reversed, on the law, with costs, and petition dismissed.

Mikoll, J.P., and Yesawich, Mercure and Crew, JJ., concur.

Before you read any further, do you understand what you've just read? It is very likely that you are confused, and that is normal. As I pointed out earlier, "legalese" — the language of legal terms — is an unfortunate consequence of the law, and it often exists in case opinions. The best way to overcome the obstacle of legalese is to understand it. Read the case over and over, if necessary, until you develop a good understanding of what is going on. After you understand the "story," write a "report" about it, using the four steps we discussed: Facts, Issue, Holding, and Reasoning. Then compare your brief with the one set forth below.

A correct answer may have many forms. It is not likely that your brief will be the same, word for word, as the one printed below. In fact, it may vary slightly or greatly. However, as long as the *main points* of each section are similar, your brief is correct.

SAMPLE CASE BRIEF

CULVER v. CULVER

594 N.Y.S.2d 68 (App. Div. 1993)

FACTS:	Respondent is the biological mother of two children. Petitioners are the children's paternal grandparents. Respondent is separated from petitioners' son and has sole custody of the children. Petitioners contend that respondent changed residences an excessive amount of times, living in unsuitable accommodations, and she gave only sporadic love and attention to her children. Accordingly, petitioners seek temporary custody of the children, until either parent has developed more stability. The trial court, while not finding the mother unfit, granted petitioners' application for custody. Respondent appeals to this court.
ISSUE:	May the State deny child custody to a biological parent where the parent is not unfit?
HOLDING:	No. The trial court's decision is reversed.
REASONING:	Where a biological parent is not declared unfit, the State does not have the right to grant custody to a nonbiological parent. Even if petitioners' allegations are true, the trial court found that the respondent's parenting does not show persistent neglect, or any other extraordinary circumstance, that would categorize her as unfit. Even if the petitioners would make "better parents" than the respondent, the State's authority goes only so far as to deny custody to an "unfit" parent, let alone a parent who should be better.

Was your brief similar to the one above? Let's examine the briefing process, beginning with the details of the story, the explanation of what happened. A husband and wife, who had two children, separated. The mother, who had sole custody of the children, moved from house to house and otherwise provided a somewhat unstable life for her children. Accordingly, the children's grandparents (the father's parents) wanted temporary custody of the children until the mother (or father) became more stable and better able to care for the children. In order for the state to take the children from the mother (biological parent) and give them to the grandparents (nonbiological parents), the mother would have to be declared unfit.

At trial, the mother was not declared unfit, although the trial court concluded that she was not a very good parent, and the grandparents were more capable of raising the children. The mother appealed the trial court's decision. The appellate court reversed the lower decision, holding that unless a mother (biological parent) is declared *unfit*, the court may not deny her custody of the children. In this case, the mother's parenting may have not been ideal, but it was not so neglectful as to warrant denial of custody.

Based on this understanding of the story — the events that took place, both before, during and after the courtroom proceedings — the sample brief reflects these events accordingly.

Did you have an easy time understanding what happened? It is possible, and quite probable, that you had some problems. We should next consider some of the mechanics of an opinion as published in a case reporter.

The Structure of a Case

Citation:
Information about a court case, including the jurisdiction, year of the decision, and in what legal reference source the case is located.

The information below the case name on page 42, 594 N.Y.S.2d 68 (App. Div. 1993), is the case **citation.** It informs the reader that this case is printed in volume 594 of the New York Supplement, 2d series, and begins on page 68 of that volume. Moreover, it informs the reader that the case was decided by the Appellate Division of the Supreme Court. Finally, the citation includes the year, 1993, in which this case was decided.

Figure 3.1 shows the opening page of Culver v. Culver as it looks in the West case reporter. Note that the opinion actually opens with a short one-paragraph summary of the case. This is often referred to as the **syllabus** or **synopsis** and briefly states the facts and the holding.

Headnote:
A note at the beginning of a court case that summarizes the legal principles that the court concluded.

Following the short summary are the **headnotes.** (You know that endnotes are found at the end of a text. Headnotes, in turn, are found at the beginning.) Headnotes summarize the legal principles that the court concluded. There is a short title (here "Parent and Child") categorizing each legal finding by subject. Next there is a small sketch of a key, followed by numbers. These "keys" are part of a research system whereby these legal principles can be looked up by number, and various cases can be found that discuss the principle referenced by the key number. In the actual

1 **Case name and citation**
2 **Court and date**
3 **Syllabus or synopsis**
4 **Headnotes and key numbers**
5 **Names of attorneys and justices**
6 **Text of opinion begins**

190 A.D.2d 960

In the Matter of Mary CULVER et al., Respondents,

v.

Faith CULVER, Appellant, et al., Respondent.

Supreme Court, Appellate Division, Third Department.

Feb. 25, 1993.

Mother opposed paternal grandparents' petition seeking temporary custody of children. The Family Court, Warren County, Austin, J., granted petition, and mother appealed. The Supreme Court, Appellate Division, Casey, J., held that: (1) trial court's findings that mother and children moved eight times in six years and that parental attention and love given to children by mother were sporadic, considered alone or cumulatively, were insufficient to establish type of gross misconduct necessary to supplant custody of children from mother to paternal grandparents, and (2) claimed psychological bond between children and their paternal grandparents had no bearing on mother's rights as natural parent, in absence of unfitness, abandonment or other gross misconduct.

Reversed.

1. Parent and Child ⇐2(3.3, 3.5)

Trial court's finding that mother lacked established household of her own and had made numerous changes of residence, most of which had unsuitable accom-modations for children, and finding that parental attention and love given to children by mother were sporadic were irrelevant and impermissible considerations in determining whether custody should be taken from mother and granted to paternal grandparents, unless they were sufficient to establish mother's persistent neglect or unfitness.

2. Parent and Child ⇐2(14)

Assuming that there was sufficient evidence to support trial court finding that parental attention and love given to children by mother were sporadic, this finding did not establish persistent neglect necessary to rise to level of extraordinary circumstance justifying change in custody from mother to paternal grandparents.

3. Parent and Child ⇐2(14)

Trial court's findings that mother and her children moved eight times in six years and that parental attention and love given to children by mother were sporadic, considered alone or cumulatively, were insufficient to establish type of gross misconduct or other behavior, evincing utter indifference and irresponsibility necessary to supplant children's custody from mother to paternal grandparents.

4. Parent and Child ⇐2(3.1)

Claimed psychological bond between children and their paternal grandparents who sought custody had no bearing on mother's rights, as natural parent, to custody of children, in absence of unfitness, abandonment, persistent neglect or other gross misconduct or grievous cause.

Gregory V. Canale, Glens Falls, for appellant.

Valerie Hughes Zahn, Middle Granville, for Mary Culver and another, respondents.

Before MIKOLL, J.P., and YESAWICH, MERCURE, CREW and CASEY, JJ.

CASEY, Justice.

Appeal from an order of the Family Court of Warren County (Austin, J.), entered September 23, 1991, which granted

Figure 3.1
Page from Case Reporter

opinion, there will be an indication of the key numbers in brackets, indicating where that key's reasoning begins.

After the headnotes, the names of the attorneys and the judges (or justices, as they are sometimes referred to) appear. Finally, there is the text of the actual opinion written by Justice Casey, which you have already read and briefed.

Look once again at the opinion, and note how the author will usually refer to cases that helped the court formulate its decision. Following each case name is the citation, enabling readers to locate that case if they desire. In addition to cases, statutes are often cited as well as other sources of law.

Finally, you may encounter certain words, often Latin terms, that are unfamiliar to you. It is a good idea to keep a law dictionary close at hand to look up definitions.

Now that you are familiar with the basic concept of reading and briefing a case, take a look at what happens when not all the judges reach the same conclusion.

Concurring and Dissenting Opinions

Concurring Opinion:
An opinion written by a judge who agrees with all or part of the judgment, but for different reasons.

Dissenting Opinion:
An opinion written by a judge who disagrees with all or part of the judgment.

In *Culver*, notice that the opinion was written by Justice Casey, and Justices Mikoll, Yesawich, Mercure, and Crew all concurred, or agreed with the decision. (This is indicated at the end of the opinion at page 44.) However, such agreement is not always the case. In fact, the bench (i.e., the group of judges hearing a case) is often bitterly divided in reaching a conclusion.

A **concurring opinion** is one where the author agrees with all or part of the judgment, or deciding opinion, but for different reasons. These reasons may be very different or reflect just a subtle nuance. In any event, where a judge agrees with the deciding opinion but nonetheless feels compelled to address certain concerns, he or she will often write a concurring opinion.

A **dissenting opinion** is one where the author disagrees with all or part of the judgment. Differences of opinion obviously occur in all aspects of life, involving both legal and nonlegal issues. In order to better illustrate this concept, consider the following example.

EXAMPLE

Suppose that an organization named the International Music Association (IMA) wants to give a lifetime achievement award to the "Greatest Rock-and-Roll Band of All Time." After several months of polling the top rock-and-roll historians, writers, disc jockeys, and musicians, the IMA was left with three finalists: the Beatles, Deep Purple, and Led Zeppelin. The IMA's executive committee took up the proposal that the award be presented to the

Beatles. Of the nine members of the executive committee, five of them issued the following opinion:

> Although the Beatles have achieved tremendous success and historical importance, after extensive study we conclude that Deep Purple is the best of the three groups in combining pure talent, songwriting ability, and stage presence. Accordingly, since we are in favor of granting the award to Deep Purple, we reject the motion of granting this award to the Beatles.

Three other members of the committee issued the following opinion:

> We agree with the majority opinion that the award should not be given to the Beatles. However, we limit our agreement to that result. We do not believe that the award should be granted to Deep Purple. Although we believe that both Deep Purple and the Beatles are two of rock and roll's truly legendary bands, we contend that Led Zeppelin has made the most significant impact in rock and roll. Led Zeppelin has influenced a greater number of young musicians than the other bands, and its popularity continues to grow years after disbanding.

Finally, the remaining member of the executive committee issued the following opinion:

> I disagree with the conclusions reached by my fellow committee members. The Beatles are the most popular band in the history of rock and roll, and are thereby the clear choice to receive our distinguished award.

Led Zeppelin: Better than the Beatles? Not as good as Deep purple?

This nonlegal example presents three different opinions. If this were a court opinion, the different statements would be analyzed as follows: In accordance with the majority opinion (five of nine votes), the award would not be given to the Beatles. The three-person vote would be known as the concurring opinion because those members agree with the majority's decision but for *different reasons*. They agree that the Beatles should not get the award, but do not endorse the majority opinion's selection of Deep Purple. The authors of the concurring opinion believe the award should be presented to Led Zeppelin.

Finally, the lone dissenter completely disagrees, arguing that the Beatles should indeed get the award.

In all probability, the Beatles would not be given the award, and it would go instead to Deep Purple, based on the majority opinion.

Majority Opinion:
In a court case, the opinion shared by more than half of the judges who adjudicated the case.

A deciding opinion is known as a **majority** if it has the most votes and represents more than half of the available votes. A **plurality** opinion has the most votes but represents less than half of the available votes. For instance, if the nine-person committee vote broke down 4-3-2, the four-person vote would be the deciding opinion, and also a *plurality* opinion since it received the most votes (four), but not more than half of the total (nine).

To sum up: A concurring opinion agrees with the deciding opinion, in whole or in part, but for different reasons. The dissenting opinion flatly disagrees, in whole or in part, with the deciding opinion. There may be more than one concurring or dissenting opinion.

Now let's take a look at an actual case involving more than one opinion, and we will brief it accordingly. First, try to brief it on your own. Then look at the sample brief below.

People v. Scott

594 N.Y.S.2d 213 (1993)

Defendant was convicted in the Supreme Court, Bronx County, Bamberger, J., of criminal possession of controlled substance in third degree, and he appealed. The Supreme Court, Appellate Division, held that defendant intentionally abandoned brown paper bag by deliberately discarding it as he hastily left taxicab.

Affirmed.

Kupferman, J., concurred in result and filed opinion.

Milonas, J., filed dissenting opinion.

Searches and Seizures [Key Number: 28]

Defendant intentionally abandoned brown paper bag by deliberately discarding it as he hastily left taxicab; his act of discarding bag was not the result of any allegedly unlawful police conduct in targeting defendant, since there was no interaction between police and defendant until after he betrayed his guilty conscience.

Before MILONAS, J.P., and KUPFERMAN, ROSS and ASCH, JJ.
MEMORANDUM DECISION.

Judgment, Supreme Court, Bronx County (Phylis Skloot Bamberger, J.), rendered October 24, 1989, convicting defendant, upon his plea of guilty, of criminal possession of a controlled substance in the third degree, and sentencing him, as a second felony offender, to a term of 4½ to 9 years, affirmed.

The suppression evidence at hearing was that two uniformed police officers stopped a taxicab in which defendant was a passenger when it unlawfully passed a stop sign. While one officer was checking the driver's license and registration, he saw defendant in the back seat bend over and move about, as if he was picking up or putting something down on the floor, and then quickly exit the cab, leaving behind a brown paper bag in open view. As the other officer, outside of the cab, asked defendant "What he was doing?" or words to that effect, the first, concerned that the bag might contain a gun, opened it and found 322 vials of cocaine.

The record supports the hearing court's finding that defendant intentionally abandoned the bag by deliberately discarding it as he hastily left the cab. Clearly, defendant's act of discarding the bag was not the result of any allegedly unlawful police conduct in targeting defendant, since "[t]here was no interaction between the police and defendant until after he betrayed his guilty conscience" (People v. Adams, 173 A.D.2d 207, 208, 569 N.Y.S.2d 88, 1v. denied, 78 N.Y.2d 1073, 577 N.Y.S.2d 236, 583 N.E.2d 948; see also, People v. Kosciusko, 149 A.D.2d 620, 621-622, 540 N.Y.S.2d 289).

All concur except Kupferman, J. who concurs in the result, and Milonas, J. who dissents, each in a separate memorandum as follows:

KUPFERMAN, Justice (Concurring in the result):

I agree with the statement in the dissent that "the probative evidence does not establish that defendant had abandoned his property, and, at most, defendant's conduct was equivocal."

Nonetheless, under the circumstances, with the stop being proper and the back of the cab now empty, and in view of the equivocal situation, good police work required that the officer open the bag that was on the floor of the back seat and, therefore, there was no violation.

MILONAS, Justice (Dissenting):

In my opinion, the conviction should be reversed and the indictment dismissed.

Defendant herein was indicted for criminal possession of a controlled substance in the second degree and resisting arrest. A pretrial hearing, at which the only witness was Police Officer James Tierney, was conducted in connection with the discovery of the narcotics. The officer who physically detained defendant did not testify. In that regard, Officer Tierney and his partner were driving in a radio patrol car when he observed a livery cab run a stop sign at the intersection of Undercliff and Boscobel Avenues in Bronx County. The police vehicle, its lights flashing, followed the taxi for approximately one-half block until the officers managed to pull it over. At that point, Officer Tierney exited the patrol car and approached the taxicab on the driver's side, his partner advancing on the passenger side. Officer Tierney requested that the driver produce his "paperwork." Another man, whom he identified as defendant, was in the back seat.

According to Officer Tierney, defendant was "bending over and moving around as if he was either picking something up or . . . putting something down on the floor, after which time he got out of the vehicle." The officer also described defendant as "fidgeting around" and stated that he "flew out the side of the car" and that he stepped out [i]n a very quick manner." Expanding his account of the incident on redirect, Officer Tierney asserted that "the door of the vehicle was still open, so the defendant was standing between the car and the door, and my partner was standing towards the end of the door." When defendant then "got out of the vehicle, he didn't have a chance to go either way. My partner was right next to him" and "in front of him." Moreover, defendant was "approximately two feet" away from the bag when he exited the cab.

While Officer Tierney's partner was questioning defendant as to what he was doing, Officer Tierney moved a few steps toward the rear of the cab and glanced through the window. On the floor of the back of the vehicle, "at the foot of where [defendant] had been motioning toward," there was a brown paper bag. The officer proceeded to open the rear passenger door on the driver's side and picked up the bag, which felt heavy. Officer Tierney asserted that "I believed there may have been a gun in the bag. When I opened the bag, I saw numerous vials of cocaine." After the officer called to his partner to cuff defendant, the latter began to put up some resistance to being arrested, but he was subdued and placed under arrest. The cabdriver was permitted to go and did not receive a summons for the traffic infraction.

Officer Tierney admitted on cross-examination that when he noticed that the taxi had failed to halt at a stop sign, it was his intention simply to issue a summons to the driver. Although he first perceived a person in the back seat of the vehicle while following it in the police car, he did not observe that individual bending down or doing anything else suspicious even when he subsequently walked by defendant in order to approach the driver. Officer Tierney also did not see a gun, knife or any other weapon. Thus, the Supreme Court, in denying the motion to suppress, upheld the search of the brown paper bag based upon nothing more than the conclusion that defendant "flew" out of the cab, thereby supposedly displaying an interest in fleeing that was only averted by the presence of Officer Tierney's partner by the door, which amounted to his abandoning the bag. Further, his furtive gestures reinforced Officer Tierney's belief that since other crimes had been committed against livery drivers in the vicinity, the bag might contain a gun.

Yet, it is clear that the record demonstrates absolutely no facts which would warrant even a suspicion that there was a weapon in the bag. The officer did not have a report of a weapon nor did he observe a weapon or see or feel the outline of a weapon. In effect, the Supreme Court accepted the proposition that whenever there have been robberies of a cab driver in a neighborhood, the presence of a passenger with a package which might conceivably have a gun or knife in it is sufficient to subject its owner to at least a further inquiry, especially if he makes a motion in the direction of the bag. There is, however, no legal authority whatever that would sanction a search of a closed container in the back seat of a taxi founded upon no more than the passenger's reaching for it, or toward it, in a vehicle that has been stopped for a traffic infraction. Indeed, such a theory is inimical to the constitutional prohibition against unlawful searches and seizures in that "[t]he officers had no information that a crime had occurred or was about to take place, had not seen defendant do anything criminal, and were confronted only by facts susceptible of innocent interpretation" (People v. Howard, 50 N.Y.2d 583, 590, 430 N.Y.S.2d 578, 408 N.E.2d 908, cert. den. 449 U.S. 1023, 101 S. Ct. 590, 66 L. Ed. 2d 484).

As for the finding that defendant intended to flee from the cab and had abandoned the bag, there is simply no evidentiary justification for this conclusion. Certainly "[p]roperty which has in fact been abandoned is outside the protection of the constitutional provisions" (People v. Howard, supra, 50 N.Y.2d at 592, 430 N.Y.S.2d 578, 408 N.E.2d 908). In People v. Howard, supra, the Court of Appeals explained that there is a presumption against the waiver of constitutional rights, and it is the People's burden to overcome that presumption (see also People v. Kelly, 172 A.D.2d 458, 568 N.Y.S.2d 804, affd. 79 N.Y.2d 899, 581 N.Y.S.2d 661, 590 N.E.2d 246).

This court stated in People v. Marrero, 173 A.D.2d 244, 245, 569 N.Y.S.2d 449, appeal dismissed 78 N.Y.2d 969, 574 N.Y.S.2d 949, 580 N.E.2d 421, that "[w]hether or not property has been abandoned is a question of intent" (173 A.D.2d at 245, 569 N.Y.S.2d 449; see also People v. Kelly, supra).

The hearing court determined that by exiting rapidly from the cab, defendant indicated an intent to depart and was only prevented from doing so by Officer Tierney's partner, who had positioned himself outside the passenger door. On the contrary, the proof shows only that as defendant stepped out of the vehicle, he was blocked by the policeman and could not have left even had he been inclined to do so. Officer Tierney then proceeded to open a bag that was in the cab only two feet from where defendant was halted. In addition, the bag was examined without Officer Tierney even asking whether it belonged to defendant or whether defendant was leaving the area. It was at least as likely that defendant, a passenger in a taxicab that had been detained by the police for a traffic infraction, was merely getting out of the vehicle to ascertain what was occurring as it was that he planned to abscond from the scene. In no manner can it reasonably be found that the evidence supported the "exclusive inference" that defendant was abandoning the bag (see People v. Howard, supra, 50 N.Y.2d at 593, 430 N.Y.S.2d 578, 408 N.E.2d 908) in the process of fleeing.

While it is true that Rios v. United States, 364 U.S. 253, 80 S. Ct. 1431, 4 L. Ed. 2d 1688, is distinguishable from the present situation, it is instructive that the United States Supreme Court did acknowledge therein that "[a] passenger who lets a package drop to the floor of the taxicab in which he is riding can hardly be said to have 'abandoned' it" (364 U.S. at 262, n.6, 80 S. Ct. at 1437, n.6). In a case that is applicable here, the Second Department recently declared that "[i]t is settled that '[t]he police may not use traffic violations as a mere pretext to investigate the defendant on an unrelated matter' " (People v. Smith, 181 A.D.2d 802, 803, 581 N.Y.S.2d 240). People v. Smith, supra, concerned a police surveillance of a "stash house" from which defendant exited carrying a canvas bag. He made a telephone call and then entered a cab. Notwithstanding that defendant was not a target of the police investigation, they followed the taxi, believing that there might be drugs in the bag, and it was thereafter stopped. Both the driver of the vehicle and defendant denied ownership of the bag. One of the officers reached into the car, grabbed the bag and opened it, discovering a gun and ammunition. The Second Department affirmed the Supreme Court's order granting suppression, deciding that the illegal U-turn made by the cab was simply not a proper reason to stop the taxi. As the court noted (at 803, 581 N.Y.S.2d 240):

> Here, the officer who testified at the hearing admitted that he was following the defendant because he thought there might be drugs in the bag. Moreover, the police did not bother to give the cab driver a summons, or even ask to see his license or registration. Thus, the alleged Vehicle and Traffic Law violation was clearly a mere pretext to stop the vehicle.
>
> In addition, the People's argument that the police had a "reasonable suspicion" that criminal activity was afoot is without merit (see, People v. Hicks, 68 N.Y.2d 234, 508 N.Y.S.2d 163, 500 N.E.2d 861; People v. Wade, 143 A.D.2d 703, 533 N.Y.S.2d 83). As the hearing court found, "[a]ll of the defendant's behavior was at least as compatible with his innocence as with his guilt."
>
> We also find no merit to the People's contention that the bag and its contents were admissible on the theory that the defendant abandoned the bag (see, People v. Howard, 50 N.Y.2d 583, 430 N.Y.S.2d 578, 408 N.E.2d 908, cert. denied 449 U.S. 1023, 101 S. Ct. 590, 66 L. Ed. 2d 484; cf., People v. Torres, 74 N.Y.2d 224, 229, n.3, 544 N.Y.S.2d 796, 543 N.E.2d 61).

It is significant that the Court of Appeals in People v. Torres, 74 N.Y.2d 224, 544 N.Y.S.2d 796, 543 N.E.2d 61, reiterated the principle that intrusions upon the personal property of citizens "must be both justified in their inception and reasonably related in scope and intensity to the circumstances which rendered their initiation permissible" (at 230, 544 N.Y.S.2d 796,543 N.E.2d 61). Consequently, deeming improper the action of the police therein in searching the passenger compartment of the suspects' automobile, the court declared (at 230, 544 N.Y.S.2d 796, 543 N.E.2d 61) that:

> In this instance, for example, the suspects had already been removed from the car, a permissible intrusion if there was reasonable suspicion of criminality in light of the need to protect the detectives' safety (Pennsylvania v. Mimms, 434 U.S. 106, 98 S. Ct. 330, 54 L. Ed. 2d 331; People v. McLaurin, 70 N.Y.2d 779, 521 N.Y.S.2d 218, 515 N.E.2d 904). Further, the suspects had been patted down without incident. At that point, there was nothing to prevent these two armed detectives from questioning the two suspects with complete safety to themselves, since the suspects had been isolated from the interior of the car, where the nylon bag that supposedly contained the gun was located. Any residual fear that the detectives might have had about the suspects' ability to break away and retrieve the bag could have been eliminated by taking the far less intrusive step of asking the suspects to move away from the vicinity of the car (see, 1 La Fave & Israel, op. cit., at 310). Finally, it is unrealistic to assume, as the Supreme Court did in Michigan v. Long (supra, 463 U.S. 1032 at 1051–1052, 103 S. Ct. 3469 at 3481-82, 77 L. Ed. 2d 1201 [1983]), that having been stopped and questioned without incident, a suspect who is about to be released and permitted to proceed on his way would, upon reentry into his vehicle, reach for a concealed weapon and threaten the departing police officer's safety.

Although the fact pattern in People v. Torres, supra, is dissimilar from the one involved here, the fact remains that the analysis by the Court of Appeals in that matter is pertinent under the circumstances of the instant case. There is no claim that defendant might have returned to the cab; rather, it is urged that he had abandoned the bag and was attempting to flee for no other reason than that he "flew" out of the vehicle and his way was obstructed by one of the officers. In effect, the Supreme Court decided that by endeavoring to remove himself rapidly from a vehicle while being blocked by a police officer, defendant might have been engaged in absconding and abandoning his property. However, the probative evidence does not establish that defendant had abandoned his property, and, at most, defendant's conduct was equivocal. Further, since the police blocked any effort by defendant to flee, assuming that this was his intention, he could not have abandoned his property, the police action having made that option impossible. The court, therefore, transformed what it perceived to be an intent to abandon property into an actual abandonment.

SAMPLE CASE BRIEF

PEOPLE v. SCOTT

594 N.Y.S.2d 313 (1993)

FACTS: Police officers stopped a taxicab for unlawfully passing a stop sign. Defendant, a passenger in the back seat, left a brown paper bag in the rear of the cab and hastily exited the cab. One of the officers, concerned that the bag might contain a gun, opened the bag and found 322 vials of cocaine. Defendant was convicted of criminal possession of a controlled substance, and appeals.

ISSUE: Did defendant's actions amount to an intentional abandonment of property, thereby rendering the search of such property lawful police conduct?

HOLDING: Yes. Defendant intentionally abandoned the bag, and the police search of the property was lawful.

REASONING:

Judgment: Defendant deliberately discarded the bag as he left the cab. Defendant's act was not the result of any unlawful police conduct, since there was no interaction between police and defendant until after defendant attempted to flee the cab and abandon the property.

Concurring: While it was not clearly established that defendant intentionally abandoned the property, good police work under the circumstances required that the bag be opened and searched. Therefore, the police did not commit any violation.

Dissenting: Police officers stopped the cab for running a stop sign. Defendant exited the cab and was standing two feet from the bag when the officers searched it. It is no more clear that defendant attempted to escape than to merely exit the cab to find out what was going on. The officers had no reasonable suspicion of defendant's wrongdoing. Absent such suspicion, there is no legal authority that would sanction the search of a closed container in the back seat of a taxi when the taxi is stopped for a traffic violation. Accordingly, the conviction should be reversed and the indictment dismissed.

How did you do? If you covered the basic points stated in the above brief, you did very well. Let's take a look at this brief, step by step.

This case is very easy to read. Apparently, two police officers noticed a taxicab unlawfully pass a stop sign. When the officers pulled the cab over, the defendant, who was a passenger in the back seat, began "fidgeting around," looked like he left something behind, and attempted to flee the cab. The officers then noticed a bag in the back seat. Fearing that it contained a gun, they opened it. The bag contained 322 vials of cocaine.

The defendant was convicted at trial. That court determined that the defendant intentionally abandoned the bag of cocaine and attempted to flee. If this were true, the officers would probably be justified in their search and arrest. Defendant, however, contended that he did not act in any manner that would give the officers probable cause to search the bag. Keep in mind that the officers originally stopped the cab due to the cab *driver's* traffic violation, not the *passenger's* (defendant's) behavior. Absent such probable cause (reasonable suspicion), the search and arrest would be unlawful.

Accordingly, the first issue that comes to mind is, "Did the defendant intentionally abandon the property (the bag containing the cocaine)?" If you wrote this as your issue, your analysis is good. However, since this issue is a question of *fact*, it is always a good idea to search for the question of *law* in an appeal.

The question of law, then, would be, "Was the search of the bag a lawful search?" If this was your issue, your analysis is even better.

In the sample brief above, the two issues are combined into one: Did defendant's actions amount to an intentional abandonment of property, thereby rendering the search of such property lawful police conduct?

★ **HINT:** Keep in mind that the issue, which is usually the toughest step to master, should be phrased in the manner that provides the most information. Although it is fine to include more than one issue, you should consolidate your questions into one issue wherever possible.

The holding, of course, is the answer to the issue. You will reach a different answer depending on how you phrase the question. Here, if the question is, "Was the police conduct a violation?" the answer is no. If the question is, "Was the police conduct lawful?" the answer is yes.

There are three parts to the reasoning: (1) the judgment, which is the deciding opinion; (2) the concurring and (3) dissenting opinions, which are labeled as such. Since these separate opinions are identified, you do not have to figure out which is which. All you have to do is summarize them.

All case briefs are essentially the same. You read the entire text and then provide the Facts, Issue, Holding, and Reasoning. If concurring or dissenting opinions exist, you can simply summarize them.

FINAL THOUGHTS

Now that you have read through this chapter and attempted to brief the sample cases, it all boils down to this: Read the case, figure out what it means, then write the facts (what happened), the issue (what the court is trying to decide), the holding (what the court has decided), and the reasoning (why the court has decided as it did). And, remember, if there is more than one reasoning, such as concurring or dissenting opinions, write those summaries too.

Now You Try It

Before you move on to the next chapter, try a few more cases on your own. See the cases in Appendix D, beginning at page 259. The first two, Johnson v. Johnson and People v. O'Keefe, are, like the two cases above, New York cases.

The third, Danielson v. Board of Higher Education, while situated in New York state, is a federal case. Unlike the others, it is quite a bit longer.

The fourth, Eisenstadt v. Baird, is a United States Supreme Court case and is the only one of the four that contains concurring and dissenting opinions. It too is rather lengthy.

Finally, two historically significant United States Supreme Court cases, Brown v. Board of Education and Roe v. Wade, provide opportunity for further experience in case briefing.

When briefing cases, especially long ones, it is a good idea to read the synopsis (or summary) and the headnotes first, just to get a basic understanding of what is going on. Then read the actual text of the case for a thorough legal analysis.

After finishing with these cases, you will have fortified your knowledge of reading and briefing case law. It's a good idea to go to a law library and brief other cases as an exercise.

Congratulations! You are now familiar with the sources of the law, and you have mastered case briefing, an important legal skill. In the next chapter, you will learn how to write like a lawyer.

Key Terms

affirmed	format	opinion
case brief	headnotes	plurality
citation	holding	reasoning
concurring opinion	issue	reversed
dissenting opinion	majority	syllabus
facts	objective	synopsis

Review Questions

1. What is a case brief and why is it important?

2. Name and describe the four main sections of a case brief.

3. What is the difference between a question of fact and a question of law?

4. Why are case briefs usually about cases on appeal?

5. Why is the length of the holding important?

6. Name and describe the different types of judicial reasoning.

7. What is the difference between a majority opinion and a plurality opinion?

8. What is the difference between a concurring opinion and a dissenting opinion?

9. What types of information may be found at the beginning of a case, prior to the actual text?

10. What does it mean when a decision has been affirmed or reversed?

Web Sites

- Findlaw
  http://www.findlaw.com
- Legal Information Institute
  http://www.law.cornell.edu/

Legal Writing: Basic Organization

4

Chapter Overview

The Four-Part Legal Answer
    Importance of Organization
The Memorandum of Law
    Format
    Sample Memorandum
The Importance of Good Writing
Make Sure Your Reader Understands Your Writing
Make Sure Your Writing Does Not Mean Something Else
Use Simple Language and Keep It Short

It is very important that you make your writing as simple as possible for your reader to understand. Keep in mind that the reason you write something is because you want somebody to read it. The person reading your document wants it to be as easy to read as possible, just as most people prefer other tasks to be as easy as possible.

For example, imagine that the weather is nice, and you decide to go to the beach. On your way out of the house, you grab your portable CD player and a couple of CDs. You turn on the player, just to make sure it is working and unfortunately discover that it isn't. You replace the old batteries with new ones and, minutes later, off you go with your music playing! Now, imagine that the solution was more complicated. Imagine instead that you had to take the player apart to repair the problem. Your goal was simply to listen to music. What would you rather do to attain that goal—spend a few seconds inserting new batteries or an entire afternoon fixing the player?

If your reader had the same problem, what do you think he or she would rather do? Obviously, anyone would prefer to accomplish a goal with as few obstacles as possible. The same holds true when reading legal documents. Your reader's goal is to understand what you are saying. For this reason, you should provide your reader with a document that is easy to read.

THE FOUR-PART LEGAL ANSWER

When you write an answer to a legal question, your answer should be organized. It's not enough to get the right answer; you must be able to express that answer in a logical manner.

EXAMPLE

Suppose that Statute 25, a local law, reads as follows: "Persons riding a motorcycle without wearing a helmet are subject to fine and/or imprisonment." Now consider the following situation.

Bob was riding his motorcycle through town. Joe, a police officer, noticed that Bob was not wearing a helmet. Joe asked Bob to pull over and issued Bob a penalty fine for riding a motorcycle without a helmet. Bob was angered and comes to your law firm the next day to see if the traffic ticket was rightfully issued. The firm's senior partner asks you to do the research and determine the outcome.

You look up Statute 25 and discover that riding a motorcycle without wearing a helmet indeed subjects a person to a fine. Accordingly, if the question posed to you is, "Was Bob rightfully issued a traffic ticket?" your answer would be yes. A simple yes, however, is not enough. Getting the answer was easy enough; *now* you have to learn to *write* the answer in a correct legal answer format. Look at the answer below.

Bob was rightfully issued a traffic ticket.
According to Statute 25, persons riding a motorcycle without a helmet are subject to a fine.
Here, Bob was riding his motorcycle through town without wearing a helmet.
Therefore, Bob was rightfully issued a traffic ticket.

As you can see, this answer is a bit more extensive than just a simple yes. There are four parts to this answer:

Conclusion
In a legal answer, a statement answering the question in the way that the question was raised.

1. First, there is the **conclusion.** The conclusion is a statement answering the question in the way that the question was raised. Therefore, if the question is "Was Bob rightfully issued a traffic ticket," and your determination is yes, then your conclusion must be "Bob was

rightfully issued a traffic ticket." You have just explained to your reader what your conclusion is. However, this is not enough. You must also explain how you arrived at this conclusion.

2. The second step is the **rule of law.** You have just told your reader that Bob was rightfully issued a traffic ticket. Why? Because *you* think so? Because "that's the way it should be"? Because "it makes sense"? NO! Because the *law* says so. Your rule of law must be "According to Statute 25, persons riding a motorcycle without a helmet are subject to a fine." Two comments on this:

Rule of Law
The reference to the law that supports the answer or conclusion to a particular issue.

- Notice that I did not copy the statute **verbatim** (word for word). I left out the part about imprisonment. Why? Because it is not relevant to the issue at hand. Bob was not imprisoned, so why even discuss what the statute says about imprisonment? If the same statute also had a provision regarding lawful operation of aircraft, should I include that as well? Of course not — it's irrelevant! This example provides a simple, one-sentence statute. If you open up some law books, however, you will easily find statutes that are several pages long. There is no need to overload your reader with every last word of a given statute. Include only the portion that is relevant to your issue.
- For this example, I named the law "Statute 25." Usually, statute references indicate more complicated and complete **citations,** including such information as volume number, state, and so on. Citations provide "locations" — that is, they direct the reader where to look up a statute if he or she needs to do so.

At this point, you have informed your reader of your conclusion and the law that you used as a source. Now you must explain to your reader how the rule of law applies to the issue at hand.

3. This third step is the **facts/analysis.** You must tell your reader that "Here, Bob was riding his motorcycle through town without wearing a helmet." This explains *why* the particular rule of law you used as your source (Statute 25) applies to this issue. If you needed more explanation, you could also use a sentence or two to clearly explain the law. In this case, however, the law is simple enough — you do not need to elaborate any further.

Facts/Analysis
A statement that bridges the rule of law with the specific facts at hand.

You now have one step to go. A legal answer states your conclusion, the rule of law supporting your conclusion, and a brief reassessment of the facts along with an analysis — where necessary — of why the law applies to the facts. You must complete an answer by restating your conclusion:

4. The fourth and final step is to repeat the **conclusion.** "Therefore, Bob was rightfully issued a traffic ticket." This allows you to once again state your position. (Notice that I inserted the word "therefore" prior to restating the exact conclusion from step 1. You may substitute

other words or phrases for "therefore," such as "accordingly," "for this reason," and so on.)

Now that I have outlined this legal answer at length, please examine it once more, with the four steps emphasized.

★ ── ★

Conclusion	Bob was rightfully issued a traffic ticket.
Rule of law	According to Statute 25, persons riding a motorcycle without a helmet are subject to a fine.
Facts/analysis	Here, Bob was riding his motorcycle through town without wearing a helmet.
Conclusion (repeated)	Therefore, Bob was rightfully issued a traffic ticket.

★ ── ★

Importance of Organization

At this point, you have probably wondered, "Why go through this long-winded repetitive process? It all sounds the same." You may think that if the question is, "Was Bob rightfully issued a traffic ticket?" you can answer:

- Yes, because he was riding his motorcycle without a helmet, which subjects him to a fine under Statute 25. OR
- Yes. He violated Statute 25 because he was riding his motorcycle without a helmet. OR
- Yes, because under Statute 25 he can be fined since he was riding his motorcycle without a helmet.

All of this seems to make sense, right? What's the difference in how you answer it? Well, you know what? There is no real difference here. Why? *Because the question is so simple, it only requires a few words to answer it!* But most problems that stump lawyers and law students throughout the country are not that simple. If they were all that simple, we would not need any lawyers. When the question is more complex, and the answer must be explained in several sentences, paragraphs, or pages, it is vital that the answer be written in a clear, organized format.

EXAMPLE

● ●

We are all familiar with the concept of alphabetizing. Suppose you were discussing the starting five players for the 1986 Boston Celtics, who won the National Basketball Association (NBA) championship that year. Listed alphabetically, the players are:

Danny **A**inge
Larry **B**ird
Dennis **J**ohnson
Kevin **Mc**Hale
Robert **P**arish

If you were to list the players by height, tallest to shortest, the result would read:

Robert Parish (7'0")
Kevin McHale (6'10")
Larry Bird (6'9")
Danny Ainge (6'5")
Dennis Johnson (6'4")

If you were to list them by team number, the list would read:

Robert Parish (00)
Dennis Johnson (3)
Kevin McHale (32)
Larry Bird (33)
Danny Ainge (44)

You can list the players in whatever order you wish. Because there are only five people on your list, you can easily find the person you are looking for.

But what if there were more than five people? What if your list included all of the Boston Celtics or all of the people who have ever played professional basketball? Now you are talking about thousands of names. How could you be sure to find a particular name in your list? **Alphabetizing.**

If you pick up a New York City telephone book, you can find any name you are looking for because the names are arranged in alphabetical order. If there were only five, or ten, or even a hundred names in the phone book, you could find the name you are looking for without much of a problem, regardless of how the names were arranged. However, can you imagine how long it would take you to find one name in thousands if they were not in alphabetical order?

Think about the following examples. The formula that I explained above—conclusion, rule of law, facts/analysis, and conclusion—may seem overly analytical, repetitive, and dry when dealing with an example as simple as the one I presented above. However, when you start with your conclusion, and five pages later you have finished explaining how you arrived at that conclusion, you will want to remind your reader of what the conclusion is.

Remember that the key to good writing is organization. Don't send your reader on a wild goose chase looking for the answer. Make your writing reader-friendly. Guide the reader along.

EXAMPLE

● ●

Suppose that Jim walks into Supershop, a well-known supermarket. While walking in the main entrance, Jim slips on the freshly mopped floor, falls to the ground, and injures his back. There was no sign or other warning to indicate that the floor was freshly mopped. Jim now wishes to sue Supershop for money damages regarding his back injury. He comes to your law firm seeking advice. Your senior partner then asks you, "Is Supershop liable for Jim's injury?"

You conduct some legal research and discover the applicable statute:

> Statute 54: Persons who do not exercise reasonable care are negligent, and thereby liable for harm resulting from their negligence.

In analyzing this law and applying it to the facts at hand, you conclude that Supershop was negligent for creating the hazardous condition (the slippery floor) without posting adequate warning and is thereby liable for Jim's injury. Now that you have determined your answer, the next step is to write the answer in an organized, lawyer-like manner.

Your first step is the conclusion. Your conclusion should provide an answer that uses the language of the question. The question was, "Is Supershop liable for Jim's injury?" Therefore, your answer should be as follows:

> Supershop is liable for Jim's injury.

The next step is the rule of law. It is not enough to merely inform your reader of *what* your conclusion is; you must now explain *why* you arrived at that conclusion. In order to explain your reasoning, you must first introduce the reader to the applicable law:

> Pursuant to Statute 54, persons who do not exercise reasonable care are negligent, and thereby liable for harm resulting from their negligence.

Next, you must explain to your reader why this law is applicable to the instant case. Your third step, facts/analysis, should read:

> Here, Jim fell and injured his back on Supershop's floor after an employee mopped the floor, causing it to be slippery. Supershop did not warn customers of this dangerous condition, thereby failing to use reasonable care, and such negligence directly resulted in Jim's injury.

Finally, your last step should repeat the conclusion. You started by stating *what* your conclusion is. Next, you explained *why* you arrived at that conclusion by citing the law and indicating how the law applies to the facts. Now, you should close your argument by repeating your conclusion—a reiteration and justification of your original conclusion:

Accordingly, Supershop is liable for Jim's injury.

Look at the answer again, with each step emphasized:

Conclusion	Supershop is liable for Jim's injury.
Rule of law	Pursuant to Statute 54, persons who do not exercise reasonable care are negligent, and thereby liable for harm resulting from their negligence.
Facts/analysis	Here, Jim fell and injured his back on Supershop'sfloorafteranemployee moppedthefloor,causingittobe slippery.Supershopdidnotwarncustomersofthisdangerouscondition,thereby failingtousereasonablecare,andsuchnegligencedirectlyresultedinJim'sinjury.
Conclusion (repeated)	Accordingly, Supershop is liable for Jim's injury.

Two things to remember: First, you've probably noticed that the facts/ analysis in this example is more extensive than in the last example. This is because the scenario in this example required more of an analysis (i.e., an application of the law to the facts).

Second, keep in mind that writing is not an exact science. There is no specific right or wrong answer. If your answer is not the same as mine, word for word, it may still be perfectly correct. As long as the basic concepts are there, don't worry if every word does not match.

EXAMPLE

Stacey signed a one-year lease to rent an apartment in George's building. Stacey realized that the heat was not working and asked George to fix it. After two months, George had done nothing. Stacey could no longer endure a cold apartment and moved out. George wants to sue Stacey for breaking the lease.

Stacey comes to your law firm seeking legal advice. Is Stacey liable for breaking the lease? The applicable law is Statute 37:

> A landlord of property leased for dwelling must provide the property in a condition that is safe and suitable for living.

Now analyze the answer below, carefully examining each of the four parts:

★ ─── ★

Conclusion Rule of law	Stacey is not liable under the lease. Under Statute 37, a landlord must provide property that is suitable for living.
Facts/analysis	Here, Stacey's apartment was without heat, and George failed to remedy the condition for over two months. Two months without heat amounts to unsuitable living conditions.
Conclusion (repeated)	Therefore, Stacey is not liable under the lease.

★ ─── ★

Legal Answer
An organized method of answering a legal question, by listing the conclusion, rule of law, facts/analysis, and repeated conclusion.

Memorandum of Law
A written document that seeks to answer legal questions presented by means of legal analysis.

Now that you have learned how to write a **legal answer** (for simplicity's sake, let's call it that), we will expand this legal answer to create a memorandum of law (or legal memorandum).

THE MEMORANDUM OF LAW

The **memorandum of law** is a legal document that contains several parts, including the legal answer. Before I begin explaining the steps involved, however, let's find out exactly what a legal memorandum is.

EXAMPLE

• •

Let's stay with our previous example of Jim slipping and falling in Supershop. On that same day, Jenny, another shopper, purchased a box of cornflakes. The next morning Jenny opened the box, poured some cornflakes into her cereal bowl, added milk and sweetener, and began eating. Suddenly, she screamed in pain and realized that she had bitten into a small

How strong is Jenny's claim against Supershop?

thumbtack that was mixed in with the cornflakes. She suffered some bruises and abrasions to her gums and wants to sue Supershop for damages.

Instead of supposing that Jim came to your firm for advice (as in the earlier example), let us suppose that the owner of Supershop asks your law firm to represent the supermarket versus both Jim and Jenny.

If your law firm is a very small organization, comprised of the senior attorney, one secretary, and you (an attorney or paralegal), then much of the interoffice communication will no doubt be verbal. It would be very simple for the client (Supershop) to speak to the senior attorney, who would then ask you face to face to find some answers. After some research, you could easily give those answers back to the attorney verbally with little or no written correspondence.

In this example you want to find out whether Supershop is liable to Jim or Jenny. By referring to the earlier example, you know that, according to Statute 54, "Persons who do not exercise reasonable care are negligent, and thereby liable for harm resulting from their negligence." From this statute you decide that Supershop is liable to Jim.

Next you find the law regarding Jenny's case in the form of Statute 76, which states: "Regarding liability for injury caused while consuming edible goods, manufacturers and distributors are strictly liable for both open and prepackaged goods, while retailers are liable for open goods only." Accordingly, you conclude that Supershop is not liable to Jenny.

After discovering both of these statutes, you approach your senior partner and explain as follows: "We can win against Jenny because the law holds us liable only for open goods. The cornflakes are prepackaged. Therefore, only the manufacturer and the distributor are liable, not us.

We are liable to Jim because our employee did not use reasonable care in leaving a floor slippery without notice." You may also want to pass along a copy of the two statutes.

In such a small firm that may be all you have to do. The senior partner (or whoever is the attorney handling the case) will then decide what to do from that point on. Your job was to find out what the law is. *Remember: Lawyers do not know all of the laws. In fact, they memorize very little of all that is out there.*

There is a common misconception that lawyers have all the law, from A to Z, stored inside their brains. That is humanly impossible. Lawyers are trained to (1) find the law and (2) interpret that law in the light most favorable to their clients. If you have a friend named Linda Johnston who lives on East 93rd Street in Manhattan, and you want to find her phone number, you do not need to memorize the entire Manhattan phone book. All you have to do is go to the letter J, look up Johnston, Linda, on East 93rd Street, and find the number. Lawyers work the same way. They do not know all of the law. They just know where to find it.

Therefore, there is a very good chance that your senior partner does not know about Statute 54 and Statute 76 off the top of his or her head. Most lawyers will only memorize the laws they deal with on a daily basis or some nationally prominent law that "everyone" knows (such as "murder is illegal").

Getting back to our example, it is very easy to just sit down and talk to your senior attorney face to face about a particular matter if your law firm is comprised of a handful of people. But what if you worked for a large firm with over 50 attorneys and 100 paralegals? If *all* of you approached the senior partner with a couple of cases per day, do you think that the senior partner would remember all that information without written documentation?

In such situations you need to write your communication. The document conveying such communication is the legal memorandum.

Format

First, let us examine the **format** of this memorandum. Please keep in mind that, whenever possible, it is beneficial to adhere to a specific format when writing various legal documents. Consistency in written format makes life easier for everyone in both legal and nonlegal writing.

For example, when mailing a letter, you (1) place a stamp in the right-hand corner of the envelope, (2) write your return address in the upper left-hand corner of the envelope, and (3) write the address of the recipient in the center of the envelope.

But what if you mixed everything up? What if you switched the locations of the mailing address and your return address? What if you placed the stamp in the center of the envelope or on the other side of the envelope? Logically, this arrangement would not be any more or less correct. However, it would probably confuse the delivery person since postal workers are used to a specific format.

Keep this example in mind every time you learn how to write a particular legal document. Now let us get back to considering the format of a legal memorandum.

There are *nine* basic steps to the legal memorandum format:

★

TO:
FROM:
RE:
DATE:

QUESTION(S) PRESENTED:

BRIEF ANSWER(S):

STATEMENT OF FACTS:

ANALYSIS:

CONCLUSION:

★

The first four steps comprise the **heading.** Quite simply, they are as follows:

- **TO** indicates the person/place you are writing to.
- **FROM** indicates the author of the memorandum (fill in your full name).
- **RE** means "regarding." This indicates your subject matter, what you are writing about.
- **DATE** is, obviously, the current date.

Questions presented are the relevant issues. A question presented is much like an "issue" in a case brief. They are the questions that you encountered when writing your legal answer. In this memorandum there are two basic issues (questions presented):

1. Is Supershop liable for Jim's injury?
2. Is Supershop liable for Jenny's injury?

As I have stated before, legal writing should be precise but not as precise as, say, a mathematical or scientific formula. My sample

Questions Presented
The legal questions that must be answered.

memorandum is one way of writing effectively, but it is not necessarily the *only* correct way. It is possible for your version to be correct, even if it does not match my version word for word.

These questions presented are the essential issues. Notice that if I wrote, "Will Supershop win against Jim?" that would be too vague (recall this discussion in Chapter 3?). We can write that question about *any* issue. We must write something a little more specific when forming our issue. Here I mentioned the word "injury" to indicate what type of potential action (i.e., lawsuit) is involved.

Brief Answers
A statement that answers the question presented using the same language in which it was raised.

Your **brief answers** must be the mirror image of your questions but in statement form. In fact, a brief answer is just like the "conclusion" of a legal answer. Therefore, for the question, "Is Supershop liable for Jim's injury?" the brief answer is not no, but instead, "Supershop is not liable for Jim's injury." Accordingly, your two brief answers (there must be two brief answers since you have two questions presented) should read this way:

1. Supershop is liable for Jim's injury.
2. Supershop is not liable for Jenny's injury.

By now, you have already informed your reader what the questions (issues) and answers (conclusions) are. Now you should inform your reader of the relevant facts.

Statement of Facts
An account of the facts that are relevant to the questions presented.

The **statement of facts,** like the facts portion of a case brief, addresses the entire fact situation that is relevant to the issue(s). Keep in mind that the statement of facts is not like the facts/analysis portion of a legal answer, which refers to only one issue at a time.

In this memorandum your statement of facts should read:

Jim was shopping in Supershop and, while walking along the main entrance area, slipped on a freshly mopped floor and injured his back. There was no sign or other indication to warn shoppers that the floor was slippery.

That same day, Jenny purchased a box of cornflakes from Supershop. She took the box home, opened it, and fixed herself a bowl, adding milk and sweetener. Moments later, she felt pain and realized that she had bitten into a thumbtack that was in the cornflakes. She suffered injury to her teeth and gums.

Jim and Jenny are now suing Supershop for damages as a result of their injuries.

These facts depict everything that happened. Not just what happened to Jim or to Jenny but what happened to both of them — that is, the entire set of facts relevant to all issues.

Moreover, notice that your facts are *objective*. At this point you are conducting research to determine whether or not Supershop will be liable to Jim, Jenny, or both. Your writing must be neutral. Using your research, you are searching for the truth as you best believe it to be. If you determine that Supershop is liable to Jim, or Jenny, or both, or neither, say so.

Once your firm decides to accept Supershop as a client, then you must be *subjective*. You must at that point do everything you can to defend your client within the bounds of the law. Your writing can then be forceful and influential, much like a newspaper editorial or a political debate. However, right now you are primarily trying to inform your reader in a neutral, objective manner. While objectivity or subjectivity is reflected in all aspects of the memorandum, it is most clearly detected in the statement of facts.

Next you have the **analysis,** which is the legal answer for each issue. Here you have two issues so the analysis will be the same exact answer previously written for each of the two issues: Remember that an analysis or legal answer is made up of a conclusion, rule of law, facts/analysis, and the conclusion repeated. You already have your conclusion because it is the same as your brief answer. Here is your analysis of the issues:

Analysis
The step that comprises a conclusion, rule of law, facts/analysis, and repeated conclusion

> 1. Supershop is liable for Jim's injury.
>
> Pursuant to Statute 54, persons who do not exercise reasonable care are egligent, and thereby liable for harm resulting from their negligence.
>
> Here, Jim slipped and fell, injuring his back on Supershop's floor, after an employee mopped the floor, causing it to be slippery. Supershop did not warn customers of this dangerous condition, thereby failing to use reasonable care, and such negligence directly resulted in Jim's injury.
>
> Accordingly, Supershop is liable for Jim's injury.
>
> 2. Supershop is not liable for Jenny's injury.
>
> According to Statute 76, retailers are strictly liable for injury caused by open goods only, not prepackaged goods.
>
> Here, Jenny was injured because of a thumbtack that was contained in a box of cornflakes. Cornflakes is a prepackaged product. Supershop has no duty to open and inspect such package, and is not liable for injury caused to the consumer by the contents of such package.
>
> Therefore, Supershop is not liable for Jenny's injury.

Keep in mind that as you deal with more issues where the law is rather vague, you will probably use previous cases as your rule of law in interpreting the statutes. In those situations your analysis will probably be longer than the one in this example.

Finally, your **conclusion** will not be like the conclusion in an analysis (or legal answer), which deals with one particular issue. Instead, your conclusion will be an *overall summary* and determination, usually no more than one or two sentences long:

Conclusion
In a memorandum of law, a statement answering a specific question presented or an overall summary of all the brief answers and specific conclusions.

> For the reasons set forth, Supershop will likely be found liable for Jim's injury but not for Jenny's.

Now take a look at this memorandum one more time:

TO: [Reader's name]

FROM: [Your name]

RE: Supershop v. Jim/Jenny

DATE: [Today's date]

QUESTIONS PRESENTED: 1. Is Supershop liable for Jim's injury?
2. Is Supershop liable for Jenny's injury?

BRIEF ANSWERS: 1. Supershop is liable for Jim's injury.
2. Supershop is not liable for Jenny's injury.

STATEMENT OF FACTS: Jim was shopping in Supershop and, while walking along the main entrance area, slipped on a freshly mopped floor and injured his back. There was no sign or other indication to warn shoppers that the floor was slippery.

That same day, Jenny purchased a box of cornflakes from Supershop. She took the box home, opened it, and fixed herself a bowl, adding milk and sweetener. Moments later, she felt pain and realized that she had bitten into a thumbtack that was in the cornflakes. She suffered injury to her teeth and gums.

Jim and Jenny are now suing Supershop for damages as a result of their injuries.

ANALYSIS: 1. Supershop is liable for Jim's injury.

Pursuant to Statute 54, persons who do not exercise reasonable care are negligent, and thereby liable for harm resulting from their negligence.

Here, Jim slipped and fell on Supershop's floor, injuring his back, after an employee mopped the floor, causing it to be slippery. Supershop did not warn customers of this dangerous condition, thereby failing to use reasonable care, and such negligence directly resulted in Jim's injury.

Accordingly, Supershop is liable for Jim's injury.

2. Supershop is not liable for Jenny's injury.

According to Statute 76, retailers are strictly liable only for injuries caused by open goods, not prepackaged goods.

Here, Jenny was injured because of a thumbtack contained in a box of cornflakes. Cornflakes is a prepackaged product. Supershop has no duty to open and inspect such package, and is not liable for injury caused to the consumer by the contents of such package.

Therefore, Supershop is not liable for Jenny's injury.

CONCLUSION: For the reasons set forth, Supershop will likely be found liable for Jim's injury but not for Jenny's.

Sample Memorandum

Let's do one more example and this time we will use a case we briefed in the previous chapter as our source of law.

Patty Smith is the 19-year-old single mother of Jessica, who is 2 years old. Patty loves Jessica very much and has done her best to care for the child, with no help from Jessica's father, who refuses to take any responsibility for the baby. Patty has a low-paying job and lives in a small basement apartment with Jessica.

Patty's parents, Mr. and Mrs. Smith, have offered to take in Patty and Jessica until Patty increases her income. Patty has refused because she gets along poorly with her parents. The Smiths, concerned for Jessica's well-being, are suing Patty in court to gain temporary custody of Jessica.

Meanwhile, the Smiths have a niece (Patty's cousin) named Tricia. Tricia is 20 years old and has no other living relatives except the Smiths, Patty, and Jessica.

Last year, Tricia gave birth to a baby boy whom she named Justin. Tricia has no idea who the father is.

Although Tricia is a heavy drug user, the baby was not born addicted to drugs. Tricia's drug habit has resulted in her not feeding Justin regularly and often beating him when he cries. Last month, Tricia passed out one night from heavy drug use, and Justin was left unattended all night.

The Smiths are very concerned about the welfare of their grandnephew, Justin. Since they have the time, money, energy, and experience to raise both Justin and Jessica, they come to your law firm seeking to gain custody of both children.

Your senior partner asks you to write a memorandum indicating the Smiths' likelihood of obtaining custody of either child. Suppose that your most vital source of law is Culver v. Culver, the case that we briefed in the previous chapter.

The following is a sample memorandum.

TO: Senior Partner

FROM: [Your name here]

RE: Smiths' motion for custody of Jessica and Justin

DATE: [Today's date]

QUESTIONS PRESENTED:	1. Is Patty an unfit mother, thereby enabling the court to grant custody of Jessica to the Smiths? 2. Is Tricia an unfit mother, thereby enabling the court to grant custody of Justin to the Smiths?
BRIEF **ANSWERS:**	1. Patty is not an unfit mother; thus, the Smiths will probably not be granted custody of Jessica. 2. Tricia is an unfit mother; thus, the Smiths will probably be granted custody of Justin.
STATEMENT OF FACTS:	The Smiths have a daughter, Patty, and a niece, Tricia. Both Patty and Tricia are single mothers with one child each: Jessica (2) and Justin (1), respectively. Patty does her best to care for Jessica but, due to her small income, lives with Jessica in a basement apartment. Tricia, a drug user, has on occasion left Justin unfed and unsupervised. In addition, she often beats him. Tricia has no living relatives other than the Smith family. The Smiths, who have the time, money, energy, and experience to raise children, are concerned with the upbringing of both children and seek custody of both accordingly.
ANALYSIS:	1. Patty is not an unfit mother; thus, the Smiths will probably not be granted custody of Jessica.

In Culver v. Culver, 594 N.Y.S.2d 68, 69 (App. Div. 1993), the court held that a biological parent will not be denied custody of a child unless the parent is declared unfit, even if there are better parents willing to care for the child.

Here, there is no reason to indicate that Patty is unfit. In *Culver*, the court held that only extraordinary circumstances would permit a question of a parent's fitness. Id. Here, no such extraordinary circumstances exist. Patty's only shortcoming is her low income, which falls short of "extraordinary circumstances." Moreover, it does not matter that the Smiths may conceivably make better parents than Patty does. Accordingly, Patty is not an unfit mother; thus, the Smiths will probably not be granted custody of Jessica.

2. Tricia is an unfit mother; thus, the Smiths will probably be granted custody of Justin.

As stated above, the *Culver* court declared that the extraordinary circumstances standard will render a parent unfit, thus denying custody to such parent. (See Culver v. Culver, 594 N.Y.S.2d 68, 69 (App. Div. 1993).)

Here, Tricia's drug use has resulted in her failing to feed or attend to Justin and to beat Justin. Such behavior would probably meet the extraordinary circumstances standard set forth in *Culver*. As the closest living relatives who have petitioned for custody of Justin, the Smiths will probably be looked upon as favorable candidates to raise the child.

Therefore, Tricia is an unfit mother; thus, the Smiths will probably be granted custody of Justin.

CONCLUSION: For the reasons set forth, the Smiths will probably not be granted custody of Jessica but will probably be granted custody of Justin.

Do you understand all of the steps taken to write this memorandum? Do you also see how Culver v. Culver was used as the source of law? If so, you have now learned how to combine legal research, case briefing, and legal writing into a well-planned legal analysis!

> ★ **HINT:** When citing the *Culver* case, the first page reference (68) indicates where the case begins in the case reporter. The second page reference (69) indicates where the information used in the citation appears. Also, "id.," which means "the same," is a Latin abbreviation used when a direct or indirect quotation is cited from exactly the same page as the previous citation. Since both points of information in this memorandum were taken from page 69 of the *Culver* case, "id." may be used instead of the final citation to indicate that it is located in the same place as the first.

Finally, you must be thinking that this memorandum is awfully repetitive. You write a brief answer, only a few sentences later to find yourself writing it again. This repetitiveness seems obvious because these sample memoranda have been kept very brief to ensure you get the basic idea of their format. Usually, such memoranda may be 10, 20, 30, or more pages long. It is necessary to repeat yourself in those circumstances, if, for example, your brief answer appears on page 4 but your analysis begins much later on page 16.

At this point you should concentrate on mastering the fundamentals of good legal writing while brushing up on your case briefing skills. Accordingly, you should pick out a couple of cases, brief them, invent a fact pattern, and write a memorandum. This is the best practice for mastering good legal writing.

THE IMPORTANCE OF GOOD WRITING

The following statement (which I firmly stand by and relay to my students every chance I get) is vital in determining your success as a member of the legal community, so pay careful attention: *The single most important thing you can learn while studying law is how to be a good writer.*

Pay attention to the word "single." I am not suggesting that you can be a first-rate lawyer or paralegal without knowing a good amount of information about various areas of the law. However, if there is *one* thing that is *most* important, it is learning to write well.

Writing is probably the most difficult skill to perfect. You can become a good writer in a short time but you will *always* have room for improvement, and you will slowly and steadily improve over the weeks, months, and years of your education and professional career. You will not only benefit in the legal field, but you will find that being a good writer reaps rewards virtually everywhere!

Writing is more than an artistic expression of your feelings. Writing is also a very powerful weapon that you must learn to use to your advantage. Let me illustrate with a very general example and, for most of us, a very real experience — trying to get a job.

EXAMPLE

Suppose that a certain company has a job opening, and you would love to be hired for the position. After verifying that you meet the requirements, you submit a resume and a letter of introduction (i.e., cover letter). You know that depending on various factors (the state of the economy, luck of timing, etc.) you can find yourself among a very large number of people applying for one position.

In fact, suppose that 150 people have applied for the position that you are seeking. Let's say that, along with all the necessary skills required for the job, you happen to have a great personality, and you are confident that you can project that personality so well during an interview that you will be a shoo-in for the job.

Chances are, however, that only a few of the 150 applicants will be interviewed. So here you are, hoping to get the chance to tell your interviewer that you are perfect for the position, and your chance of getting that interview depends on . . . your writing! The writing quality in your letter of introduction may very well be the key to your getting hired.

What we often fail to realize is that first impressions count. Maybe that is short-sighted, narrow-minded, and unjust. In many cases it certainly is. However, in the world of work think of it as reality. Think about it. When you go on a job interview, are you going to wear your old sweatpants or your best business suit? Are you going to walk in unshaven or with smeared makeup, or are you going to look well groomed? Are you going to look angry or pleasant? In short, are you going to make a good first impression or not?

Most of us would try to make the best first impression we can. It is true that the angry-looking person in sweatpants may turn out to be a better worker than the smiling, well-dressed person, but why put yourself at a disadvantage? Most job markets are competitive (the legal field certainly is), so why not try to start with as many advantages as possible?

The same holds true for your writing. It is not enough for your cover letter to be neatly typed on nice paper and to be free of any typographical errors. The words must flow. The words must invite the person you are addressing to read on. You must appear as though you control the words, not the other way around. Logically, the person with the most impressive cover letter would have the best chance to gain an interview, all other things being equal.

Accordingly, good writing is essential in one of life's most familiar challenges, trying to get a job. Now let us examine how writing is particularly important in the law.

In law, more so than in many other professions, good writing is vital. The writing of lawyers or legal assistants is their weapon. A surgeon needs steady hands. A race car driver needs sharp reflexes. Similarly, a lawyer needs good writing skills.

As I mentioned earlier, writing is a weapon that you must learn to use with authority. In countless situations writing determines the outcome of a legal decision.

Although a case will often be won on its strength, at trial it is often won by the advocacy (oral argument) skills of the lawyer, and on appeal (i.e., a motion made to a higher court) by the strength of the brief (written argument).

Before studying the following examples, keep in mind that there are many different types of writing. You will probably experience a different writing style depending on whether you are reading a poem, short story, newspaper article, medical journal, or instruction manual. Similarly, you will see a unique style in legal writing, a style that is set forth in the remainder of this chapter.

I will not teach you about nouns, verbs, independent clauses, and prepositions. That material can best be covered in an English textbook. I am going to be less technical, using instead common sense and basic concepts.

MAKE SURE YOUR READER UNDERSTANDS YOUR WRITING

First of all, always make sure that your writing can be understood by your reader. This can usually be accomplished if you know your target audience. Keep in mind that legal writing is not artistic expression; it is informative and persuasive communication. For example, a seventeenth-century poem rich in symbolism can cause one person to be overcome by emotion while another person is utterly confused as to the poem's meaning. In legal writing you cannot afford to leave your audience confused. (Your typical audience may vary depending on the type of document you are writing.) Always read over your finished product but do more than just proofread: Ask yourself if someone else will understand what you mean. The next example is again one that I believe most of us can relate to.

Have you ever taken a course where you thought you understood the material completely, but you received a mediocre grade on the final exam? Or was there a course that you feared, and where you even thought that you had failed the final, but then received an A? Well, there is a logical reason to account for this beyond good or bad luck.

In the "easy" course, you were probably very confident, and you actually enjoyed what you were writing about. You were "on a roll," churning out page after page of what you thought were brilliant observations. However, you were overconfident. The contents of your brain were not accurately reflected in your paper. You may have had good ideas but you did not adequately let your reader know what they were. You left out some important fact that you thought was obvious and, bursting with a thousand different ideas, you confused your reader. In turn, your reader had no idea that you knew as much as you did, and graded you only on the contents of your exam. Ultimately, you received a C on an exam that you thought was a certain A.

Now, in the "hard" course you no doubt encountered a difficult exam where you believed you had limited knowledge of the subject matter. You were no longer brimming with confidence, no longer excited about sputtering out a world of ideas. You cautiously limited yourself to one or two main points and concluded you had failed. However, your reader found the exam informative and easy to read, and gave you an A. See the difference? Always be sure that what is in your brain winds up on the paper. Your readers cannot read your mind. They only see what is on the paper. Anything else becomes irrelevant.

EXAMPLE

· ·

ASSIGNMENT: You are asked to write an open-ended essay regarding important presidents in American history.

WHAT TO DO: While every president has, to some extent, shaped American history, the three most important presidents were George Washington, Thomas Jefferson, and Abraham Lincoln.

George Washington, our first president, is also known as the "father of our country." He set the standard of democracy that our young nation adopted and has continued to enforce 200 years later.

Thomas Jefferson, our third president, authored the Declaration of Independence, the document that set forth the principles by which our nation was founded. His ideological leadership endured through his presidency and became the foundation of the modern-day Democratic party.

Abraham Lincoln, our sixteenth president, successfully completed two important tasks. First, he abolished slavery. Second, he fought to keep our nation together by preventing the southern states from seceding.

WHAT NOT TO DO: We have had many great presidents throughout our nation's 200-plus years, the first of whom was George Washington, followed by Thomas Jefferson and Abraham Lincoln. Lincoln freed the slaves and kept our nation together, while Jefferson continued the principles set forth in the Declaration of Independence, which he authored and which our country was founded upon. Washington became our first elected president and set the standard that all other presidents followed.

Now, there have been some presidents in between Washington and Jefferson, and Jefferson and Lincoln, and following Lincoln who have been important but not as important. For example, Franklin Roosevelt was an important president because he was the only one to be elected four times, and he helped shape many of our country's social programs. However, he was not as important as Lincoln or Washington, and he may have been as important as his cousin, Theodore Roosevelt, who, during the turn of the century, provided strong, stable leadership to this country.

Do you see the difference? One flows smoothly like a stream. The other is like a kitchen sink overflowing with dirty dishes, pots, and pans.

MAKE SURE YOUR WRITING DOES NOT MEAN SOMETHING ELSE

This advice closely relates to that in the previous section. Even if you have made sure that your reader understands your writing, you must also make sure that your writing means what you intended it to mean.

The following examples illustrate this point.

EXAMPLES

• •

1. *Jane's parents like visiting the Rocky Mountains because they are covered with snow.*

What does the above statement mean? Who or what is covered with snow? Jane's parents or the Rocky Mountains? Most people reading the sentence would assume that the Rocky Mountains are covered with snow. However, what if the facts you had to interpret were less obvious?

2. *James bought a rare painting from Stacey's art gallery, which is worth one million dollars.*

Which is worth one million dollars — the painting or the art gallery? It is quite possible that the answer could be either one. The sentence is too confusing as written. Here are some correct alternatives:

(a) If the painting is worth a million dollars, write:

James bought a rare painting worth one million dollars from Stacey's art gallery.

(b) If the art gallery is worth a million dollars, write:

James bought a rare painting from Stacey's art gallery. The gallery is worth one million dollars.

(c) If you want to communicate the point in just one sentence, write:

Stacey's art gallery, which is worth one million dollars, sold a rare painting to James.

3. Suppose you walked into a grocery store and saw a sign that stated *Soft drinks only sold here.*

In reading that sign, you would probably conclude that the only drinks sold in that grocery store were soft drinks so you couldn't, for example, buy beer there.

However, a closer examination of the sign might suggest that soft drinks are only sold in that particular grocery store—no other place in the entire world outside of that grocery store sells soft drinks. Unless you are from another planet, you have enough common sense to know that particular grocery store is not the only place in the world where you can buy soft drinks, so you know that the first meaning is probably correct.

Again, what if the facts were not so obvious? Consider the next example.

4. Suppose you walked into a store selling sports memorabilia and read a sign stating *Muhammad Ali's boxing gloves only available here*. What does this mean? This store is the only place that sells Ali's boxing gloves, or the store only sells Ali boxing gloves and nothing else? A little more confusing, isn't it? Now rewrite the sentences:

(a) If the store is the only place that sells the Ali gloves, write:

Muhammad Ali's boxing gloves are only available here.

(b) If the store only sells Ali's gloves, write:

Only Muhammad Ali's boxing gloves available here.

or

We only sell Muhammad Ali's boxing gloves.

Accordingly, you should always reread your writing and place yourself in the reader's position. By rereading, you can eliminate any statements that may sound as if they mean something different than what you intended.

USE SIMPLE LANGUAGE AND KEEP IT SHORT

This advice goes back to the book's introduction, where I stated that lawyers sometimes speak in legalese. People often try to sound more sophisticated than they really are. We have all been guilty of this at one point or another. But the secret to good writing is simplicity.

Have you ever stopped in the middle of writing something and asked, "What is another way to say . . . ?" You wanted to use smarter, dressier words to say something. It is better to just leave the original wording alone. Use the simplest words possible to say what you want to say. Consider the following examples.

EXAMPLES

• •

1. *Jason borrowed a camera that belonged to Cindy in order to take a picture of the Grand Canyon for the benefit of Molly, who collects photographs consisting of landmarks in the United States.*

Now read the edited version:

Jason borrowed Cindy's camera to photograph the Grand Canyon for Molly's photograph collection of U.S. landmarks.

See the difference? The first version is 33 words. The second is only 16. You reduce your wordload by more than half and still express the same information. Is there any information in the first sentence that is missing from the second? No.

Analyze the information. What does it consist of?

A. Jason borrowed Molly's camera.
B. In order to photograph the Grand Canyon.
C. For Molly's photograph collection of U.S. landmarks.

This is 100 percent of what was stated in the first sentence, and all of it is included in the edited version.

The only difference is **word economy.** Economy makes sense in writing, just as it does in life.

2. Let's suppose you needed to buy a container of milk, a magazine, and a basketball. The grocery store is two blocks away from your house, the newsstand is three blocks, and the sporting goods store is four blocks (all three stores are in the same direction). Now, which of these two plans would you map out?

a. Walk to the sporting goods store, buy the basketball, and on the way home, stop at the newsstand and buy the magazine, then, continuing home, go in the grocery store and buy the milk, and then go home. OR

b. Walk to the grocery store, buy the milk, walk back home, walk to the newsstand, buy the magazine, walk back home, then walk to the sporting goods store, buy the basketball, walk back home.

Unless you enjoyed the exercise, you would almost certainly pick up all the things at once, instead of making three separate trips. You would economize or consolidate your effort. Why not do the same when writing? If you can accomplish the same thing in half the time, why not?

Unlike the above examples, there is a double advantage to economy in writing. It not only saves you time and energy, but is also gives your reader less to worry about understanding. Fewer words, as long as the meaning is complete, usually amounts to less confusion. However, when you economize, make sure you are not eliminating important information. Consider the following.

EXAMPLE

• •

Jack delivered a newspaper every day to Anna, delivered a newspaper every day to Barry, and delivered a newspaper every day to Carla.

You could improve this as follows: *Every day, Jack delivered the newspaper to Anna, Barry, and Carla.* Though you are cutting down the excess wording in your sentence, you are eliminating one important bit of information. In the first example it is presumed that Jack delivers a different copy of the newspaper to Anna, Barry, and Carla. In the second version it is possible that Anna, Barry, and Carla could all live in the same house and receive one newspaper that they all share.

Accordingly, you can correct the confusion by stating: *Anna, Barry, and Carla each receive a newspaper from Jack every day.*

It is important to consolidate your sentences but not leave out important information. Moreover, don't forget to write simply. Do not use long, "sophisticated-sounding" words. If you want to make a public speech or write a poem, use a lot of rhetoric. But in legal writing, just keep it simple. The clearest statements are the simplest.

As you read through the forthcoming chapters, you will learn about different areas of the law. For best results, keep this chapter in mind throughout this book and throughout your legal career.

Key Terms

alphabetizing	format	statement of facts
analysis	heading	verbatim
brief answers	legal answer	word economy
citation	memorandum of law	
conclusion	questions presented	
facts	rule of law	

Review Questions

1. What are the four steps to writing a basic answer to a legal question?

2. Why is the format of the four-part legal answer important?

3. Why is it sometimes not necessary to restate a rule of law verbatim?

4. What is a mamorandum of law?

5. What are the nine basic steps of a memorandum of law?

6. Why is it often important to repeat information in a memorandum of law?

7. Which steps in a memorandum of law are similar to steps in a four-part legal answer?

8. Why is good writing so important in the legal profession?

9. Why is using simple language helpful when writing?

10. Why is word economy helpful when writing?

Web Sites

For more information on proper citation for your legal writing, check out:

- ALWD Citation Manual's Web site
  http://www.alwd.org
- Online tutorial designed to teach Bluebook rules
  http://www.law.cornell.edu/citation

Introduction to Law

5

By now you have learned which sources of law are useful and how to find them, how to brief a case, and how to write a memorandum based on the law and particular facts in question. You have also learned about the importance of good writing.

At this point it is time to learn a little about some aspects of the law itself. The law can be divided into various classifications or categories.

SUBSTANTIVE LAW AND PROCEDURAL LAW

Two of these classifications are **substantive law** and **procedural law**. Substantive law is the actual law itself whereas procedural law is the legal process. Sound confusing? If you're confused, you're not alone. Far too many professors attempt to teach the difference between substantive

Substantive Law:
The elements of law—that is, the actual law itself.

Procedural Law:
The law that governs legal process.

law and procedural law but leave their students baffled. To learn the difference, you must be introduced to examples.

EXAMPLES

• •

1. If Dan intentionally kills Pete, Dan will probably be charged with murder. The legal elements of murder will be compared to Dan's actions, and, if they match, Dan will be found to have committed murder. This is a *substantive law* analysis—that is, we are looking at what the actual law is.

2. If Dan is arrested, he will have the right to an attorney, the right to a jury trial, and the right to be deemed innocent until proven guilty. These are all types of *procedural law*. They deal with the legal process that comes into play after the actual act.

Notice that the actual act is classified under substantive law, and the law that governs everything revolving around that act is procedural law. Look at some additional examples to make sure you understand.

★ ── ★

Substantive

A. Amanda is guilty of reckless driving because she was speeding.
B. Richard is guilty of arson because he intentionally burned down Cindy's house.
C. Greg's will is declared invalid because there were no witnesses to the signing.

(Each specific act can be compared to elements within a law to determine their illegality.)

Procedural

A. Alan has a right to a phone call after he is arrested.
B. Brenda has the right to remain silent during and after her arrest.
C. If Leslie sues Ted, Ted has the right to file a countersuit.

(Each example deals with a legal process that happens *after* an actual act has occurred.)

★ ── ★

Now you are better capable of understanding the difference: *Substantive law* deals with the act itself, the relevant legal elements, and what makes an act legal or illegal. *Procedural law* deals with the whole legal process: the rights a person has during arrest, trial, imprisonment, issues of punishment, the right to sue, and so on.

THE BASICS OF A LAWSUIT

Let us examine procedural law a bit more closely. What happens when a person wants to sue another person? May she simply call the court and make an appointment to stop by later that evening? No. May she call in the sheriff to administer justice? No. In order to utilize the system of justice, a person must follow a certain procedure.

Pleadings

In order to sue somebody, a person must complete and serve (and file) certain pleadings. **Pleadings** are documents involved in a lawsuit. While there are numerous types of pleadings, we will deal with the most common types since we are just examining the basics.

Pleadings: Documents involved in a lawsuit.

The Complaint

A **complaint** is the document that sets forth the cause of action (the reason why a person is bringing the lawsuit). A complaint includes the names of the **plaintiff** (the person bringing the lawsuit) and the **defendant** (the person against whom the lawsuit is brought). Any additional plaintiffs and defendants must be included in the complaint.

Complaint: Along with a summons, the necessary pleading to formally begin a lawsuit.

[Caption]

COMPLAINT

Plaintiff Mary Clark complains against Defendant Kevin Johnson as follows:

1. On January 6, 2004, Plaintiff Clark and Defendant Johnson entered into a contract.

2. Clark paid Johnson $4,500 and has performed all of her obligations under the contract.

3. Johnson failed to paint Clark's house as he was required to do under the contract.

Figure 5.1
Sample Complaint

Each allegation of the complaint is generally contained in a separately numbered sentence. And, generally, the first sentences set forth the relief sought (e.g., money), along with the type of lawsuit (e.g., breach of contract). (See Figure 5.1)

Additional sentences describe what happened. Finally, the actual damages suffered are listed. Quite often, a request for a jury trial is made. A trial may be decided by a judge or by a jury. If decided by a jury, the judge serves only as the "referee," guiding and monitoring the process. Depending on the case, a plaintiff may want her fate to be in the hands of a single legal professional (a judge) or several people from all walks of life (a jury).

The complaint must then become eligible to be served on the defendant.

Summons

Summons:
Along with a complaint, the necessary pleading to formally begin a lawsuit.

In order for a complaint to be effective, it must be accompanied by a **summons** (see Figure 5.2). Consider the following example to help you remember.

Suppose you write a long, detailed letter to a friend. You place the letter in an envelope, seal it, and on the back of the envelope write your friend's address as well as your return address. Now you mail the letter. What's wrong? You forgot the stamp! Your long, flowing, powerful letter may be ten pages long or even longer. But if the letter you dropped into the mailbox is without that tiny piece of paper known as a stamp, the letter is no different than a piece of tissue paper. It is the stamp that makes the letter a document eligible for mailing from one place to another.

Similarly, a complaint is the document that contains all of the details. Without a summons to accompany it, however, a complaint is

---

SUMMONS

To: _____ *[defendant and address]* _____

    You are hereby summoned and required to serve upon _____, plaintiff's attorney, whose address is _____, an answer to the complaint that is hereby served upon you, within 20 days after service upon you, exclusive of the day of service.

    If you fail to do so, judgment by default will be taken against you for the relief demanded in the complaint.

_____
Clerk of Court

Figure 5.2
Sample Summons

powerless—just another piece of paper. The summons, like a stamp, does not contain much detail. In fact, it does not describe any facts or other circumstances of the lawsuit. It simply explains that the defendant is being sued by the plaintiff and grants a certain period of time for an answer.

Service of a summons and complaint may be made in various ways (by hand, by mail, or by other notice), depending on the particular procedural laws of the jurisdiction. Generally, it is best to serve the opposing party (i.e., the defendant) by hand. There is no substitute for face-to-face acceptance. Personal service avoids such excuses as, "It must have gotten lost in the mail."

EXAMPLE

Suppose that Lillian Lopez was driving her car south on Jones Road. At the intersection of Main Street, she stopped at a red light. Brian Downs was driving his car directly behind Lillian, and Paul Clayton was behind Brian. Paul, who had not realized that Brian had slowed down because of the red light, slammed his car into Brian's. Brian's car, in turn, smashed into Lillian's car, causing personal injury to Lillian. Lillian's car was not damaged but she suffered neck and back injuries that are valued at $10,000 in medical bills and lost earnings.

As a result, Lillian decides to sue Brian, since it was Brian's car that slammed into hers. Lillian retains Marilyn Green, an attorney, to represent her. Marilyn drafts a complaint and hires a **process server** (a nonparty to the case, who serves pleadings on parties) to serve Brian. The process server personally serves Brian by hand. Brian now has 20 days to respond.

Answer

Once service has been properly made, the defendant has a specific amount of time to **answer** the complaint. The amount of time will vary, depending on both the jurisdiction and method of service. For our purposes, let's assume the amount of time that is generally allowed for answering a complaint served personally—20 days.

Answer:
In civil procedure, a written response to a complaint.

EXAMPLE

Brian has 20 days to answer Lillian's complaint. What happens if Brian, believing the accident was not his fault, decides to ignore the complaint?

After 20 days have passed, Marilyn may make a motion (another type of pleading, which we will discuss later) for a **default judgment** (see

Default Judgment:
Judgment against a party who failed to answer or respond to, a complaint brought against that party.

Figure 5.3). This means that a judgment will be entered against Brian. Because Brian did not answer the complaint, he automatically loses the case. Since Lillian now possesses a judgment against Brian, she has a great deal of power over him.

Lillian may enforce her default judgment in many ways. First, she may be able to "freeze" Brian's bank accounts, so that Brian may not access any of his money until he pays Lillian all of the money he owes her as set forth in the complaint.

Second, if Brian works for someone, Lillian may obtain an execution to **garnish** Brian's wages. This means that on every payday Brian's employer must first deduct a specific amount from Brian's paycheck to pay Lillian. This will continue until Lillian has been paid all of the money Brian owes her.

Moreover, it is possible that Brian's personal (or, in certain instances, business) property may be sold by direction of the jurisdiction's marshal at

---

[Caption]

MOTION FOR DEFAULT

Plaintiff Lillian Lopez moves for an order finding defendant Brian Downs in default, finding that the defendant owes plaintiff the sum of $10,000 plus costs, and for judgment against defendant in that amount.

In support of her motion plaintiff states:

1. On August 22, 2003, defendant Brian Downs was personally served with the summons and the complaint, as shown by the affidavit of service on the summons.

2. Defendant has failed to answer the complaint, has failed to make an appearance, or in any way respond or defend, although over 20 days have passed since service upon him.

3. Defendant has not responded to three letters sent to him by plaintiff's attorney. Copies of these letters are attached as Exhibits A, B, and C.

4. Plaintiff is prepared to testify to her reasonable damages, which total $10,000.

WHEREFORE, plaintiff requests that the court find defendant Brian Downs in default, hold a hearing to determine the exact amount due plaintiff, and enter judgment for plaintiff and against defendant in that amount.

_____
Attorney for Plaintiff

Figure 5.3
Lillian's Motion for
Default Judgment

a public auction. The money obtained from the sale will be used to pay Lillian. In fact, Brian may actually be charged for the cost of advertising the auction sale (a sale that he certainly would not want to encourage in the first place!).

Finally, if Brian owns a business and the business is held liable for the lawsuit, the marshal may "lock out" Brian by actually placing the business under lock and chain until Brian pays the debt to Lillian.

Notice just how powerful a default judgment can be. And keep in mind that the accident was not even Brian's fault. It was Paul's fault. However, since Brian chose to ignore the summons and complaint, he must now deal with the aggravation of a default judgment being enforced against him. A paralegal or lawyer should *always* remind a client *never* to ignore a summons and complaint.

Accordingly, the correct approach is to answer the complaint in a timely manner. Suppose that Brian decides to hire Louis Reed, an attorney, to represent him. Louis will draft an answer to the complaint. The answer must address all numbered allegations made in the complaint. These allegations will either be admitted or denied. Remember this rule: *If an allegation is not denied, it is admitted.* If there are 50 allegations in a complaint and you deny only 49 of them, you are admitting the other one. Be careful and get to all of them.

Motions and Other Pleadings

Suppose that Louis believes that his client Brian should not be sued at all. He may make a **motion** for summary judgment. This is a document that asks the court to dismiss the matter because there is no basis for a lawsuit. It is as if Louis tells the judge, "Your honor, Brian was stopped in his car. He was merely pushed into Lillian's car by Paul. It was not Brian's fault at all. Why should Brian be sued?"

Motion:
A type of pleading requesting a specific action to be authorized by the court.

Additionally, there are many other types of motions. Any time either party wants to ask something of the court, this is done through a motion. (See Figure 5.4 for an example of a routine motion, requesting a court to reschedule the date of a hearing.)

What if Brian is aggravated because this lawsuit is costing him time and money? What if he believes that Lillian should be suing Paul (and even if she is, what if Brian believes she should be suing *only* Paul) and that her basis for suing Brian is greed? Brian may file a **counterclaim** against Lillian. A counterclaim is a claim responding to a claim (just as there is "point/counterpoint" or "punch/counterpunch," there is claim/counterclaim).

What if Brian chooses to sue Paul himself, since it was Paul who caused the accident? Brian may file a **cross-claim** against Paul. A cross-claim is made by a defendant in a lawsuit against yet another defendant.

UNITED STATES DISTRICT COURT FOR THE DISTRICT OF IOWA

John Smith,
     Plaintiff

    v.   No. 90 C 182

Buckley Corporation, et al.,
     Defendants

MOTION TO RESET HEARING DATE

Plaintiff John Smith moves this Court for an order continuing the hearing on defendant's motion for discovery sanctions, presently set for October 1, 2003, for 10 days.

In support of his motion, plaintiff states:

     1. . . .
     2. . . .
     3. . . .

WHEREFORE, plaintiff John Smith requests the Court to enter an order continuing the hearing, presently set for October 1, 2003, to October 11, 2003.

                                     Attorney for Plaintiff
                                     Address
                                     Telephone

Figure 5.4
Sample Motion

Discovery

Discovery:
In civil procedure, a process by which one may obtain information about the other party.

Discovery is a process by which one party (or side) may find out information about the other. There are many types of discovery methods. Let's discuss two of the most common—interrogatories and depositions.

Interrogatories are questions that one side sends to the other. They are questions about time, place, manner, and other details pertaining to the particular situation. The other side then answers the interrogatories, and may submit interrogatories of their own.

Depositions are sworn statements (made under oath) by persons (who are parties or nonparties to the case) about the case at hand. The testimony of the **deponent** (the person who is making the sworn statement) is usually taken by the opposing attorney in the presence of a court reporter, who writes everything down. Generally, the deponent's attorney is present.

One big difference between interrogatories and depositions is that depositions are conducted under oath. This adds an even more formal element to depositions. However, this is not to suggest that interrogatories may be answered less than truthfully or that they may be taken lightly.

Jury Selection

One of the most difficult and controversial parts in ensuring a fair trial is selecting a **jury**. In order to better understand the **jury** selection process, let's examine the role of a jury and the laws that make the process as fair as possible.

Jury:
A group of persons selected to decide the facts of a court case.

A jury must be made up of a certain number of **jurors** (often the number is twelve so let's use that number for our example) who will decide the facts of the case. The jury will hear both sides and make a determination as to who they believe is telling the truth.

Jurors must be open-minded and unbiased. Frequently, when people perceive the justice system to be unjust, they blame the laws. Under close examination, they discover that many problems arise not because of faulty laws but because those laws are not properly enforced.

For instance, suppose that an automobile accident involved a truck and a passenger car. The car's driver sues the truck driver. Some believe that the ideal jury of twelve for this case would be six people who are truck drivers (or friends or family of truck drivers) and six people whose cars have been hit by truck drivers (or have friends or family members whose cars have been hit by truck drivers) in order to balance the biases for or against the defendant truck driver. *This is not an ideal jury. Balancing biases is not a good idea. It is cynical and wrong.*

The ideal jury will be made up of twelve people who have no particular bias for or against truck drivers. The twelve people should be open-minded and only make up their minds after they hear the particular facts of *that* case. The jurors should not be people who have heard stories about truck drivers or have had experiences with truck drivers that would make them think that "all truck drivers are the same."

This notion does not, of course, apply solely to biases concerning truck drivers. It applies to biases about members of any profession, race, nationality, religion, and many other categories. To "pack" a jury with an even number of people representing each category may often be a necessary safeguard against bias but it is certainly not ideal. The best solution is to choose twelve open-minded people, and the other "categories" should not even be considered.

Jurors are usually selected from a pool of registered voters. If a person is selected for jury duty, he or she must comply unless excused. A person may be excused for compelling reasons, such as illness, the need to care for a small child, and so on.

If a person is not excused, he or she will be subject to questions from attorneys for *both* parties. Both attorneys must agree on each juror. A juror may be dismissed for **cause**, as determined by the answers to some questions, or by **peremptory challenge** (without cause). Consider this example to help you better understand.

EXAMPLE

• •

Suppose that a doctor is on trial for performing an operation carelessly. The doctor's lawyer may ask a potential juror, "How do you feel about doctors?" If the juror answers, "They're all incompetent quacks," that juror is very likely to be biased against the doctor in the case at hand. Accordingly, the attorney may ask the judge to dismiss that juror for cause.

What if the lawyer does not get such a straightforward response from the juror? Suppose, instead, that the juror answers, "Doctors are okay, I guess." What if the lawyer, based on the juror's tone of voice or facial expressions, gets a "hunch" that the juror may be biased against doctors? Since the lawyer has no actual proof, how may this juror be dismissed?

Each lawyer has a certain amount of "free picks," known as peremptory challenges. This means that a given number of jurors (the exact number depends on the jurisdiction) may be dismissed by a lawyer with or without cause. This way, each lawyer is given the chance to follow his or her instincts, even when jurors have not actually stated their bias.

Once the attorneys for both sides have agreed on a pool of jurors and alternates (backups), and the judge has confirmed these selections, the jurors are set for trial.

The Trial

A trial may often be a long, draining experience. Paralegals and lawyers spend a great deal of time and energy to prepare, which often costs clients a considerable amount of money. It is no wonder that the overwhelming majority of legal disputes are settled before or during trial. The number of completed trials compared to the total number of legal disputes is relatively small.

Movies and television shows have often portrayed trials as exciting, dramatic confrontations. More recently, however, television cameras have been permitted inside *real* courtrooms. Audiences now see that while a trial may sometimes be as exciting as a trip around the world, it may often be as dull as sitting in an airport terminal watching the luggage spin around a carousel as you wait for your suitcase.

Jury listens as attorney questions witness

Many trials that are extremely lengthy have their own special circumstances. Since we are discussing the basic approaches to law, we will examine the broad, general stages common in trials.

Opening Statements

Each side has the opportunity to make an **opening statement**. The plaintiff (usually through his or her lawyer) speaks first, followed by the defendant (also usually through his or her lawyer). The opening statement gives both sides a chance to introduce themselves to the jury and to give a brief explanation of what they intend to prove.

Testimony by Witnesses

Again, beginning with the plaintiff, each side has the chance to call **witnesses** to the stand. If the plaintiff, for example, calls his own witness, this is **direct examination**. If the defendant also wishes to question her opponent's witness, this testimony is **cross-examination**. Finally, **redirect** examination occurs when the plaintiff chooses to question his own witness one more time. The defendant, of course, gets the same opportunity to directly examine her own witnesses, and such witnesses are subject to the plaintiff's cross-examination and the defendant's redirect examination.

Motion for a Directed Verdict

Each side, plaintiff and defendant, may ask the judge for a **directed verdict**. This means that each side claims that the other failed to prove its

Witnesses:
In civil procedure, a person who testifies in court, usually about something he or she has seen, heard, or knows.

Directed Verdict:
A verdict ordered by a judge if the judge determines that there is no issue to

case, and so the jury should not even become involved. It is as if the attorney tells the judge, "Your honor, since opposing counsel has failed to prove its case, there is no issue for the jury to decide. We respectfully ask that you rule in our favor at this time."

Since there are many steps taken before a case actually gets to trial, both sides are usually well prepared. Accordingly, it is not often that a judge will determine that the case is so one-sided as to warrant a directed verdict.

Closing Arguments

In the **closing argument** both sides conclude their argument, summarizing what they have proven and leaving the jury with a final impression of the case. This time, the defendant usually goes first, and the plaintiff speaks last. (You will discover later that the plaintiff is the one who bears the burden of proving the case. Accordingly, he is given the opportunity to have the last word.)

Jury Instructions, Deliberations, and Verdict

Once both sides have concluded their arguments, the judge instructs the jury about the law. In a criminal trial, for instance, the judge may explain the particular law to the jurors and then instruct them, "If you think, upon reviewing the facts, that the defendant broke the law, you must find the defendant guilty. If not, then you must find the defendant not guilty."

The jury then retires to **deliberate** (i.e., discuss and decide the outcome of the case). Laws regarding the specifics of a jury verdict will vary from jurisdiction to jurisdiction.

The jury will then inform the judge of the verdict inside the courtroom. The judge will then use this information to determine judgment (including awarding money, sentencing, etc.).

These, then, are some of the basics of legal procedure. They are the general steps that a legal dispute takes all the way through trial.

CATEGORIES OF LAW: CIVIL AND CRIMINAL

Civil Law:
The category of law in which the plaintiff is a direct party to the action and the goal is to compensate the aggrieved party.

In the forthcoming chapters we will discuss various types of substantive law: contracts, torts, and types of crimes. But, first, let's look at another way the law can be categorized. Generally, there are two main types of law: civil law and criminal law.

A case under **civil law** consists of a private person (or group) bringing a lawsuit that involves civil wrongs and seeks some type of compensation.

A case under **criminal law** consists of the people (at the state or national level) bringing a lawsuit that involves crimes and seeks to punish the accused. For a clearer understanding, consider the following examples.

EXAMPLES

• •

Suppose that you are walking down the street, and a piece from an old building falls off and hits you on the shoulder and hurts you. As a result, you are hospitalized for a few days and miss work. When you leave the hospital, you are faced with a rather costly medical bill. You decide to sue the owner of the building. This is a *civil* suit, not a criminal suit. The owner certainly did not intend that you be injured by the falling piece. However, she may still be held liable for your injury. If found liable, the owner will not be *punished* (e.g., go to jail) but will be compelled to *compensate* you (e.g., pay your medical bills). Note that in this case you are the plaintiff because you are bringing the lawsuit, and the owner is the defendant because she is the person against whom you are bringing the lawsuit.

In another example, suppose you park your car on the street while you do some shopping. In the meantime, X tries to steal your car. X picks the lock and, as he is trying to start the car, the alarm goes off. Two police officers spot X in your car and arrest him. When you return to your car, the police explain what happened.

In this incident, you suffer no real damages. You are not injured in any way, your car is still there, and even the lock was neatly picked. Accordingly, there is no personal or property injury. However, X's conduct is considered by society to be wrong. In fact, it is considered to be so wrong, it goes beyond civil wrong. It is a *criminal* wrong.

Criminal wrongs are considered to be wrongs not only against the immediate victim but against society as a whole. Therefore, if this attempted car theft happened in Chicago, the people of the entire state of Illinois would be the plaintiff against X, the defendant. If X were found guilty, X would not compensate you but instead would be punished.

In the first example your priority would probably be compensation to pay your medical bills. If the owner of the building had been sent to jail for one, five, ten, or even fifty years, would that pay your medical bill? Of course not. It would not pay one penny!

In the second example you did not suffer any damages. Your car is fine, and you are fine. However, you probably want to see X punished for his actions. More important, society as a whole, acting on behalf of you and all of its other citizens, wants to see X punished for his actions. Even if you are in a forgiving mood and do not want to "press charges," it is not your lawsuit. It is society (in this case, the people of Illinois) against X. If you press charges, it only helps the people's case. Even if you don't press charges, however, the people have the right to bring a criminal lawsuit against X.

Criminal Law:
The category of law in which the plaintiffs are the people of the state or country and the goal is to punish the defendant.

Let's expand the second example a bit. Suppose that instead of picking the lock, X tried to force it open. When he failed, he smashed in the window. Accordingly, there are damages to your car totaling $150. In that case, X will probably face both civil and criminal penalties: the state versus X for the crime, and you versus X for the compensation of the $150. Same act, two lawsuits. One civil, one criminal.

Standard of Proof

Finally, you should be aware of another comparison between civil and criminal law—the **standard of proof**.

In a civil trial the defendant must be found liable (guilty) by a *preponderance of the evidence*. This simply means that the defendant must be more liable than not liable. Mathematically, if the defendant is slightly over 50 percent liable, this is enough to render a verdict.

In criminal law, however, the standard is more stringent. This is understandable since the stakes are higher. While civil penalties may be heavy at times, such as payment of a large amount of money, they are generally less severe than criminal penalties. Criminal penalties may involve heavy fines, long-term imprisonment, and even execution.

Therefore, a defendant in a criminal case cannot be found guilty simply by a preponderance of the evidence but must be found guilty *beyond a reasonable doubt*. While there is no mathematical standard to measure "reasonable doubt," proof of guilt generally requires much more than going beyond the 50 percent (preponderance) standard.

FINAL THOUGHTS

The two classifications of law you should be aware of are substantive and procedural, and civil and criminal. Starting in the next chapter, you will be introduced to substantive law, beginning with civil law.

★ **HINT:** Keep in mind that you will be learning generally applicable legal principles; however, their application may differ from state to state and jurisdiction to jurisdiction. There are 50 states with 50 different sets of laws. There is also federal law, local law, and administrative law. Therefore, these general legal principles should be considered a guideline that can be applied to the laws of a specific jurisdiction.

Key Terms

answer

cause

civil law

closing argument

complaint

counterclaim

criminal law

cross-claim

cross-examination

default judgment

defendant

deliberate

deponent

deposition

direct examination

directed verdict

discovery

garnishing

interrogatory

juror

jury

motion

opening statement

peremptory
    challenge

plaintiff

pleadings

procedural law

process server

redirect

service

standard of proof

substantive law

summons

witness

Review Questions

1. What is the difference between substantive law and procedural law? Give three examples of each.

2. What is a pleading?

3. What is a default judgment?

4. What is a peremptory challenge?

5. What is a directed verdict?

6. Define civil law and criminal law, and list some differences between them.

7. What basic documents are needed to initiate a lawsuit?

8. What is the difference between a counterclaim and a cross-claim?

9. Discuss direct, cross, and redirect examination at trail.

10. Discuss the role of the jury after closing arguments at trail.

Web Sites

- Fundamentals of a jury trial
  http://www.da.saccounty.net/info/fundamentals.htm
- Legal Information Institute, overview of appellate procedure
  http://www.law.cornell.edu/topics/appellate_procedure.html
- Information about and video clips of current trials
  http://www.courttv.com

Contracts

6

Our first venture into substantive law will be in civil law. Civil law involves many different types of law. Most can be broken down into two general categories — contracts and torts. (Torts will be examined in the next chapter.)

WHAT IS A CONTRACT?

You have undoubtedly heard the word "contract" many times during your lifetime. This is not a word exclusive to the legal community — people from all walks of life use it. In fact, people from all walks of life enter into contracts, often on a daily basis. But do you know what a contract really is?

Before I give you the definition of a contract, let me warn you that, as with all definitions, different sources will provide different explanations. For instance, the definition here may differ from that in another textbook or a law dictionary, or from a particular judge's definition in a case opinion. However, whatever version you encounter, the definitions will probably amount to essentially the same principle. Moreover, there are variations of contract law in various jurisdictions on the federal, state, and local levels. Note also that we are learning the basic, general principles of law, which may be subject to exceptions.

> ★ **HINT:** By the way, a common abbreviation for "contract" is "K." This may seem odd, since the letter *K* is not found in the word "contract." Nonetheless, it is a common legal abbreviation.

Contract:
An agreement enforceable by law.

Keeping all of this in mind, here is a simple, sensible definition: A **contract** is an agreement enforceable by law.

This straightforward definition is a valuable starting point to help you understand what a contract is. For example, some people are under the misconception that a contract must be in writing. Others feel that a contract is any promise. Some people are under the impression that a contract must be an official document. Others believe that a contract can be made by anyone.

Some of these notions are too broad, others too narrow. Let's examine the above definition: A *contract is an agreement enforceable by law*. This automatically implies that not every agreement amounts to a contract; only those agreements enforceable by law do. Therefore, let us now look at the elements necessary to create a legally valid, enforceable contract.

A valid, enforceable contract consists of

- an offer
- an acceptance
- consideration
- no defenses

An offer and an acceptance, by themselves, create an agreement. If that agreement is supported by consideration (this term will be defined later), it becomes a contract. And if that contract is not subject to any defenses, then it is a valid, enforceable contract.

Let's discuss these elements in detail.

Offer:
A proposal that, together with its acceptance, constitutes an agreement.

Offer

First of all, there is the **offer.** Simply put, an offer is an intention to enter into an agreement. Usually the offer is directly expressed orally or in writing. At times, an offer may even be implied by conduct. By itself, however, an offer does not make a contract.

EXAMPLE

• •

Charlie walks up to you and says, "I would like to buy your watch for $50." You do not respond, or you say no. Can Charlie take you to court for breach of contract? Of course not. Charlie did indeed make an offer, but an offer alone does not constitute a contract.

Acceptance

Among other things, there must be an **acceptance** to the offer, directly expressed either orally or in writing, before there is a contract.

Acceptance: Compliance with an offer that, together with the offer, constitutes an agreement.

EXAMPLE

• •

If Charlie offered to buy your watch for $50 and you accepted, you and Charlie have entered into an agreement.

Suppose, however, that Charlie had admired your watch for a long while. Then you bought a new watch and, knowing how much Charlie liked the old watch, you told Charlie that you would give him the old watch free of charge. Charlie thanked you and accepted your offer. Suppose you worked with Charlie, and you promised him on Friday afternoon that you would bring in the old watch to the office on Monday morning. But on Monday morning, you told Charlie that you had changed your mind. Could Charlie successfully sue you for breach of contract? Probably not. In order for a contract to be formed, the offer and the acceptance must be supported by consideration.

Consideration

Consideration is something of value offered in exchange for something else of value.

Consideration: Something of value offered in exchange for something else of value.

EXAMPLE

• •

In the previous example, where Charlie was going to give you $50 in exchange for the watch, there was mutual consideration. Each of you would be giving up something of value, and each would be gaining something of value. Charlie would be giving up $50 and gaining a watch. You would be giving up a watch and gaining $50.

If you were to give the watch to Charlie as a gift, however, this does not amount to consideration. Charlie is gaining something of value (the watch) but not giving up anything for it. You are giving up something of value (the watch) but not gaining anything for it. The agreement is not supported by consideration; therefore, it is not a contract.

If you changed your mind about parting with the watch, and you had promised to give the watch to Charlie, Charlie generally cannot sue you for breach of contract. However, if the agreement was that Charlie would give you $50 in exchange for the watch, and you changed your mind, Charlie would have a good case against you. In the latter example, the agreement indeed would be supported by consideration.

The term "consideration" has different meanings in the English language, but in contract law its meaning is simple: something for value in exchange for something of value. The consideration does not have to occur simultaneously with the promise. The money or goods do not have to be exchanged at the instant the agreement is made. As long as there is the promise of the bargained-for exchange, this generally amounts to valid consideration.

Defenses

Defense:
An exception that may legally excuse or justify noncompliance with a law or general rule.

Finally, in contract law (as with every type of law) a **defense** will often negate a particular condition. For example, punching someone is usually against the law, but when two professional boxers punch each other, they are not committing a crime because there is the defense of consent.

Similarly, where an offer, acceptance, and consideration will create a contract, that contract will not be enforceable if there is a valid defense. Accordingly, a contract will only be enforceable if there are no applicable defenses.

Since this book is a basic introduction to the law, we will not examine every possible contractual defense, only some of the more common ones.

Capacity

First of all, there is the **capacity defense.** There are certain types of persons who lack the capacity required to enter into a contract.

Minor:
A person who is under the legal age of capacity.

Minors. Persons under the age of majority — **minors** — fall into this category.

EXAMPLE

Suppose that on a hot, sunny day in August, you are in the park and suddenly notice that the ice cream truck has arrived. You buy a chocolate ice cream cone with chocolate sprinkles and are about to dig in and enjoy. At that point, a five-year-old girl named Michelle looks at your ice cream cone as if she would like one, too. Apparently, Michelle does not have any money, and she is not accompanied by an adult. You notice that Michelle is wearing a valuable gold chain. Let's assume you are a devious person, and you say to Michelle, "I'll trade you this yummy ice cream cone for your chain." Michelle agrees. Immediately, she takes off the chain and gives it to you, and you give her the ice cream cone. Michelle happily runs along, finds her mother, and tells her about the trade. Michelle's mother finds you and demands that you return the gold chain. You argue that you made an offer to Michelle, Michelle accepted, and the exchange of the ice cream cone for the chain was consideration. Therefore, you and Michelle entered into a contract. Is your contract with Michelle legally enforceable? No.

The contract would be unenforceable mainly because of incapacity. Michelle, as a minor, lacks the legal capacity to enter into a contract. Therefore, she (or an adult on her behalf) may void the contract at her option. Since the minor is the one who lacks capacity, she has the choice of voiding the contract. If the minor who lacks the capacity wants to void the deal, the minor may do so. However, if an adult who enters into a contract with a minor wants to void the deal, he or she cannot. The minor may say, "I am a minor and can therefore change my mind." The adult may not say, "Since you are a minor, our deal was never valid, so it's off."

There are some additional possibilities you should be aware of that could apply. Some jurisdictions would also find the contract voidable for lack of adequate consideration, citing the great discrepancy in value between the gold chain and the ice cream cone. However, this is just a possibility. Regarding contracts of necessity (such as food, shelter, etc.), some jurisdictions may hold minors liable for such dealings. Again, this is not the case with the instant example.

Illiterate persons.   The capacity defense also applies to other individuals who may lack capacity, such as **illiterate persons.** For the purposes of this definition, illiterate persons are those who cannot sufficiently read English (whether because they cannot read at all, or maybe because they are foreigners to the United States and can only read in their own native tongue).

EXAMPLE

Suppose that Bruno, who was born and raised in Italy, comes to the United States to visit his relatives in Chicago. Bruno does not speak much English.

One day, Bruno goes for a walk and enters a discount store. He sees a big, beautiful boombox on sale for $80. Bruno does not realize that the radio, which is secondhand, has a defective CD player.

Bruno begins speaking to John, the salesman, in broken English. John, realizing that Bruno is not fluent in English, sells the boombox to Bruno and asks Bruno to sign a document stating, "I have been told that this product is defective, and I choose to buy it at my own risk and waive my right to return it for a refund or exchange." John tells Bruno that this is only a typical receipt. Bruno signs the receipt, pays the $80, and takes the radio home.

When Bruno realizes that the CD player is broken, he returns to the store and demands his money back. John refuses to give him the money and produces a copy of the signed receipt. Does Bruno have a legal right to get his money back? Yes, because his contract to buy the boombox from John is not enforceable.

Although there was an offer, an acceptance, and consideration, Bruno can successfully raise the illiteracy defense. John took advantage of Bruno's illiteracy in English, and told Bruno to sign the "typical receipt," which in turn was an acknowledgment that the boombox was defective.

In reality, John never told Bruno that the boombox was defective. Accordingly, the contract is not enforceable and Bruno is entitled to a refund.

Intoxication. Another capacity defense is **intoxication**. If a person is severely intoxicated (by alcohol, drugs, etc.) and enters into a contract that he or she would not have entered into if sober, the contract may be voided.

EXAMPLE

Suppose that you were at a bar having a few drinks while wearing your beautiful gold ring. The ring was a gift from someone very close to you, and you had no intention of selling it. However, after a few more drinks, someone offered to buy it from you, and you sold it for $200. At that point, you were severely drunk. Later on, you went home and went to sleep.

The next morning, you woke up, realized that you had sold your very precious possession, and now regret your decision. You would never have sold the ring had you been sober. Are you entitled to your ring back? Yes. The contract was never enforceable due to the intoxication defense.

This is the point where a student will usually ask, "But how can you prove that you were drunk?" This is the distinction between a question of fact and a question of law that we discussed in Chapter 3.

★ **HINT:** You must first learn what the law is, always assuming that you can prove it. Then, worry about proving it.

In the example involving intoxication, you can probably prove your case if you get the bartender and bar patrons to testify to your drunkenness.

If, however, you and the person to whom you sold the ring were alone in a private home, then it is that person's word against yours; it will be very difficult to prove your case.

In either situation, the law is the same. If you were too drunk to possess the capacity to enter into a contract, then the contract cannot be enforceable. Whether or not you can prove this law depends on how successful you are at convincing the judge (or jury) of your argument.

Mental Incompetence. A fourth example of lack of capacity is **mental incompetence.** If a person lacks the mental capacity to enter into a contract, such contract may be voided. This is similar to the earlier principles, particularly the one involving age. It is easy to figure out why a 5-year-old child lacks the mental capacity to enter into a contract. But what about a 90-year-old person who has become senile? Or a 40-year-old who is mentally ill?

The mentally incompetent person must prove that his condition prevents him from possessing the capacity necessary to enter into a contract.

In all instances involving capacity, the incapacitated party may void the contract at his option. The contract is not automatically void but voidable only by the person lacking capacity. The person with capacity does not have the option to void.

EXAMPLE

• •

Marcia enters into a contract to sell a used bicycle to a minor or intoxicated or illiterate or mentally incompetent person. In each situation the other party has the option to (1) change his mind and void the contract with Marcia or (2) follow through with the contract. Marcia does not have the option to void the contract since she is not the one who lacks capacity. This defense is designed to protect those who lack capacity.

Some jurisdictions will make the contract void automatically when it involves mentally incapacitated persons who (1) have been declared mentally incapacitated by a court and (2) have a court-appointed legal guardian to care for them.

_____

These, then, are the most common examples of the capacity defense.

The Statute of Frauds

Statute of Frauds:
A rule of law that specifies when a contract must be in writing.

Another type of defense is the **statute of frauds,** which is related to unwritten contracts. As previously stated, a contract does not have to be in writing all the time. For example, if you offer to buy my skateboard for $50 and I accept, our agreement does not have to be in writing to amount to a valid, enforceable contract. If indeed it is in writing, it serves to protect both of us in case one of us goes back on his word.

Accordingly, a contract may be in writing anytime. In fact, it is advisable to execute a written contract whenever possible. In most instances, however, the contract may be either written or oral. Only in certain situations must the contract be in writing.

A contract _must_ be in writing if it involves:

★ _____ ★

1. the sale of goods $500 or more
2. the sale of land
3. marriage
4. an agreement that cannot possibly be completed within one year
5. a promise to pay or be responsible for a debt or something of value

★ _____ ★

Let us now examine each of these in detail.

Sale of goods $500 or more.   Concentrate carefully on the words "sale" and "goods." If Anna offers to rent her car to Tony for one month for $600 and Tony accepts, must the agreement be in writing? The answer is no because Anna is only renting the car, not selling it. If Anna offered to sell her car to Tony for $600, would the contract have to be in writing? Yes.

If Anna offered Tony a job as a waiter in her restaurant for $1,000 a month for three months, would the agreement have to be in writing? No, because Tony is not selling goods to Anna; he is selling (or providing) his employment services.

Once again, a contract involving _the sale of goods $500 or more_ must be in writing.

Sale of land.   The sale of land, at any price, must be in writing. Granted, most land these days will cost more than $500 anyway. So why not just combine rules 1 and 2 and say "the sale of goods and land $500 or more"? Because it is possible that some parcels of land may actually cost less than $500.

For example, imagine you offer to buy a small piece of Jim's farmland for $400, and your agreement is oral. Suppose that Jim goes back on his word. Even if you have ten witnesses that heard Jim agree to sell you the land, Jim is not legally required to sell the land to you; a contract involving the *sale of land at any price* must be in writing.

Marriage. A contract that involves marriage must be in writing. While many people marry solely based on love and trust, and do not base their commitment on legal documents, others agree to marry subject to marital agreements (such as prenuptial agreements).

For example, Maggie agrees to marry Paul as long as she retains sole interest over her own future earnings if they ever divorce. Maggie and Paul enter into a prenuptial agreement, subject to the laws of their state. In order for their agreement to be legally enforceable, it must be in writing.

Any time the contract involves *marriage*, it must be in writing. Conversely, a contract that is an agreement *not to marry* does not have to be in writing. For example, if Maggie's father tells Tony, "I'll give you $20,000 if you agree not to marry my daughter," this contract does not have to be in writing because it is not a contract to marry but a contract not to marry.

An Agreement that Cannot Possibly be Completed within one Year. If a contract by its terms cannot possibly be completed within one year, it must be in writing to be enforceable, regardless of the value amount.

For example, suppose that Jackie, a nightclub singer, agrees to perform at a certain nightclub for the club's next two New Year's Eve parties. Whatever the dollar amount Jackie will receive, the contract must be in writing because it is a contract that cannot possibly be completed within one year. (Obviously, New Year's Eve comes only once each year, and Jackie has agreed to perform for two New Year's Eve parties.)

What if you were accepted into law school, and your rich aunt and uncle, also lawyers, said to you, "If you graduate in the top 10 percent of your class, we will buy you a brand new sports car of your choice on graduation day." You say, "Wow, thanks for the offer. I accept, and I know I won't disappoint you." Now, remember, there is adequate consideration here if you work extra hard to graduate in the top 10 percent because of the offer made by your aunt and uncle. You will be giving up something of value (time and effort) in exchange for something of value (the sports car). Your aunt and uncle will be giving up something of value (the money for the sports car) in exchange for something of value (the satisfaction they derive from your having achieved excellent grades). In most jurisdictions this would be enough for mutual consideration.

Accordingly, there is an offer, an acceptance, and consideration. However, if the contract is verbal, it will not be enforceable. It must be in writing to be enforceable. Because it is impossible to complete law school in less than one year, the contract will definitely take more than one year to complete, and so must be in writing.

If a contract *may* take longer than a year to complete, it does not have to be in writing. For example, if George offers to build a house for you, it could take six months, it could take ten months, it could take a year, or longer. Since it is not certain that the contract cannot possibly be completed within one year, the contract does not have to be in writing.

A Contract to Pay or be Responsible for a Debt or Something of Value.   A person's (such as a cosigner's) promise to be responsible for another person's debt must be in writing. Again, the dollar amount is irrelevant.

For example, suppose that you have an old car you are selling for $300. Jack offers to buy your car but he can only give you $50 per week. You are not entirely convinced that Jack will pay every week. Accordingly, Jack asks his boss, Marcus, to cosign (i.e., agree to pay you the money if Jack does not).

Since you know Marcus to be trustworthy and financially secure, you agree to this condition. However, for Marcus' obligation to be binding, it must be in writing. Your contract with Jack does not have to be in writing. Nonetheless, Marcus' obligation to pay (in the event Jack does not) must be in writing.

All these conditions fall under the statute of frauds defense. This defense will only be examined if the contract is not in writing. At that point, you should ask yourself whether the contract involves:

1. a sale of goods $500 or more?
2. a sale of land?
3. marriage?
4. an agreement that by its terms cannot possibly be completed within one year?
5. a promise to pay or be responsible for another person's debt or something of value?

If the contract is oral, it will only be enforceable if the answer to all of the questions is no.

If the answer to any of the questions is yes, the contract will only be enforceable if it is in writing.

> ★ **HINT:** Again, remember that while only the above-mentioned contracts must be in writing, and all others may be oral, it is always wise, whenever possible, to execute a contract in writing in order to best protect all interested parties.

Illegality

Another important defense is **illegality.** If an agreement is made for an illegal purpose or is otherwise in violation of the law, it will not be enforceable by law. That is, it will not amount to a valid contract.

EXAMPLE

• •

If you go to the grocer and buy five pounds of freshly ground coffee but, when you get home, you discover that you were only given four pounds of coffee, you are entitled to the remaining portion. In essence, you made an offer to buy the coffee, the grocer accepted, and the exchange of money for coffee was the consideration. Therefore, you entered into a contract with the grocer, and each of you was obligated to the other. The grocer was obligated to provide you with five pounds of freshly ground coffee, and you were obligated to pay the agreed-upon price. Accordingly, when you discover that you only received four pounds of coffee, you have a right as a contracting party to enforce the terms of the contract.

Let's take a different situation. Bob offers to buy ten ounces of cocaine from Steve for an agreed-upon price. Steve accepts and gives Bob the cocaine in exchange for the money. When Bob gets home, he realizes that he only received six ounces of cocaine. Can Bob legally enforce the terms of the agreement?

No! The agreement was for the sale of an illegal drug and, therefore, the contract is not enforceable.

What happens when a person borrows money from a bank and then fails to repay it? The bank can exercise a number of legal remedies. However, have you heard of the consequences when a borrower fails to pay back a loan shark? Those "remedies" (often involving physical violence) that a loan shark uses to recover unpaid debts are illegal. In fact, the loan shark has no *legal* remedies. The loan shark cannot take the borrower to court because if the terms of the loan agreement were illegal (if, for example, the loan was given at an unlawfully high interest rate), the agreement is not a legally enforceable contract.

The illegality of the act in question may not necessarily be as notorious as drug dealing or loan sharking. For instance, suppose a college baseball team enters into an agreement with a beer distributor: The team agrees to purchase a certain amount of beer each weekend for the duration of the baseball season for an agreed-upon amount. If the team member who purchases the beer is under the legal drinking minimum age, the agreement is unenforceable. At any time, the team, or the distributor, or both may void the contract because its terms are in violation of the law.

In certain jurisdictions, if a contract contains both legal and illegal terms, only the illegal terms will be voided, and the legal portion of the contract will stand. In the above example, if the team also contracted to purchase food from the distributor, that portion of the contract would still remain valid and enforceable. Again, all of this assumes that the agreement was made in a jurisdiction that applies this legal principle.

Duress

Duress:
Corecion; it occurs when a person acts against his or her will.

Another defense to a contract is **duress.** If a contract is entered into against a person's will, that contract may be voided. Note that a contract is designed to protect contracting parties, assuming that those parties entered into the contract based on their own free will.

In contract law the courts simply look at each contract on a case-by-case basis. If it is determined that the parties have decided to commit themselves to a particular agreement, that agreement will be enforced. However, if any of the parties entered into the agreement against their will, such agreement does not amount to a valid, enforceable contract.

EXAMPLE

Suppose you own a business, and Walter approaches you one day offering to buy it. When you refuse, Walter threatens to destroy your business unless you sell to him. You think about it and decide to sell to Walter. A few weeks later, you grow more and more angry at your decision and decide to publicly expose Walter for his threats. As a result, you now want to cancel the contract and get your business back. Do you have a legal right to get your business back? Yes. As always, if you can prove your allegation—that Walter threatened you—you can establish that the contract was entered into under duress and is therefore invalid.

These, then, are some of the more common defenses that would render a contract unenforceable:

★

- CAPACITY. Includes the following categories of people:

  minors
  illiterate
  intoxicated
  mentally incompetent

- STATUTE OF FRAUDS. Contract must be in writing if it involves:

  a sale of goods $500 or more
  a sale of land
  marriage
  an agreement that cannot possibly be completed within one year
  a promise to pay or otherwise be responsible for another person's
    debt

  - ILLEGALITY
  - DURESS

★

RECOGNIZING A CONTRACT WHEN YOU SEE ONE

As I previously stated, the best way to figure out if a certain situation amounts to a valid, enforceable contract is to review the checklist at the beginning of this chapter. A valid, enforceable contract consists of:

- an offer
- an acceptance
- consideration
- no defenses

If there is an offer and an acceptance, there is an agreement. The offer and the acceptance must be identical. For instance, invitations to offer, to negotiate, to change a suggested price, and so on are meaningless. If the final acceptance matches the exact terms of the offer immediately preceding it, then the necessary meeting of the minds has been established.

EXAMPLE

Suppose Amy offers to sell her gold bracelet to Jan, and the following dialogue ensues:

Amy: Would you like to buy my bracelet?
Jan: Yes, how much?
Amy: I'll sell it to you for a hundred dollars.
Jan: How about fifty?
Amy: No way, that's too cheap. I'll come down to ninety.
Jan: That's still too expensive for me. How about sixty?
Amy: I'll go down to eighty.
Jan: Seventy-five, and you've got a deal.
Amy: Okay, seventy-five it is.

The only part of the conversation that is relevant to the contract between Amy and Jan is that Jan's last offer, to buy the bracelet for $75, was accepted by Amy. All of the other offers were rejected when a different amount was discussed. Those rejections then became counteroffers, which were also rejected. It was not until Jan's offer to buy for $75 that Amy's acceptance became the mirror image of Jan's offer.

Getting back to the elements of a contract, an agreement must be supported by consideration in order to become a contract. Consideration is value in exchange for value. In the previous example, Amy was giving up the bracelet to Jan in exchange for money. This value-for-value exchange amounts to valid consideration.

At this point, there is a contract between Amy and Jan. To be sure that the contract will be enforceable, you should compare the situation to the checklist of defenses. For example: Did both Amy and Jan have the capacity to enter into a contract? Did the contract have to be in writing? Was there anything illegal about the contract? Was either Amy or Jan under duress? (Remember that these are not the only possible defenses, just some of the more typical ones.)

When you discover that there are no defenses, you can safely conclude that a valid, enforceable contract exists.

Keep in mind that if any of the elements—offer, acceptance, consideration—is not present, there is no contract to begin with. In that case you do not even have to look at the defenses. Defenses are only a last resort when all the elements are met.

EXAMPLE

Suppose that Amy offered to give the bracelet to Jan free of charge, and Jan accepted. Now suppose that Amy changed her mind and refused to give her bracelet to Jan. Jan can enforce the exchange if she proves that there was a valid, enforceable contract. Amy will try to establish that there was no contract. It will not be necessary for Amy to bring up any defenses, for instance, if she was very drunk when she made the offer, because there is no contract to begin with. Since Amy offered to give the bracelet to Jan, there was no consideration. Therefore, the situation does not even get to the defense element. It fails once there is no consideration.

Accordingly, you should always use your checklist in the order given above. By doing so, you can proceed step by step, and only move to the next step after overcoming the preceding one.

DETRIMENTAL RELIANCE

Throughout this chapter I have been using examples of gifts as unenforceable contracts due to lack of consideration. While this is the general rule, there is a situation where the injured party may recover damages even if there is no consideration. If one party relied on the promise to his or her detriment, that party may recover as if there really were a contract. This is known as **detrimental reliance**.

EXAMPLE

You already know that if someone promises to give you a gift and you accept, but the person changes her mind, you cannot take her to court and sue her for the gift or its value. However, suppose that you live in Boston and you have an uncle who lives in San Diego, and your uncle promises to give you his old car as a gift but you first have to go pick it up from his driveway in San Diego. Suppose you take a week off from work, buy an airplane ticket, and fly to San Diego, only to discover that your uncle has changed his mind and decided to keep the car. Can you sue your uncle for the car or, at least, for reimbursement of your plane ticket and time off from work?

Probably. In that situation you detrimentally relied on your uncle's promise. Even though there was no consideration, and thus no contract, the court will probably allow you to recover anyway, since you harmed yourself (economically) because of the promise. Of course, if you were going to take time off from work and fly to San Diego anyway, then you would not be reimbursed. However, since you made all that effort because of your uncle's promise, you can recover under the theory of detrimental reliance.

These are the basic principles of contract law. Again, there may be slight variations from jurisdiction to jurisdiction, but these main ideas generally apply. By now, you probably have realized that many (if not all) of these ideas make a great deal of sense.

THE REASONABLE PERSON STANDARD

Accordingly, take some time to look again at the theory of contract law. We have defined a contract as an agreement enforceable by law. Furthermore, a contract is a legally binding commitment made by two or more parties. It is an agreement whereby each party enters into an obligation (duty) in order to receive a benefit (right). The courts merely seek to protect parties who have, by their words or conduct, entered into what would reasonably appear to be a meeting of the minds.

This **reasonable person standard** is an objective test of the theory of contract law. The court will look at the words or conduct of the person and determine whether or not such words or conduct reasonably constitute an intent to enter into a contract. At times, the *objective* test may prove more valuable than a *subjective* test. If this sounds a bit confusing, the following example should clear things up.

EXAMPLE

• •

Suppose you own a small coffee shop, and early one morning your first customer of the day walks in. Her name is Maria, and she was born and raised in a small country halfway around the world. This is her first day in the United States. Maria knows how to speak a little English, and orders eggs, toast, and coffee. After Maria eats her meal, she gets up to leave without paying. You stop Maria and politely ask her to pay. Maria appears startled and is quite puzzled at the fact that you want to receive money for giving her food.

As it turns out, Maria comes from a culture where food is free to everyone; there is no more charge for food in restaurants than in private homes. Therefore, Maria has *never* heard of the concept of "paying for food."

Assuming that you believe Maria's story to be true, you are now faced with a problem. You know that a contract consists of an offer, an acceptance, and consideration. Furthermore, there must be no defenses. In this situation there was no mention of price during the transaction. Maria simply ordered food, and you served it to her. She never specifically agreed to pay for it.

Assuming that you want to pursue this matter in court, do you have a legal right to receive payment for the meal you served to Maria? Yes. You have an excellent chance of recovering the amount. The court will apply the objective theory of contracts. A reasonable person would conclude that when a person walks into a restaurant to order a meal, it is implied that the person must pay for that meal. No words need be spoken; the implied conduct is enough to manifest an intent to enter into a contract.

In this example Maria subjectively did not wish to enter into an obligation to pay for breakfast. However, the court will look at the reasonable, objective standard rather than an individual's beliefs.

If the court did not use this objective standard but instead applied a case-by-case standard, it would be extremely difficult, if not impossible, to establish a method to hold contracting parties accountable for their mutual obligations. For example, a person could walk into a barber shop, get a haircut, and then refuse to pay for it by claiming that "the barber never mentioned money, so I didn't know that I had to pay for the haircut." Also, a person could purchase an item and return it two weeks later, stating, "I honestly believed that there was a 30-day money-back guarantee because that's the way I usually do business."

EXAMPLE

● ●

Suppose you walked into a store, bought a new watch, and a few hours later discovered that the watch did not work. You returned the watch to the store, explained that it did not work, and asked for a new one. When the owner told you that there were no others in stock, you asked for your money back. At that point, the owner told you that he has a no-refunds policy, and that none of his watches works!

You became very angry and grew even more furious when the owner said, "I sell these watches for their artistic value; none of them works. Besides, you never told me that you wanted a watch that works. I only thought you wanted the watch for its physical beauty." Do you have a legal right to a refund? Of course. Under the objective theory of contracts, the court will not only look at what was in your mind or the owner's mind, but will look at what the reasonable person would expect when buying a watch. Accordingly, the court will probably conclude that the reasonable person would expect a watch to keep time, even without the owner specifically confirming the watch's operable condition.

Because of the objective theory of contracts, the seller does not have to tell the buyer that "a pen writes," or "a clock keeps time," or "a telephone rings."

These **implied warranties of merchantability** — that is, implied assurances that a product is fit to work for its general purpose — are a small example of the objective theory of contracts.

Moreover, the courts seek to protect people who have entered into a contract fairly and honestly. Contracts that contain hidden clauses ("fine print") or clauses too vague to be clearly understood by the reasonable person are often voided for being **unconscionable** (extremely unjust).

Implied Warranty of Merchantability: Implied assurance that a product is fit to work for its general purpose.

FINAL THOUGHTS

As I mentioned in the beginning of the chapter, we enter into contracts almost every day. We do not realize that many of the simple things we do — such as ride the train, buy the newspaper, or use the telephone — are contracts.

While there are various categories of civil law, those that involve legally enforceable agreements fall under the general category of contracts.

Congratulations, you now have a basic understanding of contract law. I will venture to say that you may know more about contract law than many law students. Unfortunately, law professors often teach complex contractual theories in advanced legalese, often missing the essential points. This chapter assures that you did not miss these basics.

Now You Try It

In order to ensure your mastery of the basics you have learned, examine the following examples in which substantive contract law is combined with the essentials of good legal writing discussed in Chapter 4.

★ **HINT:** The following short fact patterns are accompanied by a question (issue) and a legal answer. Remember that a "legal answer" is the same as an analysis in a legal memorandum.

1. George wanted to sell his stereo for $600. Alex verbally agreed to buy it at that price. Two hours before the exchange was to take place, Barbara offered George $700 for the stereo. George accepted Barbara's offer. Can Alex successfully sue George for breach of contract?

Alex cannot successfully sue George for breach of contract.

Under contract law, a contract for the sale of goods of $500 or more must be in writing.

Here, Alex verbally agreed to buy George's stereo for $600. The agreement failed to become a contract because it was not in writing.

Accordingly, Alex cannot successfully sue George for breach of contract.

2. Linda and Kelly are coworkers. Linda wanted to buy a large cake for a party she was giving, but did not have much money to cover the cost. Kelly needed someone to babysit her son one night before the party. Since Kelly knows how to bake, she offered to bake a cake for Linda if Linda would babysit Kelly's son. Linda accepted. After Linda finished babysitting, Kelly thanked her and reminded her that she would bake the cake the following day. A few hours later, Kelly called Linda and said she had changed her mind and would not bake the cake for Linda.

Can Linda successfully sue Kelly for breach of contract?

Linda can successfully sue Kelly for breach of contract.

Pursuant to contract law, parties who enter into an agreement supported by consideration, with no defenses, are mutually obligated to the terms of their agreement.

Here, Kelly offered to bake a cake for Linda if Linda would babysit Kelly's son. Linda accepted, and the value of baking in exchange for the value of babysitting was sufficient consideration. Since there were no contractual defenses, Kelly failed to fulfill her obligation when she refused to bake the cake.

Therefore, Linda can successfully sue Kelly for breach of contract.

3. Jack offered to pay Peter $50 if Peter would mow Jack's lawn by Saturday. Peter, who is 12 years old, accepted. By Saturday, Peter had never shown up to mow the lawn. Jack, who had invited some guests, was embarrassed at the poor condition of his lawn. Can Jack successfully sue Peter for breach of contract?

Jack cannot successfully sue Peter for breach of contract.

Pursuant to contract law, minors lack the capacity to enter into contracts and may void their contractual obligations at their option.

In this case Peter, who agreed to mow Jack's lawn, is only 12 years old. Since Peter is a minor, he is not obligated to fulfill his contractual obligation to Jack.

Therefore, Jack cannot successfully sue Peter for breach of contract.

Did you fully understand these examples? If you

1. recognized the substantive contract law applicable to each fact pattern, and
2. remembered the legal writing format (conclusion, rule of law, facts/analysis, and repeated conclusion) as set forth in Chapter 4,

then you are doing very well in learning about the law. Congratulations! You are ready for the next chapter.

Key Terms

acceptance	duress	minor
capacity defense	illegality	offer
consideration	illiterate person	reasonable person
contract	implied warranties of	standard
defense	merchantability	statute of
detrimental	intoxication	frauds
reliance	mental incompetence	unconscionable

Review Questions

1. What are the four main elements of a valid, enforceable contract?

2. What is the statute of frauds, and what types of contracts does it apply to?

3. How are minors affected by contract law?

4. Give an example of a contract that is unenforceable because of duress.

5. Give an example of a contract that is partially unenforceable because of an illegal clause contained in it.

6. Give an example of an agreement that is enforceable because of detrimental reliance.

7. Discuss how an agreement might be unenforceable because of a missing element as opposed to a defense.

8. What is an implied warranty of merchantability?

9. Give an example of a contract that might be deemed unconscionable because of a hidden clause.

10. How is the reasonable person standard applied to contracts?

Web Sites

- GSA Board of Contract Appeals
  http://www.gsbca.gsa.gov/
- U.S. Department of Commerce
  http://www.commerce.gov/
- The Uniform Commercial Code, as revised through 2001
  http://www.law.cornell.edu/ucc/ucc.table.html
- Examples of contracts
  http://www.lectlaw.com/formb.htm

Torts

7

I n Chapter 6, you learned that civil law generally comprises two main areas, contracts and torts. You have probably heard and used the word "contract" many times in your life, even before reading this book. The word "contract" transcends the legal community and is a common word in everyday language. But you may ask, "What in the world is a tort?"

Like contracts, torts are part of our lives. While we probably enter into some form of contract on a daily basis, we (hopefully) are not **tortfeasors** (people who commit torts), nor are we usually the victims of torts. In fact, we may go through our entire lives without having committed a tort or been the victim of one. Let us then begin our lesson in torts by first defining the term.

WHAT IS A TORT?

Tort:
A civil wrong not based on a contract.

A **tort** is a civil wrong not based on a contract. Let us examine this definition.

First of all, notice that a tort is a *civil* wrong. Torts, then, are part of civil law: The remedy is compensation. There is no imprisonment involved, and the standard of proof is a preponderance of the evidence. In this respect, torts are similar to contracts.

On the other hand, a tort is a civil *wrong*. In that respect, a tort differs from a contract. A tort is necessarily a wrong, but a contract is not. Only a breach of contract is a wrong.

Moreover, a tort is a civil wrong not based on a contract. There are various forms of civil wrongs. Many are based on contracts (agreements enforceable by law), whereas others are not. A person need not enter into an agreement to become a victim of a tort or a tortfeasor. Otherwise, we would live in a society where people would be able to victimize other people and not be civilly liable as long as there was no agreement between the two.

In Chapter 5 we used an example where a person tried to steal your car and, as a result, broke the window and damaged the lock. As we discussed, that act was a crime. The person could go to jail for it. But what about paying for the damage to your car? What if the person responsible for the damage has no money? What if someone else can be held liable (e.g., a security guard hired to patrol the area)? You may be perfectly content in knowing that the criminal is behind bars, but you also want someone to pay for the damage to your car. Therefore, you commence a civil suit against the security guard (or the guard's employer).

Did you have a prior agreement with the guard or the employer? Did either make an offer to protect your car? Did the person who tried to break into your car make an agreement with you that he would never try to steal your car? No! All of these people are perfect strangers to you. However, they may still be responsible for your property damage because of the tort (civil wrong not based on a contract).

EXAMPLE

Suppose you own a large parcel of land not far from your home, and a local softball team wants to use your land to practice. You enter into a contract with the team whereby the team promises to be liable for any injury to you or to your property resulting from its activities. If you get hit in the head with the softball or the softball breaks your window, the team is liable under the contract.

What if you were simply walking in the park and were hit in the head by a softball? What if you never even saw the person who hit you before that day? Can you sue that person for breach of contract? Of course not! There was not even an offer (recall that if there is no offer, your analysis need go no further). You and that person are perfect strangers. He never came up to you and said "I hereby offer never to hit you with a softball."

Although you cannot sue this person for breach of contract, you can sue him in tort. He is liable to you even though there was no contract. (Whether the person's conduct is also a crime is a different issue altogether. Many acts are both torts and crimes, but in this chapter we will focus only on civil liability (torts), not arrests or imprisonment (crimes).)

In fact, there are situations where an act can be both a tort and a contract. For instance, in the example involving the contract whereby you rented your land to the softball team, if the players damaged your property with their actions they could be liable to you both in contract and in tort.

Note that as with contracts and other areas of law, tort law varies from state to state, jurisdiction to jurisdiction. This chapter will focus on the *general principles* of tort law, whose basic premises apply in all states. However, when dealing with a specific tort situation, you should be familiar with that specific state's law.

The consequences of a tort can include physical damage, property damage, emotional damage, and economic damage. A tort may also be committed intentionally or unintentionally.

INTENTIONAL TORTS

Let's look first at some **intentional torts.** These are torts that are committed on purpose. The tortfeasor knowingly and willingly committed the act.

Assault

Assault is the act of intentionally placing a person in apprehension of an unlawful, unprivileged, imminent offensive touching.

Assault:
The act of intentionally placing a person in apprehension of an unlawful, unprivileged, imminent offensive touching.

Let us examine this definition in detail. First of all, assault involves *intentionally* placing a person in apprehension of an imminent offensive touching. The act must be intentional; it cannot be accidental. For example, suppose that you are near a lake and toss a rock into the water. You do not realize that someone is swimming below the surface. As the swimmer stands up straight in the water, the rock almost hits her on the head, and she quickly ducks out of the way. Are you liable for assault? No, because you did not intentionally throw the rock in order to place the swimmer in apprehension of an imminent offensive touching.

Second, an assault intentionally places a person in *apprehension* of an imminent offensive touching. Apprehension indicates awareness. In order for a tortfeasor to be liable for assault, he or she must make another person aware of an imminent offensive touching.

Suppose you are standing on a street corner and someone throws a rock at you. If you see the rock coming at you, you have become aware of it; you are apprehensive of an imminent offensive touching. What if you never see the rock coming? Is the act an assault? No. Under the classic (common law) definition of a civil (tort) assault, the victim must be aware of the imminent offensive touching.

Third, the victim must be aware of an *imminent* offensive touching. "Imminent" means likely to happen at any moment. Imminent means soon, not in a few hours or in a few days.

Kevin and Danny get into an argument while sitting in a bar. Kevin says to Danny, "If you don't leave right now, I'll punch you right in the nose." Will Kevin be liable for assault? Yes, because Kevin has intentionally made Danny aware of an imminent offensive touching. What if Kevin, instead of asking Danny to leave, starts to leave himself but says to Danny, "If I see you in here again, I'll punch you right in the nose." Will Kevin be liable for assault? No, because Kevin has not made Danny aware of an imminent offensive touching. The threat is for nonimminent harm. Danny does not have to be concerned with an offensive touching likely to happen at that moment. In fact, Danny has a number of options: Call the police, hire a bodyguard, prepare to defend himself in the future, leave town, try to make peace with Kevin, and so on. Accordingly, Kevin has not made Danny aware of an imminent touching and is thereby not liable for assault.

By threatening to punch Danny next week, Kevin is not liable for assault but is probably liable for a number of other torts (or crimes). Remember that the question is not whether Kevin is liable for something, but whether he is liable for assault. Kevin's threat makes him no more liable for assault than for, say, reckless driving.

Fourth, assault is intentionally placing a person in apprehension of an imminent *offensive* touching. Note that the touching must be offensive. If you are sitting at a table and a person charges at you with a baseball bat, you will probably suspect that he is about to hurt you. The person's act will probably amount to an assault because to be hit with a baseball bat is an offensive touching. But what if you are sitting at the table, and the same person approaches you, says "hello," and extends his hand as if to shake your hand? Is this an assault? No, because he has placed you in apprehension of a touching, but not an offensive touching.

To shake someone's hand, to tap someone on the shoulder, or to pat someone on the back are touchings that our society does not generally consider to be offensive. But punching, kicking, pushing, poking, or sexually touching are considered to be offensive. Throwing an object at someone is also generally offensive.

Accordingly, if a person comes at you with a baseball bat, this will probably be an assault. If the person walks up to you and attempts to shake your hand, this will most likely not be an assault. The former touching, if completed, would be offensive; the latter would not.

The touching need not actually happen. You are placed in apprehension of an imminent offensive touching because the person intended to place you in such apprehension. This is enough to constitute an assault.

Finally, the touching must be *unlawful* and *unprivileged*. It must be against the law and without consent. Two professional karate fighters, for instance, are not liable for assault every time they try to kick each other.

EXAMPLE

• •

Suppose that you are a bank teller. A person walks up to your window and tells you that she has a bomb in her purse and will blow up the bank unless you give her $5,000. Frightened for your life, you hand over the money.

It is very possible that the woman had no bomb in her purse. Therefore, the offensive touching was not completed nor could it be completed under the circumstances. However, the woman apparently intended to place you in apprehension of an imminent offensive touching. Accordingly, this act is enough to constitute an assault; the completed touching is not necessary.

Battery

What if the offensive touching is complete? Is this a different civil wrong? Yes. The tort of **battery** is an intentional, unlawful, unprivileged, offensive touching. Since we have just finished examining the elements *intentional*, *unlawful, unprivileged,* and *offensive*, it is not necessary to repeat them. However, a word must be said about *touching*.

It is very important to remember that an offensive touching need not involve harm. The touching may be an act that does not subjectively (actually) cause harm nor is likely to objectively (reasonably) cause harm.

Battery:
An intentional, unlawful, unprivileged, offensive touching.

EXAMPLE

Suppose Walter punches Tom in the stomach. Because Tom is wearing many layers of clothing, he hardly feels the punch. No harm is done, but Walter is nonetheless liable for battery because he caused an intentional, unlawful, unprivileged, imminent offensive touching.

Moreover, suppose Walter threw a snowball at Tom. It is highly unlikely that the snowball would cause any harm to Tom. Nonetheless, if the snowball hits Tom, Walter will be liable to Tom for battery.

Accordingly, a battery is an intentional, unlawful, unprivileged, imminent offensive touching: There is no need for harm to occur. Practically speaking, however, when there is no harm (or threat of harm) there will probably not be a lawsuit. In the example where Walter punched Tom in the stomach, even though Tom was not hurt he may have been angry at Walter nevertheless. Accordingly, he is likely to bring a civil lawsuit against Walter for the tort of battery.

But what about the second example where Walter threw a snowball at Tom? Would Tom bother to go to court over a snowball? Probably not, but Walter's act is nonetheless a battery.

Moreover, a battery does not require that the victim be aware (apprehensive) of the contact. If someone threw a snowball at you from behind and hit you in the back, this act is a battery, even though you never saw the snowball coming. An assault requires awareness, and a battery requires contact.

Accordingly, an act can be

1. an assault only
2. a battery only
3. both an assault and a battery
4. neither an assault nor a battery

The following example should clear up any confusion.

EXAMPLE

Suppose you are waiting at a bus stop. Carl, a passerby, suddenly stops a few feet in front of you, makes a snowball, and throws it at you. You see the snowball coming, and you duck out of the way. Carl has committed an assault. By throwing the snowball at you, he intentionally placed you in apprehension of an imminent offensive touching.

What if you saw the snowball coming but could not get out of the way in time, and the snowball hit you? Carl has then committed both an assault and a battery. Carl committed assault because he intentionally placed you in apprehension of an imminent offensive touching, and committed battery when he completed the touching (i.e., when the snowball hit you).

Next, suppose that instead of stopping a few feet in front of you, Carl stood a few feet behind you. He made a snowball and threw it at you, hitting you in the back. In this case Carl committed only battery. He intentionally caused an imminent offensive touching. However, he never made you apprehensive (aware) of the touching. Therefore, Carl did not commit an assault, only battery.

Finally, suppose that Carl stood a few feet behind you and threw a snowball at you. His aim was bad, and he hit a mailbox with the snowball instead of you. In that case you were not hit by the snowball. In fact, you were not even aware that Carl threw the snowball at you. Accordingly, Carl committed neither an assault nor a battery. There was no awareness, and there was no contact.

> ★ **HINT:** Use this fourfold example for future reference when trying to determine the difference between assault and battery.

What Is Intent?

The general definition of **intent** is to do something knowingly and willingly — that is, to do something on purpose. Liability for an intentional tort, however, usually consists of not only intending to commit the act but intending the result.

EXAMPLE

If you are cleaning a window in your fourth-floor apartment and accidentally drop a bottle of window cleaner off your sill and onto a pedestrian's head below, you did not intend the act of dropping the bottle. But what if there was a garbage dumpster a few feet away from the pedestrian and you intended to throw the bottle into the dumpster, but your aim was bad and you hit the pedestrian? In that case you intended to commit the act (throw the bottle) but did not intend the result (to hit the pedestrian with the bottle). Will you be liable for battery? No, because you did not intend to commit an imminent offensive touching. You merely intended to throw the bottle into the garbage dumpster, not to have the bottle come in contact with another human being.

Throwing the bottle into the dumpster would not be battery, but hitting the pedestrian would. Let's assume that there are two pedestrians, Alex and Bo. If you throw the bottle at Alex, intending to hit him, but instead hit Bo, many jurisdictions will find you guilty of battery upon Bo. This is the theory of **transferred intent.**

When a person intends to commit a certain tort upon one person, but by accident commits the tort upon a second person, the tort is considered to be intentional upon the second person. Therefore, if you intended to hit Alex but instead hit Bo, you caused the same damage due to your intent. The law will not be more lenient on you because your aim was bad. However, if your aim was bad as you innocently attempted to throw the bottle into the Dumpster, the court will probably judge you less harshly than if you had intended to commit battery.

Moreover, assault (as previously stated) is intentionally placing a person in apprehension of an imminent offensive touching. Therefore, if the person has been placed in such apprehension, which you intended, you are liable.

But what if the person was placed in such apprehension, but you did not intend it? Let us look at three possibilities.

EXAMPLE

First, suppose that Alex and Bo are walking down the street. You intend to frighten Alex by throwing a rock at him. At that point Bo turns around, sees the rock, and ducks for cover. You have placed Bo in apprehension of an imminent offensive touching. Under the theory of transferred intent, you will be liable for assault upon Bo, even though you did not intend that Bo become apprehensive.

Second, suppose that you want to hit Alex in the head without Alex knowing it. You sneak up behind Alex with the plan to throw a rock at him. Suddenly, Alex turns around, sees you ready to throw the rock, and runs behind a parked car for cover. At that point you decide to leave. You obviously did not commit the battery, even though you attempted to. You never touched Alex in any way; therefore, there was no battery. But did you commit an assault?

Generally, intent for assault will be established when the intent is to make another person apprehensive of an imminent offensive touching. However, if the tortfeasor intends to commit the touching whether or not he intends the victim to be aware, and if the victim does in fact become aware, this amounts to assault.

Let me explain this again: You want to hit Alex with a rock, but you do not really care whether he sees you or not. If at the last minute he turns around and sees you, he has become aware. Even though you did not particularly care if he became aware or not, assault is involved because Alex became aware as a result of your intent to hit him.

> ★ **HINT:** Read this portion over very carefully in order to fully understand it.

Third, suppose you have just left the movie theater after seeing an action/adventure movie. You are still so caught up in the movie that you start running down the street, practicing flying karate kicks. Molly, another pedestrian, turns the corner and sees you coming toward her jumping and kicking. She becomes frightened and faints. You never intended to frighten Molly. In fact, you did not even realize that she was there. Nonetheless, Molly sues you for assault. Are you liable for assault? Probably not. Since you did not intend to make Molly aware of an imminent offensive touching, you did not commit assault. You may be liable for something else if your actions would cause a reasonable person (objective analysis) to be frightened. However, in order to commit assault, there must be intent.

Having considered these examples of intentional torts, let's take a look at some defenses to intentional torts.

Defenses

Remember that a battery is a completed offensive touching. In 1990 Evander Holyfield defeated James "Buster" Douglas to become boxing's heavyweight champion. Holyfield secured his victory when, while ducking an uppercut punch thrown by Douglas, he countered with a punch of his own, sending Douglas to the canvas. Douglas was knocked out and Holyfield became champion. With regard to the knockout punch, can Douglas sue Holyfield for battery? With regard to the uppercut, can Holyfield sue Douglas for assault? No, to both questions.

Regarding Holyfield's knockout punch, it was certainly an intentional offensive touching. However, Holyfield is not liable because he can successfully raise the defense of **consent.** Surely, Douglas did not desire to be hit but by agreeing to participate in a professional boxing match, he consented to the possibility of being hit. Therefore, any punch landed in the fight will not be a battery since it was consented to.

Regarding Douglas' uppercut, this punch placed Holyfield in apprehension of an imminent offensive touching. Again, Holyfield consented to punches being thrown at him when he agreed to fight. Accordingly, Douglas will not be liable for assault.

Consent:
Permission or authorization for a certain act to take place.

Buster Douglas being counted out moments after Evander Holyfield's knockout punch

Suppose, however, that you are shopping at a department store and suddenly notice someone running with some merchandise under his arm. A security guard immediately tackles the thief and detains him until the police arrive. Is the security guard liable for assault and battery? No! Even though the elements for assault and battery are present, the security guard's actions are **lawful** under the circumstances. It does not matter that the thief does not consent to the guard's actions. If the imminent offensive touching, or threat of such touching, is lawful, it will not amount to an assault or battery. This point is further exemplified in the defense of oneself. If someone throws a punch at you and misses, and you throw a punch back and connect, can that person successfully sue you for battery? No, because you were taking the necessary step to defend yourself, which is lawful behavior. In fact, you may sue that person for assault.

Consent and lawfulness, then, are some defenses for intentional torts.

Note: Unlawful, unprivileged acts are elements of intentional torts, but in some jurisdictions, consensual and lawful acts are *defenses*. I have mentioned the same concept in two different ways so that you continue to remember that although the general principles of laws are the same, some jurisdictions define them differently.

NONINTENTIONAL TORTS

Now that we have examined some common types of torts that are done on purpose, let us look at those torts that are done accidentally.

Negligence

Suppose, for instance, that while cleaning your window sill you accidentally drop a flowerpot out of the window and injure a pedestrian. You certainly did not intend to drop the flowerpot in order to injure the pedestrian. Nonetheless, the pedestrian is injured as a result of your having dropped the flowerpot. Will you be liable for the injuries? Yes. Even though you did not intend to create the injury, you should have been more careful in preventing it. This is the tort of negligence.

Negligence is the failure to use reasonable care when a duty of such care is owed, and the breach of this duty is the actual and proximate cause of resulting harm.

Let's take a look at this definition in detail. There must be

1. a duty of
2. reasonable care;
3. a breach of such duty; and
4. harm, which is the
5. actual and
6. proximate cause of such breach.

Notice that intent is not an element of negligence. Rather, the standard is reasonable care.

Duty

First, consider *duty* of reasonable care: If there is no duty owed, then a person will not be liable for negligence.

EXAMPLE

• •

Suppose you stop into a diner for a meal, and a person at the next table suddenly screams in pain. Apparently, she bit into a bone that was in her hamburger and chipped her tooth. Will you be held liable for her chipped tooth? Of course not! You are merely a customer, just as she is. You do not owe her any duty of reasonable care regarding the quality of food she will be served. The diner's owner, however, owes her such a duty. Therefore, a person will not be held liable for negligence unless he owed a duty of reasonable care to the person who was harmed.

Reasonable Care

Second, the duty must be one of *reasonable care*. Here the court will apply the objective standard of reasonableness.

EXAMPLE

In the previous example, the person sitting near you in the diner was injured as a result of a bone in her hamburger. The diner's owner will most likely be liable for negligence, since he owes all customers a duty of reasonable care. Such duty includes serving hamburgers with no bones in them.

Suppose you order strawberry shortcake for dessert. Unknown to you, you are allergic to strawberries. Although the cake is otherwise fresh and satisfactory, you develop a severe reaction and are hospitalized. Can you successfully sue the diner for negligence? No. It is not reasonable for the diner's employees to be aware of every person's potential allergies. As long as the food was of edible quality, the duty of reasonable care is satisfied. Your allergy to strawberries does not render the diner owner responsible for the resulting harm.

A duty of reasonable care is also owed to the public at large by all of us regarding certain actions we may undertake.

For instance, if we decide to go to the park to play baseball, we owe a duty of reasonable care to all persons in the park. If we hit someone, even though it was accidental, we will be liable for that person's injuries. However, if another person wanders into a portion of the park specifically designated for baseball and is injured, then he will have assumed the risk of injury, and the person who caused the injury will probably not be found negligent.

We may not know the persons whom we injure. Nonetheless, we owe them a duty of reasonable care not to injure them.

Breach

A person will be negligent if he or she *breaches*—that is, fails to carry out—that duty of reasonable care.

Harm

There must be some type of *harm* resulting from the breach. The harm may be physical, emotional, or economic. If there is no harm, there will be no action (lawsuit) for negligence.

Returning to an earlier example, if you accidentally drop a flowerpot from a window and injure a passerby, you will most likely be found liable for negligence. Similarly, if you drop the flowerpot on someone's car and dent it, you will be liable for negligence. Moreover, suppose the flowerpot comes within inches of hitting a small child. The child's mother, who is standing across the street, sees the entire incident. She is so shaken up at the thought that her child could have been killed, she suffers mental or emotional distress. Accordingly, she may successfully sue you for negligence.

If we change the example slightly, the tort of negligence disappears. Suppose that during the winter you open your window and, in doing so, accidentally cause a small amount of powdery snow to fall off the window sill. If this snow lands on a person, or someone's car, or a small child whose mother witnesses the entire event, you will not be liable for negligence. Even though you owe a duty of reasonable care to all of these people, and even though by causing the snow to fall you have breached that duty, there is no resulting harm. The snow does not harm the person or the car. In the scenario of the small child, the mother would not (reasonably) have worried that the small amount of snow would harm her child. Accordingly, there is no physical, economic (i.e., property), or emotional harm.

Finally, the breach of duty of reasonable care must be both the actual and proximate cause of the resulting harm.

Actual Cause.   **Actual cause,** also known as "but for" cause, means that, "but for" the act, the harm would not have resulted. Therefore, the harm must have been caused by the act.

Actual Cause: "But for" the act, the harm would not have resulted.

EXAMPLE

• •

If a person is injured by a falling flowerpot, the flowerpot was the actual cause of the injury. If the person then gets an infection from the injury, the flowerpot remains the actual cause. There would be no infection if there were no injury, and there would be no injury if the flowerpot did not fall. However, what happens when the example becomes more complex?

Suppose you accidentally drop a flowerpot and dent a person's car. The person takes the car to an automobile body shop to have the dent repaired. The car is ready one week later. As the owner approaches the body shop to pick up his car, he is hit by a bus and suffers a broken leg. Are you liable for that person's broken leg? Of course not!

Arguably, the person would not have been hit by the bus if he was not at that place at that time. He would not have been there if he did not have to pick up his car. His car would not have been in the body shop if it was not damaged by the flowerpot that you caused to fall.

Therefore, indirectly, your failure to use reasonable care caused this person's broken leg. However, the law will not hold a person liable for an unlimited chain of events that may follow a particular action.

For instance, suppose you are an auto mechanic, and you fail to adequately repair a woman's car. The woman picks up her car and drives to a job interview. On the way there, the car breaks down and she misses the interview. The employer will not give her a second chance. She then finds a job in another state. After a month on her new job, she is beaten in the lobby of her office building by a deranged person. You will not be held responsible for her injuries because her being beaten is too remote to be connected to your failure to repair the car. Where then can we draw the line? What is "too remote"?

Proximate Cause:
A test for determining whether it was reasonably foreseeable that harm would result from a particular act.

Proximate Cause.   The test for determining whether the actual cause of the harm is also the legal cause is proximate cause. A **proximate cause** test asks is it reasonably foreseeable that harm will result from a particular act.

EXAMPLE

In the previous example, you (an auto mechanic) failed to properly repair a woman's car. As a result, she missed her job interview and eventually found a job in another state. One day, she was assaulted in her office building. Was it reasonably foreseeable that your failure to fix her car would result in her being attacked in another state? No. Even though the chain of events led to that conclusion, your failure is too remote from her beating. It may be reasonably foreseeable that her car would break down or that she would get into an accident, but not much beyond that. Therefore, while your act may have been an actual cause, it was not a proximate cause of her injury. For that reason, you will not be found liable for her beating.

Keep in mind that the act must be both the actual and proximate cause of the harm. If it was reasonably foreseeable that the act would result in harm but actually did not, the person who committed the act is not negligent. If the act did in fact cause the harm, but it was not reasonably foreseeable that such an act could cause such harm, then, again, the person who committed the act is not negligent.

EXAMPLE

Suppose that you are walking home carrying a bag of groceries. Although you are behaving in a peaceful manner, a paranoid pedestrian thinks that you have a weapon in the bag and that you plan to use it to attack him. As he runs away, he slips and falls on the ground, breaking his wrist. Are you liable for his broken wrist? No! Although your act of carrying the bag in a peaceful manner was the actual cause that led the man to run, fall, and break his wrist, it was not the proximate cause. Therefore, you will not be liable for his injury.

Summary

To review the tort of negligence: In its simplest form, the term negligence indicates the failure to use reasonable care. However, for the act of negligence to become an actionable tort, there must be a duty of reasonable care, and if such duty is breached, there must be harm that is the actual and proximate result of the breach.

Compare negligence, where the element of harm is necessary, with intentional torts, where it is not. Because intentional torts are done on purpose, the intent to commit a civil wrong is, often enough, grounds for liability. Since negligent acts are accidental, however, the law does not wish to hold accidental wrongdoers liable unless their wrong has resulted in some type of harm.

Contributory and Comparative Negligence

Because some jurisdictions recognize contributory negligence and comparative negligence, you should be familiar with these theories, which, respectively, take into account the plaintiff's own negligence, and negate or diminish the defendant's negligence.

Generally, in a **contributory negligence** jurisdiction, if the plaintiff is negligent in any way, he or she will not recover damages from the defendant. For example, if the defendant is 99 percent guilty, and the plaintiff is 1 percent guilty, the plaintiff will not recover anything.

In a pure **comparative negligence** jurisdiction, the plaintiff will recover damages to the extent that he or she is not negligent. For example, if the plaintiff suffers $10,000 damages, but is found to be 70 percent guilty while the defendant is 30 percent negligent, the plaintiff will recover only $3,000. In other comparative negligence jurisdictions, the plaintiff will not recover anything if he is over 50 percent negligent, or if his negligence is greater than or equal to the defendant's.

Thus far, we have examined torts where liability is imposed because there is fault, whether intentional or unintentional. Next, we will examine liability without fault.

STRICT LIABILITY

Strict Liability:
Responsibility without intent, recklessness, or negligence.

Strict liability holds a person liable in tort where there was neither intent nor negligence. There are some instances where a person, even though he or she did not intend to commit a tort or failed to exercise reasonable care, will nonetheless be liable for ensuing harm.

Products Liability

Products Liability:
A product designer's or manufacturer's strict liability for products placed into the stream of commerce.

One type of strict liability is **products liability,** which holds a business owner strictly liable for the products that he or she places into the stream of commerce.

EXAMPLE

Suppose that a manufacturer produces an automobile, which passes a reasonably diligent inspection. However, the automobile is defective and causes a buyer to be injured. Even though the manufacturer did not intend for the injury to occur and was not negligent (since the manufacturer exercised reasonable care by conducting a diligent inspection), the manufacturer will be liable for the buyer's injuries.

Wild and Dangerous Animals

The owners of wild animals or dangerous domestic animals are strictly liable for any ensuing harm. For instance, if someone keeps a pet tiger or a pet dog that is known to be dangerous, this owner is strictly liable for any damage or personal injury that these animals cause.

EXAMPLE

Suppose that you wish to keep a pet tiger in your backyard. You purchase a thick leather leash and tie the tiger to a tree. The person who sells you the leash tells you that the tiger cannot chew through it. Unfortunately, the tiger does chew up the leash, escapes, and bites your next-door neighbor.

You certainly did not intend that the tiger bite your neighbor. You also were not negligent, since you exercised reasonable care by purchasing a leash that you were assured was strong enough to prevent the tiger from chewing it up. (Keep in mind that reasonable care does not mean perfect care—the law does not expect you to predict the future.)

Two pit bulls photographed one day after attacking and killing a wheelchair-bound neighbor in his own backyard

However, even though your actions were not intentional or negligent, you are nonetheless liable to your neighbor for the injuries caused by the tiger. As a keeper of a wild animal, you are strictly liable.

★ **HINT:** The person who told you that the leash could not be chewed through may also be liable, but that is a different issue.

Abnormally Dangerous Activities

Finally, persons who engage in abnormally dangerous activities — such as transporting dynamite or storing radioactive waste — are strictly liable for any ensuing harm.

Defenses to Strict Liability

Two common defenses to strict liability are (1) assumption of risk and (2) the harm does not result from the specific danger.

Assumption of Risk

If a person knows of a particular liability and assumes the risk, that person may not be able to successfully sue in strict liability tort.

EXAMPLE

Suppose that an automobile manufacturer builds an automobile with faulty brakes. As a result, the brakes often fail to work.

If the owner of the automobile is injured as a result of the defective brakes, the manufacturer will generally be held strictly liable.

However, if the owner previously discovered the defect but continued to drive the car anyway, the owner is deemed to have assumed the risk of injury. Accordingly, he cannot recover in strict liability tort.

Harm Not Resulting from Specific Danger

In the case of ultrahazardous activities, for instance, the activity is considered so abnormally dangerous that there is a standard higher than negligence placed on that tortfeasor. However, where the harm does not result from the specific danger, the person conducting the activity is not held strictly liable.

EXAMPLE

A person who drives a truck loaded with milk is held to a standard of reasonable care. If another driver cuts in front of the milk truck, and the truck causes injury to someone, the truck driver will probably not be ultimately liable since the accident was caused by the other driver.

However, if the driver of a dynamite truck is cut off, that driver's liability may be different. If the dynamite explodes and injures a pedestrian, that person may sue the truck driver for strict liability, even though it was someone else who caused the accident. But if the dynamite truck simply overturns and injures a pedestrian (the dynamite does not explode), then the truck driver will probably not be held ultimately liable if he did not cause the accident.

In the first instance the driver of the dynamite truck will be held strictly liable because of the dynamite's dangerous propensities. Since dynamite is more dangerous than, say, milk, the carrier of dynamite will be held to a higher standard. However, the unique abnormal danger of dynamite is its explosiveness, not the overturning of a truck storing it. Therefore, there is nothing unique about a truck carrying dynamite that is overturned and injures a person. It is no different in this regard than a truck that contains milk, furniture, or toys.

Accordingly, if the resulting harm is not the reasonably foreseeable harm that the strict liability standard intends to protect, then the person responsible for the dangerous activity will not be held strictly liable.

We have learned that negligence is the failure to use reasonable care, but strict liability means that a person is liable even when he or she did not intentionally or negligently cause something to happen. Confused? Stop. Take a deep breath, and look at one more example. It will clear things up.

EXAMPLE

If you owned a skateboard and left it on some park stairs, and a person accidentally tripped over it and was hurt, you would probably be liable for negligence. However, if you left the skateboard under a tree but a few seconds later an unforeseeable, powerful gust of wind blew it to the stairs, and then the person tripped over it, you have a good chance of being relieved of liability. In that case you did not fail to exercise reasonable care. By leaving the skateboard under the tree, you left it in a safe place. A normal gust of wind would not have carried it away. However, this particular gust of wind was so incredibly powerful that it did indeed carry the skateboard to a spot where it posed potential danger. This wind was unforeseeable. Accordingly, you are not liable for negligence.

Let's assume that instead of a skateboard, you bring a stick of dynamite to the park. (In order not to complicate matters, let's suppose that you are legally authorized to walk around with the dynamite.) As you walk along, a dog grabs the stick with its mouth and runs away from you. The dog then throws the dynamite into a campfire, causing it to go off and injure several people. Are you strictly liable for this injury? Yes. You certainly did not intend that these injuries happen. That, however, does not matter. Moreover, you would ordinarily not be found negligent if you could prove that it was not reasonably foreseeable for the dog to grab the stick of dynamite out of your hand and throw it into a lit fire. Again, this does not matter. Since carrying dynamite is an ultrahazardous activity, you are strictly liable for the consequences, regardless of the absence of intent or negligence.

Now let's change the example. Suppose that, instead of the dog throwing the stick of dynamite into a fire, the dog drops the dynamite to the ground. A few seconds later, someone trips on it and falls to the ground, breaking her wrist. Will you be held strictly liable for this injury? No. In this instance the dynamite's dangerous propensities are not key. Granted, the dynamite stick caused the injury — however, not because of its explosive potential but only because of its tubular shape. In this case, the dynamite stick is no more dangerous than, say, a candlestick. Therefore, you will not be held strictly liable. Moreover, you will not be liable for an intentional tort. Finally, you will not be liable for negligence, *if* you prove that it was not reasonably foreseeable for the dog to grab the stick of dynamite out of your hand, run with it, and drop it on the ground where someone might trip over it.

Thus far, we have examined torts that predominantly result in contact, often harmful, to both persons and property. Let us now look at the tort that deals with damage or harm to reputation.

DEFAMATION

Defamation is to intentionally or negligently make a false statement to someone who is reasonably likely to interpret the statement in a manner that will damage another person's reputation.

Suppose that Albert tells Billy that Carl cheats at their poker games. Actually, Carl does not cheat but Albert is mad at Carl for other reasons and wishes to spread false rumors about Carl's character. Here Albert has defamed Carl. Let's examine the elements in greater detail.

Intent or Negligence

First, there is the tortfeasor's state of mind. In earlier times, defamation was a strict liability tort. If defendant made a false statement to a third person about plaintiff, this was automatically defamation. Whether defendant made the false statement intentionally or negligently did not matter. However, the modern trend is, generally, that to be liable for defamation, a person must intentionally (knowingly) or negligently make a false statement.

Public vs. Private Figures

In defamation, whether intent, as opposed to negligence, is a necessary element depends on the victim. If an individual is in the public eye (i.e., considered to be a public figure), that person does not enjoy the same privileges as a private person does. A public figure may sue for defamation only if the offending statement was made with actual malice.

However, a private person may sue whether the statement was made maliciously (intentionally) or negligently. Take a look at these examples.

EXAMPLES

Suppose a reporter from your local newspaper received an anonymous telephone call that the governor of your state failed to pay the proper income tax last year. The reporter sits on the story. A week later, the reporter receives another undisclosed call confirming this information. The reporter then writes a front page story titled GOVERNOR DIDN'T PAY TAXES. It is quite probable that the reporter was negligent in printing this potentially damaging story based on two questionable telephone calls. However, the governor will not be able to sue the reporter (or the newspaper) unless he proves that the reporter wrote the story with actual malice.

The governor is a public figure. Public life certainly has its share of benefits and drawbacks. One drawback is that should a potentially damaging false statement be made against a public figure, the publication of such statement is only a tort if made with actual malice. In this example, the governor would have a valid claim for defamation only if the reporter wrote the story for the express purpose of damaging the governor's reputation. However, if the reporter wrote the story with no malice toward the governor, there is no cause of action.

Private persons do not need to prove actual malice. If a false statement is made against a private person, only negligence need be proven to establish a case of defamation. For example, suppose that someone started a false rumor that George, the milkman, is a cocaine user. If this rumor was communicated to a third person (someone other than George), George would be able to sue the person who made the statement if:

1. The tortfeasor knew that the statement was false. OR
2. The tortfeasor did not exercise reasonable care in attempting to ascertain the truth of the matter.

Publication to a Third Person

The false statement also needs to be "published." Publication here means to communicate the message to a third person. Without publication, there is no defamation. For example, if John, a restaurant owner, walks up to Sam the cashier and accuses Sam of stealing from the register, this is not defamation unless a third person hears it. Now if Kelly the waitress is also present, John has defamed Sam if the statement is false.

The published false statement will be defamatory only if it is reasonably likely that the third person will believe the statement.

EXAMPLE

• •

Consider the following dialogue involving three friends: Ian, Paul, and Tom.

Ian (speaking to Paul and Tom): Hey, have you guys heard the news? There's some nut running loose in the neighborhood, who puts on a ski mask and sexually molests old women.

Paul (speaking to Ian): You know, Ian, I'll bet it's Tom. Have you noticed how he hasn't been around at night lately?

A statement made under these particular circumstances was probably made in jest. Paul was apparently "kidding around" when he accused Tom. Suppose Paul was indeed joking and obviously made a false statement. However, the content of the statement would defame Tom if Ian might reasonably believe the statement.

In this case Ian, Paul, and Tom are friends. Paul made the statement about Tom in a rather casual, nonchalant manner and made the statement in Tom's presence. Accordingly, it is not reasonable to assume that Ian would be likely to believe Paul's statement and conclude that Tom is actually a sexual molester.

But what if, as a practical joke, Paul decided to call the police to report a suspicion that Tom is the culprit? In that instance, it is more likely that the police would believe Paul's story. The police do not know Paul. Furthermore, they do not know that Paul and Tom are friends. Finally, it is not as likely that someone would call the police department to report a false story as it is for three friends to utter amusing falsehoods about each other. Accordingly, if Paul were to carry the practical joke as far as telling the police that Tom is the molester, Paul's action would probably amount to defamation.

Damage to a Person's Reputation

Keep in mind that the statement must not only be false (the speaker knowing its falsity or negligently failing to ascertain its validity), and be communicated to a third person who is likely to believe it, but the statement must be damaging to a person's reputation.

EXAMPLE

• •

Suppose that Charlie tells Stacey that Bill's favorite food is fried chicken. Actually, Bill's favorite food is lasagna. Even if Charlie intentionally lied when making this statement or failed to use reasonable care in investigating the truth of the statement (whether fried chicken is in fact Bill's favorite), the statement is not defamatory. Suppose Charlie did lie or was negligent, and Stacey believed Charlie. Moreover, suppose Stacey told a bunch of other people that Bill's favorite food is fried chicken. As a result, many of Bill's acquaintances mistakenly believe that Bill's favorite food is fried chicken. Did Charlie defame Bill? No.

Even though this false rumor has been spread, there is no inherent damage to reputation if a person is accused of loving fried chicken. If the false statement is not reasonably likely to damage a person's reputation, it will not amount to defamation.

Let us now add to the example: Suppose that Bill happens to be president of the American Vegetarians Association. Assume that Bill is the longtime popular and successful leader of this organization, his position based on passionate speeches contrasting the moral and nutritional evils of meat with the wholesome and healthy qualities of vegetables. If a rumor were to surface that Bill's favorite food is fried chicken, Bill's reputation might be seriously damaged. It is very likely that he would be thought of as a phony or a hypocrite. In fact, he may even be removed as president of the vegetarian group. Accordingly, if Bill were indeed the president of vegetarian organization, and Charlie told Stacey that Bill's favorite food is fried chicken, this would amount to defamation *if:*

1. Charlie made the statement knowing that it was false, or without using reasonable care to determine whether it was true;
2. it was reasonable that Stacey would believe the statement; and
3. the statement was likely to damage Bill's reputation.

Whether the third person believes the statement and, more important, whether the subject's reputation is harmed are issues relating to damages, and these depend on the type of defamation.

Libel vs. Slander

Libel is written defamation; **slander** is spoken.

In earlier times, before radio, television, film, and audio/video recording technology, the two principal methods of communication were the spoken word and the printed word. People communicated either orally or by some type of publication.

The type of defamation was, and is, important as a general method of calculating potential damage. Typically, libel is more serious than slander. Slander will be spoken once. Libel can last forever.

Libel:
Written defamation.

Slander:
Spoken defamation.

EXAMPLE

• •

Suppose that Adams encounters Harrison in a saloon in a Western town and accuses Harrison of being a horse thief. There are three people in the saloon who hear the charge. After Adams speaks his piece, the matter is never referred to again. But what if Adams had this accusation printed on dozens of sheets of paper, and distributed the copies to all of the towns- people? The consequences would be more severe, for two reasons.

First, the townspeople themselves could have copies printed of the original and distribute them to even more people. Adams' written accusa- tion would probably hold more influence than people merely repeating Adams' charges, second- or thirdhand ("Did you know that last week Adams accused Harrison of being a horse thief?"). Much like the chil- dren's game "telephone," where a statement is repeated from person to person and often changes radically by the time it reaches the ears of the very last person, the spoken word often lacks the authenticity of the printed word.

Second, the accusation in the saloon may be forgotten within weeks, days, or even hours. However, when something is printed, there is a good chance it will be saved. Suppose, for example, the comment was written in the town newspaper in 1885. Over 100 years later, we happen to look at an old edition of the newspaper. We would learn, over a century later, that Adams had accused Harrison of being a horse thief, and at the very least entertain the possibility of the statement's truth. Accordingly, *authenticity* and *permanence* are two significant reasons why libel is generally more damaging than slander.

___

Long ago, communication was based on the spoken or printed word. Today, however, we live in a society of tape recorders, VCRs, and movie cameras. Accordingly, if something is spoken on the radio, uttered during a television broadcast, or stated in a film, it is likely that the statement will be *recorded* and thus retrievable at a later date. For instance, if Adams accuses Harrison on television of being a thief, the broadcast will probably be saved on videotape and can be replayed at any time. Essentially, the statement will carry the same authenticity and permanence as if it had been printed. For this reason, the general trend in tort law is to classify all methods of communication that are saved and can be rebroadcast (whether in video or audio form) as libel rather than slander.

Having considered the reasons why libel is often considered worse than slander, let us now look at the standard of proof necessary to collect damages for either type of defamation.

In a libel suit, damages will be presumed without actually having been proven. If John intentionally, recklessly, or negligently prints a false story hat Danny is mentally ill, Danny may successfully sue John in libel without having to prove damages.

In a slander suit, the plaintiff must prove actual damages, usually of an economic nature.

EXAMPLE

Suppose in the previous example that John did not print the story about Danny but merely told a third person that Danny is mentally ill. Again, if the statement is false, and made negligently or intentionally, John is liable for slander. However, Danny will only be able to successfully sue John if Danny can prove that he suffered some type of damages as a result. Typically, Danny will have to prove that he lost some economic benefit, such as his job, clients for his business, or his credit rating.

If Danny cannot prove such damages, he will probably not be able to successfully sue John for slander.

This, however, is the general rule, subject to the following exceptions.

If the slander involves one of the following categories, it is considered to be slander per se, and the plaintiff may recover as in libel, without having to prove damages. **Slander per se** is a defamatory statement that alleges:

1. plaintiff engaged in criminal activity;
2. plaintiff suffers from some loathsome, communicable disease;
3. plaintiff has engaged in sexual misconduct; or
4. plaintiff is unfit to conduct his or her profession.

Let's examine each of these in detail.

Criminal Activity

If, for instance, John tells a third person that Danny sells illegal drugs, this amounts to slander per se, if all the other elements of defamation are met.

Loathsome, Communicable Disease

If John tells a third person that Danny has venereal disease, and all the other defamation elements are met, this is slander per se.

Sexual Misconduct

If John tells a third person that Danny has committed adultery, John has committed slander per se, if all the other elements of defamation are satisfied.

Adultery is deemed to be sexual misconduct but is not generally considered criminal activity. If, however, John accuses Danny of having sexual intercourse with a minor, this would be both sexual misconduct and criminal activity.

Unfitness to Conduct Profession

If Danny is a doctor, and John refers to Danny as a "quack" or "incompetent doctor" in the presence of a third person, this amounts to slander per se if the other elements of defamation are met.

Therefore, in all four examples, if the statement is false, the tortfeasor having made it with knowledge of its falsehood or negligence as to its validity, and it is heard by a third person who might reasonably believe it to be true, then the plaintiff has an action of slander per se, and damages need not be proven.

Defenses to Defamation

There are certain exceptions under which defamatory statements are **privileged.** These privileges arise as a result of the status of the person making the statement or due to the specific situation at hand.

Statements made by *government officials* during the course of their jobs are either absolutely or partially immune. Federal officials and high state officials are generally immune, and in some instances low ranking state officials are privileged as well. For example, suppose that a federal prosecutor says in connection with a drug bust, "We've been after these guys for years; they are low-life career criminals." Even if this statement turns out to be false, and was negligently made, the prosecutor will not be liable for defamation if the statement was made during the course of duty.

Moreover, any communication made between a *husband and wife* is absolutely privileged. For example, Suzanne comes home from work and tells her husband, Peter, that her secretary, Molly, is cheating on her husband. If Suzanne has no reasonable proof of this allegation, or even if she is purposely spreading false rumor, the communication to her husband is not defamation. For the purposes of publication, a husband and a wife are the same person. Accordingly, a communication made to a spouse by the other spouse is not being made to a "third person."

Statements made by *anyone involved in judicial or legislative proceedings* are privileged. For example, if a witness at trial states before the entire court that "Mr. Jones is a known drunkard, womanizer, and compulsive gambler," this statement cannot be defamatory under any circumstances. Mr. Jones cannot sue the witness, since the statement was made during the course of judicial proceedings. Similarly, all persons involved in legislative proceedings are immune from liability for damaging false statements that they make.

Review the above sections again for the elements of defamation, in the form of libel and slander, as well as defenses to this tort.

FINAL THOUGHTS

You can now rest assured that you have been thoroughly exposed to a sound understanding of the basics of tort law. Certainly, there are many more torts, complete with conditions and exceptions. However, you now have a practical working knowledge of torts. Let us then apply this knowledge to the legal writing skills you already know.

Now You Try It

Consider the following example: Lorenzo and Evan were at a pond fishing near one another. While casting his line into the water, Lorenzo accidentally caused the hook to touch Evan, making contact with Evan's arm. Is Lorenzo liable for battery?

Now try to remember (1) the answer and (2) the legal writing formats:

Lorenzo is not liable for battery.

Battery is the intentional, offensive touching of another person.

Here, Lorenzo did not intend for his fishing hook to touch Evan. The contact was accidental.

Therefore, Lorenzo is not liable for battery.

Try another example: Mickey was rollerblading around town. As he approached a corner, Mickey did not bother to slow down. He crashed into Eleanor, who fell to the ground and sprained her wrist. Is Mickey liable for Eleanor's injury?

Mickey is liable for Eleanor's injury.

If a person fails to use reasonable care where a duty of care is owed, and the breach of that duty is the actual and proximate cause of resulting harm, that person is liable for such harm.

Here, Mickey owed a duty of reasonable care to the public at large while rollerblading. He breached that duty when he rollerbladed around a streetcorner without slowing down. As a result, he bumped into Eleanor, who fell to the ground and sprained her wrist. It was foreseeable that his negligence could have resulted in Eleanor's injury. Since Mickey's failure to use reasonable care was the actual and proximate cause of the resulting harm, Mickey is negligent.

Accordingly, Mickey is liable for Eleanor's injury.

Did that answer appear a bit longer than most of the others? It was! The facts/analysis was rather extensive, since negligence has multiple elements that must always be analyzed. By this time, you should be confident in applying your full knowledge of the law. Accordingly, you can write a thorough legal answer that consists of more than one-sentence statements for each category.

We have now concluded our analysis of civil law. Before moving on to criminal law, keep in mind the following points:

1. This was just a basic overview of the broad concepts of civil law. There are many more types of contracts and torts and specific subdivisions of each.
2. In the United States, there are 50 states and 50 codes of state law, as well as federal and local laws. Accordingly, the substantive law discussed in the civil law chapters encompasses the general principles of these laws. These laws may differ from jurisdiction to jurisdiction. However, by understanding the general principles, you will be able to adapt to the specific differences of each jurisdiction.

Key Terms

actual cause	defamation	proximate cause
assault	intent	slander
battery	intentional torts	slander per se
comparative	lawful	strict liability
negligence	libel	tort
consent	negligence	tortfeasor
contributory	privilege	transferred intent
negligence	products liability	

Review Questions

1. Give three examples of acts that can be both torts and crimes. Explain.

2. What are the differences between assault and battery?

3. Give an example of a defense to battery?

4. How is the reasonable person standard applied to negligence?

5. What is the difference between actual cause and proximate cause?

6. What is the difference between comparative negligence and contributory negligence?

7. What is strict liability?

8. What is the element of publication?

9. What is the difference between libel and slander?

10. What types of slander rise to the level of slander per se?

Web Sites

- National Safety Council, statistics on accidents
  http://www.nsc.org/lrs/statstop.htm
- U.S. Consumer Product Safety Commission, statistics on consumer products
  http://www.cpsc.gov/library/data.html
- More information on libel and slander
  http://www.expertlaw.com/library/pubarticles/Personal_Injury/defamation.html

Criminal Law

8

n the previous chapters we dealt with civil law. At its core is compensation of the plaintiff, who is generally the direct victim in some matter, and who must prove the defendant's liability by a preponderance of the evidence.

WHAT IS CRIMINAL LAW?

Criminal Law:
The category of law in which the plaintiffs are the people of the state or country and the goal is to punish the defendant.

In this chapter we will examine **criminal law.** At its core is the punishment of the defendant, who has wronged the entire people of the community, state, or nation, if the people (through their chosen representative, the prosecuting attorney) find the defendant guilty beyond a reasonable doubt.

We will deal with several crimes. Before we begin, let me once again remind you of the following:

1. This chapter will cover only a few of the many wrongs that are addressed in our criminal laws.
2. As with civil law, criminal laws exist at the federal, state, or local levels. This chapter focuses on the broad and general principles of criminal law, which can vary from jurisdiction to jurisdiction.

Accordingly, let us begin our study.

Malum in Se vs. Malum Prohibitum

What is a crime? It is an act considered to be so wrong that its victim is not only the individual immediate victim but the community at large. But what exactly does "wrong" mean? Legally wrong, morally wrong, or both?

First, let us consider **legally wrong.** If an act is not illegal, it is not a crime, even though it might still be morally wrong or emotionally devastating. Therefore, an act can be **morally wrong** but not a crime. Consider the following example.

EXAMPLE

Mike and Julie have been dating for two years and are nearing their wedding day. Although Julie is very much in love with Mike, he is interested only in her because of her family's money. Two days before the wedding, Julie's parents lose their fortune in a big stock market loss and go bankrupt. When Mike realizes that he will not "marry into money," he tells

Julie the truth and calls off the wedding. Julie is emotionally devastated. Did Mike's motive amount to a crime? Probably not. Unless there was some specific situation that legally required Mike to profess his love for Julie, his deception was not illegal. Most of us would probably consider it morally wrong. However, since it is not legally wrong, Mike cannot be charged with a crime.

After Mike breaks off his engagement with Julie, he gets in his car and starts driving home. At that point, Mike pulls a candy bar out of his coat pocket, opens it, and throws the wrapper out of the car window. Did Mike commit a crime? Probably. In many jurisdictions littering is a crime punishable by a fine. Although it is regarded as a minor offense, littering is nonetheless against the law.

Let us analyze what Mike has done:

1. He tricked Julie into marrying him, only because he was interested in her wealth. Julie, who was very much in love with him, was extremely upset when Mike told her he didn't want to marry her because her family is bankrupt.
2. Mike threw a candy wrapper out of the window.

The first act is one we would consider a horrible thing to do. Its consequences are damaging to Julie. The second act, while aesthetically and environmentally damaging, is minimal by comparison. An isolated incident of minor littering is hardly as "morally wrong" as deceiving another human being who is blinded by love.

Even though we would be more likely to chastise Mike for the first act than for the second, Mike is more likely to be guilty of a crime for the second act rather than the first.

These examples illustrate that an act that is morally wrong is not necessarily a crime, but an act that is legally wrong is always a crime whether regardless of it is morally wrong.

We have determined that an illegal act that is considered so wrong that it affects the public at large is a crime. Accordingly, we can now distinguish between legal wrongs that are also morally wrong and those that are not.

If you follow an old lady to her apartment building, sneak up behind her, hit her over the head, and steal her purse, you have committed a crime. Your actions are against the law, and they also are considered to be morally wrong by society. The community will consider your act to be a "bad" thing. If a crime is both legally and morally wrong, it is a **malum in se** crime. If, however, the crime is legally wrong but not morally wrong, it is a **malum prohibitum** crime.

★ **HINT:** Malum in se and malum prohibitum are Latin terms. Generally, you will encounter many Latin terms while studying law. In this book you will only find the Latin terms most commonly used in law. There will not be many, but those that are discussed are so widely used that they are very important for you to recognize.

EXAMPLE

If you ride a motorcycle without a helmet, and a local law requires you to wear a helmet while riding, you have committed a crime. Is the crime malum in se or malum prohibitum? Malum prohibitum. The act is a legal wrong but not a moral wrong. It is against the law, but society will not look at you as a "bad" person because you ride a motorcycle without a helmet. People will not think of you as an evil person who has committed a horrible act. At worst, they may think of you as careless and irresponsible.

Now You Try It

Take a look at the following examples and try to determine if they are malum in se or malum prohibitum crimes.

1. Albert drags Betty into an alley and rapes her.
2. Albert picks Charles' pocket in a crowded train.
3. Albert purposely sets David's car on fire.
4. Albert pulls out a knife and stabs Eddie.
5. Albert robs a local convenience store.
6. Harry drives his car without a seatbelt.
7. Harry goes fishing without a fishing license.
8. Harry walks his dog in a park where dogs are prohibited.
9. Harry sells hot dogs in the street without a license.
10. Harry drives five miles faster than the speed limit.

Assuming that each of these situations is prohibited by law and is considered to be a crime, which are malum in se crimes and which are malum prohibitum crimes?

Crimes 1-5, those committed by Albert, are all malum in se. Not only are they against the law, but they are considered to be morally wrong. They either involve unjustifiable violence, theft, or destruction of property. All such acts are considered inherently evil by society. Accordingly, they are malum in se crimes.

Crimes 6-10, those committed by Harry, are malum prohibitum. They are crimes only because they are illegal. Generally, they are not considered immoral by society. Most involve disregard for a particular ordinance. At worst, Harry may be thought to have disregard for the law, his own safety, or even the safety of others. However, he will not be considered a horrible person because of his actions. Though Harry's crimes are legal wrongs, they are not immoral. Therefore, they are malum prohibitum crimes.

Felony vs. Misdemeanor

A **felony** is a more serious crime than a **misdemeanor.** Generally, felonies are punishable by imprisonment while misdemeanors are not. Typically, but not always, felonies are malum in se crimes while misdemeanors are malum prohibitum crimes.

Felony:
A crime considered more serious than a misdemeanor and generally punishable by imprisonment.

Since jurisdictions vary as to which crimes are felonies and which are misdemeanors, it is not accurate to make a list of crimes and classify them as one or the other. The same crime might be considered a felony in one jurisdiction and a misdemeanor in another. Moreover, many jurisdictions designate the severity of felonies and misdemeanors. For example, a class "A" felony is more serious than a class "B" felony, or a class "A" misdemeanor is more serious than a class "B" misdemeanor. Again, since jurisdictions vary, I will not make a list of which crimes are class "A" felonies and misdemeanors, which are class "B," class "C," and so on. To do so would invite inaccuracy depending on the jurisdiction.

However, you should keep in mind that *a felony is more serious than a misdemeanor,* and certain crimes will *always* be one or the other. For example, something as serious as murder will always be a felony; something far less serious, like spitting on the sidewalk, will always be a misdemeanor.

Criminal Mental States

Let us now examine the mental states that will usually render a person criminally liable. (Strict liability crimes also exist, such as an adult having sexual relations with a minor, but such crimes are not part of this basic criminal law overview.)

Generally, the three criminal mental states are indicated by **intent, recklessness**, and **negligence.** You may remember some of these terms from discussions of torts or other aspects of civil law. Keep in mind that the standards indicated by these terms may be different when applied to crimes.

★ ——————————————————————————————————— ★

Criminal Mental States

Intentional = knowingly and willingly
Reckless = not purposely, but with an extremely high degree of
    probability of the outcome
Negligent = lacking reasonable care

★ ——————————————————————————————————— ★

Consider the following examples in order to master these distinctions.

EXAMPLES

• •

Suppose I am teaching in a classroom, high above a very crowded New York City street. As I look out of the window, I recognize somebody I dislike. I pick up a book from a pile sitting on the inside window sill, open the window, and throw the book at the person in order to hit him. The book hits the person on the head, killing him.

Next, suppose instead that I have no particular desire to hit anyone, but, having recently watched a football game, I am anxious to test my throwing arm. Across the street from my school is a building with a lower roof. In order to test my arm, I pick up a book and throw it out of the window. Unfortunately, the book does not make it all the way to the other roof. Instead, it falls down onto the very crowded street and hits someone on the head, killing him.

Third, imagine that I open the window to let some fresh air in, and in doing so upset the pile of books that is sloppily arranged on the inside window sill. As a result, one of the books falls out, hitting someone below on the head, killing him.

Finally, imagine that I leave the pile of books neatly arranged on the inside window sill and the window shut. After class is over and I leave the building, a mild earthquake hits the area. The earthquake causes the window's glass to shatter, and one of the books topples out of the window. The book hits a person on the head, killing him.

Notice that in each of the four situations, a person died as a result of being hit on the head by a book that was, at one time or another, in my control. No injury was any different than the others; each person suffered an equally devastating fatal injury. However, the law will treat each situation differently. Recall that criminal law seeks to punish the wrongdoer rather than compensate the plaintiff. Accordingly, my punishment will be based on my criminal mental state.

I will be punished most severely for my action in the first scenario. In that case, I *intentionally* threw the book at the person below, killing him. My action was done purposely—that is, knowingly and willingly.

In the second scenario, I will be punished, but probably not as severely as in the first, because my conduct was *reckless*, not negligent. In that case, I did not intend to hit anyone with the book. I did not intend to cause any harm or commit an otherwise "evil" act. All I wanted to do was to see how far I could throw. However, as I pointed out before, the street below was crowded. It was very risky trying to throw the book that far across the street. There was an extremely high possibility that the book would fall short and hit someone in the crowd below. While the act was not done purposely, the result was extremely likely to occur. Therefore, the act was reckless.

In the third instance, I will be punished for my action, but, again, not as severely as in the first or second scenarios. In that case, I sloppily arranged a pile of books on the window sill, causing one to fall out and hit someone on the head. Obviously, my act was not intentional; when I arranged the books as I did, I was not hoping for one of the books to fall out and hit someone walking or standing below. Moreover, the consequence was not extremely likely to occur. While the possibility of a sloppily placed book falling out of a window and harming someone on the street is foreseeable, there is not an extremely high degree of probability of such an outcome. However, since the harm is at least foreseeable, the behavior will be considered to be a failure to exercise reasonable care (owed to the public at large). Accordingly, such behavior is negligent.

Finally, in the fourth situation, I will probably not be punished at all. There, an earthquake caused a window to break and a neatly placed book to topple out the window. Although a person died as a result, my intentions when I placed the book on the inside sill, with the window closed, were certainly not bad; I did not want the earthquake to occur and cause the ensuing chain of events.

Furthermore, my action was not reckless, since there was not an extremely high degree of probability that (1) an earthquake would occur; (2) the earthquake would cause the window to break; (3) the earthquake would cause the book to fall out of the window; and (4) the book would fatally strike someone in the street below.

Finally, my action was not negligent. Not only was the above chain of events not extremely likely to occur; it was not even foreseeable. If resulting harm is not foreseeable, then failure to prevent such harm is not a failure to exercise reasonable care. Even though the person was killed by a book that I placed on the window sill and, had I not placed the book there, the person would probably not have been harmed, the earthquake that triggered the chain of events was unforeseeable. The law does not expect people to make psychic predictions of some unforeseeable event. The law only requires that people behave reasonably in order to prevent foreseeable harm. My actions in the fourth scenario were not intentional, reckless, or negligent. Accordingly, I lacked the mental state necessary to be convicted of a crime and will not be punished at all.

These examples portray an identical consequence: A person is killed after being struck on the head by a book. The first three scenarios are crimes; the fourth is not. In the first three examples, there is either an intentional, reckless, or negligent mental state present. In the fourth there is no such element, and so there is no crime.

Regarding the first three, an intentional wrong will generally be more severely punished than a reckless act, which will be considered more serious than a negligent act.

Sometimes it appears difficult to distinguish between recklessness and negligence. Intent is easy. If a person wishes to bring about a particular result, the act is intentional; otherwise, it is not. However, people sometimes have a problem in "drawing the line" separating recklessness and negligence. Quite simply, recklessness is more severe negligence. Whereas a negligent act is reasonably likely to happen, a reckless act is extremely likely to occur. For example, driving in the snow without the proper tires is negligent; driving without any brakes is reckless. Or cleaning a loaded gun in a room full of people is negligent, whereas shooting the hat off of someone's head, even without intending to harm that person, is reckless.

Keeping these three criminal mental states in mind, let us now begin to look at some substantive crimes.

SUBSTANTIVE CRIMES

Homicide

Homicide:
The killing of a human being by another.

Homicide is the killing of a human being by another human being. Therefore, both the killer and the victim must be human. For instance, if a wild animal kills a human being, the act is not considered to be a homicide, at least not by criminal standards. Moreover, if a human being kills an animal, the human being will not be charged with homicide.

There are different classifications of homicide, some criminal, some not. This chapter will cover some of the basic types of criminal homicide as well as applicable defenses.

Murder

Murder is homicide resulting from

1. intent to kill;
2. intent to cause serious bodily harm;
3. reckless disregard of such death or serious bodily harm; or
4. the commission of a felony or immediate flight thereof.

Note that if there is no homicide, there is no murder. This is so even if one, two, three, or all four of the elements are satisfied. For instance, David sees Peter walking down the street and, intending to kill Peter, David pulls out a gun and shoots Peter. The bullet only grazes Peter and he lives. Can David be charged with murder? No. Since Peter is alive, there was no homicide. If there was no homicide, there is no murder. (David may be charged with some other crime, such as attempted murder, but cannot be charged with murder.)

Not only must a homicide occur, but it must have resulted from one of the four elements. For instance, suppose Diane wants to kill Steve and walks into Steve's bedroom, finds Steve in bed, and shoots him five times. What Diane doesn't know is that Steve died of a heart attack two hours before she arrived. Can Diane be charged with murder? No.

Even though Diane had the intent to kill, which is one of the elements, Steve's death did not result from Diane's intent to kill. In fact, it did not result from Diane's intent to commit serious bodily harm, from reckless disregard of such death or serious bodily harm, or from a felony. Steve died from a heart attack. Diane's actions did not result in Steve's death. Accordingly, Diane cannot be charged with murder.

To repeat: For a person to be guilty of murder, there must be a homicide, which must have resulted from one of the four elements listed above. Let us examine these elements in greater detail.

Intent to Kill.   If a person intends to kill a particular victim, and the victim dies as a result, the killer has committed murder. For example, suppose George intends to kill Carol, and sneaks up behind Carol and strangles her. As a result of the strangling, Carol dies. George has murdered Carol.

In another example, suppose that Morris wants to kill Smith. Morris plants a bomb in Smith's car, and when Smith enters the car, the car explodes and Smith dies. Smith has died as a result of Morris' intent to kill. Therefore, Morris has murdered Smith.

Intent to Cause Serious Bodily Harm.   Suppose that a person does not intend to kill a particular victim but does intend to inflict serious bodily harm upon that particular victim. If the victim dies as a result, the attacker has committed murder.

EXAMPLE

A classic example of this is when someone simply wants to beat up someone else, without committing murder. Maybe the attacker is angry at the victim but not angry enough to kill the victim, just angry enough to cause some physical injury. Another possibility could be that the victim owes the attacker some money, and the attacker simply beats up the victim in order to induce the victim to pay the debt. Whatever the case, if serious bodily harm has been seriously inflicted on the victim, and the victim dies as a result, the attacker is liable for murder, even if he did not intend to kill the victim.

Suppose, for example, that Vinny owes Tim some money. In the presence of several witnesses, Tim approaches Gavin and says, "Will you help me find Vinny? He owes me some money. He's been a little slow in paying up. Let's give him a good beating so that he'll be sure to pay us by next week." Clearly, Tim's intentions are not to kill Vinny because, among other reasons, Tim wants Vinny to be alive so that he will eventually pay Tim the debt. Tim and Gavin find Vinny and physically assault him. As a result of multiple blows to the head, Vinny dies. Did Tim and Gavin murder Vinny? Yes. Since they intended to inflict serious bodily harm upon Vinny, and Vinny died as a result of such harm, Tim and Gavin are liable for murder.

Reckless Disregard of such Death or Serious Bodily Harm.   As you probably remember from the discussion earlier in the chapter, recklessness is action that creates an extremely high degree of probability of a particular consequence.

If a person's actions are extremely likely to cause death or serious bodily harm, and homicide results, the reckless person is guilty of murder.

EXAMPLE

Suppose that Andy is a big auto racing fan. Andy believes that he is just as good as any professional racecar driver. To prove his ability, Andy decides to climb into his sportscar and drive at top speed through ten busy intersections without stopping for red lights. Andy has no intention of harming anyone. He simply wants to prove that he can successfully dodge all obstacles in his way. Unfortunately, Andy is not as talented as he thought. During the drive, Andy strikes Maureen's car in a head-on collision, killing her. Did Andy murder Maureen? Yes. Andy did not wish to kill Maureen or cause her serious bodily harm. In fact, Andy did not wish to harm Maureen in the slightest way. However, his behavior — driving at high speeds through busy intersections without stopping at red lights — was extremely likely to cause death or serious bodily harm. Accordingly, Andy's actions were reckless. Since Maureen's death resulted from Andy's reckless behavior, Andy is liable for murder.

Commission of a Felony or Immediate Flight Thereof. If homicide results from the commission of a dangerous felony, or immediate flight thereof, the felon is also liable for murder, even if his behavior was not intentional or reckless.

EXAMPLE

Bert is going away on vacation and mentions his plans to Howard. Howard, who secretly hates Bert, plans to set fire to Bert's house while Bert is away. Howard does not want to physically harm Bert in any way but would love to see Bert lose all of his valuable antique furnishings. Therefore, Howard waits until Bert and his family have departed. Unfortunately, Howard does not realize that Bert's cousin, Floyd, is house-sitting during Bert's family vacation. While Floyd sleeps in the upstairs bedroom, Howard sets fire to Bert's house. Floyd dies in the flames. Is Howard liable for murder? Yes. Even though Howard did not intend to kill Floyd, and even though there was not an extremely high degree of probability that someone was asleep upstairs (since Howard knew that Bert and his family had departed), Howard is guilty of murder. Howard's intent to set fire to the house is a felony, and Floyd's death is a homicide resulting from the commission of a felony. Accordingly, Howard is guilty of felony murder.

Suppose, instead, that Howard does not intend to set fire to Bert's house but plans to steal Bert's stereo system. While trying to steal the stereo, Howard accidentally drops a lit cigarette, which eventually starts a fire. The fire reaches the second floor of the house where, unknown to Howard, Floyd is sleeping. If Floyd dies in the flames, Howard is guilty of felony murder. Dropping the lit cigarette was negligent, not intentional or reckless. While negligence alone will not constitute liability for murder, it will suffice if the homicide occurred during the commission of a felony (stealing the stereo system).

Suppose Howard had not been stealing the stereo but was doing something lawful, such as visiting Bert while Bert was at home. If Howard then dropped a lit cigarette by accident, which caused Floyd to die in the flames, this would not be murder. In this case, Howard's action would not be intentional or reckless (though it would be negligent). Moreover, it did not occur during the commission of a felony. Accordingly, it does not satisfy any of the elements of murder.

Felony murder is a homicide that occurs during the commission of a dangerous felony or immediate flight thereof. Suppose that while Renee is jogging, she accidentally bumps into Joyce, killing her. Renee's behavior was neither intentional nor reckless. However, suppose that Renee had just robbed a convenience store and was running away when she bumped into Joyce. If Joyce dies, Renee is guilty of murder because the homicide occurred during the commission of a felony.

Suppose further that Renee safely escaped from the convenience store, and a few hours later accidentally bumped into Joyce, killing her. In that case, Renee would not be guilty of felony murder, since the homicide did not result during the immediate flight from the felony.

Generally, many jurisdictions require that the "felony" in felony murder be a dangerous felony. Dangerous felonies are usually those likely to result in physical harm. Intentionally writing a bad check, for instance, is not a dangerous felony. Accordingly, if a person commits nonintentional, nonreckless homicide while writing a bad check (e.g., by accidentally setting a fire), such person will probably not be liable for felony murder.

Besides murder, other types of criminal homicide are voluntary manslaughter and involuntary manslaughter. From the name of each crime, you have probably figured out one major difference between the two: *Voluntary* means it was done on purpose; *involuntary* means it was done by accident.

Voluntary Manslaughter

Voluntary
Manslaughter:
Generally,
intentional homicide
with mitigating
circumstances.

Voluntary manslaughter is intentional homicide that falls short of being classified as murder. Intentional criminal homicide is usually murder. However, under certain circumstances the defendant's liability is mitigated.

Imperfect (Unreasonable) Self-Defense. **Self-defense** is justifiable when a person, reasonably believing that she is in danger, uses the amount of force reasonably necessary to avoid the danger. Basically, the same principles apply to self-defense in crimes, including homicide.

Therefore, if a person reasonably believes that he is about to be killed and, in return, commits homicide, he will probably escape liability because of a **perfect self-defense.** If, however, the person commits homicide based on an honest but unreasonable belief that he will otherwise be confronted by deadly force, he has an **imperfect self-defense** and will probably be charged with voluntary manslaughter.

EXAMPLE

Suppose that Prescott has just finished watching his favorite police drama on TV. Carrying his phony gun, he walks outside, pretending to be a crimefighter. Prescott starts popping out from alleys and pointing his gun, having a good time. Suddenly, Prescott is within a few feet of Franco, who thinks Prescott is trying to kill him. Accordingly, Franco takes out his authentic gun and kills Prescott. In this case Franco probably has a perfect self-defense: He reasonably believed that Prescott was trying to kill him and used deadly force to defend himself. Most likely, Franco will not be charged with any crime.

Suppose, however, that Prescott is not running out from alleys pointing a gun, but rather is standing in the alley singing an opera ballad. Franco, who is walking down the street, has recently seen a horror film titled *The Killer Opera Singer*. Franco was so adversely affected by the film that he honestly believes that because Prescott is singing opera, he is about to kill Franco. Accordingly, Franco pulls out his gun and fatally shoots Prescott. Even though Franco's belief about the apparent "danger" is honest, it is certainly not reasonable.

For this reason, Franco has an imperfect self-defense. He will probably be charged with voluntary manslaughter rather than murder.

Adequate Provocation with No Cooling-off Period. Another situation where a homicide that would normally be murder becomes voluntary manslaughter arises when the defendant is adequately provoked and does not have the appropriate time to cool off.

EXAMPLES

Lucas comes home from work and finds his wife in bed with another man. Lucas becomes uncontrollably enraged and kills them both. The shock of finding his wife in bed with another man, along with his lack of time to cool off, would probably render Lucas liable for voluntary manslaughter rather than murder.

Suppose, instead, that Lucas did not kill the lovers right away but plotted their death for a few days, and finally killed them both one week later. In that case, Lucas had enough time to cool off, and his charge would probably not be reduced from murder to voluntary manslaughter.

Consider another example: Suppose Lucas discovered that his wife had been overusing their credit cards. When Lucas opened the enormous credit card bill, he killed his wife. In that case, "spending too much money" will not constitute adequate provocation. Accordingly, Lucas will probably be found guilty of murder, not voluntary manslaughter.

To review the elements of voluntary manslaughter: If the homicide is committed intentionally, but the cause is either an unreasonable belief that there was justification (i.e., imperfect self-defense) or adequate provocation without a cooling-off period, the defendant will probably be charged with voluntary manslaughter, which is a lesser crime than murder.

Involuntary Manslaughter

Involuntary Manslaughter:
Homicide resulting from criminal negligence, misdemeanors, or nondangerous felonies.

Involuntary manslaughter is homicide resulting from criminal negligence, misdemeanors, or nondangerous felonies.

Criminally Negligent Homicide.   Homicide resulting from criminal negligence, rather than from intent or recklessness, is involuntary manslaughter.

EXAMPLE

Suppose that Steve, who is carrying a loaded gun, decides to play a game of tackle football with his friends. Felix, who is on the opposing team, is running with the football. As Steve grabs Felix and throws him to the ground, Steve's gun accidentally fires, killing Felix. Is Steve liable for involuntary manslaughter? Yes.

Steve certainly did not intend for the gun to go off. The act probably falls just a bit short of recklessness: While it was possible that the gun could go off, it was not extremely likely that the gun would accidentally fire or that it would kill someone if it did.

The most likely possibility is that Steve, by wearing a loaded gun on his person while playing a contact sport, did not exercise reasonable care. As a result, Felix was killed. Accordingly, this is criminally negligent homicide, which is a type of involuntary manslaughter.

Homicide Resulting from Misdemeanors or Nondangerous Felonies.   If you remember our discussion about murder earlier in the chapter, you know that felony murder is homicide resulting from the commission of a felony. Moreover, it was pointed out that the felony must be dangerous. If, however, the homicide results from a nondangerous felony or from a misdemeanor, the defendant is liable for involuntary manslaughter, and his or her mental state is irrelevant.

EXAMPLE

Suppose that Tracey, a licensed driver, was driving a car that was uninsured (a misdemeanor). Even though Tracey was driving with reasonable care, she was involved in an accident that killed Lenny. Is Tracey liable for involuntary manslaughter? Yes. Even though Tracey's act was not intentional, reckless, or negligent, the homicide resulted during the commission of a misdemeanor (driving a car without insurance). Accordingly, Tracey is liable for involuntary manslaughter.

Many jurisdictions no longer apply the manslaughter rule to misdemeanors and nondangerous felonies. Instead, they classify involuntary manslaughter only as homicide resulting from criminal negligence. However, since some jurisdictions include *both* types, it is important for you to be aware of both.

Let us consider more examples in order to better understand the difference between murder and voluntary and involuntary manslaughter.

EXAMPLES

Jeff is annoyed one morning because there is a parade marching down his street. Although Jeff lives on the fifth floor of an apartment building, the parade noise wakes him. In order to disrupt the parade, Jeff angrily throws a flowerpot down into the crowd of marchers and spectators. Jeff does not wish to harm anyone. He assumes that the paraders will see the flowerpot coming and scurry. Unfortunately, the flowerpot strikes Justin on the head, killing him. Will Jeff be liable for murder, voluntary manslaughter, or involuntary manslaughter? Jeff is liable for murder. Let's take a look at why.

Since Jeff did not intend to kill Justin, the act cannot be classified as voluntary manslaughter. As you should remember by now, voluntary manslaughter is a less serious charge than murder and applies when the defendant intended to kill his victim but, because of some other circumstances, the intent is partially mitigated.

Because Jeff did not intentionally kill Justin, the voluntary manslaughter category does not apply here. The remaining choices, then, are murder or involuntary manslaughter. Although you can make a case for both, the most probable charge will be murder.

Jeff threw a heavy object from five floors above ground into a crowd. There was an extremely high degree of probability that death or serious bodily harm would result. Accordingly, Jeff's act was reckless, and homicide resulting from a reckless disregard for death or serious bodily harm is murder.

Is Jeff also liable for involuntary manslaughter? Possibly. Remember that involuntary manslaughter is homicide resulting from negligence or during the commission of nondangerous felonies or misdemeanors. Here, Jeff's act of throwing the flowerpot into a crowd is too risky to be mere negligence. It is recklessness. Accordingly, his act is more serious than negligent homicide. However, throwing an object onto a public street is probably a misdemeanor. Accordingly, *the homicide occurred during the commission of a misdemeanor*. For this reason, Jeff may also be liable for involuntary manslaughter. Practically speaking, the prosecutor will probably attempt to convict on the murder charge.

Let's look at one more example: Suppose that Chris and Pauline, husband and wife, are walking home from the movie theater. Chris stops into a local convenience store to buy some snacks. As Chris leaves the store, he notices that Gary, a mugger, has just punched Pauline, knocking her to the ground, and that when Gary realized Pauline did not have any money on her, Gary started running away. Chris was so enraged that this man had just attacked his wife, he chased Gary and quickly caught up to him. Chris punched Gary in the face, pushed him down, and then kicked him in the head a few times, screaming "I'm going to kill you!" As a result of the blows, Gary died. Is Chris liable for murder, voluntary manslaughter, or involuntary manslaughter? Most likely, Chris will be found guilty of voluntary manslaughter.

Since Chris intended to inflict the harm upon Gary and screamed "I'm going to kill you!" Chris' actions were voluntary. Therefore, involuntary manslaughter does not apply here. The choices thus are murder or voluntary manslaughter. Because there was an intent to kill or, at least, to cause serious bodily harm, and there was resulting homicide, a murder charge would normally be likely. However, as you recall from the earlier discussion, if a person has been adequately provoked and there is no cooling-off period, the murder charge may be reduced to voluntary manslaughter. Therefore, the jury at Chris' trial may conclude that the sight of his beaten wife was adequate provocation for Chris to attack Gary and, since the attack occurred immediately after Pauline's beating, there was no cooling-off period. If the jury makes these determinations, Chris will be found guilty of voluntary manslaughter rather than murder.

If, however, the jury does not conclude that Chris was adequately provoked (that, for instance, since his wife was safe, Chris may have over-reacted), then Chris will probably be found guilty of murder. While the first determination is more likely, the second is certainly possible.

Before we move on to the next type of crime, keep in mind that homicide means the killing of one human being by another. The three main types of criminal homicide are murder, voluntary manslaughter, and involuntary manslaughter. There are situations in which homicide will not be criminal at all. For instance, if a person commits homicide without intent, recklessness, or negligence, and such homicide does not result from an unlawful act, that person will probably not be criminally liable.

Arson

Arson:
Generally, the intentional burning of the property of another person.

Arson is the intentional burning of the property of another. Arson is one of those crimes whose definition may appear different depending on the source or depending on the jurisdiction. The definition provided here is simple but must be studied carefully in order to account for exceptions and modifications.

First, there must be *intent*. For example, suppose that you invite me to your house, and we are sitting in your living room. I light up a cigar, and

When would this fire be considered an act of arson?

we continue our conversation. Eventually, I put out the cigar and throw the remains in your kitchen wastebasket. Shortly thereafter, we both leave your house. Unfortunately, I did not put out the cigar completely. As a result, your house burns down. Am I liable for arson? No. Even though I caused your house to burn down, I did not do it intentionally. It was an accident. Since there was no intent, there can be no arson.

Second, there must be a *burning*. Typically, the burning must involve some type of structural damage. If, for instance, there is some superficial discoloring or smoke damage, this does not constitute a burning. Although the property need not be completely burned, there must be damage to the structure.

Third, the burning must be of some *property*. This is where the laws differ as to what constitutes "property" with respect to arson. Traditionally, property meant a dwelling. The modern definition expanded to include any building. Most recently, several states have enacted arson laws that include personal property as well as real property. Therefore, when you are examining the elements of arson in a particular state, it is important to check the most recent arson law of that state to determine what type of property is covered. In our discussion, since we concentrate on the general principles of criminal law, we will define property as any building. A house, a restaurant, or a school would qualify as "property" within our meaning.

The property must be property of *another*. This is where you have to be careful. Property of another means property that belongs to another or property in which another (such as an insurance company) has interest.

EXAMPLE

If Aaron intentionally burns down Brian's house, Aaron has committed arson. But what if Aaron burns down his own house?

If there is a mortgage on the house, Aaron does not really own the house. Moreover, if Aaron attempts to collect insurance money, the insurance company, which has an interest in the house, is financially affected. If either of those possibilities exists, Aaron will be liable for arson. But if Aaron owns the house not subject to a mortgage, and intentionally burns it down (for whatever reason) but does not attempt to collect insurance money for it, Aaron has not committed arson. After all, the house is Aaron's property, and he has the right to do with it what he wants, including to burn it, as long as another person's interests are not affected.

Now You Try It

Take a look at the following examples and try to determine which indicate arson:

1. While cooking dinner in Sharon's house, Anna accidentally sets fire to the kitchen curtains but quickly puts the fire out before it spreads.
2. Same facts as in example 1, except Anna cannot put out the fire, and Sharon's house burns down.
3. Jessica wants to set fire to Helen's house so she starts a fire and runs out. Helen's automatic indoor sprinkler system quickly puts the fire out before any structural damage occurs.

4. John owns a field with a small barn in the middle of it. The property is not subject to mortgage. In order to create more space on the field, John sets fire to the barn. The barn burns down completely. John is not interested in collecting any insurance money as a result.

5. Ron's restaurant has been losing business for the past year, and he decides to set fire to the restaurant for the insurance money. The restaurant burns down, and Ron files a claim with his insurance company, alleging that the fire was an accident. Ron collects the insurance money and retires.

In which of these situations has arson been committed? Only in example 5.

In examples 1 and 2, Anna started the fire accidentally, not intentionally. Accordingly, she cannot be liable for arson.

In example 3, Helen's house did not burn down nor suffer any structural damage. Accordingly, Jessica cannot be charged with arson.

In example 4, John burned down property that he owned exclusively and did not attempt to collect any insurance money. Since the property did not belong to another person nor did another person have any interest in the property, John cannot be liable for arson.

Example 5 is the only one where arson has been committed. Ron intentionally burned the property in which another person had interest. The insurance company, in being responsible for fire to the property, paid Ron money. Ron fraudulently claimed that the fire was an accident. In reality, Ron set fire to the restaurant to collect the insurance money. The restaurant burned down. Therefore, Ron is liable for arson.

Larceny

Much like arson and other crimes, larceny has evolved from its common law origins, and its elements vary from jurisdiction to jurisdiction. The general principles of larceny are as follows: **Larceny** is the act of intentionally taking and carrying away another person's property, with the intent at the time of the taking to permanently deprive the rightful owner of possession. Let's analyze these elements one at a time.

As with a great number of crimes that we have reviewed, the element of *intent* is necessary to commit larceny. For example, suppose that you are enrolled in an American history course, and every student is assigned the same textbook. One day, you inadvertently place your own textbook under your chair. After class is over, you reach over and grab the nearest

Larceny:
The act of intentionally taking and carrying away another person's property, with the intent to permanently deprive the rightful owner of possession.

textbook, thinking that it is yours. You have just intentionally placed that book in your own briefcase, intending to carry it away permanently. Have you committed larceny? No.

Since you did not realize that you were taking someone else's property, you did not have the intent necessary to commit larceny. In order to be guilty of larceny, a person must realize that he or she is taking someone else's property.

Let's turn to the next element: *taking and carrying away*. How far does a person have to carry away the property in order to commit larceny? Ten miles? One mile? Two blocks? Six inches?

This is a question that varies from jurisdiction to jurisdiction. Extremes such as ten miles will generally be larceny, and six inches generally will not. If an object is carried far enough so as to constitute the intent to permanently deprive the rightful possessor, the distance will amount to larceny. For instance, a person picks up someone else's baseball glove and tries it on. Even though the glove has been moved a few inches, this will generally not be enough to constitute larceny. If, however, the person starts walking away with the glove, larceny has taken place.

Suppose, for example, that Harvey wants to steal Chuck's baseball glove. Harvey plans to grab the glove, start walking toward his car, and drive away. Harvey picks up the glove and walks a few feet toward his car. At that point, Harvey is apprehended. Did Harvey commit larceny? Yes. Under these circumstances, the "taking and carrying away" was adequate to constitute larceny.

The third element of the definition is that the property must either belong to *another person*, or another person must have rightful possession of the property. For instance, if Sandy lends her car to Barbara, and Jason steals the car while it is in Barbara's possession, Jason has committed larceny (if the other elements are present). It does not matter that the car was not in Sandy's (the owner's) possession at the time of the taking.

The trickiest element of all is establishing *the intent at the time of the taking*. Specifically, this means that the person who takes the property must have the intent at that moment to permanently deprive the owner of possession.

EXAMPLE

Suppose that Ralph wants to steal Mark's bicycle. Ralph sees the bicycle in Mark's driveway and steals it. If at the time Ralph took the bicycle, he had the intent to permanently deprive Mark of possession, Ralph committed larceny. But what if Ralph only intended to borrow it just to run a quick errand and, while using the bicycle, became so attached to it that he decided to keep it?

Many jurisdictions will hold that Ralph committed larceny at the point he decided to permanently keep the bicycle. We will continue this example while analyzing the final element of larceny.

The intent at the time of the taking must be *to permanently deprive the owner of possession.*

EXAMPLE

• •

Using the above example, suppose that Ralph took Mark's bicycle at 3 P.M. without Mark's permission. At that time, Ralph intended to use the bicycle for about one hour and return it to Mark's driveway by 4 P.M. Now, suppose that at about 3:30 P.M., Ralph decided to permanently keep the bicycle. Technically, between 3:00 and 3:30, Ralph had not yet committed larceny. However, at any point after 3:30, when Ralph decided to permanently keep the bicycle, larceny had been committed.

It may be very tempting for you to ask, "But how can you prove when Ralph formulated the intent to permanently keep the bicycle?" The key to learning about the law is to first assume that everything can be proven. Then, once you have mastered the law, you apply it to each situation and worry about proving it. For the sake of simplicity, let's assume that in this example Ralph takes the bicycle and encounters Julie, who is an undercover police officer. Julie says to Ralph, "Hey, nice bike." Ralph replies, "Thanks, but it's not mine. I just need it for awhile, so I took it. The owner will never know. I'll put it back before he gets home." Julie then arrests Ralph. While Ralph is certainly guilty of some crime for borrowing the bicycle without permission, he is not guilty of larceny. Assume that at Ralph's trial the jury believes that Ralph never intended to permanently keep the bicycle. In that case, Ralph would not be guilty of larceny.

Now let's change the scenario. Suppose instead that at 3:00 Ralph takes the bicycle, intending to return it shortly. At about 3:30, Ralph decides to keep the bicycle permanently. Five minutes later, he runs into Julie, and when she comments on the bicycle, Ralph tells Julie, "I just stole it. By the time the owner figures out that it's missing, I'll be long gone." At that point, Julie arrests Ralph. At Ralph's trial, the jury determines that Ralph did intend to permanently deprive Mark of possession. Accordingly, Ralph is found guilty of larceny. But what was the intent at the time of the taking?

Some jurisdictions would hold that the time of the taking was 3:00. Since Ralph did not, at that time, intend to permanently deprive Mark of possession, he did not commit larceny. Because Ralph formulated the intent after the time of the taking, he did not commit larceny in those jurisdictions (although he will certainly be found guilty of a related crime).

Other jurisdictions, however, will determine that since Ralph formulated the intent to permanently deprive Mark of possession at 3:30, he should be found just as guilty as if he had intended to keep the bicycle at the time of the taking. The "time of the taking" will then be 3:30, which is the time Ralph "took" the bicycle with the intent of keeping it.

By 3:30, Ralph was already in possession of Mark's bicycle. He had already "taken it and carried it away." However, some jurisdictions will hold that, nonetheless, he is guilty of larceny.

So how do you know what the law is in a particular jurisdiction? As discussed in the chapter on legal research, you should look up the law in your particular jurisdiction. And, if necessary, you should look up related court cases that interpret that law.

In any event, remember that the general principles of larceny are the elements we reviewed, and, while some of the points may have subtle variations, if you know the general principles, you are doing quite well.

Regarding **possession**, keep in mind that this is not the same as ownership. Possession is the exercise of dominion and control over property. It does not necessarily mean that the title has changed hands. For instance, if Bill steals Victor's car, Victor is still the registered and rightful owner of the car. However, it is Bill, not Victor, who is in possession of the car.

> ★ **HINT:** As you know by now, this book provides a basic introduction to the law. Accordingly, we will not cover each area of the law in tremendous detail. However, you should be aware that there are property crimes related to larceny, such as larceny by trick, embezzlement, and obtaining property by false pretenses. These are modern crimes that evolved from larceny and, again, vary from jurisdiction to jurisdiction.

Robbery

Robbery:
Larceny by force or threat.

Simply put, **robbery** is larceny by force or threat of force. Here's a more formal definition: Robbery is the taking of someone's property by force or threat of force with the intent to permanently deprive the owner of possession.

Since we have just studied larceny, you can see that within robbery is contained the crime of larceny. Accordingly, just think of robbery as larceny by force or threat of force.

EXAMPLE

• •

Suppose that Jan leaves a portable CD player in her locker. Upon returning to the locker, she notices that the player is missing. Jan begins yelling, "I've been robbed! I've been robbed!" Has Jan really been robbed? No. Let's look at the elements of robbery again. Robbery requires larceny by force or threat of force. Here, Jan's property was indeed taken. If it was taken with the intent to permanently deprive Jan of possession, this is larceny. However, the taking did not involve force or threat of force. Accordingly, Jan is not a victim of robbery.

> ★ **HINT:** The phrase "I've been robbed" is often used generically to refer to all property crimes. While this usage may be popular among laypersons, it does not suffice as a legal definition. As a member of the legal community, make sure that if you use the words "robbery, robbed, robbing, etc." you are indeed referring to the crime of robbery and not a related, but different, property crime.

Robbery includes *force or threat of force*. Force or threat of force is, basically, the crime (and, as you should remember, tort) of assault. Since we have not covered the crime of assault, and since the tort of assault may contain some subtle differences, I would not unconditionally refer to robbery as "larceny plus assault," although, for the most part, it is an accurate assessment.

The force must actually happen or be reasonably imminent. Accordingly, a typical robbery could be either of the following: Defendant knocks plaintiff to the ground and steals her purse, or defendant pulls out a gun and demands that plaintiff hand over her purse. In these cases, the taking of property is accompanied by force or threat of force.

When there is no actual force, does the threat have to be reasonable? In many jurisdictions, yes. In others, there must be an honest belief of threat of force, whether reasonable or not.

EXAMPLE

• •

Suppose that Frank pulls a gun on Wendy and demands that she hand over her diamond necklace. The gun is not loaded. Since Wendy does not know this, she has a reasonable fear of threat of force and hands over the necklace. Wendy has been robbed. Suppose, however, that Wendy (who is young and athletic) is approached by Monica, a frail,

87-year-old woman, who says to her, "Give me your necklace or I'll beat you up right now." Since Monica is old, frail, and unarmed, Wendy has no reason to fear her. If she hands over the necklace, some jurisdictions will not arrest Monica because her statement would not make a reasonable person fear her.

But suppose Monica said, "Give me your necklace right now, or I'll put a curse on you." Suppose Wendy believes in witchcraft, even though her belief is not reasonable, and perceives Monica's statement to be an actual threat of force. In that case, some jurisdictions would hold Monica liable for robbery.

Since robbery includes the crime of larceny, some jurisdictions do not find it necessary to apply the reasonable person standard. If the criminal succeeds in her threats, it does not matter whether the victim should have reasonably believed the threats. Therefore, suppose Maggie is walking down the street simply carrying an umbrella, and is spotted by Betty, who has an unreasonable fear of umbrellas. If Betty has a heart attack at the sight of Maggie's umbrella, Maggie is not liable. However, suppose Maggie demands that Betty turn over her money "or else I'll open my umbrella." While Betty's fear may not be reasonable, it is honest, and Maggie will be liable for robbery.

Practically speaking, the force or threat of force must be the type that would cause death or (serious) bodily harm. If the defendant says to the plaintiff, "give me all your money or I'll squirt you with my water gun," this will generally not constitute an assault — unless, of course, the plaintiff believed that the defendant would actually use greater force than the mere squirting of a water gun.

Now You Try It

If you are at all confused, take a look at these examples and decide which indicate robbery. Then you will better understand what is robbery and what is not.

1. While defendant and plaintiff are both standing on a crowded bus, defendant picks plaintiff's pocket, stealing his wallet. When plaintiff gets home, he realizes that his wallet is missing.
2. Defendant enters plaintiff's store and, with his hand in his jacket pocket, pretends that he has a gun and demands that plaintiff give him some money. Plantiff, afraid for his life, complies.
3. Defendant walks up to plaintiff and says, "Give me $50 right now, or I'll tell your wife that you're having an affair with your secretary." Afraid for his marriage, plaintiff gives defendant $50.

4. As plaintiff is walking down the street, defendant walks up to her and says, "Give me $20, or I'll beat you up the next time I see you." Plaintiff, fearing for her safety, gives defendant $20.

5. Defendant follows plaintiff into a public bathroom. Defendant, wielding a baseball bat, says to plaintiff, "I'd leave my wallet on the sink if I were you." Plaintiff, fearing for his safety, leaves his wallet on the sink and then leaves the bathroom.

In which of these situations has the defendant committed robbery? Examples 2 and 5. Let's look at them one by one.

Example 1 is not robbery because there was no actual force or threat of force. Obviously, there was no threat of force, since plaintiff was not even aware that defendant was stealing his wallet. But was there actual force? In most jurisdictions force (with respect to robbery) requires some resistance—that is, it must involve a physical confrontation of which the plaintiff is, at least, aware. Accordingly, in this situation there was no force.

Example 2 is robbery. Defendant intentionally took plaintiff's property by threat of force. It does not matter that defendant did not really have a gun. His actions led plaintiff to believe that defendant did in fact have one. Plaintiff's belief was both honest and reasonable, and led to his turning over his money to defendant. In this example, defendant clearly robbed plaintiff.

Example 3 is not robbery. There is no force or threat of force. The threat is that defendant will tell plaintiff's wife that plaintiff is having an affair. While fear of this exposure caused plaintiff to give defendant some money, there was never any threat by defendant to cause physical harm to plaintiff. Accordingly, there was no robbery.

Example 4 is not robbery. Remember that the threat must be a threat of *imminent* force. Here defendant threatened to beat up plaintiff "the next time I see you." "Next time" is not imminent. For this reason, defendant has not committed robbery.

Example 5 is robbery. Even though defendant did not expressly state that he wanted plaintiff's money, or that he would cause harm to plaintiff if plaintiff did not comply, defendant's conduct is sufficient to amount to robbery. Note that a person's conduct may be enough to convey a message. Here defendant's wielding the bat, coupled with the phrase, "I'd leave my wallet on the sink if I were you," is enough to suggest that if plaintiff does not comply, defendant will injure plaintiff with the bat. Plaintiff's belief is both honest and reasonable. Accordingly, example 5 is robbery.

Regarding all five examples, keep in mind that in each the defendant is guilty of some crime. However, the defendant is guilty of robbery only in examples 2 and 5.

Burglary

Burglary:
The act of intentionally breaking and entering into a building, with the intent at the time of the break-in to commit a felony while inside.

Like robbery, burglary by definition contains other crimes (or attempts of such crimes). **Burglary** is the act of intentionally breaking and entering into a building, with the intent at the time of the break-in to commit a felony while inside.

At common law, a burglary was the breaking and entering into the dwelling of another, at night, with the intent at the time of the break-in to commit a felony while inside. In modern times the building is understood to be any building—a dwelling or otherwise. Moreover, the burglary can occur at any time, day or night. Let's examine the elements one by one.

As discussed throughout this book, to have *intent* means to act knowingly and willingly. A person cannot commit a burglary recklessly, negligently, or otherwise accidentally. For instance, George tells his brother, Evan, to go into George's hotel room, which is unlocked, and bring George his camera, which is on the night table. Evan mistakenly walks into someone else's room, also unlocked, and, by coincidence, also having a camera on the night table. Evan takes the wrong camera from the wrong room and is apprehended by hotel security. Has Evan committed burglary? No.

Evan entered a room that he thought he had rightful access to. Moreover, Evan did not intend to commit a felony while inside. He thought he was in his brother's room, picking up his brother's camera at his brother's request. Accordingly, Evan did not commit burglary.

Unlike intent, which is a universal, easily distinguishable element of burglary, *breaking and entering* is a bit more vague. What does breaking and entering mean? Kicking the door down, picking the lock? Or just entering somewhere without privilege, regardless of any physical breaking?

Most jurisdictions require some physical contact to gain entry—for example, the opening of an unlocked door or window. However, walking through a completely open door or window, without needing to touch it to gain entry, does not amount to a breaking (except in a minority of jurisdictions). Therefore, while kicking in a door is not necessary to constitute a breaking, some physical contact with the door is usually required.

To successfully gain a conviction of burglary, it must be proven that the defendant, *at the time of the break-in*, intended to commit a felony while inside. Consider the following example as an explanation of this point.

Do you remember the TV show *I Dream of Jeannie*? Jeannie, the main character, was a genie with magical powers. Jeannie would often use her magic to make people still, as if they were frozen. To understand burglary, pretend that someone is about to break into someone else's house and breaks through the window. At that point, pretend the person is "frozen." Now study the frozen person. Does he now, at this point in time, have the intent to commit a felony while inside? If so, then he has already committed burglary, whether or not he actually commits the felony while inside. But if the frozen person has not yet formulated the intent to commit a felony while inside, he cannot be guilty of burglary, although he may very well be guilty of the felony he later decides to commit while inside.

Now You Try It

Confused? Take a look at these examples:

1. Defendant was running from the police and, in an attempt to lose them, broke into plaintiff's house. When the coast was clear, he left.
2. Defendant's car broke down, and she needed to use a telephone. Defendant broke into plaintiff's house, intending to use the phone to call road service. After she used the phone, defendant spotted plaintiff's portable CD player on the coffee table. Defendant stole the player on her way out.
3. Defendant broke into plaintiff's house, planning to steal some valuable items. After defendant broke in, the burglar alarm sounded. Defendant ran away without taking anything.
4. Defendant broke into plaintiff's store, planning to steal some merchandise. After defendant was in the store for a few minutes, he had a change of heart and decided not to steal the goods after all. He left the store quietly without taking anything.
5. Defendant broke into plaintiff's house, intending to rape plaintiff. Defendant walked into plaintiff's bedroom, raped plaintiff, and then hurried out the door.

Which of these situations amount to burglary? Examples 3, 4, and 5. Let's examine all of them, one by one.

Example 1 is not burglary. Let's "freeze" defendant at the point he breaks into plaintiff's house. Does he intend to commit a felony while inside? No. He breaks into the house solely to dodge the police. Since he does not have an intent at the time of the break-in to commit a felony while inside, he is not guilty of burglary.

Example 2 is also not burglary. Let's freeze defendant as she is breaking in. What is going through her mind at that point? Does she intend to commit a felony? No. She just wants to use the phone, which, by itself, is not a felony. It does not matter if she commits one, two, or twenty felonies afterwards. Since she did not intend to commit a felony at the moment she broke in, she cannot be guilty of burglary.

In example 3, defendant is guilty of burglary. At the moment he breaks in, defendant intends to steal some valuable items. Such action is a felony. Whether or not he actually goes through with it is irrelevant. Since defendant intended to commit the felony at the time of the break-in, this intent is enough to constitute burglary.

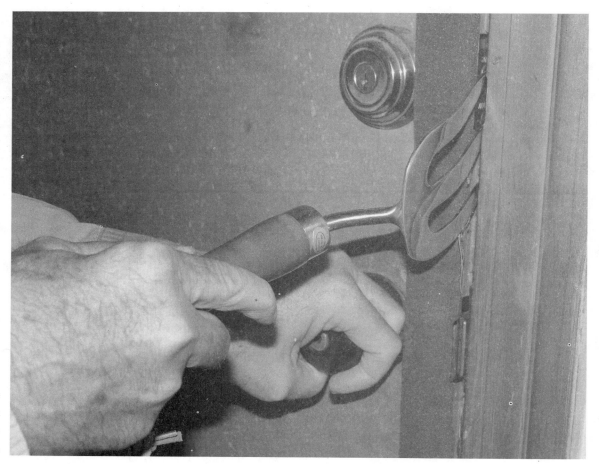

What was this man's intent at the moment of the break-in?

Example 4 is similar to example 3. Again, defendant breaks in with the intent at the time of the break-in to commit a felony while inside. In example 3, he changed his mind because of the burglar alarm. In example 4, he has a change of heart. It doesn't matter why he decides not to commit the felony, or whether he commits the felony or not. As long as at that moment when he breaks in, he intends to commit a felony while inside, he has already committed burglary.

Finally, example 5 is burglary. Defendant intentionally breaks and enters, with the intent to commit rape (a felony) while inside (and he also commits the rape). Accordingly, he will be liable for burglary (in fact, he will also be liable for rape). Notice that the "felony inside" does not necessarily have to be a property crime, such as larceny. It can be rape, murder, or any other felony.

Focus on the question: In all of these situations, is the defendant guilty of burglary? When you read this question, do not interpret it as:

Is the defendant *guilty* of burglary?

Instead, think of it as:

Is the defendant guilty of *burglary*?

Focus on the actual crime rather than on a general notion of whether the defendant is guilty.

In each situation the defendant is guilty of some crime. In all five, the defendant is guilty of breaking and entering and/or criminal trespass. Moreover, the defendant will be liable for any crimes he or she commits while inside. However, if the defendant did not have the intent at the time of the break-in to commit a felony while inside, he or she cannot be guilty of burglary. Why is this important?

Imagine that you are a juror in the case resulting from example 2, where defendant stole plaintiff's CD player. Suppose also that the prosecuting attorney is not satisfied in going for a larceny charge but is prosecuting for burglary. As the juror, you are faced with only two possibilities: burglary and innocence. Since you cannot convict for burglary, you are forced to find not guilty. Burglary is the only charge, and defendant walks away free. A diligent prosecutor would have attempted to bring a larceny charge as well. Thus, it is not only important to know whether the defendant is guilty or not guilty, but to determine what specific crime she is guilty of.

While the breaking and entering must be intentional, and during such break-in there must be an intent to commit a crime, the intent must be (1) *to commit a felony* (2) *while inside*. Let's examine both of these concepts.

As previously discussed, whether a particular crime is a *felony* may vary from jurisdiction to jurisdiction, though, certain crimes, such as murder, larceny, arson, rape, kidnapping, and other serious physical or property crimes, are felonies in every jurisdiction. The most efficient formula to follow when deciding if a particular defendant is guilty of burglary is to examine the crime he intended to commit while inside and determine whether such crime is a felony in that particular jurisdiction. For example, suppose that Tommy, who is 15 years old, broke into Agatha's house to smoke a cigarette without anyone seeing him. Smoking a cigarette is not a felony. If Tommy's intent while breaking and entering was to do nothing more than smoke a cigarette, this does not constitute a felony. Accordingly, while Tommy may be liable for the breaking and entering, and for any penalty for smoking cigarettes at the age of 15, it is highly unlikely that Tommy would be guilty of burglary.

Moreover, the felony must be committed *while inside*. The act of breaking and entering is usually a felony itself. For a charge of burglary, there must be an intent to commit a felony while inside — that is, in addition to the felony of breaking in. Again, think of "freezing" the person at the point of break-in. The felony of breaking and entering has already been committed. Now, does the person have the intent to commit an additional felony while inside? If so, he is guilty of burglary. If not, he is not guilty.

Conclusion

Some of the more common crimes basic to understanding criminal law are murder, voluntary manslaughter, involuntary manslaughter, arson, larceny, robbery, and burglary. By now, you should have mastered these basic concepts. If you have not, reread the sections and try to come up with your own examples.

ATTEMPT

To this point, we have discussed numerous crimes. Some, such as robbery and arson, require intent. Others, such as involuntary manslaughter, do not. But is it a crime to **attempt** to commit a crime and fail? Consider this example.

EXAMPLE

• •

Foster pulls out a gun and shoots at Smith, intending to kill him. Foster misses and Smith runs away unharmed. Is Foster guilty of a crime? Yes. Sometimes, the best way to answer this type of question is to imagine what the crime would be if the intent had been carried out successfully, and then look at the act as a failed attempt. In this example, if Foster had successfully shot Smith and Smith had died, Foster would be guilty of murder. Since Foster tried to commit murder and failed, Foster is guilty of attempted murder.

Before you apply this formula to all attempts, carefully consider the following definition: *Attempt requires specific intent*. For a person to be guilty of an attempted crime, he or she must have intended to commit that crime. In the previous example, Foster intended to kill Smith. Therefore, Foster is guilty of attempted murder. But consider the following example.

EXAMPLE

• •

Becky recently got into a dispute with the owners of a local bar. In order to deprive the bar of business, Becky decides to enter the bar and shoot at several of the patrons. Becky does not intend to kill or cause serious bodily harm to any of the patrons. She simply wants to create an unpleasant enough situation so as to discourage people from ever returning to that bar. Unfortunately, Becky shoots one patron, Darryl, in the head, killing him. What crime is Becky guilty of? Murder. Darryl's death resulted from Becky's reckless disregard for death or serious bodily harm. Since Becky shot at people in a bar, there was an extremely high degree of probability that her actions would result in death or serious bodily harm. Accordingly, Becky is guilty of Darryl's murder. But what if Darryl did not die but, instead, had a full recovery? In that case, would Becky be liable for attempted murder? No. Since Becky did not intend to kill Darryl, she cannot be guilty of attempted murder. While murder itself does not necessarily require specific intent, attempted murder does.

Many jurisdictions require specific intent. For example, A, trying to kill B, shoots at B but hits C instead. If C dies, A will probably be guilty of C's murder. However, if C lives, A will probably not be liable for attempting to kill C because A did not specifically intend to kill C. (Naturally, A will be liable for the attempted murder of B.)

Besides the issue of specific intent, consider another question about attempt: How far does a person have to go to be guilty of attempt? You know that robbing a bank is, among other things, larceny. But if you are sitting in a restaurant eating lunch and you are "thinking" of robbing a bank that is ten blocks away, yet you never get out of your seat to do it, are you guilty of attempted larceny? Of course not! If people fantasize about committing certain crimes, they are certainly not guilty of attempting those crimes. What would you have to do to make an attempt to rob that bank? Walk out of the restaurant? Walk toward the bank? Walk halfway to the bank? Walk all the way to the bank? Enter the bank? Enter the bank and demand money? How far would you have to go? The general definition of attempt requires intent, along with a substantial step toward committing the crime. Therefore, analyses of what constitutes a "substantial step" toward the crime must be made on a case-by-case basis.

Before we end our general introduction to criminal law, let's examine some of the more common defenses to crimes.

DEFENSES

Self-Defense

The principles of self-defense in criminal law are basically similar to those in tort law. While differences exist between crimes and torts, such differences also exist between jurisdictions within each type of law. In any event, let us briefly examine self-defense. Persons who honestly and reasonably believe that they or a third person are threatened by unlawful imminent force may use the amount of force reasonably necessary to defend themselves or third parties against such force.

First, the belief must be both actual and reasonable. It must be both subjective and objective.

Second, the force must be unlawful. This necessitates that the force be unprovoked. Any force that is provoked would indicate that the attacker is either legally empowered to apply such force (such as a police officer or security guard), or the attacker is acting in self-defense.

A person may defend himself against excessive force implemented by police officers or security guards since excessive force is, in fact, unlawful. Moreover, if A attacks B and B fights back, A cannot claim self-defense if he tries to thwart off B's attack, since B's attack is lawful.

Third, the amount of force used in self-defense must be reasonable. Anything beyond reasonable force is excessive force. This creates a tricky problem: Since the situation would often require split-second decisions in the face of life-threatening situations, what would constitute reasonableness under such circumstances?

EXAMPLE

● ●

Let's look at reasonable behavior under threatening circumstances. Suppose that you are a security guard at a small art gallery, assigned to guard a couple of expensive paintings. While you are on duty during the midnight shift (when the gallery is closed), a raging fire suddenly erupts. Although you have a few seconds to grab the paintings and run to safety, your first instinct at the sight of the flames is to run out and save yourself. The paintings are destroyed in the fire.

The next day, a few of your colleagues are discussing the fire. They believe that you could have saved the paintings, as well as yourself, without great risk. It's easy for them to talk about what was reasonable; they were not the ones in danger. They are engaging in what is commonly known as playing "Monday morning quarterback." Monday morning quarterback is a term that originated to describe football fans who, the morning after the Sunday football game, analyze what the quarterback (the team's offensive leader) should have done during the game. Monday morning quarterbacks find it easy to overlook that they didn't have a bunch of 300-pound players charging at them at the decisive moment.

The same principle holds true in the above example. Even though, when out of danger, you could gather your thoughts and conclude that it was possible for you to save the paintings and yourself, you did not have such cool, rational thoughts during the emergency. Accordingly, the law provides for some margin of error during emergencies. In an emergency, a person is required to act reasonably under the circumstances. For this reason, as a security guard who allowed the paintings to burn in the fire, you would be held to the standard of a reasonable person in such an emergency, not a reasonable person under nonemergency circumstances.

This standard applies to self-defense as well. Suppose that a person attacks you in the street, and you need only three punches to fend him off. After overpowering him by the third punch, you throw two more punches, and then walk away. Did you use excessive force? The answer to that depends on whether throwing two extra punches was reasonable under the circumstances. Since you were being attacked, your life may have been in danger. Under such circumstances, you are not expected to behave in the same manner you would during a calm, nonthreatening situation.

However, this standard does not give you free rein to use unlimited force, either. If, for instance, you knocked your attacker unconscious and then continued to pummel him, your ongoing aggression would probably be construed as excessive force, even under such circumstances. The jury would probably determine that even during a life-threatening situation, there comes a point when you can determine that the opposing force has been adequately combatted, and no additional counterattack is necessary.

Accordingly, in examining self-defense, keep in mind that the amount of force used must be just enough to combat the original force. A margin of error will be allowed to a certain extent, given the circumstances: The more compelling the emergency, the greater margin of error allowed. But, again, only up to a certain point.

Finally, the defense may be of oneself or of another person. The third party may be anyone — a family member, a friend, or a total stranger — as long as the defender honestly and reasonably believes that the third party is in danger and uses the amount of force reasonably necessary to combat the opposing force.

Duty to Retreat

Some jurisdictions require that a person faced with danger has a duty to retreat, if reasonably feasible. For instance, suppose that Bob, who is in his car, is about to be attacked by Willie, a pedestrian. If Bob has a clear path to drive away to safety, some jurisdictions will require that Bob drive away rather than defend himself. Those jurisdictions will not acknowledge complete self-defense if Bob decides to stay and fight. Other jurisdictions, however, will allow Bob the option to drive away or to stay and defend himself.

Many jurisdictions, even those that normally require retreat whenever possible, will allow for self-defense in the home, even when retreat is possible. For example, X encounters Y, an intruder, who has walked in through X's front door and is about to attack X. X has the right to fight Y, even if X can reasonably escape out the back door.

The above are the general principles of self-defense. Although they vary from jurisdiction to jurisdiction, the variations are not tremendous. Moreover, these principles are very similar to those applied in self-defense against a tort.

Minors

In legal terms, a minor is generally a person who is under the age of 18. In some instances, the age of majority is 21. When referring to criminal liability, however, the age of majority is 18. Accordingly, a person's criminal liability will sometimes depend on their age.

There are three general classifications of minors and corresponding criminal liability:

★ ─── ★

Age	Criminal Liability
under 7	None
7–under 14	Presumably none; presumption is rebuttable
14 and over	Full liability; will be tried as adult or juvenile depending on crime and jurisdiction

★ ─── ★

(Again, keep in mind that these are *general* breakdowns and may vary in some jurisdictions.)

Minors Under 7 Years of Age.   A person who is under 7 years of age is not legally capable of committing a crime. Therefore, any small child under the age of 7 who commits an act that is normally considered a crime shall not be punished as a criminal. Suppose that a 5-year-old boy picks up a rock and throws it at another child, fatally injuring that child. Normally, this would constitute murder or, at the very least, some type of manslaughter, but since the boy who threw the rock is under 7 years of age, he will not be criminally liable. (He may, however, be civilly liable in tort. In that case, his parents or legal guardians may have to pay damages to the estate of the deceased child.)

Minors Ages 7 to Under 14.   A minor from age 7 to just under age 14 is presumably incapable of possessing a criminal mental state. Accordingly, a child over 7 but under 14 will generally not be charged with committing a crime, unless such presumption is rebutted.

To do so the prosecution may introduce evidence that the child possesses a mental state not like that of the typical 7- to 14-year-old. The prosecution can argue that though the child may be chronologically young, he or she may think and behave like an adult and thus should be tried like one.

EXAMPLE

• •

Suppose that Charlie, who is 13 years old, is shooting off fireworks on the Fourth of July. Charlie accidentally injures Martha and is arrested by the police. Although Martha probably has a strong civil case against Charlie, the prosecution does not have a very easy criminal case. In a criminal trial, there will be a presumption that since Charlie is under 14 years of age, he lacks the capacity to formulate a criminal mental state. Whereas an older person would probably be found criminally negligent, a 13-year-old presumably lacks criminal capacity. Again, the key word is *presumably*. If the prosecution can prove that Charlie, unlike other children his age, possesses the mental capacity necessary to formulate a criminal mental state, Charlie will be found criminally liable.

While this is a difficult presumption to overcome, it is not impossible. By comparison, if Charlie were 6 years old, instead of 13, he would not be found criminally liable under any circumstances.

Minors 14 or Over. Generally, minors who are 14 or over are presumed to possess the same criminal capacity as adults. Suppose, then, that Charlie (from the above example) were 15 years old instead of 13. In that case, Charlie would presumably possess the capacity to formulate a criminal mental state. Whether or not his sentencing would be less severe if he were 15 rather than, say, 35 depends on the nature of the offense and on the jurisdiction. In any event, a person 14 or over will generally be presumed to be mentally capable of committing a crime and thereby liable.

Criminal Capacity vs. Criminal Guilt

Do not confuse the notion of criminal capacity with criminal guilt. Everyone is presumed innocent until proven guilty, but most people are presumed to be capable of being guilty. Adults with full mental capacity, for example, are presumed to possess the requisite criminal mental state. The only question that remains is whether they are indeed guilty of the crime. Minors, however, are only presumed to be criminally capable if they are 14 or over. If they are under 14 but at least 7, they are presumed not to be criminally capable. And if they are under 7, they are immune from criminal liability. Accordingly, there is a big difference between (1) being legally capable of committing a crime or (2) being proven guilty of committing a crime.

Duress

Duress:
Coercion; it occours when a person acts against his or her will.

Generally, if a person commits a crime in order to avoid imminent death or serious bodily harm, such person can successfully raise the defense of **duress,** thereby becoming immune from liability for the crime. Most jurisdictions will require that the threat be imminent, and that the crime committed not be homicide.

EXAMPLE

● ●

Suppose Johnny walks into the bank and tells Patty, a teller, "If you don't give me the combination to the vault, I will tell your boss that you are a drug user." Fearing for her reputation, Patty gives the combination to Johnny. Can Patty successfully raise the defense of duress?

No. Duress requires a threat of either imminent death or imminent serious bodily harm. Here, Johnny's threat did not involve either. Threat of revealing information is not enough to absolve someone of committing a crime. Accordingly, Patty cannot successfully raise the defense of duress.

If, on the other hand, Johnny says to Patty, "Give me the combination to the vault or I'll kill you," and Patty complies, she will not be criminally liable. Since Johnny threatened her with imminent death and serious bodily harm, she has a valid defense of duress.

Suppose, instead, that Johnny telephones Patty and says, "Give me the combination to the vault over the telephone or, the next time I see you, I'll kill you." If Patty complies, will she be able to successfully raise the defense of duress? Probably not, since most jurisdictions would determine that the threat of death was not "imminent" — Patty would have time to escape the danger. Other jurisdictions, however, might conclude that the threat was adequately "imminent." Therefore, though this rule is not absolute, it is prevalent in most jurisdictions.

Finally, suppose that when Johnny walks up to Patty, Patty's coworker, Wendy, is standing next to her. Suppose Johnny puts a gun to Patty's head and says, "If you don't choke Wendy to death, I will kill you." Patty, fearing for her own life, strangles Wendy. Will Patty be able to successfully raise the defense of duress? No. Though most crimes will be justified in the face of a valid duress defense, homicide will not. Even though Patty was faced with the probability of her own death, she will not be completely absolved for killing Wendy.

★ **HINT:** Keep in mind, however, that under such circumstances, Patty's liability may be reduced from murder to manslaughter.

Insanity

Finally, let's take a look at insanity. Much like many of the other aspects of criminal law, insanity has various definitions among all the jurisdictions. True to our practice, we will examine the general principles of insanity, with the understanding that the exact definition may vary from jurisdiction to jurisdiction.

A person is insane when he

1. does not understand the nature of his act,
2. or though his crime is malum in se (both legally and morally wrong), does not understand that society looks upon the act as malum in se.

Keep in mind that

1. insanity is very hard to prove and is often used as a "nothing to lose" last-resort defense in only the most serious of crimes; and
2. insanity, which is an absolute defense, is different from other levels of mental incapacity, which are often limited (mitigating) defenses.

Let's look at the definition part by part. The first possibility is an insane person *does not understand the nature of his act.* Suppose that a baby finds a live hand grenade and, picking it up, tosses it, confusing it for a ball. The hand grenade explodes, killing several people. The little baby has absolutely no concept of what just happened. The baby does not understand the nature of his act. This standard, which is very difficult to prove, is the standard that a person must usually meet to be declared legally insane.

EXAMPLE

• •

Suppose that Fred enters Roger's home and, while Roger is sleeping, shoots him in the head three times. If Fred does not understand what he did, he is insane. If, for example, he believes that, after being shot, Roger will wake from his sleep and say, "Thank you very much," then Fred obviously has no understanding of the results of shooting someone in the head. In such a case, Fred would probably be found insane.

Suppose instead that Fred understands that by shooting Roger in the head, Roger will either die or, at the very least, be seriously injured. In that case, Fred does understand the nature of his act. Accordingly, Fred will not be found insane. Unless, of course, Fred is insane under the second possibility in the definition of insanity.

The second possibility in that definition is an insane person *does not understand that the crime committed, which is malum in se, is considered by society to be malum in se.* Recall from the discussion earlier in the chapter that a malum in se crime is an act that is both legally and morally wrong. Therefore, if a particular act is a malum in se crime but the criminal does not understand that society views the act as a malum in se crime, that criminal may be considered insane.

EXAMPLE

Suppose that Fred enters Roger's house with the intention of killing Roger. Suppose, further, that Fred does realize that after he shoots Roger, Roger will be dead. But imagine that Fred does not realize that society believes that such an act is illegal and immoral. Again, this is a difficult standard to prove. In fact, if Fred takes any steps to hide the evidence of the shooting, this suggests that Fred is aware that people will find his act "wrong."

Similarly, suppose you go into a park, buy a can of soda, and sit on a bench and drink it. You are drinking the soda in broad daylight, not ashamed, not afraid. Why? Because your act is not something that society finds legally or morally wrong. But what if a criminal were to kill someone and then drag the dead body into the park in front of dozens of witnesses? Would a criminal be likely to do that? Of course not! In fact, someone would say that person is "insane." Get the picture?

For a killer to carry around the body of his victim would suggest that he does not understand that he can be arrested for his act and that the act is considered wrong by society.

This type of insanity is possible when the crime is malum in se to begin with. For example, a person riding a motorcycle without a helmet may not know that this act is illegal and may not believe that the act is considered wrong by society. Is he insane? No, because his act is not malum in se. Here, the person simply is ignorant of the law, which is not a defense.

Accordingly, insanity is commonly used in murder cases, mostly unsuccessfully as a last resort. The defense attorney tries to convince the jury that the defendant is insane. While the attempt is not successful a great deal of the time, insanity is legally proven from time to time.

Now You Try It

Let's work on the following examples, using the legal writing skills discussed earlier.

Timmy, who is 4 years old, set fire to his nursery school, because he saw a fire in a cartoon and thought it would be fun to watch the nursery school burn down. Luckily, nobody was hurt, but the nursery school burned completely. Is Timmy liable for arson?

Let's answer this question using the four-step approach: conclusion, rule of law, facts/analysis, and conclusion.

Timmy is not liable for arson.

Generally, arson is the intentional burning of another person's building. However, children under the age of 7 are not held criminally liable for the acts they commit.

In this case, Timmy intentionally burned the nursery school down. Normally, this act would amount to arson. However, since Timmy is only 4 years old, he will not be held criminally responsible for this act.

Accordingly, Timmy is not liable for arson.

Let's do another one:

Steve wants to steal Alvin's gold watch. While Alvin is out of his house, Steve breaks in, intending to steal the watch. Unknown to Steve, Alvin is wearing the watch. When Steve realizes the watch is not in Alvin's house, Steve leaves the house without taking anything else. Is Steve liable for burglary?

Steve is liable for burglary.

Burglary is the intentional breaking and entering into a building, with the intent at the time of the break-in to commit a felony while inside.

Here, Steve intentionally broke in to Alvin's house with the intent to steal Alvin's watch while inside. Steve's intent would amount to larceny, which is a felony. Steve intended to commit larceny at the time he entered Alvin's house.

Therefore, Steve is liable for burglary.

You've probably gotten the hang of legal writing by now. It gets easier and easier. Since this is our last substantive law chapter and our last opportunity to review legal writing, let's try a couple more.

Fran and Joe were riding on the subway. Joe stood behind Fran, reached into her purse, and stole her wallet. Joe got off at the next stop. Fran did not realize that her wallet was missing until she got home. Is Joe liable for robbery?

Joe is not liable for robbery.

Robbery is taking someone's property by force or threat of force.

Here, Joe took Fran's wallet without her knowing it. He never used force on her nor did he threaten her with force.

For this reason, Joe is not liable for robbery.

Samantha robbed a grocery store and dashed into her car to drive away. As she turned the first corner, she rammed into Chuck, a pedestrian, killing him. Is Samantha liable for felony murder?

Samantha is liable for felony murder.

Felony murder is homicide resulting from a felony in commission or from immediate flight thereof.

Here, Samantha robbed a grocery store, which is a felony, and was in immediate flight when she killed Chuck.

Therefore, Samantha is liable, for felony murder.

FINAL THOUGHTS

At this point in your legal education, having mastered several chapters from this book, you should be thoroughly comfortable with the legal writing format and how to apply it to each particular law you are dealing with.

A final word about criminal law: Perhaps no other area of law generates more discussion about policy and implementation. People always argue over theories of punishment, such as life imprisonment versus the death penalty. Many feel we need more prisons and tougher sentences, while others concentrate on preventive methods and rehabilitation. Some believe that the whole insanity defense is hogwash, while others contend that in certain cases it is valid and necessary. And though many believe that police officers are power-hungry and corrupt, easily capable of using excessive force, many others believe that the end justifies their means.

As you've probably noticed, this book does not offer specific viewpoints on these issues. The purpose of this book is to teach you what the law is. Once you understand the law, you can decide whether you agree or disagree with it. You cannot validly support or criticize something that you do not understand. I will not waste your time filling the book with sections titled "What Do You Think?" or "Points of View." This book is titled *Learning About the Law*. Accordingly, I advise you to first learn the law, then decide where you stand on the various legal issues.

Key Terms

arson
attempt
burglary
criminal law
duress
felony
homicide
imperfect self-defense

intent
involuntary
   manslaughter
larceny
legally wrong
malum in se
malum prohibitum
misdemeanor

morally wrong
negligence
perfect self-defense
possession
recklessness
robbery
self-defense

Review Questions

1. Define malum in se and malum prohibitum crimes, and give three examples of each.

2. Name and define the three main criminal mental states.

3. What is felony murder?

4. Give an example when an intentional break-in is not a burglary.

5. What is the criminal liability for minors?

6. What is the general legal standard for insanity?

7. What are the necessary elements of self-defense?

8. What are the elements of larceny?

9. When is intentional homicide not murder? Give an example.

10. Give an example of when intentionally burning down one's own house is arson and when it is not.

Web Sites

- Criminal justice statistics
  http://www.albany.edu/sourcebook/
- U.S. Department of Justice
  http://www.usdoj.gov/
- State criminal law statutes
  http://www.megalaw.com/top/criminal.php

Ethics

9

Chapter Overview

Ethical Conduct
    Who Is Actually Regulated?
    May Paralegals Give Legal Advice?
    Confidentiality and the Attorney/Paralegal-Client Privilege
    Conflict of Interest
    Zealously Representing Clients Within the Bounds of the
        Law
    Sharing Legal Fees
    Legal Advertising and Solicitation
    Competence
Integrity

Let us take a look at how far we've come. You have learned some very important skills—how to find the law, how to brief a case, and how to write a legal answer. You have also learned quite a bit about contracts, torts, and criminal law. Though you have more to learn, you are fast becoming a well-educated paralegal.

Being a paralegal, much like being a doctor or a police officer, is more than a job; it is a status. During an emergency, for example, it is common to hear someone exclaim, "Is there a doctor in the house?" or "Call the police!" Similarly, a person with knowledge of the law may be called on during a critical situation. Accordingly, while you are busy viewing and evaluating yourself, think also about how others see you.

More experienced members of the legal community (lawyers, judges, law professors, etc.) may see you as a "rookie" with a great deal more to learn. But your friends, family members, clients, and others who are not inside the legal circle view you as an "expert." They will rely on your knowledge even at this early stage in your legal education.

For these reasons, it is important that you conduct yourself in a manner that upholds the ethical standards of your, profession.

ETHICAL CONDUCT

Both in our personal and professional contributions to society, we live by a **code of ethics.** Typically, this ethical conduct is a combination of our own sense of values and a series of rules, laws, and regulations that we are required to follow. In this chapter we will discuss a code of ethics as it applies to the legal profession. But, you may ask, what exactly are ethics?

Generally, ethics are moral principles. Ethics are often referred to as moral ideas or a moral philosophy. But what exactly are morals? Morals are notions of what is good, right, and just. **Ethics** thus are a set of values about what is good, right, and just.

Ethics:
A set of values about what is good, right, and just.

Regrettably, the legal profession has been hampered by harsh (but often well-deserved) remarks that its members are "sharks," "ambulance chasers," and "professional liars." It is often frustrating for good, honest lawyers and paralegals to be judged by the general flaws of their profession rather than on their own merit. Such legal professionals must hope that society will exercise the good sense to judge based on conduct and not on generalized prejudices.

Fortunately, the code of ethics of the **American Bar Association (ABA)** stresses integrity and the highest moral principles. (See Figure 9.1.) Following the ABA's lead, other legal professional organizations have adopted codes of ethical conduct designed to guide all members of the profession.

Both lawyers and paralegals are covered by the ABA's code of ethics. Depending on the issue, the same ethical standard may or may not uniformly apply to both.

One hopes that enough lawyers and paralegals will take pride in themselves and restore to the profession the dignity and professionalism that the code of ethics seeks to enforce.

If enough legal professionals stand up and proudly defend their principles, they will overcome the behavior of all the "bad apples" who are responsible for the negative image of the profession.

Every lawyer and paralegal should carefully read and review the code of ethics. Most of the ethical considerations focus on serving the client's interests honestly, zealously, confidentially, competently, and without conflict of interest. Let us examine some of these notions about ethical conduct.

Figure 9.1
Canons 1-9, ABA Model Code of Professional Responsibility

Canon 1   A lawyer should assist in maintaining the integrity and competence of the legal profession.

Canon 2   A lawyer should assist the legal profession in fulfilling its duty to make legal counsel available.

Canon 3   A lawyer should assist in preventing the unauthorized practice of law.

Canon 4   A lawyer should preserve the confidences and secrets of a client.

Canon 5   A lawyer should exercise independent professional judgment on behalf of a client.

Canon 6   A lawyer should represent a client competently.

Canon 7   A lawyer should represent a client zealously within the bounds of the law.

Canon 8   A lawyer should assist in improving the legal system.

Canon 9   A lawyer should avoid even the appearance of professional impropriety.

Who Is Actually Regulated?

Generally speaking, it is lawyers, not paralegals, who are directly regulated by a code of ethics. Like many other professional organizations, the National Association of Legal Assistants (NALA), the National Federation of Paralegal Associations (NFPA), and other paralegal organizations may have a set of regulations that must be followed by their members. (See Appendix E.) Specific ethical rules, however, apply primarily to lawyers.

In any event, there are many reasons why paralegals should adhere to the same ethical conduct as attorneys. First, paralegals traditionally work for attorneys. If a paralegal engages in unethical behavior, her employer attorney will ultimately be responsible. Accordingly, employer attorneys often require specific ethical behavior from their employee paralegals.

Second, paralegals are in the business of servicing clients, whether directly or indirectly. A paralegal who engages in unethical conduct will likely cause his entire law firm to be looked on unfavorably. A freelance paralegal, in particular, who behaves unethically will probably ruin his professional reputation.

Finally, as discussed above, ethics are principles based on morality. Moral values are the difference between one's own sense of good or bad, right or wrong, and just or unjust. Morality, therefore, goes beyond legality. Something may be legally permissible but not moral.

May Paralegals Give Legal Advice?

It is important to address this question because it is often answered incompletely. As you will often discover, an incomplete answer to a question is usually an incorrect one. Many lawyers, law professors, and textbook authors insist that a paralegal may not give legal advice. The following examples illustrate why this is not always true. Nonetheless, the issue requires careful consideration.

EXAMPLE

Suppose that Charles is a paralegal in Nelson's law office. While Nelson is out to lunch one day, Charles is sitting at Nelson's desk. A client walks in and asks Charles for legal advice. Charles answers the client to the best of his knowledge. The client then leaves. Charles never actually claims to be a lawyer, but he does not explicitly state that he is not a lawyer, either. In this scenario, Charles improperly gives legal advice.

Because Charles did not clarify his professional status, it is likely that the client thought that Charles was indeed a lawyer, not a paralegal.

The reason paralegals should be careful in giving legal advice is that clients may not realize that they are dealing with a paralegal instead of a lawyer. While the paralegal's advice may often be just as good as the attorney's, a client is nonetheless entitled to know whom he is dealing with. The course of action a client takes may depend on his understanding of whose advice he is getting.

Accordingly, it is very important for paralegals to make the client understand that they are not attorneys.

EXAMPLE

Suppose that Roy asks Julie, a paralegal, for some legal advice. Julie tells Roy that she is a paralegal, not a lawyer. She then proceeds to give Roy the advice. In this case, Julie did not mislead Roy. But does this mean she may give legal advice? This answer involves more than just a simple yes or no.

Julie clearly explained to Roy that she is a paralegal, not an attorney. If a paralegal has clearly informed the client that she is indeed a paralegal, not an attorney, should the paralegal then have as much right to give out legal advice as anybody else? Do we not all have the right to give out advice on anything?

For instance, may you not relay your own "remedy" for the flu to a friend? Of course you may. Essentially, this is "medical advice" even if you are not a doctor or nurse. There is a difference, however. You are not giving this advice professionally. If you were to set up a booth and charge passersby a fee for such medical advice, you might be prohibited from doing so because you are not a medical professional.

Accordingly, Julie should be careful not to give legal advice, since this is a legal task usually reserved for lawyers. Though it may often be difficult to avoid giving some type of legal advice, paralegals should use their best efforts to direct clients' legal questions to attorneys.

Freelance or independent paralegals, however, are not usually monitored by attorneys. While there are movements to license and regulate such paralegals, for the most part they are currently unsupervised. Accordingly, it is even more likely that such paralegals will answer questions that may be construed as giving legal advice.

Accordingly, the blanket statement "a paralegal may not give legal advice" is incorrect. It implies that there are specific, across-the-board regulations prohibiting such behavior. Although paralegals are not absolutely prohibited from giving legal advice, it is inadvisable that they do so.

In any event, paralegals must clearly state to clients that they are paralegals, not attorneys, and should suggest that the client seeking advice consult an attorney as well.

Confidentiality and the Attorney/Paralegal-Client Privilege

As an aspiring paralegal, you will soon realize that you are learning important skills that will make you very valuable to many people. For instance, you may be the only person within a large group of friends or family who knows about wills, divorces, real estate closings, and criminal procedure.

Accordingly, many people you know will look at you as their resident "legal expert" and will seek your advice on various matters. Even if such a person's question involves a simple request for an attorney referral, he or she will often preface the question with a detailed account of the matter at hand. Accordingly, you should get into the habit of remembering that all information that someone shares with you while speaking to you in your professional capacity (as a lawyer or paralegal) must remain confidential.

Confidentiality is often a quality that is more than a learned professional skill. It has to do with personal behavior. Are you a person who keeps secrets or do you feel the need to tell them to someone else? Do you often promise "not to tell anyone" but then fail to keep that promise? Keep in mind that when you are dealing with information as a lawyer or paralegal, confidentiality goes beyond a personal code of conduct. It is a professional obligation.

Confidentiality: The responsibility to keep information private, such as that derived from communication between a client and a legal professional.

• •

Suppose that Walter, a stranger, walks into your law firm, and one of the attorneys speaks to him. The attorney then asks you, a paralegal, to maintain the case file. In Walter's file, you discover that he has twice been convicted of selling crack cocaine. This information is confidential: You may not share it with anyone outside the firm. This means that if a friend visits you at the firm one day when Walter is there, you may not point out Walter and whisper to your friend, "See that guy? He's a convicted drug dealer."

Let's examine another situation where the temptation to violate confidentiality may be even more difficult to resist. Suppose that you have recently graduated from college. While in college, you concentrated on paralegal studies and are now working as a paralegal. You often get together with many of your old college friends. One of your good friends, Samantha, is married to Tony. Samantha often brings Tony along when your group of friends gets together, and Tony is quite well liked by the group.

One day, Samantha calls you and asks you to meet her for lunch. During lunch, she explains to you that Tony has been physically abusing her, and that she suspects he is having an affair. She wants some information from you about the quickest and most inexpensive way to get a divorce.

A few days later, another college friend, Kelly, asks you if you've heard from Samantha. In fact, Kelly comments about how fortunate Samantha is to be so happily married. Keep in mind that you are personally upset about Samantha's marital problems, and Kelly is your good friend. You really want to tell Kelly everything. It will make you feel so much better, and it will probably help Samantha because Kelly can be very supportive during times of trouble. *Don't do it!* The temptation is there, but your professional responsibility to Samantha is to keep the information confidential.

Let's change the situation a bit. Suppose that Samantha and Tony are happily married, but Tony is a drug user who has been stealing from his employer to support his drug habit. He has not been caught. In fact, Tony's employer thinks very highly of him. One day, while you are visiting Samantha, she tells you what Tony has been doing. She speaks to you not as a client but as a friend, looking for comfort and support. Now suppose that Kelly owns her own business and wants to give Tony a good job. If you say to Kelly, "Don't hire him—he's a drug user who steals from his employer," are you violating the legal code of ethics? No.

Recall that Samantha spoke to you as a friend. Your paralegal background did not make a difference. She would have told you her secret whether you were a paralegal, lawyer, accountant, or carpenter. Accordingly, your decision whether to keep the information confidential is personal, not professional.

But what if, instead, Samantha had told you, "Tony's just been arrested for stealing from work. He often steals to support his drug habit. Can you please explain the situation to your boss?" The situation is now different. Samantha came to you not only as a friend but also because of your paralegal status and your connection to a law firm. If Kelly now informs you that she wants to give Tony a job, what do you do? You can certainly try to discourage her if you want to, but you are obligated to keep the information Samantha told you confidential. You cannot say, "Don't do it, Kelly. He steals from his employer to support his drug habit."

Suppose that Samantha had asked you to arrange for your firm to represent Tony, but she did not tell you that he stole from his employer. At a later date you find out, and your firm also decides to no longer represent him. Your firm may withdraw as Tony's attorney, but you must still abide by the code of confidentiality; you must not reveal the confidential information to anybody.

One more example. What if your firm decides to represent Tony but then Tony tells you that he is about to steal from his employer tomorrow? May you or your firm reveal this information? Yes.

A lawyer or paralegal is permitted, actually obligated, to reveal a client's intentions to commit a crime. Legal professionals may not disclose that their clients have committed crimes, but if their clients plan to commit future crimes, legal professionals have a duty to disclose this information as a method to prevent such crimes.

Keep in mind that as more and more people find out that you are a legal professional, they will come to you for advice. It is important to remember that such information is confidential. If your clients choose to publicize the information, it is their choice. You, however, may not be the one to reveal otherwise confidential information.

Because the legal code of ethics is very strict about confidentiality, clients develop a sense of security. They are encouraged to speak freely, without worry that their information will be wrongfully publicized.

Conflict of Interest

Once an attorney decides to represent a client, the attorney and her paralegals must not engage in any activity contrary to that client's best interests. This contrary activity is commonly called a **conflict of interest**. A client should feel comfortable about saying virtually anything to a lawyer or paralegal. He should be able to speak about anything and feel assured that the information will not come back to haunt him in the future.

Conflict of Interest: A legal professional's act or conduct regarding one client that is contrary to another client's best interests.

EXAMPLE

• •

Suppose that you have become an attorney. (Though adopting an attorney's perspective may make it easier to follow this example, keep in mind that this ethical conduct is expected of paralegals as well.)

You decide to represent Jim. Jim wants to open a restaurant and retains you for legal advice on how to do it. In spending a great deal of time with Jim, you learn that he is married to Jane but is having an affair with his night manager, Laurie. In fact, since you are doing a substantial amount of work for Jim, you often meet him at his house during the evening hours.

One night, while dropping off some documents at Jim's house, you learn that Jane is out of town, and you witness Jim and Laurie in the house together, both drunk and failing to properly care for Jim and Jane's two small children, Mark and Tracey.

A few months later Jane decides to divorce Jim. She asks you to represent her. Should you? No! In this case, the proper thing to do is to refer her to another law office. If you represent her, you will need to do everything legally possible to help her case. This would involve exposing information you know about Jim, and you certainly know a great deal. In fact, you may even be able to "catch" Jim and Laurie together, both drunk and neglecting Mark and Tracey—valuable evidence for Jane's child custody issues. However, exposing known information or using knowledge of Jim's propensities against him would not be in his best interests.

Representing Jane would be in conflict with the best interests of your client, Jim. Therefore, you should decline to represent Jane.

Suppose, instead, that you are a paralegal who works for an attorney. You must still avoid a conflict of interest. In that case, you should disclose any possibility of a conflict of interest involving past or present clients to your employer attorney.

Even when it seems as if there is no conflict, the best thing to do usually is to walk away if the mere possibility of conflict exists. It is possible that a thought, comment, or even a gesture that a former client made may reveal something about him that you will be able to use against him now that he is represented by an opposing attorney.

If you use the information against the former client, you are breaking the code of confidentiality and are acting in conflict with that client's best interests. If you fail to disclose the information, you are not serving the best interests of your present client. Do you see the conflict? Whenever there is even the appearance of impropriety, the best thing to do is to not get involved in such a mess at all.

Zealously Representing Clients Within the Bounds of the Law

When a client approaches a law firm for legal advice, it is the attorney, not the paralegal, who usually decides whether or not to represent that client. In order to fully appreciate the various factors that go into decisions of client representation, let us again imagine that you are an attorney.

Suppose that a client who is charged with murder comes to you for help. The client says "I did it." What do you do? To answer this question, consider the following two issues:

1. *Should* you represent this person?
2. *May* you represent this person?

The answer to the first question depends on your own personal beliefs. Do you feel comfortable representing somebody you know is guilty? As a member of the legal community, you will meet several legal professionals who have differing views on this matter. Some will tell you, "If the person is guilty, I don't want to represent him because I don't want to fight for somebody I don't believe in." This is the "say what you mean" theory.

Others will say, "Everyone is entitled to a fair trial. As a lawyer or paralegal, it is my duty to represent anyone—murderers, rapists, or armed robbers. Somebody has to do it." This is the "fair trial" theory.

Finally, others will argue, "There is no law that requires me to like or believe in my client. All I have to do is get up there and give it my best shot. This is how I choose to earn my money. As long as I am not doing anything illegal, what is the problem?" This is the "rules of the system" theory.

There are any number of additional points of view that determine whether a person decides to represent a client. The answer to "should you represent a client whom you know to be guilty" depends on you. May you represent that client? Yes. As we have just noted in describing the "rules of the system" theory, there is no law or regulation requiring you to believe in your client's innocence.

Consider the following situation. You have decided to represent a client whom you know is guilty. Your viewpoint is "Well, I know my client is guilty, so I won't give it my 'all.' I'll make some sort of effort but not 100 percent." May you do this? No! You must represent a client zealously within the bounds of the law. Whether or not you decide to represent a client is up to you, but once you make the decision to represent that person, you must zealously fight for her the way you would for your best friend or your closest family member. If at any time you feel that you are not giving it your best, you should withdraw from the case gracefully and allow somebody else to take over.

EXAMPLE

● ●

Suppose you decide to represent Marty, who has been accused of raping Linda. Initially, Marty tells you that he is innocent. A few weeks later, as the case is progressing, you realize that there are some inconsistencies in Marty's story. You approach him, and he finally confesses to you that he did in fact rape Linda. You are furious at Marty for lying to you, and you despise him for being a rapist. What do you do?

If you feel that you no longer wish to represent him, you must bow out gracefully. You may not tell people, "He confessed that he did it, so I'm withdrawing from the case." You must find a way to withdraw professionally. If you honestly believe that you can no longer do an adequate job, then withdrawing is not only good for you, it is the best thing for your client. And in that case, you are virtually obligated to withdraw. If, however, you still wish to represent Marty and will do so zealously, then you are free to do so.

In the above example, you were the attorney. This helps you work through the example easily. As a paralegal, you probably wouldn't experience exactly that type of circumstance, but you would be expected to follow the same ethical considerations nonetheless.

Sharing Legal Fees

Much of what is considered ethical or unethical will make a great deal of sense to you — that is, you would probably be able to "guess" what the ethical rule is because it seems logical. For example, imagine someone asks you, "Do you think that a paralegal is permitted to lie to her client by telling him that she is a lawyer?" Without having actually read an ethical regulation, you will no doubt answer, "No. A paralegal should not be permitted to lie," because that answer generally makes the most sense.

Some ethical standards, however, are not so apparent. There are ethical obligations that unless you are made aware of them, you would probably not think about. One of these is sharing **legal fees.**

EXAMPLE

● ●

Suppose that you are a paralegal who works in a real estate office. On a daily basis, you meet people who buy and sell real estate. When a buyer and seller decide to close (i.e., finalize) the sale, the closing must generally be supervised by an attorney.

Accordingly, you work out the following deal with Helen, a lawyer friend of yours: You will send your clients to Helen, and she will handle the closing. For every closing she completes, she will give you 20 percent of her earnings. Is this deal ethically permissible? No!

It is this type of ethical standard that is sometimes hard to understand. You may wonder, "What's wrong with the deal? It's honest and straight-forward. If both Helen and I serve the client properly, what's the problem?" Rather than just tell you, "this is the rule, and that's all there is to it," let me try to explain why this conduct is unethical. Consider the following examples.

Suppose that Helen charges $1,000 for a particular type of closing. Carrie, your client, needs an attorney to handle her closing. You refer Carrie to Helen and, as part of your usual deal, Helen will pay you 20 percent. If Helen were to charge Carrie $1,000, Helen would pay you 20 percent, which is $200, and keep the remaining $800 for herself.

But Helen may be greedy. After all, she is used to keeping the entire $1,000 for herself. Accordingly, Helen may decide to charge Carrie $1,400. Now, if Helen pays you 20 percent, which is $350, she will still keep $1,050 for herself. And Carrie has just been charged $400 more for the same service she would have received had she walked into Helen's office directly, without being referred by you. The first problem, then, is clients being overcharged.

Suppose further that Helen is not very experienced in real estate law. You send another client, Dean, to Helen's office for a closing. Dean's transaction is complicated, and a more experienced attorney would prob-ably do a better job. Nonetheless, because you know Helen will provide you with a 20 percent share of her fee, you tell Dean, "Helen is a good lawyer. She'll be perfect for your closing." On your recommendation Dean retains Helen to handle the transaction. Unfortunately, Helen does not do as good a job as a more experienced attorney would. Another problem, then, is clients not being properly served.

Accordingly, attorneys are not permitted to share their legal fees with paralegals or other nonattorneys.

What if in the above examples you were an attorney? May an attorney share her fee with another attorney? While the ethical rules here are not as strict, attorneys are discouraged, and sometimes prohibited, from paying out or collecting referral fees. Generally, attorneys may share or split fees based on the amount of work each has done, as long as the client is advised and does not object. Whether direct referral (or "forward-ing") fees between attorneys are permitted depends on the jurisdiction. Where such referrals are directly or indirectly discouraged, it is best to avoid them.

As a paralegal, you should not engage in such fee-sharing transactions with attorneys. There are plenty of alternative ways to earn a great deal of money as a freelance paralegal or to enhance your value when working for an attorney, while completely abiding by the legal code of ethics.

Legal Advertising and Solicitation

May an attorney or paralegal advertise his legal services in the same way a doctor, carpenter, or locksmith does? "Why not?" you may wonder, and you'd be right. Legal professionals may indeed advertise their services.

During most of the twentieth century legal advertising was not permitted. Today, however, **advertising** by lawyers is permitted as long as it is not misleading. For example, an attorney who has little or no experience in criminal law may not advertise that he or she is a criminal law "expert."

Accordingly, attorneys are allowed to advertise their services. However, are they allowed to solicit clients? Generally, no. The ABA prohibits **solicitation** because an attorney may have undue influence over a particularly vulnerable client.

Solicitation of Legal Services:
A legal professional's of act approaching another person to offer legal services.

EXAMPLE

• •

Suppose that Vince is injured in an automobile accident near Ron's law office. Ron happens to look out his office window and sees that a crowd has gathered where the accident took place.

Grabbing his hat, coat, and a handful of business cards, Ron dashes out of his office and to the accident scene. While Vince lies on the ground in considerable pain and discomfort, Ron "pitches" his legal services to Vince. As a result, Vince retains Ron as his attorney. Is Ron's conduct unethical? Yes.

It is possible that Vince was extremely vulnerable in this situation and unable to make a clear, rational decision. Ron's actions may be construed as overbearing and imposing, even intimidating. In an effort to protect the layperson, the ABA discourages and disallows such solicitation.

"Let me through. I'm a lawyer."

Much of the focus on advertising and solicitation is directed toward attorneys rather than paralegals. This is only natural since (1) until the latter part of this century, paralegals did not exist, and (2) even today, most paralegals work for attorneys, and thus have little need to engage in direct advertising or solicitation.

In any event, paralegals are guided and regulated in the same manner: Advertising is generally acceptable, whereas solicitation is generally not.

Competence

Competence or **capability** is another general ethical concept that the ABA reinforces through its rules. Professional competence is both a moral

"Let me through. I'm a lawyer."

*Drawing by
H. Martin; © 1989
The New Yorker
Magazine, Inc.*

and regulated obligation. Unfortunately, those "bad apples" in the legal profession whom we discussed earlier often overlook, ignore, and reject competence.

Greedy, irresponsible attorneys far too often will claim to be competent in a particular area of law when in fact they do not know what they are talking about. It is encouraging that the ABA and numerous other legal professional associations stress competence in the field.

As a lawyer or paralegal, you should always be forthright with yourself, your employer, and your client. Does this mean that you have to study something for 50 years before you dare to try it yourself? Of course not! However, it is equally true that you should not jump into undertaking a task about which you know nothing.

Ideally, you should undertake those tasks that you know you can perform well. However, everybody has to start somewhere. Accordingly, if you ever find yourself in over your head, be honest with yourself, tell your employer (or if you are self-employed, seek the advice of a more experienced colleague), and keep your client informed. Chances are that your client will not think less of you. To the contrary, your client will probably be impressed that you think enough about his concerns to seek a second opinion.

EXAMPLE

Suppose that you are a lawyer or freelance paralegal. You specialize in landlord/tenant law, but a prospective client drops by your office with a question about immigration law. If you know nothing about the subject, what should you do? The best thing would be to immediately refer the client to someone who can help him, such as an immigration attorney.

★ **HINT:** It is always a good idea to keep at hand a current referral list of legal professionals grouped by area of expertise. You will then be able to instantly and confidently refer a client to the person best suited to help her. Your client will be grateful to you and will admire your swift and confident decisionmaking.

What if you think you know how to help the person, yet after you begin the task, you run into some problems? At that point, think of the client first. Consult someone who can help you get the job done properly, even if it means sharing part (or even all) of your fee. Ethically, a good legal professional will always put her client's interests first.

Always take pride in yourself and your profession and serve your clients competently.

INTEGRITY

I have always believed, and always convey to my students, that integrity is vital to law, as it is to every profession and every aspect of life. The key to being a good lawyer or paralegal (and, I think, a good human being) is to embrace honesty and reject dishonesty. Refuse to lie, to be shady, to be underhanded. And don't be influenced by those who are. Speak the truth. Speak straight from the heart. Others will sense your honesty and be very impressed with what you have to say.

Key Terms

advertising
American Bar
   Association
capability
code of ethics

competence
confidentiality
conflict of
   interest
ethics

freelance (or
   independent)
   paralegal
legal fees
solicitation

Review Questions

1. Carefully explain whether paralegals may give legal advice.

2. What are freelance paralegals?

3. What is the attorney-client privilege?

4. Give three examples of a conflict of interest that an attorney or paralegal should avoid.

5. Explain the difference between an appearance of impropriety and actual impropriety as it applies to legal ethics.

6. Discuss the notion of zealously representing clients within the bounds of the law.

7. May attorneys share legal fees with other attorneys? With paralegals?

8. Are attorneys or paralegals permitted to advertise?

9. Are attorneys permitted to solicit potential clients?

10. Does your state have laws that specifically regulate paralegals?

Web Sites

- National Association of Legal Assistants
  http://www.nala.org/
- National Federal of Paralegal Associations
  http://www.paralegals.org/
- Legal Information Institute, ethics page
  http://www.law.cornell.edu/ethics/
- American Bar Association
  http://www.abanet.org/home.cfm

Careers

10

If you have read through all the chapters slowly and carefully and understand all of the basic principles of law within them, you have mastered those chapters. You now deserve a big *congratulations!* You have taken an important step within the legal community. Truly, you know more about the law than the average person. Even though there is still a long way to go, you are off to an excellent start.

This chapter is about legal careers. It expands on some of the notions briefly mentioned at the end of the contracts, torts, and criminal law chapters. This chapter is a collection of anecdotes and hypotheticals, as compared to the *substantive* material you have been exposed to thus far. So sit back, relax, and regard this chapter as easy reading. You've earned the break.

TYPES OF LEGAL EMPLOYMENT

First, let's look at some of the types of places where you can expect to work as a paralegal or lawyer (if you choose to work as either, or both, you will find this chapter helpful). Again, remember the perspective of this entire book. These are general principles, not to be taken as absolutes. In any event, the information is useful in helping you create your own legal career path.

Size of the Law Firm

What type of person are you? Do you like a lot of free time, or do you relish long workweeks? Would you be happy with a modest but comfortable living, or do you crave big money? Do you like a fast-paced environment, or do you prefer a more relaxed, laid-back atmosphere? Many of these working conditions can be determined by the size of the law firm you work for.

Generally, the larger the firm, the longer the hours, the higher the salary. Those lawyers and paralegals who make the "big money" usually put in very long hours. Translated, "very long hours" can mean anywhere from 60 to 80 hours per week or more. Imagine getting to the office on a Monday morning at 7 A.M. and staying until 10 P.M. That's 15 hours. Do that for five straight days, and it's 75 hours. (Not to mention work on the weekend.) Remember, however, that these attorneys also make a tremendous amount of money. To state exact figures would be misleading because they vary from city to city and may change with the times. A large firm will also have luxurious benefits — plush offices, high-profile exposure, and perhaps national and international travel.

The smaller the firm, the less the extravagance, the lower the salary, and the shorter the workweek. A midsize firm will probably mean a pay cut balanced by more time off on evenings and weekends. A very small firm could mean cramped office space, not much glamour, and closer to 9 to 5 hours. But a small firm also means more experience gained faster. In fact, the smaller the firm, the greater the chance of lawyers and paralegals learning their professions very quickly.

A law firm is, essentially, not much different from any other business. For example, suppose that you get a job in a large department store. You are placed in the electronics department, and you sell TVs, DVD players, and stereo systems. Most probably, you will work in that department every day, and you will soon become proficient in selling electronic goods. Eventually, you may become manager of the department. Is it likely that your supervisor will ask you to work in or manage the shoe department one day? No, because in department stores people usually specialize in one area and remain there. (It is possible, of course, for persons to transfer from one department to the other; however, this is the exception to the general rule.) In all likelihood, you will remain in electronics for the duration of your employment at that department store.

What if, instead, you work in a small grocery store? In that case, you may have to do various tasks: open and close the store, work the cash register, sweep the floor, display the merchandise, organize the stockroom, make signs for the window, etc. Accordingly, when you leave the large department store, you will have experience in one area — electronics. When you leave the grocery store, you will know how to do a great many things.

Much like retail stores, law firms vary in the type of experience their employees receive. For example, as a lawyer or paralegal for a large firm, you may be assigned to one department — criminal, real estate, personal injury, etc. — and you may specialize in one specific area of law. As a paralegal, furthermore, you may be assigned to perform one type of task — interviews, research, proofreading. The large law firms enjoy the luxury of employing many people and, accordingly, these firms make sure that each person does one thing (or a few things) very well, rather than having to do many things less expertly.

The small law firms, however, are much like the small grocery stores. In such firms, you may be a member of a staff of at best two or three employees. Accordingly, you will have to be involved in all the areas of law, and do everything from writing a memorandum to making the coffee. While these firms do not have the luxury of a large number of employees, the benefit to you is that you gain a great deal of experience very quickly.

Keep in mind that I am giving examples of two extremes: very large and very small law firms. Within these extremes there are midsized firms that represent a compromise between the characteristics of the extremes — for example, moderate hours, moderate pay, moderate duties, moderate experience.

Let us next examine the types of employers who usually hire lawyers and paralegals.

Types of Careers

Keeping in mind that the size of the law firm will make some difference to your salary and overall quality of work life, take a look at the different types of career options available to you.

Private Law Firms

Private law firms are those where the client pays the legal fee. Large companies and wealthy individuals often hire large private law firms, while middle-class and working-class clients go to the smaller firms.

Private law firms are in business for the purpose of practicing law, and take on clients and cases spanning all types of law (though some firms limit their practice to certain areas).

Public Law

In **public law,** the government pays the bill. A lawyer or paralegal may work directly for the government either by representing the government in a lawsuit or by working for a branch of government or a government agency.

The **District Attorney's (D.A.'s) office** prosecutes criminal suspects. On the other side, there is the **Public Defender's Office,** which represents criminal suspects and defendants in civil suits who cannot afford to pay for legal services. Moreover, plaintiffs who cannot afford to initiate a lawsuit are often represented on a pro bono basis. **Pro bono** (which means "for the good") services include free legal representation. Although pro bono is often provided by private firms, various states require that all their practicing attorneys undertake a minimal amount of pro bono work periodically.

One of the most heartfelt and passionate legal professions is **public interest law,** particularly in criminal matters. There are a great number of aspiring attorneys and paralegals who have a strong desire to either "put criminals behind bars" or "give criminals a fair defense." Accordingly, these individuals wind up on different sides of criminal law, either for the prosecution or for the defense.

Corporate/In-House Practice

Whereas the primary reason law firms are in business is to practice law, most companies are in business for other purposes and employ legal professionals for preventive measures. In fact, corporate lawyers are very much like fire extinguishers. You may keep a fire extinguisher in your house, but you hope you never have to use it. Companies do not want lawsuits but are often faced with them. Accordingly, they have lawyers and paralegals on staff rather than having to go out and find legal professionals whenever they need them.

Much like a secretary, security guard, or maintenance person, a legal professional may be a paid staff employee of a company. Again, the size of the company may determine the size and characteristics of its law department. However, the company is the one and only client of the attorney or paralegal. Typically, corporate matters can involve employment disputes, real estate transactions, and tax advice. Quite often, the legal professional may take an interest in the business end of the company and may choose to undertake nonlegal responsibilities.

Nonlegal Careers

Two questions come to mind regarding nonlegal careers for lawyers and paralegals:

1. What type of nonlegal careers are open to a person with a legal background?

2. Why would a person who completed a legal education choose to enter a nonlegal career? That is, why would a person study to become a lawyer or paralegal and then not pursue that career?

Let's take a look at the first question. Within all nonlegal careers, there are careers that are law-related and those that are completely independent of the legal field.

Law-related careers include teaching law in a law school, college, or professional school (such as a school that trains paralegals or legal secretaries); training paralegals for a law firm or corporation; writing, editing, or promoting legal publications; placing individuals in legal positions; and working in a law library.

Careers unrelated to law include anything from being a doctor, accountant, or advertising agent to coaching football, selling hot dogs, or being a rock-and-roll musician. For those choosing any one of the above occupations, why in the world would they train to become a paralegal or go on to law school?

These questions can be answered most easily when dealing with the law-related professions. Some people love learning about the law but are not very happy practicing it. They may enjoy teaching, writing, or librarianship, and their legal background is their vehicle for landing such a position. Suppose, for example, that you enjoy learning about the law and would like to teach in a college, train paralegals, or help edit a casebook. Your legal education will come in very handy. In fact, it will be a vital tool in your being hired.

But why would someone go to law school and then pursue a career, for example, as a journalist? Things are not always what they seem. Maybe the person started law school and during (or shortly after) the law school experience decided that she preferred being a journalist. Accordingly, the person finished law school and then went to work as a journalist. In that case, was law school a waste? Absolutely not! A legal education is extremely valuable. More valuable, in fact, than the legal career itself. As unbelievable as it may sound, in some cases a person with a legal education may be more marketable in the fields of journalism, politics, economics, as well as other professions, than a person who studied those subjects while in school. How is that possible, you may ask? Think of people who were in the military. Do you know how impressive a military career looks on a resume? Very impressive. Did you ever wonder why a department store looking for a manager in the furniture department would actually care if someone flew jets for the U.S. Navy? "What does flying airplanes have to do with selling furniture?" you may ask. Absolutely nothing. However, a former military person has mastered the skills of discipline, responsibility, and leadership. These are skills vital to any employer. Generally speaking, an employer may have more confidence in an ex-soldier to open a store on time, keep records in order, and settle internal disputes than a person without a military background.

A legal education, much like military training, requires hard work, discipline, and sharpening of the mind. When you have completed your legal education, be proud! You have sharpened your mind, enhanced your endurance, improved your ability to think on your feet and work under pressure, and become a well-seasoned problem solver.

These are timeless, indispensable skills. Because you possess these skills, you will probably be very marketable in both legal and nonlegal fields.

Accordingly, with a paralegal education or a law degree, there is a wide-open market for you. Despite the fact that during a bad economy the legal profession, like most others, suffers high rates of unemployment, the education is never out of date and will be very lucrative when times get better.

TIPS FOR GAINING EMPLOYMENT

As stated earlier, this book is primarily devoted to learning about the law. This chapter is designed to provide a few helpful hints, once you have learned about the law, on how you may go about putting that knowledge to professional use.

There are two excellent ways of getting your "foot in the door" — temp agencies and internships.

Temp Agencies

Temp agencies are agencies that hire **temporary employees (temps)** for short-term or long-term assignments. Choose the largest business area (city, town) within reasonable commuting distance from where you live, and look through the yellow pages and the largest daily newspaper for as many legal temp agencies as you can find.

Next send a cover letter and resume to each of these agencies, discussing your credentials, aspirations, and availability.

Quite often, these agencies have plenty of entry-level positions available. At first, the work may appear mundane, and you may feel that you are overqualified. However, think of it as a stepping stone. If your employers like you, they will hire you rather than an outside stranger when a better position opens up.

Internships

Whenever I bring up the marketability of a legal education, people often respond, "In a bad economy, it's very hard to find a job no matter what your education is." This statement has a great deal of truth to it. For that reason, it is important to recognize that in a bad economy where there is high unemployment, it is crucial to make the most of what you have.

An **internship,** particularly a nonpaying internship, is an excellent trade-off for both the employer and the employee. It is particularly easy to obtain one during a bad economy. When business is bad, employers do not make a great deal of money. Under such circumstances, which would they prefer—paid help or free help? Free help, of course. This explains why an employer will hire you, but what is the benefit to you in all of this?

Even though paid employment is certainly more appealing than free employment, a nonpaying internship is certainly better than nothing. In fact, it is better in the long run than a paying nonlegal position. An internship will reap two great rewards: the inside track to a paying position and general legal experience.

First, if the employer likes your work, when a paying position opens up, you will probably have a great chance of obtaining it. Why would the employer take a chance on someone else when you are already there and perfect for the job?

Second, even if you do not land a paying position with that particular employer, you will have gained valuable legal experience. Such experience will be more valuable than if you had a nonlegal paying position during that time.

For example, suppose that Andy is a criminal lawyer who needs to hire a paralegal. Two people apply for the position. The first applicant, Ben, took paralegal courses while in college but has worked as a waiter in a local pizzeria for the past two years. As a waiter, Ben earned a good hourly wage and excellent tips.

The second applicant, Charles, took the same type of paralegal courses as Ben did. For the past two years, Charles has worked as a nonpaid intern in the District Attorney's Office. While Charles did not earn a penny during this time, he gained a great deal of valuable criminal law experience. All other things being equal, who has the better chance of getting the job? Charles does. Even though Charles did not earn any money during this time, the employer does not care. The employer cares about relevant experience, and Charles has a great deal more relevant experience than Ben does.

★ **HINT:** Many people cannot afford the luxury of working for free. In reality, people need money to pay their bills, and this is no less true for students. In any event, whenever possible, an aspiring paralegal or law student should do *some* type of legal work to gain experience, however minimal. If, for example, you need to earn money, why not work twenty hours a week as a retail clerk, bartender, or construction worker, and then put in five hours as a nonpaid legal intern? In that way, you can earn money, yet at least gain some valuable long-term experience as well. Keep in mind that nonpaying internships do not reap short-term gains; they are a long-term self-investment.

These hints and tips about the world of legal employment describe general principles, but quite often apply directly to specific situations. The bottom line is get to know yourself and what you want from a job. Then be aggressive in trying to land such a job by (1) making the most of what you presently have and (2) constantly striving to improve your credentials.

Key Terms

District Attorney's
  (D.A.'s) Office
freelance
internship

private law firm
pro bono
Public Defender's
  Office

public interest law
public law
temporary employee
  (temp)

Review Questions

1. Would you like to become a paralegal or an attorney, or both? Explain your answer.

2. Are you interested in becoming a judge?

3. Would you like to be a trial lawyer or a paralegal working on a court case? Why or why not?

4. Would you be interested in a career in contract law? Why or why not?

5. Discuss whether you would like to be a tort lawyer or paralegal.

6. In which area of law would you prefer to work, civil or criminal?

7. If you were a criminal law attorney or paralegal, would you prefer to work for the prosecution or for the defense? Explain your answer.

8. Buy all of the local newspapers in your area and check the job postings for paralegal positions. What are the qualifications and Salary range?

9. Join two or three paralegal temp agencies in your area.

10. Try to obtain an internship in a law firm or company where you would really like to work.

Web Sites

- Job search directory and other career advice
  http://careers.findlaw.com/
- ABA Career Counsel, the ABA's central source for online information on finding jobs and enhancing lawyers' careers
  http://www.abanet.org/careercounsel/home.html
- U.S. Department of Labor, statistics on legal careers
  http://stats.bls.gov/oco/ocos053.htm

Afterword: Is the Law for You?

One last time, let me say *congratulations!* You have just completed a basic introductory guide to the law. You know where to find the law, how to brief a court case, and how to write a logical, organized answer to a legal question. Moreover, you have a general understanding of contracts, torts, and criminal law. Finally, you have an idea about career avenues open to you once you have completed your legal education.

Throughout this book, I have tried to present the law for what it is: basic, uncomplicated ideas based on everyday principles. I explained to you that the law need not be difficult to learn. Those who do not use this basic approach in teaching the law make the law appear more complicated than it really is because they do not know how to make learning easy.

I hope that I have succeeded in making it easy for you to learn about the law. Before you put this book down, however, I have one more question for you, one that you probably began thinking about while reading Chapter 1, and even long before that: Is the law for you?

Actually, this is a question that may take a long time for you to answer. In arriving at an honest, educated answer to this question, you may want to consider some additional questions:

1. Why do you want to study law?
2. Do you want to be a lawyer, a paralegal, a judge, a law professor — that is, what type of job do you want from your legal education?
3. Have you considered the time, money, and energy necessary to successfully complete a legal education? If so, are you willing to devote the time, money, and energy to fulfill your goal?

4. Is a legal education the best method of achieving your ultimate career goal?

You may never fully answer these questions. You may find yourself entering law school, for example, without being fully aware of why you are there. Although you should try to know yourself and understand the reason why you chose a legal career, it is perfectly natural and quite common if you do not.

Finally, let me leave you with a couple of reminders. If you do indeed decide to pursue a legal career, whether as a paralegal or lawyer, consider the following course of action:

1. Map out a plan for achieving your career goal. Make a list of schools, time, money, etc. Try to plan ahead rather than "winging it." While this may be too safe and predictable for some of you, in the long run it will make you a better prepared legal scholar.

2. Speak to as many legal professionals as possible to get the most complete spectrum of points of view. Talk to lawyers, judges, paralegals, legal secretaries, law professors, law clerks, and anyone else in the legal profession. Speak to male and female legal professionals of all ages, races, and nationalities to get their perspective. Also, speak to people from various backgrounds with various interests. Remember that the more points of view you get, the better informed you will probably be.

3. Note that the legal profession is as much respected as it is ridiculed. Many people think of lawyers as "smart," while others call them "crooks." There is probably good reason for both statements. If you really want to be a lawyer or paralegal, don't be ashamed of your choice. Don't let the negative talk bother you, but don't behave in a manner to justify it, either. The legal profession needs honorable people: people who place honesty and integrity *above all*, and who will strive to maintain these ideals *with no exception*. If you are this type of person, then I sincerely hope that you join the professional legal community because your services are much needed.

In conclusion, I hope that you have enjoyed reading this book as much as I have enjoyed writing it, and I wish you the best of luck in your future. For those of you settled in your careers, who are reading this book for nonvocational purposes, I hope that you found it helpful. Keep it handy so you can refer to it whenever you need to.

Being a Paralegal

Appendix

A

Overview

What Is a Paralegal?
What Do Paralegals Do?
    Summarizing Court Cases and Other Court Documents
    Filling Out Legal Forms
    Preparing Drafts of Wills, Leases, and Other Agreements
    Proofreading
    Filing Papers in Court
    Client Contact
    Legal Research
What Is the Difference Between a Paralegal and a Lawyer?
How Does Someone Become a Paralegal?
If You Want to Become a Lawyer, Should You First Become a
    Paralegal?
Final Thoughts

Now that we have learned quite a bit about the law, let's take a look at the legal professional, particularly the paralegal. Whether you want to become a lawyer, paralegal, or legal secretary, or simply wish to have a basic, well-rounded understanding of the law, it is important to know a thing or two about paralegals.

In reading this chapter, you will learn a great deal about the various categories of people who make up the legal profession.

WHAT IS A PARALEGAL?

So what exactly is a **paralegal?** Consider the following example to better understand the answer. In the classic sitcom *The Honeymooners* starring Jackie Gleason as Ralph Kramden and Art Carney as his pal Ed Norton, Norton often refers to himself as "an underground engineer" and Ralph is always quick to point out that Norton "works in a sewer."

How does a sewer worker proclaiming himself an underground engineer relate to the legal profession? First, it helps us understand that the

Underground engineer?

same job is often given different titles by different people. Also, the same job title can entail different job descriptions in different workplaces.

Suppose, for example, that Amy, Bob, and Carrie each work for a different law firm. All three have the exact same job description: They maintain the firm's litigation calendar (i.e., the schedule of upcoming court appearances). But each firm assigns a different job title to this job description: Amy is a "paralegal," Bob is a "law clerk," and Carrie is an "office manager." Same job, different titles.

Now consider David, Ellen, and Frank, each of whom works at a different law firm. All three are referred to as "paralegals" by their firms. David spends all day in the library doing legal research. He never sees or talks to clients. Ellen, on the other hand, interviews clients all day. She never does any legal research. Frank spends each day typing, filing, and answering phones. Different jobs, same job title.

So what is the answer to our question, what is a paralegal? The answer is . . . there is no exact answer. And don't let anyone tell you otherwise! The above examples describe some types of paralegal duties, but there are many others. Accordingly, to describe a paralegal as someone who "interviews clients" is an incomplete answer because, as we have just seen, Ellen interviews clients quite often but David and Frank never do. Accordingly, the term "paralegal" covers such a broad range of jobs and duties that a specific definition may be too narrow.

WHAT DO PARALEGALS DO?

Since a specific definition is not possible, let's focus on describing the functions paralegals typically perform. Remember that the category of people considered to be "paralegals" is very broad. Accordingly, the range of job descriptions is equally broad. Some typical paralegal duties include:

- summarizing court cases and court documents
- filling out legal forms
- preparing drafts of wills, leases, or other agreements
- proofreading
- filing papers in court
- client contact
- legal research

Summarizing Court Cases and Other Court Documents

By the time a single case has concluded, the client's file may become extremely large. Quite often, an attorney will be assigned to a case in its later stages. Because this attorney needs to become familiar with the file as soon as possible, it is essential for paralegals to **summarize the file.**

A paralegal will write a brief description of what the case is about and outline the various documents in the case, thereby providing a valuable guideline for the attorney. The paralegal will also briefly summarize court cases relevant to the matter at hand.

Filling Out Legal Forms

In many legal matters the bulk of the work involves completing certain **forms**— preprinted applications covering every sort of transaction from name changes to obtaining vendor licenses to becoming an American citizen. In these situations there will probably be no trial or other oral argument. Most of the work will involve completing forms. See Figure A.1 for an example. Typically, a paralegal will complete the forms, and the supervising attorney will review the work. If the paralegal is experienced, the attorney will merely need to formally validate the work by signing the documents.

Preparing Drafts of Wills, Leases, and Other Agreements

A **will** or a **lease** is a bit different than a form because it is often an original draft and is dependent on the client's particular situation— that is, preparing a will or lease or other such agreement does not involve answering existing questions but rather summarizing the client's intent in original language.

EXAMPLE

Imagine you are taking a multiple choice test and one question is, "Which animal is most likely to be found in a zoo?"

a. dog   b. cat   c. goldfish   d. elephant

The correct answer, apparently, is "d. elephant."

In a multiple choice test you have a specific set of questions to answer. This is much like completing a form. Imagine now that your test is in essay form, and the question is

Please write an essay describing four types of animals. Discuss whether they are typical household pets or likely to be found in a zoo.

Here, you do not have all of your facts set. You need to think about the types of animals you will write about. This task is not like completing a form but more like drafting a document.

Figure A.1   Sample Form

REAL ESTATE LEASE

Agreement made this _____ day of _____, 20 _____, between X, Inc., a _____ corporation (Lessor), and _____, an individual (Lessee).

The Lessor hereby devises and lets to the Lessee the premises known as _____ for the term of one year, commencing on the _____ day of _____, 20 ____, and ending on the ____ day of ____, 20 ____, for which the Lessee agrees to pay the Lessor, at his place of business, promptly on the first day of each month, in advance, a monthly rental of _____ dollars ($ ____). On the failure of the Lessee to pay said rent when due, all further rent under this contract shall immediately become due and payable, and the Lessor has the right, at his option, to declare this lease void, cancel the same, enter and take possession of the premises.

It is further agreed that:

(Indicate all specific covenants the parties agree to, for example:
Allocation of cost of repairs
Maintenance of premises
Right of Lessor to enter
Subletting
Destruction of property due to fire or act of God
Alteration of premises
Payment of damages due to negligence
Notice to quit
Security deposit)

All of the aforementioned agreements, covenants, and conditions shall apply to and be binding upon the parties hereto, their heirs, executors, administrators, and assigns.

IN WITNESS WHEREOF, the parties hereto have set their hands and seals this _____ day of _____, 20 _____.

Lessor
By: _____
_____
Lessee

In any event, drafting documents, like completing forms, is often done by the paralegal. As a paralegal, you will complete the work, then present it to the lawyer, who will proofread the content and make any necessary revisions.

Proofreading

Just as a lawyer will **proofread** a paralegal's work, the reverse is true. A lawyer will often ask a paralegal to proofread various work that the lawyer has done. While a secretary usually proofreads for typographical errors, a paralegal will typically check for proper form, accurate use of the law, and proper presentation of the facts.

Filing Papers in Court

As we learned in Chapter 5, there is a procedure involved in beginning and maintaining a lawsuit or other legal matter in court. Paralegals are often placed in charge of making sure that all of the proper documents have been completed and filed with the court. As a paralegal, for instance, you may have to file a certain paper in court instructing the sheriff to collect money that your client is owed.

Client Contact

As demonstrated in the examples set forth above, paralegals are often extensively involved in preparing various documents. Accordingly, they often need to stay in close contact with clients. The contact may range from client interviews and summarizing a client's **deposition** (a type of sworn statement) to routinely calling clients to keep them informed about the status of their case. As we learned in Chapter 9, it is important that paralegals, when dealing with clients, identify themselves as paralegals. Clients should never be led to believe that they are speaking to an attorney when that is not the case.

Legal Research

In Chapter 2 we learned that the key to a successful lawsuit or other legal matter is a strong command of the relevant law. Quite often, attorneys send their paralegals to do legal "detective work" — that is, find the law to "solve" the issues at hand.

Keep in mind that this is by no means a complete list of all the things a paralegal does because the nature of the work is up to the employer and may involve anything connected to the legal profession, no matter how remote the connection. Naturally, someone who only answers telephones is not a "traditional" paralegal in the same sense as someone who does legal research, but both may be considered paralegals by their respective employers.

WHAT IS THE DIFFERENCE BETWEEN A PARALEGAL AND A LAWYER?

First and foremost, a lawyer is a person who is licensed to practice law, whereas a paralegal is not. Generally, a paralegal may not appear before a judge on a client's behalf or prepare certain legal documents (the types of documents vary from state to state). Moreover, paralegals often perform tasks that lawyers usually do not, such as payroll management or computerized billing.

Paralegals did not even *exist* until late in this century. The notion of legal assistants was developed and expanded sometime in the early 1970s. Since then the profession has grown tremendously. Although paralegals are not formally regulated, there are movements supporting such regulation. The debate over paralegal regulation will likely endure, as will the continued growth of the profession.

HOW DOES SOMEONE BECOME A PARALEGAL?

There is no specific path one must follow to become a paralegal. To become a lawyer, for instance, you must (1) graduate from law school and (2) pass the bar examination in the particular jurisdiction (usually, each state) in which you wish to practice law. But a paralegal may be anyone from a high school dropout to a law school graduate who has yet to pass the bar. Since the category of paralegal job descriptions is so broad, the requirements for employment will vary from job to job.

Generally, the more education and experience you have, the better your chances of getting hired and being successful in the profession. A strong background in writing is helpful, along with a basic knowledge of law. As computers influence our daily lives more and more each day, it is wise to be computer literate—particularly regarding legal research.

Moreover, some national and local paralegal associations grant **paralegal certificates** based on successful performance on a paralegal examination. Such examinations are unpredictable criteria for employment. Some employers do not even look at them at all. However, it certainly will not hurt you if you have successfully scored on such a test.

Completing a specific course of study thus is not *required* to become a paralegal, though it is certainly very helpful. Think about it. If *you* were hiring a paralegal, wouldn't you want that person to have received formal training in that field? Wouldn't you prefer that the person indeed has been learning about the law? Accordingly, if you want to become a paralegal, learning about the law certainly is the right way to go about it.

IF YOU WANT TO BECOME A LAWYER, SHOULD YOU FIRST BECOME A PARALEGAL?

Contrary to popular belief, you do not have to major in pre-law or political science or any other specific area in order to become a lawyer. In fact, you can become a successful lawyer just as easily if your college major is in any nonlegal field from art history to zoology. Accordingly, you certainly do not start out as a paralegal in order to ultimately become a lawyer.

However, you should keep in mind that law school is a heavy investment of both time and money. If you make the decision to go, you should have a good idea of what it is all about. Sometimes a paralegal education and/or work experience will help you make up your mind one way or the other. If you have learned enough about the law prior to entering law school and conclude that it's not for you, then you have saved yourself a great deal of time, money, and aggravation.

But if you believe that becoming an attorney is the right career for you, then a paralegal background will give you a big advantage. Law school is full of exciting challenges, but such challenges take time to master. As a paralegal, you will have the edge over those who have never tried. This advantage can set the tone for a smooth, steady ride through law school, with a promising future at the end of the road.

FINAL THOUGHTS

You now have some ideas about lawyers and paralegals. In the next chapter we will begin to explore the world of law. Remember that the law is a large collection of basic ideas. So just relax, read everything slowly and carefully, and you will enjoy the journey.

Key Terms

deposition	paralegal	summarizing the file
form	paralegal certificate	will
lease	proofreading	

Review Questions

1. Name five things that a paralegal may be assigned to do in a law office.

2. Is there a uniform definition of a "paralegal"? Explain.

3. Does your city or town have a local paralegal organization?

4. What advantage would a law school applicant have if he or she first became a paralegal?

5. What are some differences between a lawyer and a paralegal?

The Constitution of the United States

We the People of the United States, in Order to form a more perfect Union, establish Justice, insure domestic Tranquility, provide for the common defence, promote the general Welfare, and secure the Blessings of Liberty to ourselves and our Posterity, do ordain and establish this Constitution for the United States of America.

ARTICLE I

Section 1. All legislative Powers herein granted shall be vested in a Congress of the United States which shall consist of a Senate and House of Representatives.

Section 2. [1] The House of Representatives shall be composed of Members chosen every second Year by the People of the several States, and the Electors in each State shall have the Qualifications requisite for Electors of the most numerous Branch of the State Legislature.

[2] No Person shall be a Representative who shall not have attained to the Age of twenty five Years, and been seven Years a Citizen of the United States, and who shall not, when elected, be an Inhabitant of that State in which he shall be chosen.

[3] Representatives and direct Taxes shall be apportioned among the several States which may be included within this Union, according to their respective Numbers, which shall be determined by adding to the whole Number of free Persons, including those bound to Service for a Term of Years, and excluding Indians not taxed, three fifths of all other Persons. The actual Enumeration shall be made within three Years after the first Meeting of the Congress of the United States, and within every subsequent Term of ten Years, in such Manner as they shall by Law direct. The Number of Representatives shall not exceed one for every thirty Thousand, but each State shall have at Least One Representative; and until such enumeration shall be made, the State of New Hampshire

shall be entitled to chuse three, Massachusetts eight, Rhode Island and Providence Plantations one, Connecticut five, New York six, New Jersey four, Pennsylvania eight, Delaware one, Maryland six, Virginia ten, North Carolina five, South Carolina five, and Georgia three.

[4] When vacancies happen in the Representation from any State, the Executive Authority thereof shall issue Writs of Election to fill such Vacancies.

[5] The House of Representatives shall chuse their Speaker and other Officers; and shall have the sole Power of Impeachment.

Section 3. [1] The Senate of the United States shall be composed of two Senators from each State, chosen by the Legislature thereof, for six Years; and each Senator shall have one Vote.

[2] Immediately after they shall be assembled in Consequence of the first Election, they shall be divided as equally as may be into three Classes. The Seats of the Senators of the first Class shall be vacated at the Expiration of the second Year, of the second Class at the Expiration of the fourth Year, and of the third Class at the Expiration of the sixth Year, so that one third may be chosen every second Year; and if Vacancies happen by Resignation, or otherwise, during the Recess of the Legislature of any State, the Executive thereof may make temporary Appointments until the next Meeting of the Legislature, which shall then fill such Vacancies.

[3] No Person shall be a Senator who shall not have attained to the Age of thirty Years, and been nine Years a Citizen of the United States, and who shall not, when elected, be an Inhabitant of that State for which he shall be chosen.

[4] The Vice President of the United States shall be President of the Senate, but shall have no Vote, unless they be equally divided.

[5] The Senate shall chuse their other Officers, and also a President pro tempore, in the absence of the Vice President, or when he shall exercise the Office of President of the United States.

[6] The Senate shall have the sole Power to try all Impeachments. When sitting for that Purpose, they shall be on Oath or Affirmation. When the President of the United States is tried, the Chief Justice shall preside: And no Person shall be convicted without the Concurrence of two thirds of the Members present.

[7] Judgment in Cases of Impeachment shall not extend further than to removal from Office, and disqualification to hold and enjoy any Office of honor, Trust or Profit under the United States: but the Party convicted shall nevertheless be liable and subject to Indictment, Trial, Judgment and Punishment, according to Law.

Section 4. [1] The Times, Places and Manner of holding Elections for Senators and Representatives, shall be prescribed in each State by the Legislature thereof; but the Congress may at any time by Law make or alter such Regulations, except as to the Places of chusing Senators.

[2] The Congress shall assemble at least once in every Year, and such Meeting shall be on the first Monday in December, unless they shall by Law appoint a different Day.

Section 5. [1] Each House shall be the Judge of the Elections, Returns and Qualifications of its own Members, and a Majority of each shall constitute a Quorum to do Business; but a smaller Number may adjourn from day to day, and may be authorized to compel the Attendance of absent Members, in such Manner, and under such Penalties as each House may provide.

[2] Each House may determine the Rules of its Proceedings, punish its Members for disorderly Behavior, and, with the Concurrence of two thirds, expel a Member.

[3] Each House shall keep a Journal of its Proceedings, and from time to time publish the same, excepting such Parts as may in their Judgment require Secrecy; and the Yeas and Nays of the Members of either House on any question shall, at the Desire of one fifth of those Present, be entered on the Journal.

[4] Neither House, during the Session of Congress, shall, without the Consent of the other, adjourn for more than three days, nor to any other Place than that in which the two Houses shall be sitting.

Section 6. [1] The Senators and Representatives shall receive a Compensation for their Services, to be ascertained by Law, and paid out of the Treasury of the United States. They shall in all Cases, except Treason, Felony and Breach of the Peace, be privileged from Arrest during their Attendance at the Session of their respective Houses, and in going to and returning from the same; and for any Speech or Debate in either House, they shall not be questioned in any other Place.

[2] No Senator or Representative shall, during the Time for which he was elected, be appointed to any civil Office under the Authority of the United States, which shall have been created, or the Emoluments whereof shall have been encreased during such time; and no Person holding any Office under the United States, shall be a Member of either House during his Continuance in Office.

Section 7. [1] All Bills for raising Revenue shall originate in the House of Representatives; but the Senate may propose or concur with Amendments as on other Bills.

[2] Every Bill which shall have passed the House of Representatives and the Senate, shall, before it becomes a Law, be presented to the President of the United States; If he approve he shall sign it, but if not he shall return it, with his Objections to the House in which it shall have originated, who shall enter the Objections at large on their Journal, and proceed to reconsider it. If after such Reconsideration two thirds of that House shall agree to pass the Bill, it shall be sent, together with the Objections, to the other House, by which it shall likewise be reconsidered, and if approved by two thirds of that House, it shall become a Law. But in all such Cases the Votes of both Houses shall be determined by Yeas and Nays, and the Names of the Persons voting for and against the Bill shall be entered on the Journal of each House respectively. If any Bill shall not be returned by the President within ten Days (Sundays excepted) after it shall

have been presented to him, the Same shall be a Law, in like Manner as if he had signed it, unless the Congress by their Adjournment prevents its Return, in which Case it shall not be a Law.

[3] Every Order, Resolution, or Vote to Which the Concurrence of the Senate and House of Representatives may be necessary (except on a question of Adjournment) shall be presented to the President of the United States; and before the Same shall take Effect, shall be approved by him, or being disapproved by him, shall be repassed by two thirds of the Senate and House of Representatives, according to the Rules and Limitations prescribed in the Case of a Bill.

Section 8. [1] The Congress shall have Power To lay and collect Taxes, Duties, Imposts and Excises, to pay the Debts and provide for the common Defence and general Welfare of the United States; but all Duties, Imposts and Excises shall be uniform throughout the United States;

[2] To borrow money on the credit of the United States;

[3] To regulate Commerce with foreign Nations, and among the several States, and with the Indian Tribes;

[4] To establish an uniform Rule of Naturalization, and uniform Laws on the subject of Bankruptcies throughout the United States;

[5] To coin Money, regulate the value thereof, and of foreign Coin, and fix the Standard of Weights and Measures;

[6] To provide the Punishment of counterfeiting the Securities and current Coin of the United States;

[7] To establish Post Offices and post Roads;

[8] To promote the Progress of Science and useful Arts, by securing for limited Times to Authors and Inventors the exclusive Right to their respective Writings and Discoveries;

[9] To constitute Tribunals inferior to the supreme Court;

[10] To define and punish Piracies and Felonies committed on the high Seas, and Offenses against the Law of Nations;

[11] To declare War, grant Letters of Marque and Reprisal, and make Rules concerning Captures on Land and Water;

[12] To raise and support Armies, but no Appropriation of Money to that Use shall be for a longer Term than two Years;

[13] To provide and maintain a Navy;

[14] To make Rules for the Government and Regulation of the land and naval Forces;

[15] To provide for calling forth the Militia to execute the Laws of the Union, suppress Insurrections and repel Invasions;

[16] To provide for organizing, arming, and disciplining, the Militia, and for governing such Part of them as may be employed in the Service of the United States, reserving to the States respectively, the Appointment of the Officers, and the Authority of training the Militia according to the discipline prescribed by Congress;

[17] To exercise exclusive Legislation in all Cases whatsoever, over such District (not exceeding ten Miles square) as may, by Cession of

particular States, and the Acceptance of Congress, become the Seat of the Government of the United States, and to exercise like Authority over all Places purchased by the Consent of the Legislature of the State in which the Same shall be, for the Erection of Forts, Magazines, Arsenals, dock-Yards, and other needful Buildings; — And

[18] To make all Laws which shall be necessary and proper for carrying into Execution the foregoing Powers, and all other Powers vested by this Constitution in the Government of the United States, or in any Department or Officer thereof.

Section 9. [1] The Migration or Importation of such Persons as any of the States now existing shall think proper to admit, shall not be prohibited by the Congress prior to the Year one thousand eight hundred and eight, but a Tax or duty may be imposed on such Importation, not exceeding ten dollars for each Person.

[2] The privilege of the Writ of Habeas Corpus shall not be suspended, unless when in Cases of Rebellion or Invasion the public Safety may require it.

[3] No Bill of Attainder or ex post facto Law shall be passed.

[4] No Capitation, or other direct, Tax shall be laid, unless in Proportion to the Census or Enumeration herein before directed to be taken.

[5] No Tax or Duty shall be laid on Articles exported from any State.

[6] No Preference shall be given by any Regulation of Commerce or Revenue to the Ports of one State over those of another: nor shall Vessels bound to, or from, one State, be obliged to enter, clear, or pay Duties in another.

[7] No Money shall be drawn from the Treasury, but in Consequence of Appropriations made by Law; and a regular Statement and Account of the Receipts and Expenditures of all public Money shall be published from time to time.

[8] No Title of Nobility shall be granted by the United States: And no Person holding any Office of Profit or Trust under them, shall, without the Consent of the Congress, accept of any present, Emolument, Office, or Title, of any kind whatever, from any King, Prince, or foreign State.

Section 10. [1] No State shall enter into any Treaty, Alliance, or Confederation; grant Letters of Marque and Reprisal; coin Money; emit Bills of Credit; make any Thing but gold and silver Coin a Tender in Payment of Debts; pass any Bill of Attainder, ex post facto Law, or Law impairing the Obligation of Contracts, or grant any Title of Nobility.

[2] No State shall, without the Consent of the Congress, lay any Imposts or Duties on Imports or Exports, except what may be absolutely necessary for executing its inspection Laws: and the net Produce of all Duties and Imposts, laid by any State on Imports or Exports, shall be for the Use of the Treasury of the United States; and all such Laws shall be subject to the Revision and Controul of the Congress.

[3] No State shall, without the Consent of Congress, lay any Duty of Tonnage, keep Troops, or Ships of War in time of Peace, enter into any Agreement or Compact with another State, or with a foreign Power, or engage in War, unless actually invaded, or in such imminent Danger as will not admit of delay.

ARTICLE II

Section 1. [1] The executive Power shall be vested in a President of the United States of America. He shall hold his Office during the Term of four Years, and, together with the Vice President, chosen for the same Term, be elected, as follows:

[2] Each State shall appoint, in such Manner as the Legislature thereof may direct, a Number of Electors, equal to the whole Number of Senators and Representatives to which the State may be entitled in the Congress: but no Senator or Representative, or Person holding an Office of Trust or Profit under the United States, shall be appointed an Elector.

[3] The Electors shall meet in their respective States, and vote by Ballot for two Persons, of whom one at least shall not be an Inhabitant of the same State with themselves. And they shall make a List of all the Persons voted for, and of the Number of Votes for each; which List they shall sign and certify, and transmit scaled to the Seat of the Government of the United States, directed to the President of the Senate. The President of the Senate shall, in the Presence of the Senate and House of Representatives, open all the Certificates, and the Votes shall then be counted. The Person having the greatest Number of Votes shall be the President, if such Number be a Majority of the whole Number of Electors appointed; and if there be more than one who have such Majority, and have an equal Number of Votes, then the House of Representatives shall immediately chuse by Ballot one of them for President; and if no Person have a Majority, then from the five highest on the List the said House shall in like Manner chuse the President. But in chusing the President, the Votes shall be taken by States, the Representation from each State having one Vote; a quorum for this Purpose shall consist of a Member or Members from two thirds of the States, and a Majority of all the States shall be necessary to a Choice. In every Case, after the Choice of the President, the Person having the greatest Number of Votes of the Electors shall be the Vice President. But if there should remain two or more who have equal Votes, the Senate shall chuse from them by Ballot the Vice President.

[4] The Congress may determine the Time of chusing the Electors, and the Day on which they shall give their Votes; which Day shall be the same throughout the United States.

[5] No person except a natural born Citizen, or a Citizen of the United States, at the time of the Adoption of this Constitution, shall be eligible to

the Office of President; neither shall any Person be eligible to that Office who shall not have attained to the Age of thirty five Years, and been fourteen Years a Resident within the United States.

[6] In case of the removal of the President from Office, or of his Death, Resignation or Inability to discharge the Powers and Duties of the said Office, the Same shall devolve on the Vice President, and the Congress may by Law provide for the Case of Removal, Death, Resignation or Inability, both of the President and Vice President, declaring what Officer shall then act as President, and such Officer shall act accordingly, until the Disability be removed, or a President shall be elected.

[7] The President shall, at stated Times, receive for his Services, a Compensation, which shall neither be increased nor diminished during the Period for which he shall have been elected, and he shall not receive within that Period any other Emolument from the United States, or any of them.

[8] Before he enter on the Execution of his Office, he shall take the following Oath or Affirmation: "I do solemnly swear (or affirm) that I will faithfully execute the Office of President of the United States, and will to the best of my Ability, preserve, protect and defend the Constitution of the United States."

Section 2. [1] The President shall be Commander in Chief of the Army and Navy of the United States, and of the Militia of the several States, when called into the actual Service of the United States; he may require the Opinion; in writing, of the principal Officer in each of the executive Departments, upon any subject relating to the Duties of their respective Offices, and he shall have Power to grant Reprieves and Pardons for Offenses against the United States, except in Cases of Impeachment.

[2] He shall have Power, by and with the Advice and Consent of the Senate, to make Treaties, provided two thirds of the Senators present concur; and he shall nominate, and by and with the Advice and Consent of the Senate, shall appoint Ambassadors, other public Ministers and Consuls, Judges of the supreme Court, and all other Officers of the United States, whose Appointments are not herein otherwise provided for, and which shall be established by Law: but the Congress may by Law vest the Appointment of such inferior Officers, as they think proper, in the President alone, to the Courts of Law, or in the Heads of Departments.

[3] The President shall have Power to fill up all Vacancies that may happen during the Recess of the Senate, by granting Commissions which shall expire at the End of their next Session.

Section 3. He shall from time to time give to the Congress Information of the State of the Union, and recommend to their Consideration such Measures as he shall judge necessary and expedient; he may, on extraordinary occasions, convene both Houses, or either of them, and in Case of Disagreement between them, with Respect to the time of Adjournment, he may adjourn them to such Time as he shall think proper; he shall receive

Ambassadors and other public Ministers; he shall take Care that the Laws be faithfully executed, and shall Commission all the Officers of the United States.

Section 4. The President, Vice President and all civil Officers of the United States, shall be removed from Office on Impeachment for, and Conviction of, Treason, Bribery, or other high Crimes and Misdemeanors.

ARTICLE III

Section 1. The judicial Power of the United States, shall be vested in one supreme Court, and in such inferior Courts as the Congress may from time to time ordain and establish. The Judges, both of the supreme and inferior Courts, shall hold their Offices during good Behaviour, and shall, at stated Times, receive for their Services, a Compensation, which shall not be diminished during their Continuance in Office.

Section 2. [1] The Judicial Power shall extend to all Cases, in Law and Equity, arising under this Constitution, the Laws of the United States, and Treaties made, or which shall be made, under their Authority;—to all Cases affecting Ambassadors, other public Ministers and Consuls;—to all Cases of admiralty and maritime Jurisdiction;—to Controversies to which the United States shall be a Party;—to Controversies between two or more States;—between a State and Citizens of another State;—between Citizens of different States;—between Citizens of the same State claiming Lands under Grants of different States, and between a State, or the Citizens thereof, and foreign States, Citizens or Subjects.

[2] In all Cases affecting Ambassadors, other public Ministers and Consuls, and those in which a State shall be a Party, the supreme Court shall have original Jurisdiction. In all the other Cases before mentioned, the supreme Court shall have appellate Jurisdiction, both as to Law and Fact, with such Exceptions, and under such Regulations as the Congress shall make.

[3] The trial of all Crimes, except in Cases of Impeachment, shall be by Jury; and such Trial shall be held in the State where the said Crimes shall have been committed; but when not committed within any State, the Trial shall be at such Place or Places as the Congress may by Law have directed.

Section 3. [1] Treason against the United States, shall consist only in levying War against them, or in adhering to their Enemies, giving them Aid and Comfort. No person shall be convicted of Treason unless on the Testimony of two Witnesses to the same overt Act, or on Confession in open Court.

[2] The Congress shall have Power to declare the Punishment of Treason, but no Attainder of Treason shall work Corruption of Blood, or Forfeiture except during the Life of the Person attainted.

ARTICLE IV

Section 1. Full Faith and Credit shall be given in each State to the public Acts, Records, and judicial Proceedings of every other State. And the Congress may by general Laws prescribe the Manner in which such Acts, Records and Proceedings shall be proved, and the Effect thereof.

Section 2. [1] The Citizens of each State shall be entitled to all Privileges and Immunities of Citizens in the several States.

[2] A Person charged in any State with Treason, Felony, or other Crime, who shall flee from Justice, and be found in another State, shall on demand of the executive Authority of the State from which he fled, be delivered up, to be removed to the State having Jurisdiction of the Crime.

[3] No Person held to Service or Labour in one State, under the Laws thereof, escaping into another, shall, in Consequence of any Law or Regulation therein, be discharged from such Service or Labour, but shall be delivered up on Claim of the Party to whom such Service or Labour may be due.

Section 3. [1] New States may be admitted by the Congress into this Union; but no new State shall be formed or erected within the Jurisdiction of any other State; nor any State be formed by the Junction of two or more States, or Parts of States, without the Consent of the Legislatures of the States concerned as well as of the Congress.

[2] The Congress shall have Power to dispose of and make all needful Rules and Regulations respecting the Territory or other Property belonging to the United States; and nothing in this Constitution shall be so construed as to Prejudice any Claims of the United States, or of any particular State.

Section 4. The United States shall guarantee to every State in this Union a Republican Form of Government, and shall protect each of them against Invasion; and on Application of the Legislature, or of the Executive (when the Legislature cannot be convened) against domestic Violence.

ARTICLE V

The Congress, whenever two thirds of both Houses shall deem it necessary, shall propose Amendments to this Constitution, or, on the Application of the Legislatures of two thirds of the several States, shall call a Convention for proposing Amendments, which, in either Case, shall be valid to all Intents and Purposes, as part of this Constitution, when ratified by the Legislatures of three fourths of the several States, or by Conventions in three fourths thereof, as the one of the other Mode of Ratification may be proposed by the Congress; Provided that no Amendment which may be made prior to the Year One thousand eight hundred and eight shall in any Manner affect the first and fourth Clauses in the Ninth Section of the first Article; and that no State, without its Consent, shall be deprived of its equal Suffrage in the Senate.

ARTICLE VI

[1] All Debts contracted and Engagements entered into, before the Adoption of this Constitution, shall be as valid against the United States under this Constitution, as under the Confederation.

[2] This Constitution, and the Laws of the United States which shall be made in Pursuance thereof; and all Treaties made, or which shall be made, under the Authority of the United States, shall be the supreme Law of the Land; and the Judges in every State shall be bound thereby, any Thing in the Constitution or Laws of any State to the Contrary notwithstanding.

[3] The Senators and Representatives before mentioned, and the Members of the several State Legislatures, and all executive and judicial Officers, both of the United States and of the several States, shall be bound by Oath or Affirmation, to support this Constitution; but no religious Test shall ever be required as a Qualification to any Office or public Trust under the United States.

ARTICLE VII

The Ratification of the Conventions of nine States shall be sufficient for the Establishment of this Constitution between the States so ratifying the Same.

Done in Convention by the Unanimous Consent of the States present the Seventeenth Day of September in the Year of our Lord one thousand seven hundred and Eighty seven and of the Independence of the United States of America the Twelfth.

ARTICLES IN ADDITION TO, AND AMENDMENT OF, THE CONSTITUTION OF THE UNITED STATES OF AMERICA, PROPOSED BY CONGRESS, AND RATIFIED BY THE LEGISLATURES OF THE SEVERAL STATES, PURSUANT TO THE FIFTH ARTICLE OF THE ORIGINAL CONSTITUTION

AMENDMENT I [1791]

Congress shall make no law respecting an establishment of religion, or prohibiting the free exercise thereof; or abridging the freedom of speech, or of the press; or the right of the people peaceably to assemble, and to petition the Government for a redress of grievances.

AMENDMENT II [1791]

A well regulated Militia, being necessary to the security of a free State, the right of the people to keep and bear Arms, shall not be infringed.

AMENDMENT III [1791]

No Soldier shall, in time of peace be quartered in any house, without the consent of the Owner, nor in time of war, but in a manner to be prescribed by law.

AMENDMENT IV [1791]

The right of the people to be secure in their persons, houses, papers, and effects, against unreasonable searches and seizures, shall not be violated, and no Warrants shall issue, but upon probable cause, supported by Oath or affirmation, and particularly describing the place to be searched, and the persons or things to be seized.

AMENDMENT V [1791]

No person shall be held to answer for a capital, or otherwise infamous crime, unless on a presentment or indictment of a Grand Jury, except in cases arising in the land or naval forces, or in the Militia, when in actual service in time of War or public danger; nor shall any person be subject for the same offence to be twice put in jeopardy of life or limb; nor shall be compelled in any criminal case to be a witness against himself, nor be deprived of life, liberty, or property, without due process of law; nor shall private property be taken for public use, without just compensation.

AMENDMENT VI [1791]

In all criminal prosecutions, the accused shall enjoy the right to a speedy and public trial, by an impartial jury of the State and district wherein the crime shall have been committed, which district shall have been previously ascertained by law, and to be informed of the nature and cause of the accusation; to be confronted with the witnesses against him; to have compulsory process for obtaining witnesses in his favor, and to have the Assistance of Counsel for his defence.

AMENDMENT VII [1791]

In Suits at common law, where the value in controversy shall exceed twenty dollars, the right of trial by jury shall be preserved, and no fact tried by a jury, shall be otherwise re-examined in any Court of the United States, than according to the rules of the common law.

AMENDMENT VIII [1791]

Excessive bail shall not be required, nor excessive fines imposed, nor cruel and unusual punishments inflicted.

AMENDMENT IX [1791]

The enumeration in the Constitution, of certain rights, shall not be construed to deny or disparage others retained by the people.

AMENDMENT X [1791]

The powers not delegated to the United States by the Constitution, nor prohibited by it to the States, are reserved to the States respectively, or to the people.

AMENDMENT XI [1798]

The Judicial power of the United States shall not be construed to extend to any suit in law or equity, commenced or prosecuted against one of the United States by Citizens of another State, or by Citizens or Subjects of any Foreign State.

AMENDMENT XII [1804]

The Electors shall meet in their respective states and vote by ballot for President and Vice-President, one of whom, at least, shall not be an inhabitant of the same state with themselves; they shall name in their ballots the person voted for as President, and in distinct ballots the person voted for as Vice-President, and they shall make distinct lists of all persons voted for as President, and of all persons voted for as Vice-President, and of the number of votes for each, which lists they shall sign and certify, and transmit sealed to the seat of the government of the United States, directed to the President of the Senate;—The President of the Senate shall, in the presence of the Senate and House of Representatives, open all the certificates and the votes shall then be counted;—The person having the greatest number of votes for President, shall be the President, if such number be a majority of the whole number of Electors appointed; and if no person have such majority, then from the persons having the highest numbers not exceeding three on the list of those voted for as President, the House of Representatives shall choose immediately, by ballot, the President. But in choosing the President, the votes shall be taken by states, the representation from each state having one vote; a quorum for this purpose shall consist of a member or members from two-thirds of the states, and a majority of all the states shall be necessary to a choice. And if the House of Representatives shall not choose a President whenever the right of choice shall devolve upon them, before the fourth day of March next following, then the Vice-President shall act as President, as in the case of the death or other constitutional disability of the President.—The person having the greatest number of votes as Vice-President, shall be the Vice-President, if such number be a majority of the whole number of Electors appointed, and if no person have a majority, then from the two highest numbers on the list, the Senate shall choose the Vice-President; a quorum for the purpose shall consist of two-thirds of the whole number of Senators, and a majority of the whole number shall be necessary to a choice. But no person constitutionally ineligible to the office of President shall be eligible to that of Vice-President of the United States.

AMENDMENT XIII [1865]

Section 1. Neither slavery nor involuntary servitude, except as a punishment for crime whereof the party shall have been duly convicted, shall exist within the United States, or any place subject to their jurisdiction.

Section 2. Congress shall have power to enforce this article by appropriate legislation.

AMENDMENT XIV [1868]

Section 1. All persons born or naturalized in the United States, and subject to the jurisdiction thereof, are citizens of the United States and of the State wherein they reside. No State shall make or enforce any law which shall abridge the privileges or immunities of citizens of the United States; nor shall any State deprive any person of life, liberty, or property, without due process of law; nor deny to any person within its jurisdiction the equal protection of the laws.

Section 2. Representatives shall be apportioned among the several States according to their respective numbers, counting the whole number of persons in each State, excluding Indians not taxed. But when the right to vote at any election for the choice of electors for President and Vice President of the United States, Representatives in Congress, the Executive and Judicial officers of a State, or the members of the Legislature thereof, is denied to any of the male inhabitants of such State, being twenty-one years of age, and citizens of the United States, or in any way abridged, except for participation in rebellion, or other crime, the basis of representation therein shall be reduced in the proportion which the number of such male citizens shall bear to the whole number of male citizens twenty-one years of age in such State.

Section 3. No person shall be a Senator or Representative in Congress, or elector of President and Vice President, or hold any office, civil or military, under the United States, or under any State, who, having previously taken an oath, as a member of Congress, or as an officer of the United States, or as a member of any State legislature, or as an executive or judicial officer of any State, to support the Constitution of the United States, shall have engaged in insurrection or rebellion against the same, or given aid or comfort to the enemies thereof. But Congress may by a vote of two-thirds of each House, remove such disability.

Section 4. The validity of the public debt of the United States, authorized by law, including debts incurred for payment of pensions and bounties for services in suppressing insurrection or rebellion, shall not be questioned. But neither the United States nor any State shall assume or pay any debt or obligation incurred in aid of insurrection or rebellion against the United States, or any claim for the loss of emancipation of any slave; but all such debts, obligations and claims shall be held illegal and void.

Section 5. The Congress shall have power to enforce, by appropriate legislation, the provisions of this article.

AMENDMENT XV [1870]

Section 1. The right of citizens of the United States to vote shall not be denied or abridged by the United States or by any State on account of race, color, or previous condition of servitude.

Section 2. The Congress shall have power to enforce this article by appropriate legislation.

AMENDMENT XVI [1913]

The Congress shall have power to lay and collect taxes on incomes, from whatever source derived, without apportionment among the several States, and without regard to any census or enumeration.

AMENDMENT XVII [1913]

[1] The Senate of the United States shall be composed of two Senators from each State, elected by the people thereof, for six years, and each Senator shall have one vote. The electors in each State shall have the qualifications requisite for electors of the most numerous branch of the State legislatures.

[2] When vacancies happen in the representation of any State in the Senate, the executive authority of such State shall issue writs of election to fill such vacancies: *Provided,* That the legislature of any State may empower the executive thereof to make temporary appointments until the people fill the vacancies by election as the legislature may direct.

[3] This amendment shall not be so construed as to affect the election or term of any Senator chosen before it becomes valid as part of the Constitution.

AMENDMENT XVIII [1919]

Section 1. After one year from the ratification of this article the manufacture, sale, or transportation of intoxicating liquors within, the importation thereof into, or the exportation thereof from the United States and all territory subject to the jurisdiction thereof for beverage purposes is hereby prohibited.

Section 2. The Congress and the several States shall have concurrent power to enforce this article by appropriate legislation.

Section 3. This article shall be inoperative unless it shall have been ratified as an amendment to the Constitution by the legislatures of the several States, as provided in the Constitution, within seven years from the date of the submission hereof to the States by the Congress.

AMENDMENT XIX [1920]

[1] The right of citizens of the United States to vote shall not be denied or abridged by the United States or by any State on account of sex.

[2] Congress shall have power to enforce this article by appropriate legislation.

AMENDMENT XX [1933]

Section 1. The terms of the President and Vice President shall end at noon on the 20th day of January, and the terms of Senators and Representatives at noon on the 3d day of January, of the years in which such terms would have ended if this article had not been ratified; and the terms of their successors shall then begin.

Section 2. The Congress shall assemble at least once in every year, and such meeting shall begin at noon on the 3d day of January, unless they shall by law appoint a different day.

Section 3. If, at the time fixed for the beginning of the term of the President, the President elect shall have died, the Vice President elect shall become President. If a President shall not have been chosen before the time fixed for the beginning of his term, or if the President elect shall have failed to qualify, then the Vice President elect shall act as President until a President shall have qualified; and the Congress may by law provide for the case wherein neither a President elect nor a Vice President elect shall have qualified, declaring who shall then act as President, or the manner in which one who is to act shall be selected, and such person shall act accordingly until a President or Vice President shall have qualified.

Section 4. The Congress may by law provide for the case of the death of any of the persons from whom the House of Representatives may choose a President whenever the right of choice shall have devolved upon them, and for the case of the death of any of the persons from whom the Senate may choose a Vice President whenever the right of choice shall have devolved upon them.

Section 5. Sections 1 and 2 shall take effect on the 15th day of October following the ratification of this article.

Section 6. This article shall be inoperative unless it shall have been ratified as an amendment to the Constitution by the legislatures of three-fourths of the several States within seven years from the date of its submission.

AMENDMENT XXI [1933]

Section 1. The eighteenth article of amendment to the Constitution of the United States is hereby repealed.

Section 2. The transportation or importation into any State, Territory, or possession of the United States for delivery or use therein of intoxicating liquors, in violation of the laws thereof, is hereby prohibited.

Section 3. This article shall be inoperative unless it shall have been ratified as an amendment to the Constitution by conventions in the several States, as provided in the Constitution, within seven years from the date of the submission hereof to the States by the Congress.

AMENDMENT XXII [1951]

Section 1. No person shall be elected to the office of the President more than twice, and no person who has held the office of President, or acted as President, for more than two years of a term to which some other person was elected President shall be elected to the office of the President more than once. But this Article shall not apply to any person holding the office of President when this Article was proposed by the Congress, and shall not prevent any person who may be holding the office of President, or acting as President, during the term within which the Article becomes operative from holding the office of President or acting as President during the remainder of such term.

Section 2. This article shall be inoperative unless it shall have been ratified as an amendment to the Constitution by the legislatures of three-fourths of the several States within seven years from the date of its submission to the States by the Congress.

AMENDMENT XXIII [1961]

Section 1. The District constituting the seat of Government of the United States shall appoint in such manner as the Congress may direct:

A number of electors of President and Vice President equal to the whole number of Senators and Representatives in Congress to which the District would be entitled if it were a State, but in no event more than the least populous State; they shall be in addition to those appointed by the States, but they shall be considered, for the purposes of the election of President and Vice President, to be electors appointed by a State; and they shall meet in the District and perform such duties as provided by the twelfth article of amendment.

Section 2. The Congress shall have power to enforce this article by appropriate legislation.

AMENDMENT XXIV [1964]

Section 1. The right of citizens of the United States to vote in any primary or other election for President or Vice President, for electors for President or Vice President, or for Senator or Representative in Congress, shall not be denied or abridged by the United States or any State by reason of failure to pay any poll tax or other tax.

Section 2. The Congress shall have power to enforce this article by appropriate legislation.

AMENDMENT XXV [1967]

Section 1. In case of the removal of the President from office or of his death or resignation, the Vice President shall become President.

Section 2. Whenever there is a vacancy in the office of the Vice President, the President shall nominate a Vice President who shall take office upon confirmation by a majority vote of both Houses of Congress.

Section 3. Whenever the President transmits to the President pro tempore of the Senate and the Speaker of the House of Representatives his written declaration that he is unable to discharge the powers and duties of his office, and until he transmits to them a written declaration to the contrary, such powers and duties shall be discharged by the Vice President as Acting President.

Section 4. Whenever the Vice President and a Majority of either the principal officers of the executive departments or of such other body as Congress may by law provide, transmit to the President pro tempore of the Senate and the Speaker of the House of Representatives their written declaration that the President is unable to discharge the powers and duties of his office, the Vice President shall immediately assume the powers and duties of the office as Acting President.

Thereafter, when the President transmits to the President pro tempore of the Senate and the Speaker of the House of Representatives his written declaration that no inability exists, he shall resume the powers and duties of his office unless the Vice President and a majority of either the principal officers of the executive department or of such other body as Congress may by law provide, transmit within four days to the President pro tempore of the Senate and the Speaker of the House of Representatives their written declaration that the President is unable to discharge the powers and duties of his office. Thereupon Congress shall decide the issue, assembling within forty-eight hours for that purpose if not in session. If the Congress, within twenty-one days after receipt of the latter written declaration, or, if Congress is not in session, within twenty-one days after Congress is required to assemble, determines by two-thirds vote of both Houses that the President is unable to discharge the powers and duties of his office, the Vice President shall continue to discharge the same as Acting President; otherwise, the President shall resume the powers and duties of his office.

AMENDMENT XXVI [1971]

Section 1. The right of citizens of the United States, who are eighteen years of age or older, to vote shall not be denied or abridged by the United States or by any State on account of age.

Section 2. The Congress shall have power to enforce this article by appropriate legislation.

AMENDMENT XXVII [1992]

No law varying the Compensation for the services of the Senators and Representatives shall take effect, unless an election of Representatives shall have intervened.

The Emancipation Proclamation

Whereas on the 22d day of September, A.D. 1862, a proclamation was issued by the President of the United States, containing, among other things, the following, to wit:

"That on the 1st day of January, A.D. 1863, all persons held as slaves within any State or designated part of a State the people whereof shall then be in rebellion against the United States shall be then, thenceforward, and forever free; and the executive government of the United States, including the military and naval authority thereof, will recognize and maintain the freedom of such persons and will do no act or acts to repress such persons, for any of them, in any efforts they may make for their actual freedom.

"That the executive will on the 1st day of January aforesaid, by proclamation, designate the States and parts of States, if any, in which the people thereof, respectively, shall then be in rebellion against the United States; and the fact that any State or the people thereof shall on that day be in good faith represented in the Congress of the United States by members chosen thereto at elections wherein a majority of the qualified voters of such States shall have participated shall, in the absence of strong countervailing testimony, be deemed conclusive evidence that such State and the people thereof are not then in rebellion against the United States."

Now, therefore, I, Abraham Lincoln, President of the United States, by virtue of the power in me vested as Commander-in-Chief of the Army and Navy of the United States in time of actual armed rebellion against the authority and government of the United States, and as a fit and necessary war measure for suppressing said rebellion, do, on this 1st day of January, A.D. 1863, and in accordance with my purpose so to do, publicly proclaimed for the full period of one hundred days from the first day above mentioned, order and designate as the States and parts of States wherein the people thereof, respectively, are this day in rebellion against the United States the following, to wit:

Arkansas, Texas, Louisiana (except the parishes of St. Bernard, Plaquemines, Jefferson, St. John, St. Charles, St. James, Ascension, Assumption, Terrebonne, Lafourche, St. Mary, St. Martin, and Orleans, including the city of New Orleans), Mississippi, Alabama, Florida, Georgia, South Carolina, North Carolina, and Virginia (except the forty-eight counties designated as West Virginia, and also the counties of Berkeley, Accomac, Northhampton, Elizabeth City, York, Princess Anne, and Norfolk, including the cities of Norfolk and Portsmouth), and which excepted parts are for the present left precisely as if this proclamation were not issued.

And by virtue of the power and for the purpose aforesaid, I do order and declare that all persons held as slaves within said designated States and parts of States are, and henceforward shall be, free; and that the Executive Government of the United States, including the military and naval authorities thereof, will recognize and maintain the freedom of said persons.

And I hereby enjoin upon the people so declared to be free to abstain from all violence, unless in necessary self-defense; and I recommend to them that, in all cases when allowed, they labor faithfully for reasonable wages.

And I further declare and make known that such persons of suitable condition will be received into the armed service of the United States to garrison forts, positions, stations, and other places, and to man vessels of all sorts in said service.

And upon this act, sincerely believed to be an act of justice, warranted by the Constitution upon military necessity, I invoke the considerate judgment of mankind and the gracious favor of Almighty God.

Court Cases

Johnson v. Johnson

594 N.Y.S.2d 259 (App. Div. 1993)

In action on contract, the Supreme Court, New York County, Moskowitz, J., granted summary judgment for plaintiff, declaring plaintiff to be joint owner of winning lottery ticket with defendant. Defendant appealed. The Supreme Court, Appellate Division, held that: (1) agreement was supported by consideration, and (2) defendant ratified agreement.

Affirmed.

1. Lotteries [Key Number: 12]

Agreement to share joint ownership of proceeds of winning lottery ticket was supported by consideration, i.e., forbearance and mutual promises made by the party to surrender their respective rights to claim entire prize as their own due to lottery's "sole claimant" rule and their agreement to share equally the related tax liabilities.

2. Contracts [Key Number: 97(2)]

Defendant's conduct, by voluntarily adhering to terms of agreement to share joint ownership of proceeds of any winning lottery ticket for four years and accepting benefits of plaintiff's performance ratified the agreement and prevented him from attacking its validity.

Before Milonas, J.P., and Rosenberger, Kupferman and Ross, JJ.
Memorandum Decision.

Order and judgment (one paper), Supreme Court New York County (Karla Moskowitz, J.), entered June 17, 1992, which inter alia, granted plaintiff's motion for summary judgment, and declared plaintiff to be joint owner of the subject winning lottery ticket with defendant, unanimously affirmed, without costs.

[1,2] The IAS court properly granted summary judgment. The signed and witnessed agreement clearly establishes the intent of the parties to share joint ownership of the proceeds (see Slatt v. Slatt, 64 N.Y.2d 966, 488 N.Y.S.2d 645, 477 N.E.2d 1099) and is supported by consideration, i.e., the forebearance and mutual promises made by the parties to surrender their respective rights to claim the entire prize as their own due to the lottery's "sole claimant" rule and their agreement to share equally the related tax liabilities (see Weiner v. McGraw-Hill, Inc., 57 N.Y.2d 458, 464, 457 N.Y.S.2d 193, 443 N.E.2d 441). Further, defendant's conduct, by voluntarily adhering to the terms of the agreement for four years (in each of which lottery payments were made) and accepting the benefits of plaintiff's performance ratified the agreement and prevents him from now attacking its validity (see Stacom v. Wunsch, 162 A.D.2d 170, 171, 556 N.Y.S.2d 303, appeal dismissed, 77 N.Y.2d 873, 568 N.Y.S.2d 915, 571 N.E.2d 85).

People v. O'Keefe

594 N.Y.S.2d 265 (App. Div. 1993)

Defendant was convicted in the County Court, Suffolk County, Weissman, J., of attempted burglary in the second degree, criminal mischief in the third degree, and resisting arrest, and he appealed. The Supreme Court, Appellate Division, held that: (1) defendant's intoxication did not rise to the level of "mania" as required for suppression of statements because of intoxication, and (2) evidence supported jury's determination that defendant's intoxication did not prevent him from forming the requisite intent necessary to sustain the convictions for attempted burglary in the second degree, criminal mischief in the third degree, and resisting arrest.

Affirmed.

1. Criminal Law [Key Number: 412.1(1)]

For a statement to be suppressed because defendant was intoxicated when it was made, degree of inebriation must have risen to the level of "mania."

2. Criminal Law [Key Number: 414]

Defendant was not entitled to suppression of statements made in police custody on the grounds he was intoxicated; evidence supported People's claim that statements were freely volunteered and were not made in response to any questioning or coercion, and there was no evidence that defendant's intoxication rose to level of "mania."

3. Criminal Law [Key Number: 739(5)]

Question of whether defendant was so intoxicated as to be unable to form the requisite intent to be guilty of the crimes of attempted burglary, criminal mischief and resisting arrest of which he was convicted, presented issues of facts and credibility for jury.

4. Criminal Law [Key Number: 570(1)]

Sufficient evidence supported jury's determination that, despite defendant's intoxication, he was able to form requisite intent to sustain convictions for attempted burglary in second degree, criminal mischief in third degree, and resisting arrest.

Ethel P. Ross, Rye, for appellant.

James M. Catterson, Jr., Dist. Atty., Riverhead (Demetri M. Jones of counsel; James F. Creighton, on the brief), for respondent.

Before THOMPSON, J.P., and BRACKEN, EIBER and PIZZUTO, JJ.
MEMORANDUM BY THE COURT.

Appeal by the defendant from a judgment of the County Court, Suffolk County (Weissman, J.), rendered January 17, 1991, convicting him of attempted burglary in the second degree, criminal mischief in the third degree, and resisting arrest, upon a jury verdict, and imposing sentence. The appeal brings up for review the denial, after a hearing, of that branch of the defendant's omnibus motion which was to suppress statements made by him to law enforcement officials.

Ordered that the judgment is affirmed.

[1, 2] We reject the defendant's contention that the statements he made while he was in police custody should have been suppressed. The evidence fully supports the People's claim that those statements were freely volunteered and were not made in response to any questioning or coercion. For a statement to be suppressed because the defendant was intoxicated when it was made, the degree of inebriation must have risen to the level of "mania" (People v. Schompert, 19 N.Y.2d 300, 279 N.Y.S.2d 515, 226 N.E.2d 305, cert. denied, 389 U.S. 874, 88 S. Ct. 164, 19 L. Ed. 2d 157). There was no clear evidence at the hearing that the defendant's intoxication reached that stage (see People v. McClaney, 135 A.D.2d 901, 521 N.Y.S.2d 894).

[3, 4] The defendant claims that due to his intoxication he was unable to form the requisite intent necessary to sustain the convictions for attempted burglary in the second degree, criminal mischief in the third degree, and resisting arrest. "While it is true that a defendant may offer evidence of his intoxication whenever it is relevant to negative an element of the crime charged (see Penal Law §15.15), it has likewise been held that even an inebriated individual may be capable of forming an intent" (People v. Lang, 143 A.D.2d 685, 532 N.Y.S.2d 927). The question of whether the defendant was so intoxicated as to be unable to form the requisite intent to be guilty of the crimes he was convicted of presents issues of fact and credibility for the jury to resolve (see People v. Merrill, 132 A.D.2d

573, 517 N.Y.S.2d 553; People v. Lyng, 154 A.D.2d 787, 546 N.Y.S.2d 464; People v. Shapiro, 96 A.D.2d 626, 464 N.Y.S.2d 880). Based upon the record in this case, we find that the jury's resolution of these issues had sufficient evidentiary support and should not be disturbed.

We find the defendant's remaining contention to be without merit.

Danielson v. Board of Higher Education
358 F. Supp. 22 (S.D.N.Y. 1972)

College lecturer brought action seeking declaration that maternity leave provision was unconstitutional on its face and as applied to male faculty members and seeking injunction restraining defendants from discharging lecturer or otherwise penalizing him for having taken child-care leave. Lecturer's wife who was also a lecturer sought declaratory judgment that refusal to treat her 12-day leave, during which she gave birth, as sick leave, deprived her of property in violation of Fourteenth Amendment and also sought award of her back pay. On plaintiffs' motion for summary judgment and on defendants' motion to dismiss or for summary judgment, the District Court, Motley, J., held that complaint alleging that husband's right to equal protection had been violated by refusal to extend to him the same child-care leave privilege extended to women solely because he was a man, alleging that refusal to pay wife for period in question deprived her of property in violation of Fourteenth Amendment and alleging denial of right of personal liberty and invasion of right to privacy raised "colorable" constitutional claims and thus stated claims on which relief could be granted, notwithstanding assertion that claims pertained to deprivation of "profits or emoluments."

Motions denied.

1. Federal Civil Procedure [Key Number: 2481]

In action in which male lecturer in college challenged constitutionality of college's maternity leave provision assertedly permitting women faculty members to take leave of absence in connection with pregnancy up to three semesters without adversely affecting tenure on ground that provision denied same child-care leave privileges to men, issues of fact as to defendants' policies and as to whether women were permitted such leaves where there was no unusual medical disability resulting from birth of child and, during such period, could also do work toward Ph.D. degree without loss of time served, as it related to tenure, precluded summary judgment.

2. Federal Civil Procedure [Key Number: 2481]

In action in which lecturer at college challenged constitutionality of defendants' refusal to treat her 12-day leave, during which she gave birth, as sick leave, issue of fact as to whether period immediately following childbirth unattended by other complications was a medical disability or illness for which a woman was entitled to sick leave under policy of college precluded summary judgment. U.S.C.A. Const. Amend. 14.

3. Federal Civil Procedure [Key Number: 1827]

On motion to dismiss action based on contention that maternity leave provision of college was unconstitutional, it was only necessary to determine whether allegations raised "colorable" constitutional claims.

4. Civil Rights [Key Number: 13.12(7)]

Complaint alleging that male college lecturer's right to equal protection had been violated by refusal to extend to him the same child-care leave privilege extended to women solely because he was a man, alleging that refusal to pay lecturer's wife, who was also a lecturer, for 12-day period during which she gave birth, deprived her of property in violation of Fourteenth Amendment and alleging denial of right of personal liberty and invasion of right to privacy raised "colorable" constitutional claims and stated claims on which relief could be granted, notwithstanding assertion that claims pertained to deprivation of "profits or emoluments." U.S.C.A Const. Amends. 9,14; 28 U.S.C.A §1343 (3); 42 U.S.C.A. §1983.

5. Federal Civil Procedure [Key Number: 1773]

Motion to dismiss for failure to state a claim need be granted only when it appears that plaintiffs could prove no set of facts in support of their claim which would entitle them to relief.

Nancy Stearns, Center for Constitutional Rights, Veronika Kraft, New York City, for plaintiffs.

J. Lee Rankin, Corp. Counsel, City of New York, by Yvette Harmon, Asst. Corp. Counsel, New York City, for defendants.

MOTLEY, District Judge.

Opinion on Motion to Dismiss and for Summary Judgment

This is an action by Ross Danielson, a lecturer in sociology at City College, a branch of the City University of New York. Mr. Danielson's challenge is to the constitutionality of defendants' maternity leave provision on its face and as applied. The essence of Danielson's claim is that women faculty members are permitted to take a leave of absence in connection with pregnancy, up to three semesters, for the purpose, among others, of caring for a new born infant, without adversely affecting their tenure rights, but the same child care leave privilege is denied to men.

This action is also brought by Mr. Danielson's wife, Susan Danielson, who is a lecturer in English at Lehman College, another branch of the City University of New York. Her challenge is to the constitutionality of defendants' refusal to treat her 12-day leave, during which she gave birth to a child, as sick leave.

Defendants are the Board of Higher Education which governs the City University of New York, the chairman of that Board, the chancellor of the University, the president of City College, and the dean of faculties of Lehman College.

Jurisdiction is predicated upon 28 U.S.C. §§1331 and 1343. Declaratory and injunctive relief are sought. Ross Danielson seeks a declaration that the maternity leave provision is unconstitutional on its face and as applied to male faculty members. He also seeks an injunction enjoining defendants from discharging him or otherwise penalizing him for having taken child-care leave. Mrs. Danielson seeks a declaratory judgment that defendants' actions in withholding her pay for the period December 8 through 23, 1970 deprived her of her property in violation of the Fourteenth Amendment She also seeks an award of her back pay in the amount of $180, plus interest.

[1] The action is presently before the court on the motion of plaintiffs for summary judgment in their favor and the motion of defendants to dismiss or, alternatively, for summary judgment in their favor. Defendants have moved to dismiss the complaint on two grounds: (1) the court lacks jurisdiction of the subject matter and, (2) the complaint fails to state a claim upon which relief may be granted. For the reasons set forth below, the motion to dismiss is denied. The motions for summary judgment are also denied on the ground that there are several disputed issues of fact.

Mr. Danielson commenced teaching in the City College in the fall semester of 1969. His wife, Susan Danielson, who was teaching at Lehman College at the same time became pregnant in the early spring of 1970. Upon discovering her pregnancy, Susan and her husband discussed the matter at great length. They weighed the options available to them with respect to the care of their child and the pursuit of their respective careers. They decided that Susan would continue her teaching duties throughout her pregnancy and after childbirth. Then, for at least the first six months after the child was born, Mr. Danielson would stay home and assume the primary responsibility for the care of their infant. Susan Danielson consulted her physician who assured her that such conduct on her part would in no way be injurious to her health.

Mr. Danielson then made every effort to obtain "parental leave of absence" from City College. He claims such "parental leave" is available for women faculty members pursuant to Article XIII, Section 13.4, of the By-Laws of the Board of Higher Education and should be equally available to men.

This section provides in pertinent part as follows:

> *Maternity Leave.*   a. As soon as a member of the instructional staff shall become aware of her pregnancy, she shall forthwith notify the president

and *may* apply for a leave of absence. Such leave shall begin on February 1 or September 1, unless the conditions of the pregnancy require that the leave begin sooner. The duration of the leave shall be at least one full semester. In exceptional cases, if approved by the college physician, the president may terminate a maternity leave during a college term, provided there is an appropriate opening in which the applicant's service may be utilized. An extension of maternity leave shall be permitted on request for a period not in excess of one year from the end of the original leave. No further extentions [sic] shall be permitted.

b. Maternity leaves shall be granted without pay during the period of the leave, including the vacation period concomitant to the leave. If the leave is for one semester only, the loss of paid vacation shall be for one month only. If the leave is for two semesters, both months of vacation shall be without pay. If the duration of a maternity leave is one year or more, it shall not be credited towards salary increments. [Emphasis added.]

It is agreed that women are not compelled by this section to take maternity leave. This case is therefore unlike the companion case of Monell v. Department of Social Services, D.C., 357 F Supp. 1051, decided this same date, involving the constitutionality of New York City agency regulations which allegedly compel women to take a maternity leave at the end of the seventh month of pregnancy.

Mr. Danielson applied for a leave of absence for the spring semester of 1971, by letter dated October 5, 1970, to the acting chairman of his department. In that letter he stated as follows:

The purpose of my leave of absence would be two-fold: (1) to care for a new baby and, (2) engage in serious work on a PHD.

(Complaint, Appendix B.) The acting chairman rejected the requested leave of absence by letter dated October 28, 1970. He stated: "... there is no provision for a 'leave of absence' (for any reason) for persons who do not have tenure." The acting chairman also advised Mr. Danielson that his letter of October 5 amounted to a resignation as of January 31, 1971. (Complaint, Appendix C.) On November 10, 1970, Mr. Danielson applied for "maternity leave of absence" to the president of City College. He submitted the appropriate form under Section 13.4 with a letter stating his reasons for the requested maternity leave.

In that letter Mr. Danielson stated:

Men should have the same rights as women to care for young infants, especially where the mother chooses to work full time (as is true in my case.) If a husband is not entitled to a leave of absence, then the mother is virtually forced to take a leave of absence and hence the woman's maternity leave is rendered less a right than an obligation, contrary to the spirit, as I see it, of the maternity leave provisions and of various interpretations of equal rights legislation and constitutional guarantees. If not granted a leave of absence, a husband who wishes to care for a young infant must suffer greater hardship (such as termination of employment and loss, even with reappointment, of certain contract provisions, tenure credits, etc.) than a woman who may take a leave of absence; therefore the non-application of the maternity leave provision to men is unfair to men and tends to keep women in the home where they are *burdened* with the traditional child-care role in order to secure the employment of the husband. There can be no equal rights for women without equal rights for men.

(Complaint, Appendix D.)

On or about December 21, 1970 Mr. Danielson learned that the president's Review Committee had rejected his application without stating any reason. Mr. Danielson appealed to the chancellor of the University and the chairman of the Board of Higher Education but received no reply to his letters.

Ross Danielson took a leave during the spring 1971 semester and alleges he assumed primary responsibility for the care of his child. His wife resumed her teaching duties. His application for maternity leave was treated as a resignation. Thus, although he was rehired for the fall 1971 term, the computation of his continuous service time has been affected.

Susan Danielson, who had a right to do so, did not request the maternity leave permitted under Section 13.4. The president's office, however, sent her a form for such leave on numerous occasions. Maternity leaves which are granted under Section 13.4 are leaves without pay. If Mrs. Danielson had chosen to take maternity leave as of September 1, 1970 and had requested the one year extension, she could have remained away from her post until February 1, 1972 without loss of accrued time towards tenure requirements. It appears that no doctor's certificate in support of her request for extension would have been required. However, there is no proof one way or the other on this question. During this time away from her position, Mrs. Danielson apparently would have been free to devote all her time to the care of her newborn infant or, it appears, she could also have worked on her Ph.D. But, again, there is no firm proof one way or the other on this crucial question.

Defendants say that "... Ross Danielson might have obtained a leave for special purposes under Section 13.6 if he so requested, for the purpose of taking care of his child." (Defendants' Brief, p.18.) They also assert that "If *any* parent desires to take leave solely for childrearing purposes, they must proceed under By-Law §13.6, leave for special purposes." (Id. p.24.)

Section 13.6b provides:

> On the recommendation of the relevant departmental committee concerned with appointments, the relevant college committee and the president, the Board may grant to members of the instructional staff leaves of absence for special purposes such as study, writing, research, the carrying out of a creative project or a public service of reasonable duration. Such leaves shall be *without* pay. [Emphasis added.]

Mr. Danielson was not advised of this "administrative procedure ... available to accommodate him" prior to suit (Id. pp. 18-19). Such leave, of course, does affect the computation of the five years of continuous service required for tenure.

It should be noted also that defendants' statement, that *any* parent who desires leave "solely" for childrearing purposes may apply for same under Section 13.6, does not square with defendants' assertion on the same page of their brief (p.24) which reads as follows: "Defendant's By-Law provides a mother with the option to recuperate from pregnancy. If she utilizes this leave period to also care for her child, this is her own determination." This latter statement is consistent with the former if the former refers to women who desire to take child-care leave unconnected with childbirth. Thus from reading defendants' brief, it is clear to this court that defendants have not made up their collective minds as to what their child-care leave policies really are in the face of this men's liberation request for equal treatment with women.

Consequently, summary judgment cannot be granted for either party. Not only is it unclear what defendants' policies really are, but the central fact is plainly in dispute, i.e., whether women faculty members are permitted leaves up to three semesters under Section 13.4 to care for their newborn children when there is no unusual medical disability resulting from the birth of the child and, during this period, may also do work toward a Ph.D. degree without loss of time served, as it relates to tenure.

Mrs. Danielson made arrangements with other teachers to cover her classes during her brief leave for the birth of her child. She was absent from work for 12 days, from December 8, 1970 to December 23, 1970. She requested that her absence be credited against her allotted sick leave with pay. Instead of treating her absence as sick leave, Lehman College recorded the leave as a "special leave without pay for emergency purposes (maternity)." The special leave section, Section 13.6a, provides for special leaves for personal emergencies of not more than 10 working days *with pay* at the discretion of the president. Despite the express terms of this provision, Mrs. Danielson was not paid.

[2] Again it is clear defendants were confused about their own policy. Mrs. Danielson's claim that the leave which she took should be treated as any other illness is disputed by defendants on the ground that pregnancy is not an illness. With respect to Mrs. Danielson's claim we thus have another central disputed issue of fact, i.e., whether the period immediately following childbirth unattended by other complications is a medical disability or illness for which a woman is entitled to sick leave. Mrs. Danielson's claim for sick leave pay is a claim which has been previously recognized by a federal court, Cohen v. Chesterfield County School Board, 326 F. Supp. 1159 (E.D. Va. 1971), and has been bolstered by recently adopted Rules and Regulations of the Equal Employment Opportunity Commission. 37 Fed. Reg. 6837 (April 5,1972).[1]

---

1. This regulation provides in pertinent part as follows:

§1604.10(b) "Disabilities caused or contributed to by pregnancy, miscarriage, abortion, childbirth, *and recovery therefrom* are, for all job-related purposes, temporary disabilities and should be treated as such under any

[3] On this motion to dismiss it is only necessary to determine whether Mr. and Mrs. Danielson's allegations raise "colorable" constitutional claims. Roberson v. Harder, 440 F.2d 687 (2d Cir. 1971); Campagnuolo v. Harder, 440 F.2d 1225 (2d Cir. 1971); Johnson v. Harder, 438 F.2d 7 (2d Cir. 1971).

[4] Mr. Danielson's primary claim is that his right to equal protection of the laws has been violated by defendants' refusal to extend to him the same child-care leave privilege which they extend to women solely because he is a man. He claims that by so discriminating against men who seek to fully participate in the care of their children, defendants are effectively denying men the right to play a full and equal role in their families. He then argues that the fact that child care has traditionally been considered women's work is no more an answer here than were the use of such sex stereotypes in an attempt to bar women from certain kinds of employment. Sail'ers Inn Inc. v. Kirby, 5 Cal. 3d 1, 95 Cal. Rptr. 329, 485 P.2d 529 (1971) (invalidating state ban on female bartenders); Weeks v. Southern Bell Telephone & Telegraph Co., 408 F.2d 228 (5th Cir. 1969) (invalidating ban on women as telephone switchmen); Bowe v. Colgate-Palmolive Co., 416 F.2d 711 (7th Cir. 1969) (invalidating ban on women in jobs requiring the lifting of weights). He also argues that he and other men are perfectly capable of caring for infant children and have a right to elect to do so without arbitrary interference with this choice by the state.

Very recently, the Supreme Court ruled that a state may not arbitrarily prefer men over women similarly situated in determining appointments to positions of administrator of decedent's estates. Reed v. Reed, 404 U.S. 71, 92 S. Ct. 251, 30 L. Ed. 2d 225 (1971). There the Court ruled that where the state provides that different treatment be accorded to persons similarly situated, such a classification is subject to scrutiny under the equal protection clause. The Court held that a classification must be reasonable, not arbitrary, and must rest upon some ground of difference having a fair and substantial relation to the object of the legislation, so that all persons similarly circumstanced shall be treated alike. If upon a trial it is proved that the purpose of Section 13.4 leave is to give women an opportunity to care for infant children, and since it is not claimed that Mr. Danielson is incapable of such child care, then Mr. Danielson would have presented at least a "colorable" constitutional claim. Whether he will succeed with his claim is another matter not here decided.

Even more recently the Supreme Court in Stanley v. Illinois, 405 U.S. 645, 92 S. Ct. 1208, 31 L. Ed. 2d 551 (1972), held that an Illinois dependency statute that presumes parental unfitness of unwed fathers by excluding them from the definition of parents and which thereby deprives them of custody of their children without a hearing on their fitness accorded to all

health or temporary disability insurance or sick leave plan available in connection with employment." (Emphasis added)

other parents violates both the equal protection and due process clauses of the Fourteenth Amendment.

Moreover, in determining the precise nature of the private interest there affected by governmental action the Court said:

> The private interest here, that a man has in the children he has sired and raised, undeniably warrants deference and, absent a powerful countervailing interest, protection. It is plain that the interest of a parent in companionship, care, custody, and management of his or her children come[s] to this Court with a momentum for respect lacking when appeal is made to liberties which derive merely from shifting economic arrangement. . . .
>
> The Court has frequently emphasized the importance of the family. The rights to conceive and to raise one's children have been deemed "essential" . . . "basic civil rights of man" . . . and "[r]ights far more precious . . . than property rights." . . . "It is cardinal with us that the custody, care and nurture of the child reside first in the parents, whose primary function and freedom include preparation for obligations the state can neither supply nor hinder." . . . The integrity of the family unit has found protection in the Due Process Clause of the Fourteenth Amendment . . . the Equal Protection Clause of the Fourteenth Amendment . . . , and the Ninth Amendment. . . .

Here plaintiffs also rely on the right of personal liberty guaranteed by the due process clause of the Fourteenth Amendment as well as a claimed invasion of their right to privacy under the Ninth Amendment.

[5] The complaint, therefore, cannot be dismissed as to either plaintiff for failure to state a claim upon which relief may be granted. It is only when it appears that plaintiffs could prove no set of facts in support of their claim which would entitle them to relief that a motion to dismiss for failure to state a claim must be granted. Conley v. Gibson, 355 U.S. 41, 45-46, 78 S. Ct. 99, 2 L. Ed. 2d 80 (1957); Jenkins v. McKeithen, 395 U.S. 411, 421-422,89 S. Ct. 1843, 23 L. Ed. 2d 404 (1969); Build of Buffalo, Inc. v. Sedita, 441 F.2d 284, 287 (2d Cir. 1971). "Particularly when an action is brought under the Civil Rights Act, we are chary of permitting dismissal where plaintiffs might obtain relief on facts suggested, but inarticulately stated, by the complaint." United States ex rel. Hyde v. McGinnis, 429 F.2d 864, 865 (2d Cir. 1970).

Defendants asserted that plaintiffs' claims amount to little more than that they have been or are about to be deprived of the "profits or emoluments" derived from their employment and since this court is without jurisdiction under the Civil Rights Acts of a claim of infringement of personal liberty which is predicated upon a property right, the complaint must be dismissed. In moving to dismiss on the ground that the court is without jurisdiction under the civil rights statutes, 42 U.S.C. §1983 and 28 U.S.C. §1343(3), defendants relied upon the Second Circuit decision in Eisen v. Eastman, 421 F.2d 560 (2d Cir. 1969) which was recently overruled by the Supreme Court in Lynch v. Household Finance Corp., 405 U.S. 538,

92 S. Ct. 1113, 31 L. Ed. 2d 424 (1972). There the Court held that it had never adopted the Second Circuit's distinction between property rights and personal liberties for the purpose of determining §1343(3) jurisdiction, and expressly rejected it.

For all of the foregoing reasons, the motions for summary judgment and to dismiss are denied.

Submit order on 5 days' notice.

Eisenstadt v. Baird

405 U.S. 438 (1972)

Habeas corpus proceeding. The United States District Court for the District of Massachusetts, 310 F. Supp. 951, dismissed petition, and petitioner appealed. The United States Court of Appeals for the First Circuit, 429 F.2d 1398, vacated the order of dismissal and remanded with instructions, and county sheriff appealed. The Supreme Court, Mr. Justice Brennan, held that Massachusetts statute permitting married persons to obtain contraceptives to prevent pregnancy but prohibiting distribution of contraceptives to single persons for that purpose violates equal protection clause.

Affirmed.

Mr. Justice DOUGLAS filed a concurring opinion.

Mr. Justice WHITE concurred in result and filed an opinion in which Mr. Justice BLACKMUN joined.

Mr. Chief Justice BURGER filed a dissenting opinion.

Mr. Justice POWELL and Mr. Justice REHNQUIST took no part in consideration or decision of the case.

1. Courts [Key Number: 365(2)]

Construction of state law by state's highest court was binding on United States Supreme Court.

2. Constitutional Law [Key Number: 42.1(1)]

Even though petitioner convicted of violating state statute by giving woman vaginal foam was not authorized distributor of contraceptives within the statute nor a single person unable to obtain contraceptives under it, he had standing to attack the statute as unconstitutional, where relationship between petitioner and those whose rights he sought to assert was not simply that between distributor and potential distributees, but that between advocate of rights of persons to obtain contraceptives and those desirous of doing so and where the statute denied unmarried persons access to contraceptives but did not subject them to prosecution so they were denied a forum in which to assert their own rights. U.S.C.A. Const. art. 3, §2; M.G.L.A. c.272 §21A.

3. Constitutional Law [Key Number: 211]

The equal protection clause of the Fourteenth Amendment does not deny to states the power to treat different classes of persons in different ways; it does, however, deny to states the power to legislate that different treatment be accorded to persons placed by statute into different classes on basis of criteria wholly unrelated to the object of that statute. U.S.C.A. Const. Amend. 14.

4. Constitutional Law [Key Number: 208(3)]

Statutory classification must be reasonable, not arbitrary, and must rest on some ground of difference having fair and substantial relation to the object of legislation, so that all persons similarly circumstanced shall be treated alike. U.S.C.A. Const. Amend. 14.

5. Constitutional Law [Key Number: 211] Health and Environment [Key Number: 21]

Massachusetts statute permitting married persons to obtain contraceptives to prevent pregnancy but prohibiting distribution of contraceptives to single persons for that purpose violates equal protection clause. U.S.C.A. Const. Amend. 14; M.G.L.A. c.272 §§21, 21A.

6. Health and Environment [Key Number: 21]

Difference in treatment provided for by Massachusetts statute permitting married persons to obtain contraceptives to prevent pregnancy but prohibiting distribution of contraceptives to single persons for that purpose was not justified on basis that it deterred premarital sex, where it could not be assumed that state had prescribed pregnancy and birth of unwanted child as punishment for fornication, distribution of contraceptives to unmarried persons had at best a marginal relation to the proffered objective, and fornication was a misdemeanor, entailing a $30 fine or three months in jail but offense of providing contraceptives to unmarried person was a felony, punishable by five years' imprisonment. U.S.C.A. Const. Amend. 14; M.G.L.A. c.272 §§21, 21A.

7. Health and Environment [Key Number: 21]

Different treatment accorded married and unmarried persons under statute permitting married persons to obtain contraceptives by prescription to prevent pregnancy but prohibiting dispensing of contraceptives to single persons for that purpose was not justified on theory that it served health needs of community by regulating distribution of potentially harmful articles, where any need to have physician prescribe and pharmacist dispense contraceptives was as great for unmarried persons as for married persons, not all contraceptives are potentially dangerous, so that statute would be overbroad as to married persons, and other state laws and federal laws regulated distribution of harmful drugs. U.S.C.A. Const. Amend. 14; M.G.L.A. c.94 §187A; c.272 §§21, 21A; Federal Food, Drug, and Cosmetic Act, §503 as amended 21 U.S.C.A. §353.

8. Constitutional Law [Key Number: 82]

Under right of privacy, individual, married or single, has right to be free from unwarranted governmental intrusion into matters so fundamentally affecting a person as decision whether to bear or beget a child. U.S.C.A. Const. Amend. 14.

Syllabus*

Appellee attacks his conviction of violating Massachusetts law for giving a woman a contraceptive foam at the close of his lecture to students on contraception. That law makes it a felony for anyone to give away a drug, medicine, instrument, or article for the prevention of conception except in the case of (1) a registered physician administering or prescribing it for a married person or (2) an active registered pharmacist furnishing it to a married person presenting a registered physician's prescription. The District Court dismissed appellee's petition for a writ of habeas corpus. The Court of Appeals vacated the dismissal, holding that the statute is a prohibition on contraception per se and conflicts "with fundamental human rights" under Griswold v. Connecticut, 381 U.S. 479, 85 S. Ct. 1678, 14 L. Ed. 2d 510. Appellant, inter alia, argues that appellee lacks standing to assert the rights of unmarried persons denied access to contraceptives because he was neither an authorized distributor under the statute nor a single person unable to obtain contraceptives. *Held:*

1. If, as the Court of Appeals held, the statute under which appellee was convicted is not a health measure, appellee may not be prevented, because he was not an authorized distributor, from attacking the statute in its alleged discriminatory application to potential distributees. Appellee, furthermore, has standing to assert the rights of unmarried persons denied access to contraceptives because their ability to obtain them will be materially impaired by enforcement of the statute. Cf. *Griswold*, supra; Barrows v. Jackson, 346 U.S. 249, 73 S. Ct. 1031, 97 L. Ed. 1586.

2. By providing dissimilar treatment for married and unmarried persons who are similarly situated, the statute violates the Equal Protection Clause of the Fourteenth Amendment.

(a) The deterrence of fornication, a 90-day misdemeanor under Massachusetts law, cannot reasonably be regarded as the purpose of

---

* The syllabus constitutes no part of the opinion of the Court but has been prepared by the Reporter of Decisions for the convenience of the reader. See United States v. Detroit Timber & Lumber Co., 200 U.S. 321, 337, 26 S. Ct. 282, 287, 50 L. Ed. 499.

the statute, since the statute is riddled with exceptions making contraceptives freely available for use in premarital sexual relations and its scope and penalty structure are inconsistent with that purpose.

(b) Similarly, the protection of public health through the regulation of the distribution of potentially harmful articles cannot reasonably be regarded as the purpose of the law, since, if health were the rationale, the statute would be both discriminatory and overbroad, and federal and state laws already regulate the distribution of drugs unsafe for use except under the supervision of a licensed physician.

(c) Nor can the statute be sustained simply as a prohibition on contraception per se, for whatever the rights of the individual to access to contraceptives may be, the rights must be the same for the unmarried and the married alike. If under *Griswold*, supra, the distribution of contraceptives to married persons cannot be prohibited, a ban on distribution to unmarried persons would be equally impermissible, since the constitutionally protected right of privacy inheres in the individual, not the marital couple. If, on the other hand, *Griswold* is no bar to a prohibition on the distribution of contraceptives, a prohibition limited to unmarried persons would be underinclusive and invidiously discriminatory.

429 F.2d 1398, affirmed.

Joseph R. Nolan, Boston, Mass., for appellant.

Joseph D. Tydings, Baltimore, Md., for appellee.

Mr. Justice BRENNAN delivered the opinion of the Court.

Appellee William Baird was convicted at a bench trial in the Massachusetts Superior Court under Massachusetts General Laws Ann., c.272, §21, first, for exhibiting contraceptive articles in the course of delivering a lecture on contraception to a group of students at Boston University and, second, for giving a young woman a package of Emko vaginal foam at the close of his address.[1] The Massachusetts Supreme Judicial Court unanimously set aside the conviction for exhibiting contraceptives on the ground that it violated Baird's First Amendment rights, but by a four-to-three vote sustained the conviction for giving away the foam. Commonwealth v. Baird, 355 Mass. 746, 247 N.E.2d 574 (1969). Baird subsequently filed a petition for a federal writ of habeas corpus, which the District Court dismissed. 310F. Supp. 951 (1970). On appeal, however, the Court of Appeals for the First Circuit vacated the dismissal and remanded the action with directions to grant the writ discharging Baird. 429 F.2d 1398 (1970). This appeal by the Sheriff of Suffolk County, Massachusetts, followed, and we noted probable jurisdiction. 401 U.S. 934, 91 S. Ct. 921, 28 L. Ed. 2d 213 (1971). We affirm.

---

1. The Court of Appeals below described the recipient of the foam as "an unmarried adult woman." 429 F.2d 1398, 1399 (1970). However, there is no evidence in the record about her marital status.

[1] Massachusetts General Laws Ann., c.272, §21, under which Baird was convicted, provides a maximum five-year term of imprisonment for "whoever . . . gives away . . . any drug, medicine, instrument or article whatever for the prevention of conception," except as authorized in §21A. Under §21A, "[a] registered physician may administer to or prescribe for any married person drugs or articles intended for the prevention of pregnancy or conception. [And a] registered pharmacist actually engaged in the business of pharmacy may furnish such drugs or articles to any married person presenting a prescription from a registered physician."[2] As interpreted by the State Supreme Judicial Court, these provisions make it a felony for anyone, other than a registered physician or pharmacist acting in accordance with the terms of §21A, to dispense any article with the intention that it be used for the prevention of conception. The statutory scheme distinguishes among three distinct classes of distributees — *first*, married persons may obtain contraceptives to prevent pregnancy, but only from doctors or druggists on prescription; *second*, single persons may not obtain contraceptives from anyone to prevent pregnancy; and, *third*, married or single persons may obtain contraceptives from anyone to prevent, not pregnancy, but the spread of disease. This construction of state law is, of course, binding on us. E.g., Groppi v. Wisconsin, 400 U.S. 505, 507, 91 S. Ct. 490, 491, 27 L. Ed. 2d 571 (1971).

2. Section 21 provides in full:

> Except as provided in section twenty-one A, whoever sells, lends, gives away, exhibits or offers to sell, lend or give away an instrument or other article intended to be used for self-abuse, or any drug, medicine, instrument or article whatever for the prevention of conception or for causing unlawful abortion, or advertises the same, or writes, prints, or causes to be written or printed a card, circular, book, pamphlet, advertisement or notice of any kind stating when, where, how, of whom or by what means such article can be purchased or obtained, or manufactures or makes any such article shall be punished by imprisonment in the state prison for not more than five years or in jail or the house of correction for not more than two and one half years or by a fine of not less than one hundred nor more than one thousand dollars.

Section 21A provides in full:

> A registered physician may administer to or prescribe for any married person drugs or articles intended for the prevention of pregnancy or conception. A registered pharmacist actually engaged in the business of pharmacy may furnish such drugs or articles to any married person presenting a prescription from a registered physician.
>
> A public health agency, a registered nurse, or a maternity health clinic operated by or in an accredited hospital may furnish information to any married person as to where professional advice regarding such drugs or articles may be lawfully obtained.
>
> This section shall not be construed as affecting the provisions of sections twenty and twenty-one relative to prohibition of advertising of drugs or articles intended for the prevention of pregnancy or conception; nor shall this section be construed so as to permit the sale or dispensing of such drugs or articles by means of any vending machine or similar device.

The legislative purposes that the statute is meant to serve are not altogether clear. In Commonwealth v. Baird, supra, the Supreme Judicial Court noted only the State's interest in protecting the health of its citizens: "[T]he prohibition in §21," the court declared, "is directly related to" the State's goal of "preventing the distribution of articles designed to prevent conception which may have undesirable, if not dangerous, physical consequences." 355 Mass., at 753, 247 N.E.2d, at 578. In a subsequent decision, Sturgis v. Attorney General, 358 Mass. 37, 260 N.E.2d 687, 690 (1970), the court, however, found "a second and more compelling ground for upholding the statute"—namely, to protect morals through "regulating the private sexual lives of single persons."[3] The Court of Appeals, for reasons that will appear, did not consider the promotion of health or the protection of morals through the deterrence of fornication to be the legislative aim. Instead, the court concluded that the statutory goal was to limit contraception in and of itself—a purpose that the court held conflicted "with fundamental human rights" under Griswold v. Connecticut, 381 U.S. 479, 85 S. Ct. 1678, 14 L. Ed. 2d 510 (1965), where this Court struck down Connecticut's prohibition against the use of contraceptives as an unconstitutional infringement of the right of marital privacy. 429 F.2d, at 1401-1402.

We agree that the goals of deterring premarital sex and regulating the distribution of potentially harmful articles cannot reasonably be regarded as legislative aims of §§21 and 21A. And we hold that the statute, viewed as a prohibition on contraception per se, violates the rights of single persons under the Equal Protection Clause of the Fourteenth Amendment.

I

[2] We address at the outset appellant's contention that Baird does not have standing to assert the rights of unmarried persons denied access to contraceptives because he was neither an authorized distributor under §21A nor a single person unable to obtain contraceptives. There can be no question, of course, that Baird has sufficient interest in challenging the statute's validity to satisfy the "case or controversy" requirement of Article III of the Constitution.[4] Appellant's argument, however, is that this case is governed by the Court's self-imposed rules of restraint, *first*, that "one to

---

3. Appellant suggests that the purpose of the Massachusetts statute is to promote marital fidelity as well as to discourage premarital sex. Under §21A, however, contraceptives may be made available to married persons without regard to whether they are living with their spouses or the uses to which the contraceptives are to be put. Plainly the legislation has no deterrent effect on extramarital sexual relations.

4. This factor decisively distinguishes Tileston v. Ullman, 318 U.S. 44, 63 S. Ct. 493, 87 L. Ed. 603 (1943), where the Court held that a physician lacked standing to bring an action for declaratory relief to challenge, on behalf of his patients, the Connecticut law prohibiting the use of contraceptives. The patients were fully able to bring their own action. Underlying the decision was the concern that "the standards of 'case or controversy' in Article HI of the Constitution [not] become blurred," Griswold v. Connecticut, 381 U.S. 479, 481, 85 S. Ct. 1678, 1679, 14 L. Ed. 2d 510 (1965)—a problem that is not at all involved in this case.

whom application of a statute is constitutional will not be heard to attack the statute on the ground that impliedly it might also be taken as applying to other persons or other situations in which its application might be unconstitutional," United States v. Raines, 362 U.S. 17, 21, 80 S. Ct. 519, 522, 4 L. Ed. 2d 524 (1960), and, *second*, the "closely related corollary that a litigant may only assert his own constitutional rights or immunities," id., at 22, 80 S. Ct., at 523. Here, appellant contends that Baird's conviction rests on the restriction in 21A on permissible distributors and that that restriction serves a valid health interest independent of the limitation on authorized distributees. Appellant urges, therefore, that Baird's action in giving away the foam fell squarely within the conduct that the legislature meant and had power to prohibit and that Baird should not be allowed to attack the statute in its application to potential recipients. In any event, appellant concludes, since Baird was not himself a single person denied access to contraceptives, he should not be heard to assert their rights. We cannot agree.

The Court of Appeals held that the statute under which Baird was convicted is not a health measure. If that view is correct, we do not see how Baird may be prevented, because he was neither a doctor nor a druggist, from attacking the statute in its alleged discriminatory application to potential distributees. We think, too, that our self-imposed rule against the assertion of third-party rights must be relaxed in this case just as in Griswold v. Connecticut, supra. There the Executive Director of the Planned Parenthood League of Connecticut and a licensed physician who had prescribed contraceptives for married persons and been convicted as accessories to the crime of using contraceptives were held to have standing to raise the constitutional rights of the patients with whom they had a professional relationship. Appellant here argues that the absence of a professional or aiding-and-abetting relationship distinguishes this- case from *Griswold*. Yet, as the Court's discussion of prior authority in *Griswold*, 381 U.S., at 481, 85 S. Ct., at 1679, 14 L. Ed. 2d 510, indicates, the doctor-patient and accessory-principal relationships are not the only circumstances in which one person has been found to have standing to assert the rights of another. Indeed, in Barrows v. Jackson, 346 U.S. 249, 73 S. Ct. 1031, 97 L. Ed. 1586 (1953), a seller of land was entitled to defend against an action for damages for breach of a racially restrictive covenant on the ground that enforcement of the covenant violated the equal protection rights of prospective non Caucasian purchasers. The relationship there between the defendant and those whose rights he sought to assert was not simply the fortuitous connection between a vendor and potential vendees, but the relationship between one who acted to protect the rights of a minority and the minority itself. Sedler, Standing to Assert Constitutional Jus Tertii in the Supreme Court, 71 Yale L.J. 599, 631 (1962). And so here the relationship between Baird and those whose rights he seeks to assert is not simply that between a distributor and potential distributees, but that between an advocate of the rights of persons to obtain contraceptives and those desirous of doing so. The very point of Baird's giving away the vaginal foam was to challenge the Massachusetts statute that limited access to contraceptives.

In any event, more important than the nature of the relationship between the litigant and those whose rights he seeks to assert is the impact of the litigation on the third-party interests.[5] In *Griswold*, 381 U.S., at 481, 85 S. Ct., at 1680, 14 L. Ed. 2d 510, the Court stated: "The rights of husband and wife, pressed here, are likely to be diluted or adversely affected unless those rights are considered in a suit involving those who have this kind of confidential relation to them." A similar situation obtains here. Enforcement of the Massachusetts statute will materially impair the ability of single persons to obtain contraceptives. In fact, the case for according standing to assert third-party rights is stronger in this regard here than in *Griswold* because unmarried persons denied access to contraceptives in Massachusetts, unlike the users of contraceptives in Connecticut, are not themselves subject to prosecution and, to that extent, are denied a forum in which to assert their own rights. Cf. NAACP v. Alabama, 357 U.S. 449, 78 S. Ct. 1163, 2 L. Ed. 2d 1488 (1958); Burrows v. Jackson, supra.[6] The Massachusetts statute, unlike the Connecticut law considered in *Griswold*, prohibits, not use, but distribution.

For the foregoing reasons we hold that Baird, who is now in a position, and plainly has an adequate incentive, to assert the rights of unmarried persons denied access to contraceptives, has standing to do so. We turn to the merits.

II

[3-5] The basic principles governing application of the Equal Protection Clause of the Fourteenth Amendment are familiar. As the Chief Justice only recently explained in Reed v. Reed, 404 U.S. 71, 75-76, 92 S. Ct. 251, 253, 30 L. Ed. 2d 225 (1971):

> In applying that clause, this Court has consistently recognized that the Fourteenth Amendment does not deny to States the power to treat different classes of persons in different ways. Barbier v. Connolly, 113 U.S. 27, 5 S. Ct. 357, 28 L. Ed. 923 (1885); Lindsley v. Natural Carbonic Gas Co., 220 U.S. 61, 31 S. Ct. 337, 55 L. Ed. 369 (1911); Railway Express Agency v.

5. Indeed, in First Amendment cases we have relaxed our rules of standing without regard to the relationship between the litigant and those whose rights he seeks to assert precisely because application of those rules would have an intolerable, inhibitory effect on freedom of speech. E.g., Thornhill v. Alabama, 310 U.S. 88, 97-98, 60 S. Ct. 736, 741-742, 84 L. Ed. 1093 (1940). See United States v. Raines, 362 U.S. 17, 22, 80 S. Ct. 519, 523, 4 L. Ed. 2d 524 (1960).

6. See also Prince v. Massachusetts, 321 U.S. 158, 64 S. Ct. 438, 88 L. Ed. 645 (1944), where a custodian, in violation of state law, furnished a child with magazines to distribute on the streets. The Court there implicitly held that the custodian had standing to assert alleged freedom of religion and equal protection rights of the child that were threatened in the very litigation before the Court and that the child had no effective way of asserting herself.

New York, 336 U.S. 106, 69 S. Ct. 463, 93 L. Ed. 533 (1949); McDonald v. Board of Election Commissioners, 394 U.S. 802, 89 S. Ct. 1404, 22 L. Ed. 2d 739 (1969). The Equal Protection Clause of that amendment does, however, deny to States the power to legislate that different treatment be accorded to persons placed by a statute into different classes on the basis of criteria wholly unrelated to the objective of that statute. A classification "must be reasonable, not arbitrary, and must rest upon some ground of difference having a fair and substantial relation to the object of the legislation, so that all persons similarly circumstanced shall be treated alike." Royster Guano Co. v. Virginia, 253 U.S. 412, 415, 40 S. Ct. 560, 64 L. Ed. 989 (1920).

The question for our determination in this case is whether there is some ground of difference that rationally explains the different treatment accorded married and unmarried persons under Massachusetts General Laws Ann., c.272, §§21 and 21A.[7] For the reasons that follow, we conclude that no such ground exists.

First. Section 21 stems from Mass. Stat. 1879, c.159, §1, which prohibited without exception, distribution of articles intended to be used as contraceptives. In Commonwealth v. Allison, 227 Mass. 57, 62, 116 N.E. 265, 266 (1917), the Massachusetts Supreme Judicial Court explained that the law's "plain purpose is to protect purity, to preserve chastity, to encourage continence and self restraint, to defend the sanctity of the home, and thus to engender in the State and nation a virile and virtuous race of men and women." Although the State clearly abandoned that purpose with the enactment of §21A, at least insofar as the illicit sexual activities of married persons are concerned, see n.3, supra, the court reiterated in Sturgis v. Attorney General, supra, that the object of the legislation is to discourage premarital sexual intercourse. Conceding that the State could, consistently with the Equal Protection Clause, regard the problems of extramarital and premarital sexual relations as "[e]vils . . . of different dimensions and proportions, requiring different remedies," Williamson v. Lee Optical Co., 348 U.S. 483, 489, 75 S. Ct. 461, 465, 99 L. Ed. 563 (1955), we cannot agree that the deterrence of premarital sex may reasonably be regarded as the purpose of the Massachusetts law.

[6] It would be plainly unreasonable to assume that Massachusetts has prescribed pregnancy and the birth of an unwanted child as punishment for fornication, which is a misdemeanor under Massachusetts General Laws Ann., c.272, §18. Aside from the scheme of values that assumption

---

7. Of course, if we were to conclude that the Massahusetts statute impinges upon fundamental freedoms under *Griswold*, the statutory classification would have to be not merely *rationally related* to a valid public purpose but *necessary* to the achievement of a *compelling* state interest. E.g., Shapiro v. Thompson, 394 U.S. 618, 89 S. Ct. 1322, 22 L. Ed. 2d 600 (1969); Loving v. Virginia, 388 U.S. 1, 87 S. Ct. 1817, 18 L. Ed. 2d 1010 (1967). But just as in Reed v. Reed, 404 U.S. 71, 92 S. Ct. 251, 30 L. Ed. 2d 225 (1971), we do not have to address the statute's validity under that test because the law fails to satisfy even the more lenient equal protection standard.

would attribute to the State, it is abundantly clear that the effect of the ban on distribution of contraceptives to unmarried persons has at best a marginal relation to the proffered objective. What Mr. Justice Goldberg said in Griswold v. Connecticut, supra, 381 U.S., at 498, 85 S. Ct., at 1689,14 L. Ed. 2d 510 (concurring opinion), concerning the effect of Connecticut's prohibition on the use of contraceptives in discouraging extramarital sexual relations, is equally applicable here. "The rationality of this justification is dubious, particularly in light of the admitted widespread availability to all persons in the State of Connecticut, unmarried as well as married, of birth-control devices for the prevention of disease, as distinguished from the prevention of conception." See also id., at 505-507, 85 S. Ct., at 1689 (White, J., concurring in judgment). Like Connecticut's laws, §§21 and 21A do not at all regulate the distribution of contraceptives when they are to be used to prevent, not pregnancy, but the spread of disease. Commonwealth v. Corbett, 307 Mass. 7,29 N.E.2d 151 (1940), cited with approval in Commonwealth v. Baird, 355 Mass., at 754,247 N.E.2d, at 579. Nor, in making contraceptives available to married persons without regard to their intended use, does Massachusetts attempt to deter married persons from engaging in illicit sexual relations with unmarried persons. Even on the assumption that the fear of pregnancy operates as a deterrent to fornication, the Massachusetts statute is thus so riddled with exceptions that deterrence of premarital sex cannot reasonably be regarded as its aim.

Moreover, §§21 and 21A on their face have a dubious relation to the State's criminal prohibition on fornication. As the Court of Appeals explained, "Fornication is a misdemeanor [in Massachusetts], entailing a thirty dollar fine, or three months in jail. Massachusetts General Laws Ann. c.272 §18. Violation of the present statute is a felony, punishable by five years in prison. We find it hard to believe that the legislature adopted a statute carrying a five-year penalty for its possible, obviously by no means fully effective, deterrence of the commission of a ninety-day misdemeanor." 429 F.2d, at 1401. Even conceding the legislature a full measure of discretion in fashioning means to prevent fornication, and recognizing that the State may seek to deter prohibited conduct by punishing more severely those who facilitate than those who actually engage in its commission, we, like the Court of Appeals, cannot believe that in this instance Massachusetts has chosen to expose the aider and abetter who simply *gives away* a contraceptive to *20* times the *90-day* sentence of the offender himself. The very terms of the State's criminal statutes, coupled with the de minimis effect of §§21 and 21A in deterring fornication, thus compel the conclusion that such deterrence cannot reasonably be taken as the purpose of the ban on distribution of contraceptives to unmarried persons.

[7] *Second.* Section 21A was added to the Massachusetts General Laws by Stat. 1966, c.265, §1. The Supreme Judicial Court in Commonwealth v. Baird, supra, held that the purpose of the amendment was to serve the health needs of the community by regulating the distribution of potentially harmful articles. It is plain that Massachusetts had no such purpose

in mind before the enactment of §21A. As the Court of Appeals remarked, "Consistent with the fact that the statute was contained in a chapter dealing with 'Crimes Against Chastity, Morality, Decency and Good Order,' it was cast only in terms of morals. A physician was forbidden to prescribe contraceptives even when needed for the protection of health. Commonwealth v. Gardner, 1938, 300 Mass. 372, 15 N.E.2d 222." 429 F.2d, at 1401. Nor did the Court of Appeals "believe that the legislature [in enacting §21A] suddenly reversed its field and developed an interest in health. Rather, it merely made what it thought to be the precise accommodation necessary to escape the *Griswold* ruling." Ibid.

Again, we must agree with the Court of Appeals. If health were the rationale of §21A, the statute would be both discriminatory and overbroad. Dissenting in Commonwealth v. Baird, 355 Mass., at 758, 247 N.E.2d, at 581, Justices Whittemore and Cutter stated that they saw "in §21 and §21 A, read together, no public health purpose. If there is need to have a physician prescribe (and a pharmacist dispense) contraceptives, that need is as great for unmarried persons as for married persons." The Court of Appeals added: "If the prohibition [on distribution to unmarried persons] . . . is to be taken to mean that the same physician who can prescribe for married patients does not have sufficient skill to protect the health of patients who lack a marriage certificate, or who may be currently divorced, it is illogical to the point of irrationality." 429 F.2d, at 1401.[8] Furthermore, we must join the Court of Appeals in noting that not all contraceptives are potentially dangerous.[9] As a result, if the Massachusetts statute were a health measure, it would not only invidiously discriminate against the unmarried, but also be overbroad with respect to the married, a fact that the Supreme Judicial Court itself seems to have conceded in Sturgis v. Attorney General, Mass., 260 N.E.2d, at 690, where it noted that "it may well be that certain contraceptive medication and devices constitute no hazard to health, in which event it could be argued that the statute swept too broadly in its prohibition." "In this posture," as the Court of

---

8. Appellant insists that the unmarried have no right to engage in sexual intercourse and hence no health interest in contraception that needs to be served. The short answer to this contention is that the same devices the distribution of which the State purports to regulate when their asserted purpose is to forestall pregnancy are available without any controls whatsoever so long as their asserted purpose is to prevent the spread of disease. It is inconceivable that the need for health controls varies with the purpose for which the contraceptive is to be used when the physical act in all cases is one and the same.

9. The Court of Appeals stated, 429 F.2d, at 1401:

> [W]e must take notice that not all contraceptive devices risk "undesirable . . . [or] dangerous physical consequences." It is 200 years since Casanova recorded the ubiquitous article which, perhaps because of the birthplace of its inventor, he termed a "redingote anglais." The reputed nationality of the condom has now changed, but we have never heard criticism of it on the side of health. We cannot think that the legislature was unaware of it, or could have thought that it needed a medical prescription. We believe the same could be said of certain other products.

Appeals concluded, "it is impossible to think of the statute as intended as a health measure for the unmarried, and it is almost as difficult to think of it as so intended even as to the married." 429 F.2d, at 1401.

But if further proof that the Massachusetts statute is not a health measure is necessary, the argument of Justice Spiegel, who also dissented in Commonwealth v. Baird, 355 Mass., at 759, 247 N.E.2d, at 582, is conclusive: "It is at best a strained conception to say that the Legislature intended to prevent the distribution of articles 'which may have undesirable, if not dangerous, physical consequences.' If that was the Legislature's goal, §21 is not required" in view of the federal and state laws *already* regulating the distribution of harmful drugs. See Federal Food, Drug, and Cosmetic Act, §503, 52 Stat. 1051, as amended, 21 U.S.C. §353; Mass. Gen. Laws Ann., c.94, §187A, as amended. We conclude, accordingly, that, despite the statute's superficial earmarks as a health measure, health, on the face of the statute, may no more reasonably be regarded as its purpose than the deterrence of premarital sexual relations.

Third. If the Massachusetts statute cannot be upheld as a deterrent to fornication or as a health measure, may it, nevertheless, be sustained simply as a prohibition on contraception? The Court of Appeals analysis "led inevitably to the conclusion that, so far as morals are concerned, it is contraceptives per se that are considered immoral — to the extent that *Griswold* will permit such a declaration." 429 F.2d, at 1401-1402. The Court of Appeals went on to hold, id., at 1402:

> To say that contraceptives are immoral as such, and are to be forbidden to unmarried persons who will nevertheless persist in having intercourse, means that such persons must risk for themselves an unwanted pregnancy, for the child, illegitimacy, and for society, a possible obligation of support. Such a view of morality is not only the very mirror image of sensible legislation; we consider that it conflicts with fundamental human rights. In the absence of demonstrated harm, we hold it is beyond the competency of the state.

We need not and do not, however, decide that important question in this case because, whatever the rights of the individual to access to contraceptives may be, the rights must be the same for the unmarried and the married alike.

[8] If under *Griswold* the distribution of contraceptives to married persons cannot be prohibited, a ban on distribution to unmarried persons would be equally impermissible. It is true that in *Griswold* the right of privacy in question inhered in the marital relationship. Yet the marital couple is not an independent entity with a mind and heart of its own, but an association of two individuals each with a separate intellectual and emotional makeup. If the right of privacy means anything, it is the right of the *individual*, married or single, to be free from unwarranted governmental intrusion into matters so fundamentally affecting a person as the decision whether to bear or beget a child. See Stanley v. Georgia, 394

U.S. 557, 89 S. Ct. 1243, 22 L. Ed. 2d 542 (1969).[10] See also Skinner v. Oklahoma ex rel. Williamson, 316 U.S. 535, 62 S. Ct. 1110, 86 L. Ed. 1655 (1942); Jacobson v. Massachusetts, 197 U.S. 11, 29, 25 S. Ct. 358, 362, 49 L. Ed. 643 (1905).

On the other hand, if *Griswold* is no bar to a prohibition on the distribution of contraceptives, the State could not, consistently with the Equal Protection Clause, outlaw distribution to unmarried but not to married persons. In each case the evil, as perceived by the State, would be identical, and the underinclusion would be invidious. Mr. Justice Jackson, concurring in Railway Express Agency v. New York, 336 U.S. 106, 112-113, 69 S. Ct. 463, 466, 93 L. Ed. 533 (1949), made the point:

> The framers of the Constitution knew, and we should not forget today, that there is no more effective practical guaranty against arbitrary and unreasonable government than to require that the principles of law which officials would impose upon a minority must be imposed generally. Conversely, nothing opens the door to arbitrary action so effectively as to allow those officials to pick and choose only a few to whom they will apply legislation and thus to escape the political retribution that might be visited upon them if larger numbers were affected. Courts can take no better measure to assure that laws will be just than to require that laws be equal in operation.

Although Mr. Justice Jackson's comments had reference to administrative regulations, the principle he affirmed has equal application to the legislation here. We hold that by providing dissimilar treatment for married and unmarried persons who are similarly situated, Massachusetts General Laws Ann., c.272, §§21 and 21A, violate the Equal Protection Clause. The judgment of the Court of Appeals is affirmed.

Affirmed.

Mr. Justice POWELL and Mr. Justice REHNQUIST took no part in the consideration or decision of this case.

---

10. In *Stanley*, 394 U.S., at 564, 89 S. Ct., at 1247, the Court stated:

> [A]lso fundamental is the right to be free, except in very limited circumstances, from unwanted governmental intrusions into one's privacy.
> "The makers of our Constitution undertook to secure conditions favorable to the pursuit of happiness. They recognized the significance of man's spiritual nature, of his feelings and of his intellect. They knew that only a part of the pain, pleasure and satisfactions of life are to be found in material things. They sought to protect Americans in their beliefs, their thoughts, their emotions, and their sensations. They conferred, as against the Government, the right to be let alone—the most comprehensive of rights and the right most valued by civilized man." Olmstead v. United States, 277 U.S. 438, 478, 48 S. Ct. 564, 572, 72 L. Ed. 944 (1928) (Brandeis, J., dissenting).
> See Griswold v. Connecticut, supra; cf. NAACP v. Alabama [ex rel. Patterson], 357 U.S. 449, 462, 78 S. Ct. 1163, 1171, 2 L. Ed. 2d 1488 (1958).

Mr. Justice DOUGLAS, concurring.

While I join the opinion of the Court, there is for me a narrower ground for affirming the Court of Appeals. This to me is a simple First Amendment case, that amendment being applicable to the States by reason of the Fourteenth. Stromberg v. California, 283 U.S. 359, 51 S. Ct. 532, 75 L. Ed. 1117.

Under no stretch of the law as presently stated could Massachusetts require a license for those who desire to lecture on planned parenthood, contraceptives, the rights of women, birth control, or any allied subject, or place a tax on that privilege. As to license taxes on First Amendment rights we said in Murdock v. Pennsylvania, 319 U.S. 105, 115, 63 S. Ct. 870, 876, 87 L. Ed. 1292:

> A license tax certainly does not acquire constitutional validity because it classifies the privileges protected by the First Amendment along with the wares and merchandise of hucksters and peddlers and treats them all alike. Such equality in treatment does not save the ordinance. Freedom of press, freedom of speech, freedom of religion are in a preferred position.

We held in Thomas v. Collins, 323 U.S. 516, 65 S. Ct. 315, 89 L. Ed. 430, that a person speaking at a labor union rally could not be required to register or obtain a license:

> As a matter of principle a requirement of registration in order to make a public speech would seem generally incompatible with an exercise of the rights of free speech and free assembly. Lawful public assemblies, involving no element of grave and immediate danger to an interest the State is entitled to protect, are not instruments of harm which require previous identification of the speakers. And the right either of workmen or of unions under these conditions to assemble and discuss their own affairs is as fully protected by the Constitution as the right of businessmen, farmers, educators, political party members or others to assemble and discuss their affairs and to enlist the support of others.
>
> . . . If one who solicits support for the cause of labor may be required to register as a condition to the exercise of his right to make a public speech, so may he who seeks to rally support for any social, business, religious or political cause. We think a requirement that one must register before he undertakes to make a public speech to enlist support for a lawful movement is quite incompatible with the requirements of the First Amendment.

Id., at 539, 540, 65 S. Ct., at 327.

Baird addressed an audience of students and faculty at Boston University on the subject of birth control and overpopulation. His address was approximately one hour in length and consisted of a discussion of various contraceptive devices displayed by means of diagrams on two demonstration boards, as well as a display of contraceptive devices in their original packages. In addition, Baird spoke of the respective merits of various contraceptive devices; overpopulation in the world; crises throughout the world due to overpopulation; the large number of abortions performed on unwed mothers; and quack abortionists and the potential harm to women resulting from abortions performed by quack abortionists. Baird also urged members of the audience to petition the Massachusetts Legislature and to make known their feelings with regard to birth control laws in order to bring about a change in the laws. At the close of the address Baird invited members of the audience to come to the stage and help themselves to the contraceptive articles. We do not know how many accepted Baird's invitation. We only know that Baird personally handed one woman a package of Emko Vaginal Foam. He was then arrested and indicted (1) for exhibiting contraceptive devices and (2) for giving one such device away. The conviction for the first offense was reversed, the Supreme Judicial Court of Massachusetts holding that the display of the articles was essential to a graphic representation of the lecture. But the conviction for the giving away of one article was sustained. 355 Mass. 746, 247 N.E.2d 574. The case reaches us by federal habeas corpus.

Had Baird not "given away" a sample of one of the devices whose use he advocated, there could be no question about the protection afforded him by the First Amendment. A State may not "contract the spectrum of available knowledge." Griswold v. Connecticut, 381 U.S. 479, 482, 85 S. Ct. 1678,1680,14 L. Ed. 2d 510. See also Thomas v. Collins, supra; Pierce v. Society of Sisters, 268 U.S. 510, 45 S. Ct. 571, 69 L. Ed. 1070; Meyer v. Nebraska, 262 U.S. 390, 43 S. Ct. 625, 67 L. Ed. 1042. However noxious Baird's ideas might have been to the authorities, the freedom to learn about them, fully to comprehend their scope and portent, and to weigh them against the tenets of the "conventional wisdom," may not be abridged. Terminiello v. Chicago, 337 U.S. 1, 69 S. Ct. 894, 93 L. Ed. 1131. Our system of government requires that we have faith in the ability of the individual to decide wisely, if only he is fully apprised of the merits of a controversy.

> "Freedom of discussion, if it would fulfill its historic function in this nation, must embrace all issues about which information is needed or appropriate to enable the members of society to cope with the exigencies of their period." Thornhill v. Alabama, 310 U.S. 88,102, 60 S. Ct. 736, 744, 84 L. Ed. 1093.

The teachings of Baird and those of Galileo might be of a different order; but the suppression of either is equally repugnant.

As Milton said in the Areopagitica, "Give me the liberty to know, to utter, and to argue freely according to conscience, above all liberties."

It is said that only Baird's conduct is involved and United States v. O'Brien, 391 U.S. 367, 88 S. Ct. 1673, 20 L. Ed. 2d 672, is cited. That case involved a registrant under the Selective Service Act burning his Selective Service draft card. When prosecuted for that act, he defended his conduct as "symbolic speech." The Court held it was not.

Whatever may be thought of that decision on the merits,[1] *O' Brien* is not controlling here. The distinction between "speech" and "conduct" is a valid one, insofar as it helps to determine in a particular case whether the purpose of the activity was to aid in the communication of ideas, and whether the form of the communication so interferes with the rights of others that reasonable regulations may be imposed.[2] See Public Utilities Comm'n v. Pollak, 343 U.S. 451, 467, 72 S. Ct. 813, 823, 96 L. Ed. 1068 (Douglas, J., dissenting). Thus, excessive noise might well be "conduct" — a form of pollution — which can be made subject to precise, narrowly drawn regulations. See Adderley v. Florida, 385 U.S. 39, 54, 87 S. Ct. 242, 250, 17 L. Ed. 2d 149 (Douglas, J., dissenting). But "this Court has repeatedly stated, [First Amendment] rights are not confined to verbal expression. They embrace appropriate types of action. . . ." Brown v. Louisiana, 383 U.S. 131, 141-142, 86 S. Ct. 719, 724, 15 L. Ed. 2d 637.

Baird gave an hour's lecture on birth control and as an aid to understanding the ideas which he was propagating he handed out one sample of one of the devices whose use he was endorsing. A person giving a lecture on coyote-getters would certainly improve his teaching technique if he passed one out to the audience; and he would be protected in doing so unless of course the device was loaded and ready to explode, killing or injuring people. The same holds true in my mind for mousetraps, spray guns, or any other article not dangerous per se on which speakers give educational lectures.

It is irrelevant to the application of these principles that Baird went beyond the giving of information about birth control and advocated the use of contraceptive articles. The First Amendment protects the opportunity to persuade to action whether that action be unwise or immoral, or whether the speech incites to action. See, e.g., Brandenburg v. Ohio, 395 U.S. 444, 89 S. Ct. 1827, 23 L. Ed. 2d 430; Edwards v. South Carolina, 372 U.S. 229, 83 S. Ct. 680, 9 L. Ed. 2d 697; Terminiello v. Chicago, supra.

In this case there was not even incitement to action.[3] There is no evidence or finding that Baird intended that the young lady take the foam

---

1. I have earlier expressed my reasons for believing that the *O'Brien* decision was not consistent with First Amendment rights. See Brandenburg v. Ohio, 395 U.S. 444, 455, 89 S. Ct. 1827, 1833, 23 L. Ed. 2d 430 (concurring opinion).

2. In Giboney v. Empire Storage & Ice Co., 336 U.S. 490, 69 S. Ct. 684, 93 L. Ed. 834, the Court upheld a state court injunction against peaceful picketing carried on in violation of a state "anti-restraint-of-trade" law. *Giboney*, however, is easily distinguished from the present case. Under the circumstances there present, "There was clear danger, imminent and immediate, that unless restrained, appellants would succeed in making [state antitrust] policy a dead letter . . . They were exercising their economic power together with that of their allies to *compel* Empire to abide by union rather than by state regulation of trade." Id., at 503, 69 S. Ct., at 691 (footnote omitted; emphasis supplied). There is no such coercion in the instant case nor is there a similar frustration of state policy, see text at n. 4, infra. For an analysis of the state policies underlying the Massachusetts statute which Baird was convicted of having violated, see Dienes, The Progeny of Comstockery — Birth Control Laws Return to Court, 21 Am. U.L. Rev. 1, 3-44 (1971).

3. Even under the restrictive meaning which the Court has given the First Amendment, as applied to the States by the Fourteenth, advocacy of law violation is permissible "except

home with her when he handed it to her or that she would not have examined the article and then returned it to Baird, had he not been placed under arrest immediately upon handing the article over.[4]

First Amendment rights are not limited to verbal expression.[5] The right to petition often involves the right to walk. The right of assembly may mean pushing or jostling. Picketing involves physical activity as well as a display of a sign. A sit-in can be a quiet, dignified protest that has First Amendment protection even though no speech is involved, as we held in Brown v. Louisiana, supra. Putting contraceptives on display is certainly an aid to speech and discussion. Handing an article under discussion to a member of the audience is a technique known to all teachers and is commonly used. A handout may be on such a scale as to smack of a vendor's marketing scheme. But passing one article to an audience is merely a projection of the visual aid and should be a permissible adjunct of free speech. Baird was not making a prescription nor purporting to give medical advice. Handing out the article was not even a suggestion that the lady use it. At most it suggested that she become familiar with the product line.

I do not see how we can have a Society of the Dialogue, which the First Amendment envisages, if time-honored teaching techniques are barred to those who give educational lectures.

Mr. Justice WHITE, with whom Mr. Justice BLACKMUN joins, concurring in the result.

In Griswold v. Connecticut, 381 U.S. 479, 85 S. Ct. 1678, 14 L. Ed. 2d 510 (1965), we reversed criminal convictions for advising married persons with respect to the use of contraceptives. As there applied, the Connecticut law, which forbade using contraceptives or giving advice on the subject, unduly invaded a zone of marital privacy protected by the Bill of Rights. The Connecticut law did not regulate the manufacture or sale of such products and we expressly left open any question concerning the permissible scope of such legislation. 381 U.S., at 485, 85 S. Ct., at 1682.

Chapter 272, §21, of the Massachusetts General Laws makes it a criminal offense to distribute, sell, or give away any drug, medicine, or article for the prevention of conception. Section 21A excepts from this prohibition registered physicians who prescribe for and administer such articles to

where such advocacy is directed to inciting or producing imminent lawless action and is likely to incite or produce such action." Brandenburg v. Ohio, supra, n.1, 395 U.S., at 447, 89 S. Ct., at 1829.

4. This factor alone would seem to distinguish *O'Brien*, supra as that case turned on the Court's judgment that O'Brien's "conduct" frustrated a substantial governmental interest.

5. For a partial collection of cases involving action that comes under First Amendment protection see Brandenburg v. Ohio, supra, n.1, 395 U.S., at 455-456, 89 S. Ct., at 1833-1834 (concurring opinion).

married persons and registered pharmacists who dispense on medical prescription.[1]

Appellee Baird was indicted for giving away Emko Vaginal Foam, a "medicine and article for the prevention of conception. . . ."[2] The State did not purport to charge or convict Baird for distributing to an unmarried person. No proof was offered as to the marital status of the recipient. The gravamen of the offense charged was that Baird had no license and therefore no authority to distribute to anyone. As the Supreme Judicial Court of Massachusetts noted, the constitutional validity of Baird's conviction rested upon his lack of status as a "distributor and not . . . the marital status of the recipient." Commonwealth v. Baird, 355 Mass. 746, 753, 247 N.E.2d 574, 578 (1969). The Federal District Court was of the same view.[3]

1. Section 21 provides as follows:

> Except as provided in section twenty-one A, whoever sells, lends, gives away, exhibits or offers to sell, lend or give away an instrument or other article intended to be used for self-abuse, or any drug, medicine, instrument or article whatever for the prevention of conception or for causing unlawful abortion, or advertises the same, or writes, prints, or causes to be written or printed a card, circular, book, pamphlet, advertisement or notice of any kind stating when, where, how, of whom or by what means such article can be purchased or obtained, or manufactures or makes any such article shall be punished by imprisonment in the state prison for not more than five years or in jail or the house of correction for not more than two and one half years or by a fine of not less than one hundred nor more than one thousand dollars.

Section 21 A makes these exceptions:

> A registered physician may administer to or prescribe for any married person drugs or articles intended for the prevention of pregnancy or conception. A registered pharmacist actually engaged in the business of pharmacy may furnish such drugs or articles to any married person presenting a prescription from a registered physician.
>
> A public health agency, a registered nurse, or a maternity health clinic operated by or in an accredited hospital may furnish information to any married person as to where professional advice regarding such drugs or articles may be lawfully obtained.
>
> This section shall not be construed as affecting the provisions of sections twenty and twenty-one relative to prohibition of advertising of drugs or articles intended for the prevention of pregnancy or conception; nor shall this section be construed so as to permit the sale or dispensing of such drugs or articles by means of any vending machine or similar device.

2. The indictment states:

> The Jurors for the Commonwealth of Massachusetts on their oath present that William R. Baird, on the sixth day of April, in the year of our Lord one thousand nine hundred and sixty-seven, did unlawfully give away a certain medicine and article for the prevention of conception to wit: Emko Vaginal Foam, the giving away of the said medicine and article by the said William R. Baird not being in accordance with, or authorized or permitted by, the provisions of Section 21A of Chapter 272, of the General Laws of the said Commonwealth.

3. "Had §21A authorized registered physicians to administer or prescribe contraceptives for unmarried as well as for married persons, the legal position of the petitioner would

I assume that a State's interest in the health of its citizens empowers it to restrict to medical channels the distribution of products whose use should be accompanied by medical advice. I also do not doubt that various contraceptive medicines and articles are properly available only on prescription, and I therefore have no difficulty with the Massachusetts court's characterization of the statute at issue here as expressing "a legitimate interest in preventing the distribution of articles designed to prevent conception which may have undesirable, if not dangerous, physical consequences." Id., at 753, 247 N.E.2d, at 578. Had Baird distributed a supply of the so-called "pill," I would sustain his conviction under this statute.[4] Requiring a prescription to obtain potentially dangerous contraceptive material may place a substantial burden upon the right recognized in *Griswold*, but that burden is justified by a strong state interest and does not, as did the statute at issue in *Griswold*, sweep unnecessarily broadly or seek "to achieve its goals by means having a maximum destructive impact upon" a protected relationship. Griswold v. Connecticut, 381 U.S., at 485, 85 S. Ct., at 1682.

Baird, however, was found guilty of giving away vaginal foam. Inquiry into the validity of this conviction does not come to an end merely because some contraceptives are harmful and their distribution may be restricted. Our general reluctance to question a State's judgment on matters of public health must give way where, as here, the restriction at issue burdens the constitutional rights of married persons to use contraceptives. In these circumstances we may not accept on faith the State's classification of a particular contraceptive as dangerous to health. Due regard for protecting constitutional rights requires that the record contain evidence that a restriction on distribution of vaginal foam is essential to achieve the statutory purpose, or the relevant facts concerning the product must be such as to fall within the range of judicial notice.

Neither requirement is met here. Nothing in the record even suggests that the distribution of vaginal foam should be accompanied by medical advice in order to protect the user's health. Nor does the opinion of the Massachusetts court or the State's brief filed here marshal facts demonstrating that the hazards of using vaginal foam are common knowledge or so incontrovertible that they may be noticed judicially. On the contrary, the State acknowledges that Emko is a product widely available without prescription. Given Griswold v. Connecticut, supra, and absent proof of the probable hazards of using vaginal foam, we could not sustain appellee's conviction had it been for selling or giving away foam to a married person. Just as in *Griswold*, where the right of married persons to use

not have been in any way altered. Not being a physician he would still have been prohibited by §21 from 'giving away' the contraceptive." 310 F. Supp. 951, 954 (Mass. 1970).

4. The Food and Drug Administration has made a finding that birth control pills pose possible hazards to health. It therefore restricts distribution and receipt of such products in interstate commerce to properly labeled packages that must be sold pursuant to a prescription. 21 CFR §130.45. A violation of this law is punishable by imprisonment for one year, a fine of not more than $10,000, or both. 21 U.S.C. §§331, 333.

contraceptives was "diluted or adversely affected" by permitting a conviction for giving advice as to its exercise, id., at 481, 85 S. Ct., at 1679, so here, to sanction a medical restriction upon distribution of a contraceptive not proved hazardous to health would impair the exercise of the constitutional right.

That Baird could not be convicted for distributing Emko to a married person disposes of this case. Assuming, arguendo, that the result would be otherwise had the recipient been unmarried, nothing has been placed in the record to indicate her marital status. The State has maintained that marital status is irrelevant because an unlicensed person cannot legally dispense vaginal foam either to married or unmarried persons. This approach is plainly erroneous and requires the reversal of Baird's conviction; for on the facts of this case, it deprives us of knowing whether Baird was in fact convicted for making a constitutionally protected distribution of Emko to a married person.

The principle established in Stromberg v. California, 283 U.S. 359, 51 S. Ct. 532, 75 L. Ed. 1117 (1931), and consistently adhered to is that a conviction cannot stand where the "record fail[s] to prove that the conviction was not founded upon a theory which could not constitutionally support a verdict." Street v. New York, 394 U.S. 576, 586, 89 S. Ct. 1354, 1362, 22 L. Ed. 2d 572 (1969). To uphold a conviction even "though we cannot know that it did not rest on the invalid constitutional ground . . . would be to countenance a procedure which would cause a serious impairment of constitutional rights." Williams v. North Carolina, 317 U.S. 287, 292, 63 S. Ct. 207, 210, 87 L. Ed. 279 (1942).

Because this case can be disposed of on the basis of settled constitutional doctrine, I perceive no reason for reaching the novel constitutional question whether a State may restrict or forbid the distribution of contraceptives to the unmarried. Cf. Ashwander v. Tennessee Valley Authority, 297 U.S. 288, 345-348, 56 S. Ct. 466, 482-483, 80 L. Ed. 688 (1936) (Brandeis, J., concurring).

Mr. Chief Justice BURGER, dissenting.

The judgment of the Supreme Judicial Court of Massachusetts in sustaining appellee's conviction for dispensing medicinal material without a license seems eminently correct to me and I would not disturb it. It is undisputed that appellee is not a physician or pharmacist and was prohibited under Massachusetts law from dispensing contraceptives to anyone, regardless of marital status. To my mind the validity of this restriction on dispensing medicinal substances is the only issue before the Court, and appellee has no standing to challenge that part of the statute restricting the persons to whom contraceptives are available. There is no need to labor this point, however, for everyone seems to agree that if Massachusetts has validly required, as a health measure, that all contraceptives be dispensed by a physician or pursuant to a physician's prescription, then the statutory distinction based on marital status has no bearing on this case. United States v. Raines, 362 U.S. 17, 21, 80 S. Ct. 519, 522, 4 L. Ed. 2d 524 (1960).

The opinion of the Court today brushes aside appellee's status as an unlicensed layman by concluding that the Massachusetts Legislature was not really concerned with the protection of health when it passed this statute. Mr. Justice White acknowledges the statutory concern with the protection of health, but finds the restriction on distributors overly broad because the State has failed to adduce facts showing the health hazards of the particular substance dispensed by appellee as distinguished from other contraceptives. Mr. Justice Douglas' concurring opinion does not directly challenge the power of Massachusetts to prohibit laymen from dispensing contraceptives, but considers that appellee rather than dispensing the substance was resorting to a "time-honored teaching technique" by utilizing a "visual aid" as an adjunct to his protected speech. I am puzzled by this third characterization of the case. If the suggestion is that appellee was merely displaying the contraceptive material without relinquishing his ownership of it, then the argument must be that the prosecution failed to prove that appellee had "given away" the contraceptive material. But appellee does not challenge the sufficiency of the evidence, and himself summarizes the record as showing that "at the close of his lecture he invited members of the audience . . . to come and help themselves." On the other hand, if the concurring opinion means that the First Amendment protects the distribution of all articles "not dangerous per se" when the distribution is coupled with some form of speech, then I must confess that I have misread certain cases in the area. See e.g., United States v. O'Brien, 391 U.S. 367, 376, 88 S. Ct. 1673, 1678, 20 L. Ed. 2d 672 (1968); Cox v. Louisiana, 379 U.S. 536, 555, 85 S. Ct. 453, 464, 13 L. Ed. 2d 471 (1965); Giboney v. Empire Storage & Ice Co., 336 U.S. 490, 502, 69 S. Ct. 684, 690, 93 L. Ed. 834 (1949).

My disagreement with the opinion of the Court and that of Mr. Justice White goes far beyond mere puzzlement, however, for these opinions seriously invade the constitutional prerogatives of the States and regrettably hark back to the heyday of substantive due process.

In affirming appellee's conviction, the highest tribunal in Massachusetts held that the statutory requirement that contraceptives be dispensed only through medical channels served the legitimate interest of the State in protecting the health of its citizens. The Court today blithely hurdles this authoritative state pronouncement and concludes that the statute has no such purpose. Three basic arguments are advanced: First, since the distribution of contraceptives was prohibited as a moral matter in Massachusetts prior to 1966, it is impossible to believe that the legislature was concerned with health when it lifted the complete ban but insisted on medical supervision. I fail to see why the historical predominance of an unacceptable legislative purpose makes incredible the emergence of a new and valid one.[1] See McGowan v. Maryland, 366 U.S. 420, 445-449, 81 S. Ct. 1101,

---

1. The Court places some reliance on the opinion of the Supreme Judicial Court of Massachusetts in Sturgis v. Attorney General, 358 Mass. 37, 260 N.E.2d 687 (1970), to show

1115-1117,6 L. Ed. 2d 393 (1961). The second argument, finding its origin in a dissenting opinion in the Supreme Judicial Court of Massachusetts, rejects a health purpose because, "[i]f there is need to have a physician prescribe . . . contraceptives, that need is as great for unmarried persons as for married persons." 355 Mass. 746, 758, 247 N.E.2d 574, 581. This argument confuses the validity of the restriction on distributors with the validity of the further restriction on distributees, a part of the statute not properly before the Court. Assuming the legislature too broadly restricted the class of persons who could obtain contraceptives, it hardly follows that it saw no need to protect the health of all persons to whom they are made available. Third, the Court sees no health purpose underlying the restriction on distributors because other state and federal laws regulate the distribution of harmful drugs. I know of no rule that all enactments relating to a particular purpose must be neatly consolidated in one package in the statute books for, if so, the United States Code will not pass muster. I am unable to draw any inference as to legislative purpose from the fact that the restriction on dispensing contraceptives was not codified with other statutory provisions regulating the distribution of medicinal substances. And the existence of nonconflicting, nonpreemptive federal laws is simply without significance in judging the validity or purpose of a state law on the same subject matter.

It is possible, of course, that some members of the Massachusetts Legislature desired contraceptives to be dispensed only through medical channels in order to minimize their use, rather than to protect the health of their users, but I do not think it is the proper function of this Court to dismiss as dubious a state court's explication of a state statute absent overwhelming and irrefutable reasons for doing so.

Mr. Justice White, while acknowledging a valid legislative purpose of protecting health, concludes that the State lacks power to regulate the distribution of the contraceptive involved in this case as a means of protecting health.[2] The opinion grants that appellee's conviction would be valid if he had given away a potentially harmful substance, but rejects the State's placing this particular contraceptive in that category. So far as I am aware, this Court has never before challenged the police power of a State to protect the public from the risks of possibly spurious and deleterious substances sold within its borders. Moreover, a statutory-classification is not invalid.

---

that §21A is intended to regulate morals rather than public health. In *Sturgis* the state court rejected a challenge by a group of physicians to that part of the statute prohibiting the distribution of contraceptives to unmarried women. The court accepted the State's interest in "regulating the private sexual lives of single persons," that interest being expressed in the restriction on distributees. Mass., 260 N.E.2d., at 690. The purpose of the restriction on distributors was not in issue.

2. The opinion of the Court states in passing that if the restriction on distributors were in fact intended as a health measure, it would be overly broad. Since the Court does not develop this argument in detail, my response is addressed solely to the reasoning in the opinion of Mr. Justice White, concurring in the result.

"simply because some innocent articles or transactions may be found within the proscribed class. The inquiry must be whether, considerating the end in view, the statute passes the bounds of reason and assumes the character of a merely arbitrary fiat." Purity Extract & Tonic Co. v. Lynch, 226 U.S. 192, 204, 33 S. Ct. 44, 47, 57 L. Ed. 184 (1912).

But since the Massachusetts' statute seeks to protect health by regulating contraceptives, the opinion invokes Griswold v. Connecticut, 381 U.S. 479, 85 S. Ct. 1678, 14 L. Ed. 2d 510 (1965), and puts the statutory classification to an unprecedented test: either the record must contain evidence supporting the classification or the health hazards of the particular contraceptive must be judicially noticeable. This is indeed a novel constitutional doctrine and not surprisingly no authority is cited for it.

Since the potential harmfulness of this particular medicinal substance has never been placed in issue in the state or federal courts, the State can hardly be faulted for its failure to build a record on this point. And it totally mystifies me why, in the absence of some evidence in the record, the factual underpinnings of the statutory classification must be "incontrovertible" or a matter of "common knowledge."

The actual hazards of introducing a particular foreign substance into the human body are frequently controverted, and I cannot believe that unanimity of expert opinion is a prerequisite to a State's exercise of its police power, no matter what the subject matter of the regulation. Even assuming no present dispute among medical authorities, we cannot ignore that it has become commonplace for a drug or food additive to be universally regarded as harmless on one day and to be condemned as perilous on the next. It is inappropriate for this Court to overrule a legislative classification by relying on the present consensus among leading authorities. The commands of the Constitution cannot fluctuate with the shifting tides of scientific opinion.

Even if it were conclusively established once and for all that the product dispensed by appellee is not actually or potentially dangerous in the somatic sense, I would still be unable to agree that the restriction on dispensing it falls outside the State's power to regulate in the area of health. The choice of a means of birth control, although a highly personal matter, is also a health matter in a very real sense, and I see nothing arbitrary in a requirement of medical supervision.[3] It is generally acknowledged that contraceptives vary in degree of effectiveness and potential harmfulness.[4]

3. For general discussions of the need for medical supervision before choosing a means of birth control, see Manual of Family Planning and Contraceptive Practice 47-53 (M. Calderone ed. 1970); Advanced Concepts in Contraception 22-24 (F. Hoffman & R. Kleinman ed. 1968).

4. See U.S. Commission on Population Growth and the American Future, Population and the American Future, pt. II, pp. 38-39 (Mar. 16, 1972); Manual of Family Planning, supra, at 268-274, 316, 320, 342, 346; Jaffe, Toward the Reduction of Unwanted Pregnancy, 174 Science 119, 121 (Oct. 8, 1971); G. Hardin, Birth Control 128 (1970); E. Havemann, Birth Control (1967). The contraceptive substance dispensed by appellee, vaginal foam, is

There may be compelling health reasons for certain women to choose the most effective means of birth control available, no matter how harmless the less effective alternatives.[5] Others might be advised not to use a highly effective means of contraception because of their peculiar susceptibility to an adverse side effect.[6] Moreover, there may be information known to the medical profession that a particular brand of contraceptive is to be preferred or avoided, or that it has not been adequately tested. Nonetheless, the concurring opinion would hold, as a constitutional matter, that a State must allow someone without medical training the same power to distribute this medicinal substance as is enjoyed by a physician.

It is revealing, I think, that those portions of the majority and concurring opinions rejecting the statutory limitation on distributors rely on no particular provision of the Constitution. I see nothing in the Fourteenth Amendment or any other part of the Constitution that even vaguely suggests that these medicinal forms of contraceptives must be available in the open market. I do not challenge Griswold v. Connecticut, supra, despite its tenuous moorings to the text of the Constitution, but I cannot view it as controlling authority for this case. The Court was there confronted with a statute flatly prohibiting the use of contraceptives, not one regulating their distribution. I simply cannot believe that the limitation on the class of lawful distributors has significantly impaired the right to use contraceptives in Massachusetts. By relying on *Griswold* in the present context, the Court has passed beyond the penumbras of the specific guarantees into the uncircumscribed area of personal predilections.

The need for dissemination of information on birth control is not impinged in the slightest by limiting the distribution of medicinal substances to medical and pharmaceutical channels as Massachusetts has done by statute. The appellee has succeeded, it seems, in cloaking his activities in some new permutation of the First Amendment although his conviction rests in fact and law on dispensing a medicinal substance without a license. I am constrained to suggest that if the Constitution can be strained to invalidate the Massachusetts statute underlying appellee's conviction, we could quite as well employ it for the protection of a "curbstone quack," reminiscent of the "medicine man" of times past, who attracted a crowd of the curious with a soapbox lecture and then plied them with "free samples" of some unproved remedy. Massachusetts presumably outlawed such activities long ago, but today's holding seems to invite their return.

---

thought to be between 70% and 80% effective. See Jaffe, supra, at 121; Dingle & Tietze, Comparative Study of Three Contraceptive Methods, 85 Amer. J. Obst. & Gyn. 1012, 1021 (1963). The birth control pill, by contrast, is thought to be better than 99% effective. See Havemann, Birth Control, supra.

5. See Perkin, Assessment of Reproductive Risk in Nonpregnant Women — A Guide to Establishing Priorities for Contraceptive Care, 101 Amer. J. Obst. & Gyn. 709 (1968).

6. See Manual of Family Planning, supra, at 301, 332-333, 336-340.

Brown v. Board of Education

347 U.S. 483 (1954)

No. 1. Appeal from the United States District Court for the District of Kansas.*

Segregation of white and Negro children in the public schools of a State solely on the basis of race, pursuant to state laws permitting or requiring such segregation, denies to Negro children the equal protection of the laws guaranteed by the Fourteenth Amendment — even though the physical facilities and other "tangible" factors of white and Negro schools may be equal.

(a) The history of the Fourteenth Amendment is inconclusive as to its intended effect on public education.

(b) The question presented in these cases must be determined, not on the basis of conditions existing when the Fourteenth Amendment was adopted, but in the light of the full development of public education and its present place in American life throughout the Nation.

(c) Where a State has undertaken to provide an opportunity for an education in its public schools, such an opportunity is a right which must be made available to all on equal terms.

(d) Segregation of children in public schools solely on the basis of race deprives children of the minority group of equal educational opportunities, even though the physical facilities and other "tangible" factors may be equal.

(e) The "separate but equal" doctrine adopted in Plessy v. Ferguson, 163 U.S. 537, has no place in the field of public education.

(f) The cases are restored to the docket for further argument on specified questions relating to the forms of the decrees.

[Attorneys' names omitted.]

Mr. Chief Justice WARREN delivered the opinion of the Court.

These cases come to us from the States of Kansas, South Carolina, Virginia, and Delaware. They are premised on different facts and different local conditions, but a common legal question justifies their consideration together in this consolidated opinion.[1]

---

*Together with No. 2, Briggs et al. v. Elliott et al., on appeal from the United States District Court for the Eastern District of South Carolina, argued December 9-10, 1952, reargued December 7-8, 1953; No. 4, Davis et al. v. County School Board of Prince Edward County, Virginia, et al., on appeal from the United States District Court for the Eastern District of Virginia, argued December 10, 1952, reargued December 7-8, 1953; and No. 10, Gebhart et al. v. Belton et al., on certiorari to the Supreme Court of Delaware, argued December 11, 1952, reargued December 9, 1953.

1. In the Kansas case, Brown v. Board of Education, the plaintiffs are Negro children of elementary school age residing in Topeka. They brought this action in the United States District Court for the District of Kansas to enjoin enforcement of a Kansas statute which

In each of the cases, minors of the Negro race, through their legal representatives, seek the aid of the courts in obtaining admission to the public schools of their community on a nonsegregated basis. In each

permits, but does not require, cities of more than 15,000 population to maintain separate school facilities for Negro and white students. Kan. Gen. Stat. §72-1724 (1949). Pursuant to that authority, the Topeka Board of Education elected to establish segregated elementary schools. Other public schools in the community, however, are operated on a nonsegregated basis. The three-judge District Court, convened under 28 U.S.C. §§2281 and 2284, found that segregation in public education has a detrimental effect upon Negro children, but denied relief on the ground that the Negro and white schools were substantially equal with respect to buildings, transportation, curricula, and educational qualifications of teachers. 98 F. Supp. 797. The case is here on direct appeal under 28 U.S.C. §1253.

In the South Carolina case, Briggs v. Elliott, the plaintiffs are Negro children of both elementary and high school age residing in Clarendon County. They brought this action in the United States District Court for the Eastern District of South Carolina to enjoin enforcement of provisions in the state constitution and statutory code which require the segregation of Negroes and whites in public schools. S.C. Const., Art. XI, §7; S.C. Code §5377 (1942). The three-judge District Court, convened under 28 U.S.C. §§2281 and 2284, denied the requested relief. The court found that the Negro schools were inferior to the white schools and ordered the defendants to begin immediately to equalize the facilities. But the court sustained the validity of the contested provisions and denied the plaintiffs admission to the white schools during the equalization program. 98 F. Supp. 529. This Court vacated the District Court's judgment and remanded the case for the purpose of obtaining the court's views on a report filed by the defendants concerning the progress made in the equalization program. 342 U.S. 350. On remand, the District Court found that substantial equality had been achieved except for buildings and that the defendants were proceeding to rectify this inequality as well. 103 F. Supp. 920. The case is again here on direct appeal under 28 U.S.C. §1253.

In the Virginia case, Davis v. County School Board, the plaintiffs are Negro children of high school age residing in Prince Edward County. They brought this action in the United States District Court for the Eastern District of Virginia to enjoin enforcement of provisions in the state constitution and statutory code which require the segregation of Negroes and whites in public schools. Va. Const., §140; Va. Code §22-221 (1950). The three-judge District Court, convened under 28 U.S.C. §§2281 and 2284, denied the requested relief. The court found the Negro school inferior in physical plant, curricula, and transportation, and ordered the defendants forthwith to provide substantially equal curricula and transportation and to "proceed with all reasonable diligence and dispatch to remove" the inequality in physical plant. But, as in the South Carolina case, the court sustained the validity of the contested provisions and denied the plaintiffs admission to the white schools during the equalization program. 103 F. Supp. 337. The case is here on direct appeal under 28 U.S.C. §1253.

In the Delaware case, Gebhart v. Belton, the plaintiffs are Negro children of both elementary and high school age residing in New Castle County. They brought this action in the Delaware Court of Chancery to enjoin enforcement of provisions in the state constitution and statutory code which require the segregation of Negroes and whites in public schools. Del. Const., Art. X, §2; Del. Rev. Code §2631 (1935). The Chancellor gave judgment for the plaintiffs and ordered their immediate admission to schools previously attended only by white children, on the ground that the Negro schools were inferior with respect to teacher training, pupil-teacher ratio, extracurricular activities, physical plant, and time and distance involved in travel. 87 A.2d 862. The Chancellor also found that segregation itself results in an inferior education for Negro children (see note 10, infra) but did not rest his decision on that ground. Id., at 865. The Chancellor's decree was affirmed by the Supreme Court of Delaware, which intimated, however, that the defendants might be able to obtain a modification of the decree after equalization of the Negro and white schools had been accomplished. 91 A.2d 137,152. The defendants, contending only that the Delaware courts had erred in ordering the immediate admission of the Negro plaintiffs to the white schools, applied to this Court for certiorari. The writ was granted, 344 U.S. 891. The plaintiffs, who were successful below, did not submit a cross-petition.

instance, they had been denied admission to schools attended by white children under laws requiring or permitting segregation according to race. This segregation was alleged to deprive the plaintiffs of the equal protection of the laws under the Fourteenth Amendment. In each of the cases other than the Delaware case, a three-judge federal district court denied relief to the plaintiffs on the so-called "separate but equal" doctrine announced by this Court in Plessy v. Ferguson, 163 U.S. 537. Under that doctrine, equality of treatment is accorded when the races are provided substantially equal facilities, even though these facilities be separate. In the Delaware case, the Supreme Court of Delaware adhered to that doctrine, but ordered that the plaintiffs be admitted to the white schools because of their superiority to the Negro schools.

The plaintiffs contend that segregated public schools are not "equal" and cannot be made "equal," and that hence they are deprived of the equal protection of the laws. Because of the obvious importance of the question presented, the Court took jurisdiction.[2] Argument was heard in the 1952 Term, and reargument was heard this Term on certain questions propounded by the Court.[3]

Reargument was largely devoted to the circumstances surrounding the adoption of the Fourteenth Amendment in 1868. It covered exhaustively consideration of the Amendment in Congress, ratification by the states, then existing practices in racial segregation, and the views of proponents and opponents of the Amendment. This discussion and our own investigation convince us that, although these sources cast some light, it is not enough to resolve the problem with which we are faced. At best, they are inconclusive. The most avid proponents of the post-War Amendments undoubtedly intended them to remove all legal distinctions among "all persons born or naturalized in the United States." Their opponents, just as certainly, were antagonistic to both the letter and the spirit of the Amendments and wished them to have the most limited effect. What others in Congress and the state legislatures had in mind cannot be determined with any degree of certainty.

An additional reason for the inconclusive nature of the Amendment's history, with respect to segregated schools, is the status of public education at that time.[4] In the South, the movement toward free common

2. 344 U.S. 1, 141, 891.

3. 345 U.S. 972. The Attorney General of the United States participated both Terms as amicus curiae.

4. For a general study of the development of public education prior to the Amendment, see Butts and Cremin, A History of Education in American Culture (1953), Pts. I, II; Cubberley, Public Education in the United States (1934 ed.), cc. II-XII. School practices current at the time of the adoption of the Fourteenth Amendment are described in Butts and Cremin, supra, at 269-275; Cubberley, supra, at 288-339, 408-431; Knight, Public Education in the South (1922), cc. VIII, IX. See also H. Ex. Doc. No. 315, 41st Cong., 2d Sess. (1871). Although the demand for free public schools followed substantially the same pattern in both the North and the South, the development in the South did not begin to gain momentum until about 1850, some twenty years after that in the North. The reasons for the somewhat slower development in the South (e.g., the rural character of

schools, supported by general taxation, had not yet taken hold. Education of white children was largely in the hands of private groups. Education of Negroes was almost non-existent, and practically all of the race were illiterate. In fact, any education of Negroes was forbidden by law in some states. Today, in contrast, many Negroes have achieved outstanding success in the arts and sciences as well as in the business and professional world. It is true that public school education at the time of the Amendment had advanced further in the North, but the effect of the Amendment on Northern States was generally ignored in the congressional debates. Even in the North, the conditions of public education did not approximate those existing today. The curriculum was usually rudimentary; ungraded schools were common in rural areas; the school term was but three months a year in many states; and compulsory school attendance was virtually unknown. As a consequence, it is not surprising that there should be so little in the history of the Fourteenth Amendment relating to its intended effect on public education.

In the first cases in this Court construing the Fourteenth Amendment, decided shortly after its adoption, the Court interpreted it as proscribing all state-imposed discriminations against the Negro race.[5] The doctrine of "separate-but-equal" did not make its appearance in this Court until 1896 in the case of Plessy v. Ferguson, supra, involving not education but transportation.[6] American courts have since labored with the doctrine for over

the South and the different regional attitudes toward state assistance) are well explained in Cubberley, supra, at 408-423. In the country as a whole, but particularly in the South, the War virtually stopped all progress in public education. Id., at 427-428. The low status of Negro education in all sections of the country, both before and immediately after the War, is described in Beale, A History of Freedom of Teaching in American Schools (1941), 112-132, 175-195. Compulsory school attendance laws were not generally adopted until after the ratification of the Fourteenth Amendment, and it was not until 1918 that such laws were in force in all the states. Cubberley, supra, at 563-565.

5. Slaughter-House Cases, 16 Wall. 36, 67-72 (1873); Strauder v. West Virginia, 100 U.S. 303, 307-308 (1880):

> It ordains that no State shall deprive any person of life, liberty, or property, without due process of law, or deny to any person within its jurisdiction the equal protection of the laws. What is this but declaring that the law in the States shall be the same for the black as for the white; that all persons, whether colored or white, shall stand equal before the laws of the States, and, in regard to the colored race, for whose protection the amendment was primarily designed, that no discrimination shall be made against them by law because of their color? The words of the amendment, it is true, are prohibitory, but they contain a necessary implication of a positive immunity, or right, most valuable to the colored race, — the right to exemption from unfriendly legislation against them distinctively as colored, — exemption from legal discriminations, implying inferiority in civil society, lessening the security of their enjoyment of the rights which others enjoy, and discriminations which are steps towards reducing them to the condition of a subject race.

See also Virginia v. Rives, 100 U.S. 313, 318 (1880); Ex parte Virginia, 100 U.S. 339, 344-345 (1880).

6. The doctrine apparently originated in Roberts v. City of Boston, 59 Mass. 198, 206 (1850), upholding school segregation against attack as being violative of a state constitutional

half a century. In this Court, there have been six cases involving the "separate but equal" doctrine in the field of public education.[7] In Cumming v. County Board of Education, 175 U.S. 528, and Gong Lum v. Rice, 275 U.S. 78, the validity of the doctrine itself was not challenged.[8] In more recent cases, all on the graduate school level, inequality was found in that specific benefits enjoyed by white students were denied to Negro students of the same educational qualifications. Missouri ex rel. Gaines v. Canada, 305 U.S. 337; Sipuel v. Oklahoma, 332 U.S. 631; Sweatt v. Painter, 339 U.S. 629; McLaurin v. Oklahoma State Regents, 339 U.S. 637. In none of these cases was it necessary to re-examine the doctrine to grant relief to the Negro plaintiff. And in Sweatt v. Painter, supra, the Court expressly reserved decision on the question whether Plessy v. Ferguson should be held inapplicable to public education.

In the instant cases, that question is directly presented. Here, unlike Sweatt v. Painter, there are findings below that the Negro and white schools involved have been equalized, or are being equalized, with respect to buildings, curricula, qualifications and salaries of teachers, and other "tangible" factors.[9] Our decision, therefore, cannot turn on merely a comparison of these tangible factors in the Negro and white schools involved in each of the cases. We must look instead to the effect of segregation itself on public education.

In approaching this problem, we cannot turn the clock back to 1868 when the Amendment was adopted, or even to 1896 when Plessy v. Ferguson was written. We must consider public education in the light of its full development and its present place in American life throughout the Nation. Only in this way can it be determined if segregation in public schools deprives these plaintiffs of the equal protection of the laws.

Today, education is perhaps the most important function of state and local governments. Compulsory school attendance laws and the great expenditures for education both demonstrate our recognition of the

---

guarantee of equality. Segregation in Boston public schools was eliminated in 1855. Mass. Acts 1855, c.256. But elsewhere in the North segregation in public education has persisted in some communities until recent years. It is apparent that such segregation has long been a nationwide problem, not merely one of sectional concern.

7. See also Berea College v. Kentucky, 211 U.S. 45 (1908).

8. In the *Cumming* case, Negro taxpayers sought an injunction requiring the defendant school board to discontinue the operation of a high school for white children until the board resumed operation of a high school for Negro children. Similarly, in the *Gong Lum* case, the plaintiff, a child of Chinese descent, contended only that state authorities had misapplied the doctrine by classifying him with Negro children and requiring him to attend a Negro school.

9. In the Kansas case, the court below found substantial equality as to all such factors. 98 F. Supp. 797,798. In the South Carolina case, the court below found that the defendants were proceeding "promptly and in good faith to comply with the court's decree." 103 F. Supp. 920, 921. In the Virginia case, the court below noted that the equalization program was already "afoot and progressing" (103 F. Supp. 337, 341); since then, we have been advised, in the Virginia Attorney General's brief on reargument, that the program has now been completed. In the Delaware case, the court below similarly noted that the state's equalization program was well under way. 91 A.2d 137, 149.

importance of education to our democratic society. It is required in the performance of our most basic public responsibilities, even service in the armed forces. It is the very foundation of good citizenship. Today it is a principal instrument in awakening the child to cultural values, in preparing him for later professional training, and in helping him to adjust normally to his environment. In these days, it is doubtful that any child may reasonably be expected to succeed in life if he is denied the opportunity of an education. Such an opportunity, where the state has undertaken to provide it, is a right which must be made available to all on equal terms.

We come then to the question presented: Does segregation of children in public schools solely on the basis of race, even though the physical facilities and other "tangible" factors may be equal, deprive the children of the minority group of equal educational opportunities? We believe that it does.

In Sweatt v. Painter, supra, in finding that a segregated law school for Negroes could not provide them equal educational opportunities, this Court relied in large part on "those qualities which are incapable of objective measurement but which make for greatness in a law school." In McLaurin v. Oklahoma State Regents, supra, the Court, in requiring that a Negro admitted to a white graduate school be treated like all other students, again resorted to intangible considerations: " . . . his ability to study, to engage in discussions and exchange views with other students, and, in general, to learn his profession." Such considerations apply with added force to children in grade and high schools. To separate them from others of similar age and qualifications solely because of their race generates a feeling of inferiority as to their status in the community that may affect their hearts and minds in a way unlikely ever to be undone. The effect of this separation on their educational opportunities was well stated by a finding in the Kansas case by a court which nevertheless felt compelled to rule against the Negro plaintiffs:

> Segregation of white and colored children in public schools has a detrimental effect upon the colored children. The impact is greater when it has the sanction of the law; for the policy of separating the races is usually interpreted, as denoting the inferiority of the negro group. A sense of inferiority affects the motivation of a child to learn. Segregation with the sanction of law, therefore, has a tendency to [retard] the educational and mental development of negro children and to deprive them of some of the benefits they would receive in a racial[ly] integrated school system.[10]

Whatever may have been the extent of psychological knowledge at the time of Plessy v. Ferguson, this finding is amply supported by modern

10. A similar finding was made in the Delaware case: "I conclude from the testimony that in our Delaware society, State-imposed segregation in education itself results in the Negro children, as a class, receiving educational opportunities which are substantially inferior to those available to white children otherwise similarly situated." 87 A.2d 862, 865.

authority.[11] Any language in Plessy v. Ferguson contrary to this finding is rejected.

We conclude that in the field of public education the doctrine of "separate but equal" has no place. Separate educational facilities are inherently unequal. Therefore, we hold that the plaintiffs and others similarly situated for whom the actions have been brought are, by reason of the segregation complained of, deprived of the equal protection of the laws guaranteed by the Fourteenth Amendment. This disposition makes unnecessary any discussion whether such segregation also violates the Due Process Clause of the Fourteenth Amendment.[12]

Because these are class actions, because of the wide applicability of this decision, and because of the great variety of local conditions, the formulation of decrees in these cases presents problems of considerable complexity. On reargument, the consideration of appropriate relief was necessarily subordinated to the primary question—the constitutionality of segregation in public education. We have now announced that such segregation is a denial of the equal protection of the laws. In order that we may have the full assistance of the parties in formulating decrees, the cases will be restored to the docket, and the parties are requested to present further argument on Questions 4 and 5 previously propounded by the Court for the reargument this Term.[13] The Attorney General of the United States is again invited to participate. The Attorneys General of the states requiring or permitting segregation in public education will also be permitted to

11. K.B. Clark, Effect of Prejudice and Discrimination on Personality Development (Midcentury White House Conference on Children and Youth, 1950); Witmer and Kotinsky, Personality in the Making (1952), c. VI; Deutscher and Chein, The Psychological Effects of Enforced Segregation: A Survey of Social Science Opinion, 26 J. Psychol. 259 (1948); Chein, What Are the Psychological Effects of Segregation Under Conditions of Equal Facilities?, 3 Int. J. Opinion and Attitude Res. 229 (1949); Brameld, Educational Costs, in Discrimination and National Welfare (MacIver, ed., 1949), 44-48; Frazier, The Negro in the United States (1949), 674-681. And see generally Myrdal, An American Dilemma (1944).

12. See Bolling v. Sharpe concerning the Due Process Clause of the Fifth Amendment.

13. "4. Assuming it is decided that segregation in public schools violates the Fourteenth Amendment

"(a) would a decree necessarily follow providing that, within the limits set by normal geographic school districting, Negro children should forthwith be admitted to schools of their choice, or

"(b) may this Court, in the exercise of its equity powers, permit an effective gradual adjustment to be brought about from existing segregated systems to a system not based on color distinctions?

"5. On the assumption on which questions 4 (a) and (b) are based, and assuming further that this Court will exercise its equity powers to the end described in question 4 (b),

"(a) should this Court formulate detailed decrees in these cases;

"(b) if so, what specific issues should the decrees reach;

"(c) should this Court appoint a special master to hear evidence with a view to recommending specific terms for such decrees;

"(d) should this Court remand to the courts of first instance with directions to frame decrees in these cases, and if so what general directions should the decrees of this Court include and what procedures should the courts of first instance follow in arriving at the specific terms of more detailed decrees?"

appear as amici curiae upon request to do so by September 15, 1954, and submission of briefs by October 1, 1954.[14]

It is so ordered.

Roe v. Wade

410 U.S. 113 (1973)

Action was brought for a declaratory and injunctive relief respecting Texas criminal abortion laws which were claimed to be unconstitutional. A three-judge United States District Court for the Northern District of Texas, 314 F. Supp. 1217, entered judgment declaring laws unconstitutional and an appeal was taken. The Supreme Court, Mr. Justice Blackmun, held that the Texas criminal abortion statutes prohibiting abortions at any stage of pregnancy except to save the life of the mother are unconstitutional; that prior to approximately the end of the first trimester the abortion decision and its effectuation must be left to the medical judgment of the pregnant woman's attending physician, subsequent to approximately the end of the first trimester the state may regulate abortion procedure in ways reasonably related to maternal health, and at the stage subsequent to viability the state may regulate and even proscribe abortion except where necessary in appropriate medical judgment for preservation of life or health of mother.

Affirmed in part and reversed in part.

Mr. Chief Justice BURGER, Mr. Justice DOUGLAS and Mr. Justice STEWART filed concurring opinions.

Mr. Justice WHITE filed a dissenting opinion in which Mr Justice REHNQUIST joined.

Mr. Justice REHNQUIST filed a dissenting opinion.

1. Courts [Key Number 385(7)]

Supreme Court was not foreclosed from review of both the injunctive and declaratory aspects of case attacking constitutionality of Texas criminal abortion statutes where case was properly before Supreme Court on direct appeal from decision of three-judge district court specifically denying injunctive relief and the arguments as to both aspects were necessarily identical. 28 U.S.C.A. §1253.

2. Constitutional Law [Key Numbers 42.1(3), 46(1)]

With respect to single, pregnant female who alleged that she was unable to obtain a legal abortion in Texas, when viewed as of the time of filing of case and for several months thereafter, she had standing to challenge constitutionality of Texas criminal abortion laws, even though record did not disclose that she was pregnant at time of district court hearing or when the opinion and judgment were filed, and she presented a justiciable

14. See Rule 42, Revised Rules of this Court (effective July 1, 1954).

controversy; the termination of her pregnancy did not render case moot. Vernon's Ann. Tex P.C. arts. 1191-1194, 1196.

3. Courts [Key Numbers 383(1), 385(1)]

Usual rule in federal cases is that an actual controversy must exist at stages of appellate or certiorari review and not simply at date action is initiated.

4. Action [Key Number 6]

Where pregnancy of plaintiff was a significant fact in litigation and the normal human gestation period was so short that pregnancy would come to term before usual appellate process was complete, and pregnancy often came more than once to the same woman, fact of that pregnancy provided a classic justification for conclusion of nonmootness because of termination.

5. Federal Civil Procedure [Key Number 331]

Texas physician, against whom there were pending indictments charging him with violations of Texas abortion laws who made no allegation of any substantial and immediate threat to any federally protected right that could not be asserted in his defense against state prosecutions and who had not alleged any harassment or bad faith prosecution, did not have standing to intervene in suit seeking declaratory and injunctive relief with respect to Texas abortion statutes which were claimed to be unconstitutional. Vernon's Ann. Tex. P.C. arts. 1191-1194, 1196.

6. Courts [Key Number 508(7)]

Absent harassment and bad faith, defendant in pending state criminal case cannot affirmatively challenge in federal court the statutes under which state is prosecuting him.

7. Federal Civil Procedure [Key Number 321]

Application for leave to intervene making certain assertions relating to a class of people was insufficient to establish party's desire to intervene on behalf of class, where the complaint failed to set forth the essentials of class suit.

8. Constitutional Law [Key Number 42.1(3)]

Childless married couple alleging that they had no desire to have children at the particular time because of medical advice that the wife should avoid pregnancy and for other highly personal reasons and asserting an inability to obtain a legal abortion in Texas were not, because of the highly speculative character of their position, appropriate plaintiffs in federal district court suit challenging validity of Texas criminal abortion statutes. Vernon's Ann. Tex. P.C. arts. 1191-1194, 1196.

9. Constitutional Law [Key Number 82]

Right of personal privacy or a guarantee of certain areas or zones of privacy does exist under Constitution, and only personal rights that can be deemed fundamental or implicit in the concept of ordered liberty are included in this guarantee of personal privacy; the right has some extension to activities relating to marriage. U.S.C.A. Const. Amends. 1, 4, 5, 9, 14, 14, §1.

10. Constitutional Law [Key Number 82]

Constitutional right of privacy is broad enough to encompass woman's decision whether or not to terminate her pregnancy, but the woman's right to terminate pregnancy is not absolute since state may properly assert important interests in safeguarding health, in maintaining medical standards and in protecting potential life, and at some point in pregnancy these respective interests become sufficiently compelling to sustain regulation of factors that govern the abortion decision. U.S.C.A. Const. Amends. 9, 14.

11. Constitutional Law [Key Number 82]

Where certain fundamental rights are involved, regulation limiting these rights may be justified only by a compelling state interest and the legislative enactments must be narrowly drawn to express only legitimate state interests at stake.

12. Constitutional Law [Key Numbers 210, 252]

Word "person" as used in the Fourteenth Amendment does not include the unborn. U.S.C.A Const. Amend. 14.

13. Abortion [Key Number 1]

Prior to approximately the end of the first trimester of pregnancy the attending physician in consultation with his patient is free to determine, without regulation by state, that in his medical judgment the patient's pregnancy should be terminated, and if that decision is reached such judgment may be effectuated by an abortion without interference by the state.

14. Abortion [Key Number 1]

From and after approximately the end of the first trimester of pregnancy a state may regulate abortion procedure to extent that the regulation reasonably relates to preservation and protection of maternal health.

15. Abortion [Key Number 1]

If state is interested in protecting fetal life after viability it may go so far as to proscribe abortion during that period except when necessary to preserve the life or the health of the mother.

16. Abortion [Key Number 1] Constitutional Law
[Key Number 258(3)]

State criminal abortion laws like Texas statutes making it a crime to procure or attempt an abortion except an abortion on medical advice for purpose of saving life of the mother regardless of stage of pregnancy violate due process clause of Fourteenth Amendment protecting right to privacy against state action. U.S.C.A. Const. Amend. 14; Vernon's Ann. Tex. P.C. arts. 1191-1194, 1196.

17. Abortion [Key Number 1]

State in regulating abortion procedures may define "physician" as a physician currently licensed by State and may proscribe any abortion by a person who is not a physician as so defined.

18. Statutes [Key Number 64(6)]

Conclusion that Texas criminal abortion statute proscribing all abortions except to save life of mother is unconstitutional meant that the abortion statutes as a unit must fall, and the exception could not be struck down separately for then the state would be left with statute proscribing all abortion procedures no matter how medically urgent the case. Vernon's Ann. Tex. P.C. arts. 1191-1194, 1196.

Syllabus*

A pregnant single woman (Roe) brought a class action challenging the constitutionality of the Texas criminal abortion laws, which proscribe procuring or attempting an abortion except on medical advice for the purpose of saving the mother's life. A licensed physician (Hallford), who had two state abortion prosecutions pending against him, was permitted to intervene. A childless married couple (the Does), the wife not being pregnant, separately attacked the laws, basing alleged injury on the future possibilities of contraceptive failure, pregnancy, unpreparedness for parenthood, and impairment of the wife's health. A three-judge District Court, which consolidated the actions, held that Roe and Hallford, and members of their classes, had standing to sue and presented justiciable controversies. Ruling that declaratory, though not injunctive, relief was warranted, the court declared the abortion statutes void as vague and overbroadly infringing those plaintiffs' Ninth and Fourteenth Amendment rights. The court ruled the Does' complaint not justiciable.

---

*The syllabus constitutes no part of the opinion of the Court but has been prepared by the Reporter of Decisions for the convenience of the reader. See United States v. Detroit Timber & Lumber Co., 200 U.S. 321, 337, 26 S. Ct. 282, 287, 50 L. Ed. 499.

Appellants directly appealed to this Court on the injunctive rulings, and appellee cross-appealed from the District Court's grant of declaratory relief to Roe and Hallford. *Held:*

1. While 28 U.S.C. §1253 authorizes no direct appeal to this Court from the grant or denial of declaratory relief alone, review is not foreclosed when the case is properly before the Court on appeal from specific denial of injunctive relief and the arguments as to both injunctive and declaratory relief are necessarily identical.

2. Roe has standing to sue: the Does and Hallford do not.

(a) Contrary to appellee's contention, the natural termination of Roe's pregnancy did not moot her suit. Litigation involving pregnancy, which is "capable of repetition, yet evading review," is an exception to the usual federal rule that an actual controversy must exist at review stages and not simply when the action is initiated.

(b) The District Court correctly refused injunctive, but erred in granting declaratory, relief to Hallford, who alleged no federally protected right not assertable as a defense against the good-faith state prosecutions pending against him. Samuels v. Mackell, 401 U.S. 66, 91 S. Ct. 764, 27 L. Ed. 2d 688.

(c) The Does' complaint, based as it is on contingencies, any one or more of which may not occur, is too speculative to present an actual case or controversy.

3. State criminal abortion laws, like those involved here, that except from criminality only a life-saving procedure on the mother's behalf without regard to the stage of her pregnancy and other interests involved violate the Due Process Clause of the Fourteenth Amendment, which protects against state action the right to privacy, including a woman's qualified right to terminate her pregnancy. Though the State cannot override that right, it has legitimate interests in protecting both the pregnant woman's health and the potentiality of human life, each of which interests grows and reaches a "compelling" point at various stages of the woman's approach to term.

(a) For the stage prior to approximately the end of the first trimester, the abortion decision and its effectuation must be left to the medical judgment of the pregnant woman's attending physician.

(b) For the stage subsequent to approximately the end of the first trimester, the State, in promoting its interest in the health of the mother, may, if it chooses, regulate the abortion procedure in ways that are reasonably related to maternal health.

(c) For the stage subsequent to viability the State, in promoting its interest in the potentiality of human life, may, if it chooses, regulate, and even proscribe, abortion except where necessary, in appropriate medical judgment, for the preservation of the life or health of the mother.

4. The State may define the term "physician" to mean only a physician currently licensed by the State, and may proscribe any abortion by a person who is not a physician as so defined.

5. It is unnecessary to decide the injunctive relief issue since the Texas authorities will doubtless fully recognize the Court's ruling that the Texas criminal abortion statutes are unconstitutional.

314 F. Supp. 1217, affirmed in part and reversed in part.

Sarah R. Weddington, Austin, Tex., for appellants.

Robert C. Flowers, Asst. Atty. Gen. of Texas, Austin, Tex., for appellee on reargument.

Jay Floyd, Asst. Atty. Gen., Austin, Tex., for appellee on original argument.

Mr. Justice BLACKMUN delivered the opinion of the Court.

This Texas federal appeal and its Georgia companion, Doe v. Bolton, 410 U.S. 179, 93 S. Ct. 739, 35 L. Ed. 2d 201, present constitutional challenges to state criminal abortion legislation. The Texas statutes under attack here are typical of those that have been in effect in many States for approximately a century. The Georgia statutes, in contrast, have a modern cast and are a legislative product that, to an extent at least, obviously reflects the influences of recent attitudinal change, of advancing medical knowledge and techniques, and of new thinking about an old issue.

We forthwith acknowledge our awareness of the sensitive and emotional nature of the abortion controversy, of the vigorous opposing views, even among physicians, and of the deep and seemingly absolute convictions that the subject inspires. One's philosophy, one's experiences, one's exposure to the raw edges of human existence, one's religious training, one's attitudes toward life and family and their values, and the moral standards one establishes and seeks to observe, are all likely to influence and to color one's thinking and conclusions about abortion.

In addition, population growth, pollution, poverty, and racial overtones tend to complicate and not to simplify the problem.

Our task, of course, is to resolve the issue by constitutional measurement, free of emotion and of predilection. We seek earnestly to do this, and, because we do, we have inquired into, and in this opinion place some emphasis upon, medical and medical-legal history and what that history reveals about man's attitudes toward the abortion procedure over the centuries. We bear in mind, too, Mr. Justice Holmes' admonition in his now-vindicated dissent in Lochner v. New York, 198 U.S. 45, 76, 25 S. Ct. 539, 547, 49 L. Ed. 937 (1905):

> [The Constitution] is made for people of fundamentally differing views, and the accident of our finding certain opinions natural and familiar, or novel, and even shocking, ought not to conclude our judgment upon the question whether statutes embodying them conflict with the Constitution of the United States.

I

The Texas statutes that concern us here are Arts. 1191-1194 and 1196 of the State's Penal Code,[1] Vernon's Ann. P.C. These make it a crime to "procure an abortion," as therein defined, or to attempt one, except with respect to "an abortion procured or attempted by medical advice for the purpose of saving the life of the mother." Similar statutes are in existence in a majority of the States.[2]

Texas first enacted a criminal abortion statute in 1854. Texas Laws 1854, c. 49, §1, set forth in 3 H. Gammel, Laws of Texas 1502 (1898). This was

1. "Article 1191. Abortion
"If any person shall designedly administer to a pregnant woman or knowingly procure to be administered with her consent any drug or medicine, or shall use towards her any violence or means whatever externally or internally applied, and thereby procure an abortion, he shall be confined in the penitentiary not less than two nor more than five years; if it be done without her consent, the punishment shall be doubled. By 'abortion' is meant that the life of the fetus or embryo shall be destroyed in the woman's womb or that a premature birth thereof be caused.
"Art. 1192. Furnishing the means
"Whoever furnishes the means for procuring an abortion knowing the purpose intended is guilty as an accomplice.
"Art. 1193. Attempt at abortion
"If the means used shall fail to produce an abortion, the offender is nevertheless guilty of an attempt to produce abortion, provided it be shown that such means were calculated to produce that result, and shall be fined not less than one hundred nor more than one thousand dollars.
"Art. 1194. Murder in producing abortion
"If the death of the mother is occasioned by an abortion so produced or by an attempt to effect the same it is murder."
"Art. 1196. By medical advice
"Nothing in this chapter applies to an abortion procured or attempted by medical advice for the purpose of saving the life of the mother."
The foregoing Articles, together with Art. 1195, compose Chapter 9 of Title 15 of the Penal Code. Article 1195, not attacked here, reads:
"Art. 1195. Destroying unborn child
"Whoever shall during parturition of the mother destroy the vitality or life in a child in a state of being born and before actual birth, which child would otherwise have been born alive, shall be confined in the penitentiary for life or for not less than five years."
2. Ariz. Rev. Stat. Ann. §13-211 (1956): Conn. Pub. Act No. 1 (May 1972 special session) (in 4 Conn. Leg. Serv. 677 (1972)), and Conn. Gen. Stat. Rev. §§53-29, 53-30 (1968) (or unborn child); Idaho Code §18-601 (1948); 111. Rev. Stat. c.38, §23-1 (1971); Ind. Code §35-1-58-1 (1971); Iowa Code §701.1 (1971); Ky. Rev. Stat. §436.020 (1962); La. Rev. Stat. §37:1285(6) (1964) (loss of medical license) (but see §14-87 (Supp. 1972) containing no exception for the life of the mother under the criminal statute); Me. Rev. Stat. Ann., Tit. 17, §51 (1964); Mass. Gen. Laws Ann., c.272, §19 (1970) (using the term "unlawfully," construed to exclude an abortion to save the mother's life, Kudish v. Bd. of Registration, 356 Mass. 98, 248 N.E.2d 264 (1969)); Mich. Comp. Laws §750.14 (1948); Minn. Stat. §617.18 (1971); Mo. Rev. Stat. §559.100 (1969); Mont. Rev. Codes Ann. §94-401 (1969); Neb. Rev. Stat. §28-405 (1964); Nev. Rev. Stat. §200.220 (1967); N.H. Rev. Stat. Ann. §585:13 (1955); N.J. Stat. Ann. §2A.87-1 (1969) ("without lawful justification"): N.D. Cent. Code §§12-25-01, 12-25-02 (1960); Ohio Rev. Code Ann. §2901.16 (1953); Okla. Stat. Ann., Tit. 21, §861 (1972-1973 Supp.); Pa. Stat. Ann., Tit. 18, §§4718, 4719 (1963) ("unlawful"); R.I. Gen. Laws Ann. §11-3-1 (1969); S.D. Comp. Laws Ann. §22-17-1 (1967); Tenn. Code Ann. §§39-301, 39-302 (1956); Utah Code Ann. §§76-2-1, 76-2-2 (1953); Vt. Stat. Ann., Tit. 13, §101 (1958); W. Va. Code Ann. §61-2-8 (1966); Wis. Stat. §940.04 (1969); Wyo. Stat. Ann. §§6-77, 6-78 (1957).

soon modified into language that has remained substantially unchanged to the present time. See Texas Penal Code of 1857, c.7, Arts. 531-536; G. Paschal, Laws of Texas, Arts. 2192-2197 (1866); Texas Rev. Stat., c.8, Arts. 536-541 (1879); Texas Rev. Crim. Stat., Arts. 1071-1076 (1911). The final article in each of these compilations provided the same exception, as does the present Article 1196, for an abortion by "medical advice for the purpose of saving the life of the mother."[3]

II

Jane Roe,[4] a single woman who was residing in Dallas County, Texas, instituted this federal action in March 1970 against the District Attorney of the county. She sought a declaratory judgment that the Texas criminal abortion statutes were unconstitutional on their face, and an injunction restraining the defendant from enforcing the statutes.

Roe alleged that she was unmarried and pregnant; that she wished to terminate her pregnancy by an abortion "performed by a competent, licensed physician, under safe, clinical conditions"; that she was unable to get a "legal" abortion in Texas because her life did not appear to be threatened by the continuation of her pregnancy; and that she could not afford to travel to another jurisdiction in order to secure a legal abortion under safe conditions. She claimed that the Texas statutes were unconstitutionally vague and that they abridged her right of personal privacy, protected by the First, Fourth, Fifth, Ninth, and Fourteenth Amendments. By an amendment to her complaint Roe purported to sue "on behalf of herself and all other women" similarly situated.

James Hubert Hallford, a licensed physician, sought and was granted leave to intervene in Roe's action. In his complaint he alleged that he had

3. Long ago, a suggestion was made that the Texas statutes were unconstitutionally vague because of definitional deficiencies. The Texas Court of Criminal Appeals disposed of that suggestion peremptorily, saying only, "It is also insisted in the motion in arrest of judgment that the statute is unconstitutional and void, in that it does not sufficiently define or describe the offense of abortion. We do not concur with counsel in respect to this question." Jackson v. State, 55 Tex. Cr. R. 79, 89, 115 S.W. 262, 268 (1908).

The same court recently has held again that the State's abortion statutes are not unconstitutionally vague or overbroad. Thompson v. State, 493 S.W.2d 913 (1971), appeal docketed, No. 71-1200. The court held that "the State of Texas has a compelling interest to protect fetal life"; that Art. 1191 "is designed to protect fetal life"; that the Texas homicide statutes, particularly Art. 1205 of the Penal Code, are intended to protect a person "in existence by actual birth" and thereby implicitly recognize other human life that is not "in existence by actual birth"; that the definition of human life is for the legislature and not the courts; that Art. 1196 "is more definite than the District of Columbia statute upheld in [United States v.] Vuitch" (402 U.S. 62, 91 S. Ct. 1294, 28 L. Ed. 2d 601); and that the Texas statute "is not vague and indefinite or overbroad." A physician's abortion conviction was affirmed.

In 493 S.W 2d, at 920 n.2, the court observed that any issue as to the burden of proof under the exemption of Art. 1196 "is not before us." But see Veevers v. State, 172 Tex. Cr. R. 162, 168-169, 354 S.W.2d 161, 166-167 (1962). Cf. United States v. Vuitch, 402 U.S. 62, 69-71, 91 S. Ct. 1294, 1298-1299, 28 L. Ed. 2d 601 (1971).

4. The name is a pseudonym.

been arrested previously for violations of the Texas abortion statutes and that two such prosecutions were pending against him. He described conditions of patients who came to him seeking abortions, and he claimed that for many cases he, as a physician, was unable to determine whether they fell within or outside the exception recognized by Article 1196. He alleged that, as a consequence, the statutes were vague and uncertain, in violation of the Fourteenth Amendment, and that they violated his own and his patients' rights to privacy in the doctor-patient relationship and his own right to practice medicine, rights he claimed were guaranteed by the First, Fourth, Fifth, Ninth, and Fourteenth Amendments.

John and Mary Doe,[5] a married couple, filed a companion complaint to that of Roe. They also named the District Attorney as defendant, claimed like constitutional deprivations, and sought declaratory and injunctive relief. The Does alleged that they were a childless couple; that Mrs. Doe was suffering from a "neural-chemical" disorder; that her physician had "advised her to avoid pregnancy until such time as her condition has materially improved" (although a pregnancy at the present time would not present "a serious risk" to her life); that, pursuant to medical advice, she had discontinued use of birth control pills; and that if she should become pregnant, she would want to terminate the pregnancy by an abortion performed by a competent, licensed physician under safe, clinical conditions. By an amendment to their complaint, the Does purported to sue "on behalf of themselves and all couples similarly situated."

The two actions were consolidated and heard together by a duly convened three-judge district court. The suits thus presented the situations of the pregnant single woman, the childless couple, with the wife not pregnant, and the licensed practicing physician, all joining in the attack on the Texas criminal abortion statutes. Upon the filing of affidavits, motions were made for dismissal and for summary judgment. The court held that Roe and members of her class, and Dr. Hallford, had standing to sue and presented justiciable controversies, but that the Does had failed to allege facts sufficient to state a present controversy and did not have standing. It concluded that, with respect to the requests for a declaratory judgment, abstention was not warranted. On the merits, the District Court held that the "fundamental right of single women and married persons to choose whether to have children is protected by the Ninth Amendment, through the Fourteenth Amendment," and that the Texas criminal abortion statutes were void on their face because they were both unconstitutionally vague and constituted an overbroad infringement of the plaintiffs' Ninth Amendment rights. The court then held that abstention was warranted with respect to the requests for an injunction. It therefore dismissed the Does' complaint, declared the abortion statutes void, and dismissed the application for injunctive relief. 314 F. Supp. 1217, 1225 (N.D. Tex. 1970).

---

5. These names are pseudonyms.

The plaintiffs Roe and Doe and the intervenor Hallford, pursuant to 28 U.S.C. §1253, have appealed to this Court from that part of the District Court's judgment denying the injunction. The defendant District Attorney has purported to cross-appeal, pursuant to the same statute, from the court's grant of declaratory relief to Roe and Hallford. Both sides also have taken protective appeals to the United States Court of Appeals for the Fifth Circuit. That court ordered the appeals held in abeyance pending decision here. We postponed decision on jurisdiction to the hearing on the merits. 402 U.S. 941, 91 S. Ct. 1610, 29 L. Ed. 2d 108 (1971).

III

[1] It might have been preferable if the defendant, pursuant to our Rule 20, had presented to us a petition for certiorari before judgment in the Court of Appeals with respect to the granting of the plaintiffs' prayer for declaratory relief. Our decisions in Mitchell v. Donovan, 398 U.S. 427, 90 S. Ct. 1763, 26 L. Ed. 2d 378 (1970), and Gunn v. University Committee, 399 U.S. 383, 90 S. Ct. 2013, 26 L. Ed. 2d 684 (1970), are to the effect that §1253 does not authorize an appeal to this Court from the grant or denial of declaratory relief alone. We conclude, nevertheless, that those decisions do not foreclose our review of both the injunctive and the declaratory aspects of a case of this kind when it is properly here, as this one is, on appeal under §1253 from specific denial of injunctive relief, and the arguments as to both aspects are necessarily identical. See Carter v. Jury Commn., 396 U.S. 320, 90 S. Ct. 518, 24 L. Ed. 2d 549 (1970); Florida Lime and Avocado Growers, Inc. v. Jacobsen, 362 U.S. 73; 80–81, 80 S. Ct. 568, 573–574, 4 L. Ed. 2d 568 (1960). It would be destructive of time and energy for all concerned were we to rule otherwise. Cf. Doe v. Bolton, 410 U.S. 179, 93 S. Ct. 739, 35 L. Ed. 2d 201.

IV

We are next confronted with issues of justiciability, standing, and abstention. Have Roe and the Does established that "personal stake in the outcome of the controversy," Baker v. Carr, 369 U.S. 186, 204, 32 S. Ct. 691, 703, 7 L. Ed. 2d 663 (1962), that insures that "the dispute sought to be adjudicated will be presented in an adversary context and in a form historically viewed as capable of judicial resolution," Flast v. Cohen, 392 U.S. 83, 101, 88 S. Ct. 1942, 1953, 20 L. Ed. 2d 947 (1968), and Sierra Club v. Morton, 405 U.S. 727, 732, 92 S. Ct. 1361, 1364, 31 L. Ed. 2d 636 (1972)? And what effect did the pendency of criminal abortion charges against Dr. Hallford in state court have upon the propriety of the federal court's granting relief to him as a plaintiff-intervenor?

[2] A. *Jane Roe*. Despite the use of the pseudonym, no suggestion is made that Roe is a fictitious person. For purposes of her case, we accept as true, and as established, her existence; her pregnant state, as of the inception of

her suit in March 1970 and as late as May 21 of that year when she filed an alias affidavit with the District Court; and her inability to obtain a legal abortion in Texas.

Viewing Roe's case as of the time of its filing and thereafter until as late as May, there can be little dispute that it then presented a case or controversy and that, wholly apart from the class aspects, she, as a pregnant single woman thwarted by the Texas criminal abortion laws, had standing to challenge those statutes. Abele v. Markle, 452 F.2d 1121, 1125 (CA2 1971); Crossen v. Breckenridge, 446 F.2d 833, 838-839 (CA6 1971); Poe v. Menghini, 339 F. Supp. 986, 990-991 (D.C. Kan. 1972). See Truax v. Raich, 239 U.S. 33, 36 S. Ct. 7, 60 L. Ed. 131 (1915). Indeed, we do not read the appellee's brief as really asserting anything to the contrary. The "logical nexus between the status asserted and the claim sought to be adjudicated," Flast v. Cohen, 392 U.S., at 102, 88 S. Ct., at 1953, and the necessary degree of contentiousness, Golden v. Zwickler, 394 U.S. 103, 89 S. Ct. 956, 22 L. Ed. 2d 113 (1969), are both present.

The appellee notes, however, that the record does not disclose that Roe was pregnant at the time of the District Court hearing on May 22, 1970,[6] or on the following June 17 when the court's opinion and judgment were filed. And he suggests that Roe's case must now be moot because she and all other members of her class are no longer subject to any 1970 pregnancy.

[3] The usual rule in federal cases is that an actual controversy must exist at stages of appellate or certiorari review, and, not simply at the date the action is initiated. United States v. Munsingwear, Inc., 340 U.S. 36, 71 S. Ct. 104, 95 L. Ed. 36 (1950); Golden v. Zwickler, supra; SEC v. Medical Committee for Human Rights, 404 U.S. 403, 92 S. Ct. 577, 30 L. Ed. 2d 560 (1972).

[4] But when, as here, pregnancy is a significant fact in the litigation, the normal 266-day human gestation period is so short that the pregnancy will come to term before the usual appellate process is complete. If that termination makes a case moot, pregnancy litigation seldom will survive much beyond the trial stage, and appellate review will be effectively denied. Our law should not be that rigid. Pregnancy often comes more than once to the same woman, and in the general population, if man is to survive, it will always be with us. Pregnancy provides a classic justification for a conclusion of nonmootness. It truly could be "capable of repetition, yet evading review." Southern Pacific Terminal Co. v. ICC, 219 U.S. 498, 515, 31 S. Ct. 279, 283, 55 L. Ed. 310 (1911). See Moore v. Ogilvie, 394 U.S. 814, 816, 89 S. Ct. 1493, 1494, 23 L. Ed. 2d 1 (1969); Carroll v. President and Commissioners of Princess Anne, 393 U.S. 175,

---

6. The appellee twice states in his brief that the hearing before the District Court was held on July 22,1970. Brief for Appellee 13. The docket entries, App. 2, and the transcript, App. 76, reveal this to be an error. The July date appears to be the time of the reporter's transcription. See App 77.

178-179, 89 S. Ct. 347, 350, 351, 21 L. Ed. 2d 325 (1968); United States v. W.T. Grant Co., 345 U.S. 629, 632-633, 73 S. Ct. 894, 897-898, 97 L. Ed. 1303 (1953).

We, therefore, agree with the District Court that Jane Roe had standing to undertake this litigation, that she presented a justiciable controversy, and that the termination of her 1970 pregnancy has not rendered her case moot.

[5] B. *Dr. Hallford.* The doctor's position is different. He entered Roe's litigation as a plaintiff-intervenor, alleging in his complaint that he:

> [I]n the past has been arrested for violating the Texas Abortion Laws and at the present time stands charged by indictment with violating said laws in the Criminal District Court of Dallas County, Texas to-wit: (1) The State of Texas vs. James H. Hallford, No. C-69-5307-IH, and (2) The State of Texas vs. James H. Hallford, No. C-69-2524-H. In both cases the defendant is charged with abortion. . . .

In his application for leave to intervene, the doctor made like representations as to the abortion charges pending in the state court. These representations were also repeated in the affidavit he executed and filed in support of his motion for summary judgment.

[6] Dr. Hallford is, therefore, in the position of seeking, in a federal court, declaratory and injunctive relief with respect to the same statutes under which he stands charged in criminal prosecutions simultaneously pending in state court. Although he stated that he has been arrested in the past for violating the State's abortion laws, he makes no allegation of any substantial and immediate threat to any federally protected right that cannot be asserted in his defense against the state prosecutions. Neither is there any allegation of harassment or bad-faith prosecution. In order to escape the rule articulated in the cases cited in the next paragraph of this opinion that, absent harassment and bad faith, a defendant in a pending state criminal case cannot affirmatively challenge in federal court the statutes under which the State is prosecuting him, Dr. Hallford seeks to distinguish his status as a present state defendant from his status as a "potential future defendant" and to assert only the latter for standing purposes here.

We see no merit in that distinction. Our decision in Samuels v. Mackell, 401 U.S. 66, 91 S. Ct. 764, 27 L. Ed. 2d 688 (1971), compels the conclusion that the District Court erred when it granted declaratory relief to Dr. Hallford instead of refraining from so doing. The court, of course, was correct in refusing to grant injunctive relief to the doctor. The reasons supportive of that action, however, are those expressed in Samuels v. Mackell, supra, and in Younger v. Harris, 401 U.S. 37, 91 S. Ct. 746, 27 L. Ed. 2d 669 (1971); Boyle v. Landry, 401 U.S. 77, 91 S. Ct. 758, 27 L. Ed. 2d 696 (1971); Perez v. Ledesma, 401 U.S. 82, 91 S. Ct. 674, 27 L. Ed. 2d 701 (1971); and Byrne v. Karalexis, 401 U.S. 216, 91 S. Ct. 777, 27 L. Ed. 2d 792 (1971). See also Dombrowski v. Pfister, 380 U.S. 479, 85 S. Ct. 1116, 14 L. Ed.

2d 22 (1965). We note, in passing, that *Younger* and its companion cases were decided after the three-judge District Court decision in this case.

[7] Dr. Hallford's complaint in intervention, therefore, is to be dismissed.[7] He is remitted to his defenses in the state criminal proceedings against him. We reverse the judgment of the District Court insofar as it granted Dr. Hallford relief and failed to dismiss his complaint in intervention.

[8] C. *The Does.* In view of our ruling as to Roe's standing in her case, the issue of the Does' standing in their case has little significance. The claims they assert are essentially the same as those of Roe, and they attack the same statutes. Nevertheless, we briefly note the Does' posture.

Their pleadings present them as a childless married couple, the woman not being pregnant, who have no desire to have children at this time because of their having received medical advice that Mrs. Doe should avoid pregnancy, and for "other highly personal reasons." But they "fear . . . they may face the prospect of becoming parents." And if pregnancy ensues, they "would want to terminate" it by an abortion. They assert an inability to obtain an abortion legally in Texas and, consequently, the prospect of obtaining an illegal abortion there or of going outside Texas to some place where the procedure could be obtained legally and competently.

We thus have as plaintiffs a married couple who have, as their asserted immediate and present injury, only an alleged "detrimental effect upon [their] marital happiness" because they are forced to "the choice of refraining from normal sexual relations or of endangering Mary Doe's health through a possible pregnancy." Their claim is that sometime in the future Mrs. Doe might become pregnant because of possible failure of contraceptive measures, and at that time in the future she might want an abortion that might then be illegal under the Texas statutes.

This very phrasing of the Does' position reveals its speculative character. Their alleged injury rests on possible future contraceptive failure, possible future pregnancy, possible future unpreparedness for parenthood, and possible future impairment of health. Any one or more of these several possibilities may not take place and all may not combine. In the Does' estimation, these possibilities might have some real or imagined impact upon their marital happiness. But we are not prepared to say that the bare allegation of so indirect an injury is sufficient to present an actual case or controversy. Younger v. Harris, 401 U.S., at 41–42, 91 S. Ct., at 749; Golden v.

---

7. We need not consider what different result, if any, would follow if Dr. Hallford's intervention were on behalf of a class. His complaint in intervention does not purport to assert a class suit and makes no reference to any class apart from an allegation that he "and others similarly situated" must necessarily guess at the meaning of Art. 1196. His application for leave to intervene goes somewhat further, for it asserts that plaintiff Roe does not adequately protect the interest of the doctor "and the class of people who are physicians . . . [and] the class of people who are . . . patients. . . ." The leave application, however, is not the complaint. Despite the District Court's statement to the contrary, 314 F. Supp., at 1225, we fail to perceive the essentials of a class suit in the Hallford complaint.

Zwickler, 394 U.S., at 109-110, 89 S. Ct., at 960; Abele v. Markle, 452 F.2d, at 1124-1125; Crossen v. Breckenridge, 446 F.2d, at 839. The Does' claim falls far short of those resolved otherwise in the cases that the Does urge upon us, namely, Investment Co. Institute v. Camp, 401 U.S. 617, 91 S. Ct. 1091, 28 L. Ed. 2d 367 (1971); Association of Data Processing Service Organizations, Inc. v. Camp, 397 U.S. 150, 90 S. Ct. 827, 25 L. Ed. 2d 184 (1970); and Epperson v. Arkansas, 393 U.S. 97, 89 S. Ct. 266, 21 L. Ed. 2d 228 (1968). See also Truax v. Raich, 239 U.S. 33, 36 S. Ct. 7, 60 L. Ed. 131 (1915).

The Does therefore are not appropriate plaintiffs in this litigation. Their complaint was properly dismissed by the District Court, and we affirm that dismissal.

V

The principal thrust of appellant's attack on the Texas statutes is that they improperly invade a right, said to be possessed by the pregnant woman, to choose to terminate her pregnancy. Appellant would discover this right in the concept of personal "liberty" embodied in the Fourteenth Amendment's Due Process Clause; or in personal, marital, familial, and sexual privacy said to be protected by the Bill of Rights or its penumbras, see Griswold v. Connecticut, 381 U.S. 479, 85 S. Ct. 1678, 14 L. Ed. 2d 510 (1965); Eisenstadt v. Baird, 405 U.S. 438 (1972); id., at 460, 92 S. Ct. 1029, at 1042, 31 L. Ed. 2d 349 (White, J., concurring in result); or among those rights reserved to the people by the Ninth Amendment, Griswold v. Connecticut, 381 U.S., at 486, 85 S. Ct., at 1682 (Goldberg, J., concurring). Before addressing this claim, we feel it desirable briefly to survey, in several aspects, the history of abortion, for such insight as that history may afford us, and then to examine the state purposes and interests behind the criminal abortion laws.

VI

It perhaps is not generally appreciated that the restrictive criminal abortion laws in effect in a majority of States today are of relatively recent vintage. Those laws, generally proscribing abortion or its attempt at any time during pregnancy except when necessary to preserve the pregnant woman's life, are not of ancient or even of common-law origin. Instead, they derive from statutory changes effected, for the most part, in the latter half of the 19th century.

1. *Ancient attitudes.* These are not capable of precise determination. We are told that at the time of the Persian Empire abortifacients were known and that criminal abortions were severely punished.[8] We are also told, however, that abortion was practiced in Greek times as well as in the Roman

---

8. A. Castiglioni, A History of Medicine 84 (2d ed. 1947), E. Krumbhaar, translator and editor (hereinafter Castiglioni).

Era,[9] and that "it was resorted to without scruple."[10] The Ephesian, Soranos, often described as the greatest of the ancient gynecologists, appears to have been generally opposed to Rome's prevailing free-abortion practices. He found it necessary to think first of the life of the mother, and he resorted to abortion when, upon this standard, he felt the procedure advisable.[11] Greek and Roman law afforded little protection to the unborn. If abortion was prosecuted in some places, it seems to have been based on a concept of a violation of the father's right to his offspring. Ancient religion did not bar abortion.[12]

2. *The Hippocratic Oath.* What then of the famous Oath that has stood so long as the ethical guide of the medical profession and that bears the name of the great Greek (460(?)-377(?) B.C.), who has been described as the Father of Medicine, the "wisest and the greatest practitioner of his art," and the "most important and most complete medical personality of antiquity," who dominated the medical schools of his time, and who typified the sum of the medical knowledge of the past?[13] The Oath varies somewhat according to the particular translation, but in any translation the content is clear: "I will give no deadly medicine to anyone if asked, nor suggest any such counsel; and in like manner I will not give to a woman a pessary to produce abortion,"[14] or "I will neither give a deadly drug to anybody if asked for it, nor will I make a suggestion to this effect. Similarly, I will not give to a woman an abortive remedy."[15]

Although the Oath is not mentioned in any of the principal briefs in this case or in Doe v. Bolton, 410 U.S. 179, 93 S. Ct. 739, 35 L. Ed. 2d 201, it represents the apex of the development of strict ethical concepts in medicine, and its influence endures to this day. Why did not the authority of Hippocrates dissuade abortion practice in his time and that of Rome? The late Dr. Edelstein provides us with a theory:[16] The Oath was not uncontested even in Hippocrates' day; only the Pythagorean school of philosophers frowned upon the related act of suicide. Most Greek thinkers, on the other hand, commended abortion, at least prior to viability. See Plato, Republic, V, 461; Aristotle, Politics, VII, 1335b 25. For the Pythagoreans, however, it was a matter of dogma. For them the embryo was animate from

9. J. Ricci, The Genealogy of Gynaecology 52, 84, 113, 149 (2d ed. 1950) (hereinafter Ricci); L. Lader, Abortion 75-77 (1966) (hereinafter Lader); K. Niswander, Medical Abortion Practices in the United States, in Abortion and the Law 37, 38-40 (D. Smith ed. 1967); G. Williams, The Sanctity of Life and the Criminal Law 148 (1957) (hereinafter Williams); J. Noonan, An Almost Absolute Value in History, in The Morality of Abortion 1, 3-7 (J. Noonan ed. 1970) (hereinafter Noonan); Quay, Justifiable Abortion — Medical and Legal Foundations, (pt. 2), 49 Geo. L. J. 395, 406-422 (1961) (hereinafter Quay).

10. L. Edelstein, The Hippocratic Oath 10 (1943) (hereinafter Edelstein). But see Castiglioni 227.

11. Edelstein 12; Ricci 113-114, 118-119; Noonan 5.

12. Edelstein 13-14.

13. Castiglioni 148.

14. Id., at 154.

15. Edelstein 3.

16. Id., at 12, 15-18.

the moment of conception, and abortion meant destruction of a living being. The abortion clause of the Oath, therefore, "echoes Pythagorean doctrines," and "[i]n no other stratum of Greek opinion were such views held or proposed in the same spirit of uncompromising austerity."[17]

Dr. Edelstein then concludes that the Oath originated in a group representing only a small segment of Greek opinion and that it certainly was not accepted by all ancient physicians. He points out that medical writings down to Galen (A.D. 130-200) "give evidence of the violation of almost every one of its injunctions."[18] But with the end of antiquity a decided change took place. Resistance against suicide and against abortion became common. The Oath came to be popular. The emerging teachings of Christianity were in agreement with the Pythagorean ethic. The Oath "became the nucleus of all medical ethics" and "was applauded as the embodiment of truth." Thus, suggests Dr. Edelstein, it is "a Pythagorean manifesto and not the expression of an absolute standard of medical conduct."[19]

This, it seems to us, is a satisfactory and acceptable explanation of the Hippocratic Oath's apparent rigidity. It enables us to understand, in historical context, a long-accepted and revered statement of medical ethics.

3. *The common law.* It is undisputed that at common law, abortion performed *before* "quickening" — the first recognizable movement of the fetus in *utero*, appearing usually from the 16th to the 18th week of pregnancy[20] — was not an indictable offense.[21] The absence of a common-law crime for pre-quickening abortion appears to have developed from a confluence of earlier philosophical, theological, and civil and canon law concepts of when life begins. These disciplines variously approached the question in terms of the point at which the embryo or fetus became "formed" or recognizably human, or in terms of when a "person" came into being, that is, infused with a "soul" or "animated." A loose concensus evolved in early English law that these events occurred at some point between conception and live birth.[22] This was "mediate animation."

17. Id., at 18; Lader 76.
18. Edelstein 63.
19. Id., at 64.
20. Dorland's Illustrated Medical Dictionary 1261 (24th ed. 1965).
21. E. Coke, Institutes III *50; 1 W. Hawkins, Pleas of the Crown, c.31, §16 (4th ed. 1762); 1 W. Blackstone, Commentaries *129-130; M. Hale, Pleas of the Crown 433 (1st Amer. ed. 1847). For discussions of the role of the quickening concept in English common law, see Lader 78; Noonan 223-226; Means, The Law of New York Concerning Abortion and the Status of the Foetus, 1664-1968: A Case of Cessation of Constitutionality (pt. 1), 14 N.Y.L.F. 411, 418-428 (1968) (hereinafter Means I); Stern, Abortion: Reform and the Law, 59 J. Crim. L.C. & P.S. 84 (1968) (hereinafter Stern); Quay 430-432; Williams 152.
22. Early philosophers believed that the embryo or fetus did not become formed and begin to live until at least 40 days after conception for a male, and 80 to 90 days for a female. See, for example, Aristotle, Hist. Anim. 7.3.5.83b; Gen. Anim. 2.3.736, 2.5.741; Hippocrates, Lib. de Nat. Puer., No 10. Aristotle's thinking derived from his three-stage theory of life: vegetable, animal, rational. The vegetable stage was reached at conception, the animal at "animation," and the rational soon after live birth. This theory, together with the 40/80 day view, came to be accepted by early Christian thinkers.

Although Christian theology and the canon law came to fix the point of animation at 40 days for a male and 80 days for a female, a view that persisted until the 19th century, there was otherwise little agreement about the precise time of formation or animation. There was agreement, however, that prior to this point the fetus was to be regarded as part of the mother, and its destruction, therefore, was not homicide. Due to continued uncertainty about the precise time when animation occurred, to the lack of any empirical basis for the 40-80-day view, and perhaps to Aquinas' definition of movement as one of the two first principles of life, Bracton focused upon quickening as the critical point. The significance of quickening was echoed by later common-law scholars and found its way into the received common law in this country.

Whether abortion of a *quick* fetus was a felony at common law, or even a lesser crime, is still disputed. Bracton, writing early in the 13th century, thought it homicide.[23] But the later and predominant view, following the great common-law scholars, has been that it was, at most, a lesser offense. In a frequently cited passage, Coke took the position that abortion of a woman "quick with childe" is "a great misprision, and no murder."[24] Blackstone followed, saying that while abortion after quickening had once been considered manslaughter (though not murder), "modern law" took a less severe view.[25] A recent review of the common-law precedents argues, however, that those precedents contradict Coke and that even post-quickening abor-tion was never established as a common-law crime.[26] This is of some importance because while most American courts

The theological debate was reflected in the writings of St. Augustine, who made a distinction between *embryo inanimatus*, not yet endowed with a soul, and *embryo animatus*. He may have drawn upon Exodus 21:22. At one point, however, he expressed the view that human powers cannot determine the point during fetal development at which the critical change occurs. See Augustine, De Origine Animae 4.4 (Pub. Law 44.527). See also W. Reany, The Creation of the Human Soul, c.2 and 83-86 (1932); Huser, The Crime of Abortion in Canon Law 15 (Catholic Univ. of America, Canon Law Studies No. 162, Washington, D.C., 1942).

Galen, in three treaties related to embryology, accepted the thinking of Aristotle and his followers. Quay 426-427. Later, Augustine on abortion was incorporated by Gratian into the Decretum, published about 1140. Decretum Magistri Gratiani 2.32.2.7 to 2.32.2.10, in 1 Corpus Juris Canonici 1122,1123 (A. Friedberg, 2d ed. 1879). This Decretal and the Decretals that followed were recognized as the definitive body of canon law until the new Code of 1917.

For discussions of the canon-law treatment, see Means I, pp. 411-412; Noonan 20-26; Quay 426-430; see also J. Noonan, Contraception: A History of Its Treatment by the Catholic Theologians and Canonists 18-20 (1965).

23. Bracton took the position that abortion by blow or poison was homicide "if the foetus be already formed and animated, and particularly if it be animated," 2 H. Bracton, De Legibus et Consuetudinibus Angliae 279 (T. Twiss ed. 1879), or, as a later translation puts it, "if the foetus is already formed or quickened, especially if it is quickened," 2 H. Bracton, On the Laws and Customs of England 341 (S. Thorne ed. 1968). See Quay 431; see also 2 Fleta 60-61 (Book 1, c.23) (Selden Society ed. 1955).

24. E. Coke, Institutes III *50.

25. 1 W. Blackstone, Commentaries *129-130.

26. Means, The Phoenix of Abortional Freedom: Is a Penumbral or Ninth-Amendment Right About to Arise from the Nineteenth-Century Legislative Ashes of a Fourteenth-Century

ruled, in holding or dictum, that abortion of an unquickened fetus was not criminal under their received common law,[27] others followed Coke in stating that abortion of a quick fetus was a "misprision," a term they translated to mean "misdemeanor."[28] That their reliance on Coke on this aspect of the law was uncritical and, apparently in all the reported cases, dictum (due probably to the paucity of common-law prosecutions for post-quickening abortion), makes it now appear doubtful that abortion was ever firmly established as a common-law crime even with respect to the destruction of a quick fetus.

4. *The English statutory law.* England's first criminal abortion statute, Lord Ellenborough's Act, 43 Geo. 3, c.58, came in 1803. It made abortion of a quick fetus, §1, a capital crime, but in §2 it provided lesser penalties for the felony of abortion before quickening, and thus preserved the "quickening" distinction. This contrast was continued in the general revision of 1828, 9 Geo. 4, c.31, §13. It disappeared, however, together with the death penalty, in 1837, 7 Will. 4 & 1 Vict., c.85, §6, and did not reappear in the Offenses Against the Person Act of 1861, 24 and 25 Vict., c.100, §59, that formed the core of English anti-abortion law until the liberalizing reforms of 1967. In 1929, the Infant Life (Preservation) Act, 19 & 20 Geo. 5, c.34, came into being. Its emphasis was upon the destruction of "the life of a child capable of being born alive." It made a willful act performed with the necessary intent a felony. It contained a proviso that one was not to be found guilty of the offense "unless it is proved that the act which caused the death of the child was not done in good faith for the purpose only of preserving the life of the mother."

A seemingly notable development in the English law was the case of Rex v. Bourne, [1939] 1 K.B. 687. This case apparently answered in

Common-Law Liberty?, 17 N.Y.L.F. 335 (1971) (hereinafter Means II). The author examines the two principal precedents cited marginally by Coke, both contrary to his dictum, and traces the treatment of these and other cases by earlier commentators. He concludes that Coke, who himself participated as an advocate in an abortion case in 1601, may have intentionally misstated the law. The author even suggests a reason: Coke's strong feelings against abortion, coupled with his determination to assert common-law (secular) jurisdiction to assess penalties for an offense that traditionally had been an exclusively ecclesiastical or canon-law crime. See also Lader 78-79, who notes that some scholars doubt that the common law ever was applied to abortion; that the English ecclesiastical courts seem to have lost interest in the problem after 1527; and that the preamble to the English legislation of 1803, 43 Geo. 3, c.58, §1, referred to in the text, infra, states that "no adequate means have been hitherto provided for the prevention and punishment of such offenses."

27. Commonwealth v. Bangs, 9 Mass. 387, 388 (1812); Commonwealth v. Parker, 50 Mass. (9 Metc.) 263, 265-266 (1845); State v. Cooper, 22 N.J.L. 52, 58 (1849); Abrams v. Foshee, 3 Iowa 274, 278-280 (1856); Smith v. Gaffard, 31 Ala. 45, 51 (1857); Mitchell v. Commonwealth, 78 Ky. 204, 210 (1879); Eggart v. State, 40 Fla. 527, 532, 25 So. 144, 145 (1898); State v. Alcorn, 7 Idaho 599, 606, 64 P. 1014, 1016 (1901); Edwards v. State, 79 Neb. 251, 252, 112 N.W. 611, 612 (1907); Gray v. State, 77 Tex. Cr. R. 221, 224, 178 S.W. 337, 338 (1915); Miller v. Bennett, 190 Va. 162, 169, 56 S.E.2d 217, 221 (1949). Contra, Mills v. Commonwealth, 13 Pa. 631, 633 (1850); State v. Slagle, 83 N.C. 630, 632 (1880).

28. See Smith v. State, 33 Me. 48, 55 (1851); Evans v. People, 49 N.Y. 86, 88 (1872); Lamb v. State, 67 Md. 524, 533, 10 A. 208 (1887).

the affirmative the question whether an abortion necessary to preserve the life of the pregnant woman was excepted from the criminal penalties of the 1861 Act. In his instructions to the jury, Judge Macnaghten referred to the 1929 Act, and observed that that Act related to "the case where a child is killed by a willful act at the time when it is being delivered in the ordinary course of nature." Id., at 691. He concluded that the 1861 Act's use of the word "unlawfully," imported the same meaning expressed by the specific proviso in the 1929 Act, even though there was no mention of preserving the mother's life in the 1861 Act. He then construed the phrase "preserving the life of the mother" broadly, that is, "in a reasonable sense," to include a serious and permanent threat to the mother's *health*, and instructed the jury to acquit Dr. Bourne if it found he had acted in a good-faith belief that the abortion was necessary for this purpose. Id., at 693-694. The jury did acquit.

Recently, Parliament enacted a new abortion law. This is the Abortion Act of 1967, 15 & 16 Eliz. 2, c.87. The Act permits a licensed physician to perform an abortion where two other licensed physicians agree (a) "that the continuance of the pregnancy would involve risk to the life of the pregnant woman, or of injury to the physical or mental health of the pregnant woman or any existing children of her family, greater than if the pregnancy were terminated," or (b) "that there is a substantial risk that if the child were born it would suffer from such physical or mental abnormalities as to be seriously handicapped." The Act also provides that, in making this determination, "account may be taken of the pregnant woman's actual or reasonably foreseeable environment." It also permits a physician, without the concurrence of others, to terminate a pregnancy where he is of the good-faith opinion that the abortion "is immediately necessary to save the life or to prevent grave permanent injury to the physical or mental health of the pregnant woman."

5. *The American law.* In this country, the law in effect in all but a few States until mid-19th century was the pre-existing English common law. Connecticut, the first State to enact abortion legislation, adopted in 1821 that part of Lord Ellenborough's Act that related to a woman "quick with child."[29] The death penalty was not imposed. Abortion before quickening was made a crime in that State only in 1860.[30] In 1828, New York enacted legislation[31] that, in two respects, was to serve as a model for early anti-abortion statutes. First, while barring destruction of an unquickened fetus as well as a quick fetus, it made the former only a misdemeanor, but the latter second-degree manslaughter. Second, it incorporated a concept of therapeutic abortion by providing that an abortion was excused if it "shall have been necessary to preserve the life of such mother, or shall have been advised by two physicians to be necessary for such purpose."

29. Conn. Stat., tit. 20, §14 (1821).
30. Conn. Pub. Acts, c.71, §1 (1860).
31. N.Y. Rev. Stat., pt. 4, c.1 or tit. 2, art. 1, §9, p. 661, and tit. 6, §21, p. 694 (1829).

By 1840, when Texas had received the common law,[32] only eight American States had statutes dealing with abortion.[33] It was not until after the War Between the States that legislation began generally to replace the common law. Most of these initial statutes dealt severely with abortion after quickening but were lenient with it before quickening. Most punished attempts equally with completed abortions. While many statutes included the exception for an abortion thought by one or more physicians to be necessary to save the mother's life, that provision soon disappeared and the typical law required that the procedure actually be necessary for that purpose.

Gradually, in the middle and late 19th century the quickening distinction disappeared from the statutory law of most States and the degree of the offense and the penalties were increased. By the end of the 1950's a large majority of the jurisdictions banned abortion, however and whenever performed, unless done to save or preserve the life of the mother.[34] The exceptions, Alabama and the District of Columbia, permitted abortion to preserve the mother's health.[35] Three States permitted abortions that were not "unlawfully" performed or that were not "without lawful justification," leaving interpretation of those standards to the courts.[36] In the past several years, however, a trend toward liberalization of abortion statutes has resulted in adoption, by about one-third of the States, of less stringent laws, most of them patterned after the ALI Model Penal Code, §230.3,[37] set forth as Appendix B to the opinion in Doe v. Bolton, 410 U.S. 205, 93 S. Ct. 754.

32. Act of Jan. 20, 1840, §1, set forth in 2 H. Gammel, Laws of Texas 177-178 (1898); see Grigsby v. Reib, 105 Tex. 597, 600, 153 S.W. 1124, 1125 (1913).

33. The early statutes are discussed in Quay 435-438. See also Lader 85-88; Stern 85-86; and Means II 375-376.

34. Criminal abortion statutes in effect in the States as of 1961, together with historical statutory development and important judicial interpretations of the state statutes, are cited and quoted in Quay 447-520. See Comment, A Survey of the Present Statutory and Case Law on Abortion: The Contradictions and the Problems, 1972 U. Ill. L.F. 177, 179, classifying the abortion statutes and listing 25 States as permitting abortion only if necessary to save or preserve the mother's life.

35. Ala. Code, tit. 14, §9 (1958); D.C. Code Ann. §22-201 (1967).

36. Mass. Gen. Laws Ann., c.272, §19 (1970); N.J. Stat. Ann. §2A:87-1 (1969); Pa. Stat. Ann., tit. 18, §§4718, 4719 (1963).

37. Fourteen States have adopted some form of the ALI statute. See Ark. Stat. Ann. §§41-303 to 41-310 (Supp. 1971); Calif. Health & Safety Code §§25950-25955.5 (Supp. 1972); Colo. Rev. Stat. Ann. §§40-2-50 to 40-2-53 (Cum. Supp. 1967); Del. Code Ann., Tit. 24, §§1790-1793 (Supp. 1972); Florida Law of Apr. 13, 1972, c.72-196, 1972 Fla. Sess. Law Serv., pp. 380-382; Ga. Code §§26-1201 to 26-1203 (1972); Kan. Stat. Ann. §21-3407 (Supp. 1971); Md. Ann. Code, art. 43, §§137-139 (1971); Miss. Code Ann. §2223 (Supp. 1972); N.M. Stat. Ann. §§40A-5-1 to 40A-5-3 (1972); N.C. Gen. Stat. §14-45.1 (Supp. 1971); Ore. Rev. Stat. §§435.405 to 435.495 (1971); S.C. Code Ann. §§16-82 to 16-89 (1962 and Supp. 1971); Va. Code Ann. §§18.1-62 to 18.1-62.3 (Supp. 1972). Mr. Justice Clark described some of these States as having "led the way." Religion, Morality, and Abortion: A Constitutional Appraisal, 2 Loyola U. (L.A.) L. Rev. 1, 11 (1969).

By the end of 1970, four other States had repealed criminal penalties for abortions performed in early pregnancy by a licensed physician, subject to stated procedural and health requirements. Alaska Stat. §11.15.060 (1970); Haw. Rev. Stat. §453-16 (Supp. 1971); N.Y. Penal Code §125.05, subd. 3 (Supp. 1972-1973); Wash. Rev. Code §§9.02.060 to 9.02.080 (Supp. 1972).

It is thus apparent that at common law, at the time of the adoption of our Constitution, and throughout the major portion of the 19th century, abortion was viewed with less disfavor than under most American statutes currently in effect. Phrasing it another way, a woman enjoyed a substantially broader right to terminate a pregnancy than she does in most States today. At least with respect to the early stage of pregnancy, and very possibly without such a limitation, the opportunity to make this choice was present in this country well into the 19th century. Even later, the law continued for some time to treat less punitively an abortion procured in early pregnancy.

6. *The position of the American Medical Association.* The anti-abortion mood prevalent in this country in the late 19th century was shared by the medical profession. Indeed, the attitude of the profession may have played a significant role in the enactment of stringent criminal abortion legislation during that period.

An AMA Committee on Criminal Abortion was appointed in May 1857. It presented its report, 12 Trans. of the Am. Med. Assn. 73-78 (1859), to the Twelfth Annual Meeting. That report observed that the Committee had been appointed to investigate criminal abortion "with a view to its general suppression." It deplored abortion and its frequency and it listed three causes of "this general demoralization":

> The first of these causes is a wide-spread popular ignorance of the true character of the crime—a belief, even among mothers themselves, that the foetus is not alive till after the period of quickening.
>
> The second of the agents alluded to is the fact that the profession themselves are frequently supposed careless of foetal life. . . .
>
> The third reason of the frightful extent of this crime is found in the grave defects of our laws, both common and statute, as regards the independent and actual existence of the child before birth, as a living being. These errors, which are sufficient in most instances to prevent conviction, are based, and only based, upon mistaken and exploded medical dogmas. With strange inconsistency, the law fully acknowledges the foetus in utero and its inherent rights, for civil purposes; while personally and as criminally affected, it fails to recognize it, and to its life as yet denies all protection.

Id., at 75-76. The Committee then offered, and the Association adopted, resolutions protesting "against such unwarrantable destruction of human life," calling upon state legislatures to revise their abortion laws, and requesting the cooperation of state medical societies "in pressing the subject." Id., at 28, 78.

In 1871 a long and vivid report was submitted by the Committee on Criminal Abortion. It ended with the observation, "We had to deal with

---

The precise status of criminal abortion laws in some States is made unclear by recent decisions in state and federal courts striking down existing state laws, in whole or in part.

human life. In a matter of less importance we could entertain no compromise. An honest judge on the bench would call things by their proper names. We could do no less." 22 Trans. of the Am. Med. Assn. 258 (1871). It proffered resolutions, adopted by the Association, id., at 38-39, recommending, among other things, that it "be unlawful and unprofessional for any physician to induce abortion or premature labor, without the concurrent opinion of at least one respectable consulting physician, and then always with a view to the safety of the child — if that be possible," and calling "the attention of the clergy of all denominations to the perverted views of morality entertained by a large class of females — aye, and men also, on this important question."

Except for periodic condemnation of the criminal abortionist, no further formal AMA action took place until 1967. In that year, the Committee on Human Reproduction urged the adoption of a stated policy of opposition to induced abortion, except when there is "documented medical evidence" of a threat to the health or life of the mother, or that the child "may be born with incapacitating physical deformity or mental deficiency," or that a pregnancy "resulting from legally established statutory or forcible rape or incest may constitute a threat to the mental or physical health of the patient," two other physicians "chosen because of their recognized professional competency have examined the patient and have concurred in writing," and the procedure "is performed in a hospital accredited by the Joint Commission on Accreditation of Hospitals." The providing of medical information by physicians to state legislatures in their consideration of legislation regarding therapeutic abortion was "to be considered consistent with the principles of ethics of the American Medical Association." This recommendation was adopted by the House of Delegates. Proceedings of the AMA House of Delegates 40-51 (June 1967).

In 1970, after the introduction of a variety of proposed resolutions, and of a report from its Board of Trustees, a reference committee noted "polarization of the medical profession on this controversial issue"; division among those who had testified; a difference of opinion among AMA councils and committees; "the remarkable shift in testimony" in six months, felt to be influenced "by the rapid changes in state laws and by the judicial decisions which tend to make abortion more freely available;" and a feeling "that this trend will continue." On June 25, 1970, the House of Delegates adopted preambles and most of the resolutions proposed by the reference committee. The preambles emphasized "the best interests of the patient," "sound clinical judgment," and "informed patient consent," in contrast to "mere acquiescence to the patient's demand." The resolutions asserted that abortion is a medical procedure that should be performed by a licensed physician in an accredited hospital only after consultation with two other physicians and in conformity with state law, and that no party to the procedure should be required to violate personally held moral principles.[38] Proceedings of the AMA House of Delegates 220 (June 1970). The AMA Judicial Council rendered a complementary opinion.[39]

7. *The position of the American Public Health Association.* In October 1970, the Executive Board of the APHA adopted Standards for Abortion Services. These were five in number:

a. Rapid and simple abortion referral must be readily available through state and local public health departments, medical societies, or other nonprofit organizations.

b. An important function of counseling should be to simplify and expedite the provision of abortion services; it should not delay the obtaining of these services.

c. Psychiatric consultation should not be mandatory. As in the case of other specialized medical services, psychiatric consultation should be sought for definite indications and not on a routine basis.

d. A wide range of individuals from appropriately trained, sympathetic volunteers to highly skilled physicians may qualify as abortion counselors.

e. Contraception and/or sterilization should be discussed with each abortion patient.

Recommended Standards for Abortion Services, 61 Am. J. Pub. Health 396 (1971). Among factors pertinent to life and health risks associated with abortion were three that "are recognized as important":

a. the skill of the physician.

b. the environment in which the abortion is performed, and above all

c. the duration of pregnancy, as determined by uterine size and confirmed by menstrual history.

38. "Whereas, Abortion, like any other medical procedure, should not be performed when contrary to the best interests of the patient since good medical practice requires due consideration for the patient's welfare and not mere acquiescence to the patient's demand; and

"Whereas, The standards of sound clinical judgment, which, together with informed patient consent should be determinative according to the merits of each individual case; therefore be it

"RESOLVED, That abortion is a medical procedure and should be performed only by a duly licensed physician and surgeon in an accredited hospital acting only after consultation with two other physicians chosen because of their professional competency and in conformance with standards of good medical practice and the Medical Practice Act of his State: and be it further

"RESOLVED, That no physician or other professional personnel shall be compelled to perform any act which violates his good medical judgment. Neither physician, hospital, nor hospital personnel shall be required to perform any act violative of personally-held moral principles. In these circumstances good medical practice requires only that the physician or other professional personnel withdraw from the case so long as the withdrawal is consistent with good medical practice." Proceedings of the AMA House of Delegates 220 (June 1970).

39. "The Principles of Medical Ethics of the AMA do not prohibit a physician from performing an abortion that is performed in accordance with good medical practice and under circumstances that do not violate the laws of the community in which he practices.

"In the matter of abortions, as of any other medical procedure, the Judicial Council becomes involved whenever there is alleged violation of the Principles of Medical Ethics as established by the House of Delegates."

Id., at 397. It was said that "a well-equipped hospital" offers more protection "to cope with unforeseen difficulties than an office or clinic without such resources. . . . The factor of gestational age is of overriding importance." Thus, it was recommended that abortions in the second trimester and early abortions in the presence of existing medical complications be performed in hospitals as in-patient procedures. For pregnancies in the first trimester, abortion in the hospital with or without overnight stay "is probably the safest practice." An abortion in an extramural facility, however, is an acceptable alternative "provided arrangements exist in advance to admit patients promptly if unforeseen complications develop." Standards for an abortion facility were listed. It was said that at present abortions should be performed by physicians or osteopaths who are licensed to practice and who have "adequate training." Id., at 398.

8. *The position of the American Bar Association.* At its meeting in February 1972 the ABA House of Delegates approved, with 17 opposing votes, the Uniform Abortion Act that had been drafted and approved the preceding August by the Conference of Commissioners on Uniform State Laws. 58 A.B.A.J. 380 (1972). We set forth the Act in full in the margin.[40] The Conference has appended an enlightening Prefatory Note.[41]

40. "UNIFORM ABORTION ACT
"Section 1. [*Abortion Defined; When Authorized.*]
"(a) 'Abortion' means the termination of human pregnancy with an intention other than to produce a live birth or to remove a dead fetus.
"(b) An abortion may be performed in this state only if it is performed:
"(1) by a physician licensed to practice medicine [or osteopathy] in this state or by a physician practicing medicine [or osteopathy] in the employ of the government of the United States or of this state, [and the abortion is performed [in the physician's office or in a medical clinic, or] in a hospital approved by the [Department of Health] or operated by the United States, this state, or any department, agency, or political subdivision of either;] or by a female upon herself upon the advice of the physician; and
"(2) within [20] weeks after the commencement of the pregnancy [or after [20] weeks only if the physician has reasonable cause to believe (i) there is a substantial risk that continuance of the pregnancy would endanger the life of the mother or would gravely impair the physical or mental health of the mother, (ii) that the child would be born with grave physical or mental defect, or (iii) that the pregnancy resulted from rape or incest, or illicit intercourse with a girl under the age of 16 years].
"Section 2. [*Penalty.*] Any person who performs or procures an abortion other than authorized by this Act is guilty of a [felony] and, upon conviction thereof, may be sentenced to pay a fine not exceeding [$1,000] or to imprisonment [in the state penitentiary] not exceeding [5 years], or both.
"Section 3. [*Uniformity of Interpretation.*] This Act shall be construed to effectuate its general purpose to make uniform the law with respect to the subject of this Act among those states which enact it.
"Section 4. [*Short Title.*] This Act may be cited as the Uniform Abortion Act.
"Section 5. [*Severability.*] If any provision of this Act or the application thereof to any person or circumstance is held invalid, the invalidity does not affect other provisions or applications of this Act which can be given effect without the invalid provision or application, and to this end the provisions of this Act are severable.
"Section 6. [*Repeal.*] The following acts and parts of acts are repealed:
"(1)
"(2)
"(3)
"Section 7. [*Time of Taking Effect.*] This Act shall take effect _____."

VII

Three reasons have been advanced to explain historically the enactment of criminal abortion laws in the 19th century and to justify their continued existence.

It has been argued occasionally that these laws were the product of a Victorian social concern to discourage illicit sexual conduct. Texas, however, does not advance this justification in the present case, and it appears that no court or commentator has taken the argument seriously.[42] The appellants and amici contend, moreover, that this is not a proper state purpose at all and suggest that, if it were, the Texas statutes are overbroad in protecting it since the law fails to distinguish between married and unwed mothers.

A second reason is concerned with abortion as a medical procedure. When most criminal abortion laws were first enacted, the procedure was a hazardous one for the woman.[43] This was particularly true prior to the development of antisepsis. Antiseptic techniques, of course, were based on discoveries by Lister, Pasteur, and others first announced in 1867, but were not generally accepted and employed until about the turn of the century. Abortion mortality was high. Even after 1900, and perhaps until as late as the development of antibiotics in the 1940's, standard modern techniques such as dilation and curettage were not nearly so safe as they are today. Thus, it has been argued that a State's real concern in enacting a criminal abortion law was to protect the pregnant woman, that is, to restrain her from submitting to a procedure that placed her life in serious jeopardy.

41. "This Act is based largely upon the New York abortion act following a review of the more recent laws on abortion in several states and upon recognition of a more liberal trend in laws on this subject. Recognition was given also to the several decisions in state and federal courts which show a further trend toward liberalization of abortion laws, especially during the first trimester of pregnancy.

"Recognizing that a number of problems appeared in New York, a shorter time period for 'unlimited' abortions was advisable. The time period was bracketed to permit the various states to insert a figure more in keeping with the different conditions that might exist among the states. Likewise, the language limiting the place or places in which abortions may be performed was also bracketed to account for different conditions among the states. In addition, limitations on abortions after the initial 'unlimited' period were placed in brackets so that individual states may adopt all or any of these reasons, or place further restrictions upon abortions after the initial period.

"This Act does not contain any provision relating to medical review committees or prohibitions against sanctions imposed upon medical personnel refusing to participate in abortions because of religious or other similar reasons, or the like. Such provisions, while related, do not directly pertain to when, where, or by whom abortions may be performed; however, the Act is not drafted to exclude such a provision by a state wishing to enact the same."

42. See, for example, YWCA v. Kugler, 342 F. Supp. 1048, 1074 (D.C.N.J. 1972); Abele v. Markle, 342 F. Supp. 800, 805-806 (D.C. Conn. 1972) (Newman, J., concurring in result), appeal docketed, No. 72-56; Walsingham v. State, 250 So. 2d 857, 863 (Ervin, J., concurring) (Fla. 1971); State v. Gedicke, 43 N.J.L. 86, 90 (1881); Means II 381-382.

43. See C. Haagensen & W. Lloyd, A Hundred Years of Medicine 19 (1943).

Modern medical techniques have altered this situation. Appellants and various amici refer to medical data indicating that abortion in early pregnancy, that is, prior to the end of the first trimester, although not without its risk, is now relatively safe. Mortality rates for women undergoing early abortions, where the procedure is legal, appear to be as low as or lower than the rates for normal childbirth.[44] Consequently, any interest of the State in protecting the woman from an inherently hazardous procedure, except when it would be equally dangerous for her to forgo it, has largely disappeared. Of course, important state interests in the areas of health and medical standards do remain. The State has a legitimate interest in seeing to it that abortion, like any other medical procedure, is performed under circumstances that insure maximum safety for the patient. This interest obviously extends at least to the performing physician and his staff, to the facilities involved, to the availability of after-care, and to adequate provision for any complication or emergency that might arise. The prevalence of high mortality rates at illegal "abortion mills" strengthens, rather than weakens, the State's interest in regulating the conditions under which abortions are performed. Moreover, the risk to the woman increases as her pregnancy continues. Thus, the State retains a definite interest in protecting the woman's own health and safety when an abortion is proposed at a late stage of pregnancy.

The third reason is the State's interest — some phrase it in terms of duty — in protecting prenatal life. Some of the argument for this justification rests on the theory that a new human life is present from the moment of conception.[45] The State's interest and general obligation to protect life then extends, it is argued, to prenatal life. Only when the life of the pregnant mother herself is at stake, balanced against the life she carries within her, should the interest of the embryo or fetus not prevail. Logically, of course, a legitimate state interest in this area need not stand or fall on acceptance of the belief that life begins at conception or at some other point prior to live birth. In assessing the State's interest, recognition may be given to the less rigid claim that as long as at least *potential* life is involved, the State may assert interests beyond the protection of the pregnant woman alone.

Parties challenging state abortion laws have sharply disputed in some courts the contention that a purpose of these laws, when enacted, was to

44. Potts, Postconceptive Control of Fertility, 8 Intl. J. of G. & O. 957, 967 (1970) (England and Wales), Abortion Mortality, 20 Morbidity and Mortality 208, 209 (June 12, 1971) (U.S. Dept. of HEW, Public Health Service) (New York City); Tietze, United States: Therapeutic Abortions, 1963-1968, 59 Studies in Family Planning 5, 7 (1970); Tietze, Mortality with Contraception and Induced Abortion, 45 Studies in Family Planning 6 (1969) (Japan, Czechoslovakia, Hungary); Tietze & Lehfeldt, Legal Abortion in Eastern Europe, 175 J.A.M.A. 1149, 1152 (April 1961). Other sources are discussed in Lader 17-23.

45. See Brief of Amicus National Right to Life Committee: R. Drinan. The Inviolability of the Right to Be Born, in Abortion and the Law 107 (D. Smith ed. 1967); Louisell, Abortion, The Practice of Medicine and the Due Process of Law, 16 U.C.L.A. L. Rev. 233 (1969); Noonan 1.

protect prenatal life.[46] Pointing to the absence of legislative history to support the contention, they claim that most state laws were designed solely to protect the woman. Because medical advances have lessened this concern, at least with respect to abortion in early pregnancy, they argue that with respect to such abortions the laws can no longer be justified by any state interest. There is some scholarly support for this view of original purpose.[47] The few state courts called upon to interpret their laws in the late 19th and early 20th centuries did focus on the State's interest in protecting the woman's health rather than in preserving the embryo and fetus.[48] Proponents of this view point out that in many States, including Texas,[49] by statute or judicial interpretation, the pregnant woman herself could not be prosecuted for self-abortion or for cooperating in an abortion performed upon her by another.[50] They claim that adoption of the "quickening" distinction through received common law and state statutes tacitly recognizes the greater health hazards inherent in late abortion and impliedly repudiates the theory that life begins at conception.

It is with these interests, and the weight to be attached to them, that this case is concerned.

VIII

[9] The Constitution does not explicitly mention any right of privacy. In a line of decisions, however, going back perhaps as far as Union Pacific R. Co. v. Botsford, 141 U.S. 250, 251, 11 S. Ct. 1000, 1001, 35 L. Ed. 734 (1891), the Court has recognized that a right of personal privacy, or a guarantee of certain areas or zones of privacy, does exist under the Constitution. In varying contexts, the Court or individual Justices have, indeed, found at least the roots of that right in the First Amendment, Stanley v. Georgia, 394 U.S. 557, 564, 89 S. Ct. 1243, 1247, 22 L. Ed. 2d 542 (1969); in the Fourth and Fifth Amendments, Terry v. Ohio, 392 U.S. 1, 8-9, 88 S. Ct. 1868, 1872-1873, 20 L. Ed. 2d 889 (1968), Katz v. United States, 389 U.S. 347, 350, 88 S. Ct. 507, 510, 19 L. Ed. 2d 576 (1967); Boyd v. United States, 116 U.S. 616, 6 S. Ct. 524, 29 L. Ed. 746 (1886), see Olmstead v. United States, 277 U.S. 438, 478, 48 S. Ct. 564, 572, 72 L. Ed. 944 (1928) (Brandeis, J., dissenting); in the penumbras of the Bill of Rights, Griswold v. Connecticut, 381 U.S., at 484-485, 85 S. Ct., at

46. See, e.g., Abele v. Markle, 342 F. Supp. 800 (D.C. Conn. 1972), appeal docketed, No. 72-56.

47. See discussion in Means I and Means II.

48. See, e.g., State v. Murphy, 27 N.J.L. 112, 114 (1858).

49. Watson v. State, 9 Tex. App. 237, 244-245 (1880); Moore v. State, 37 Tex. Cr. R. 352, 561, 40 S.W. 287, 290 (1897); Shaw v. State, 73 Tex. Cr. R. 337, 339, 165 S.W. 930, 931 (1914); Fondren v. State, 74 Tex. Cr. R. 552, 537, 169 S.W. 411, 414 (1914); Gray v. State, 77 Tex. Cr. R. 221, 229, 178 S.W. 337, 341 (1915). There is no immunity in Texas for the father who is not married to the mother. Hammett v. State, 84 Tex. Cr. R. 635, 209 S.W. 661 (1919); Thompson v. State, Tex. Cr. App., 493 S.W.2d 913 (1971), appeal pending.

50. See Smith v. State, 33 Me., at 55; In re Vince, 2 N.J. 443, 450, 67 A.2d 141, 144 (1949). A short discussion of the modern law on this issue is contained in the Comment to the ALI's Model Penal Code §207.11, at 158 and nn.35-37 (Tent. Draft No. 9, 1959).

1681-1682; in the Ninth Amendment, id., at 486, 85 S. Ct. at 1682 (Goldberg, J., concurring); or in the concept of liberty guaranteed by the first section of the Fourteenth Amendment, see Meyer v. Nebraska, 262 U.S. 390, 399, 43 S. Ct. 625, 626, 67 L. Ed. 1042 (1923). These decisions make it clear that only personal rights that can be deemed "fundamental" or "implicit in the concept of ordered liberty," Palko v. Connecticut, 302 U.S. 319, 325, 58 S. Ct. 149, 152, 82 L. Ed. 288 (1937), are included in this guarantee of personal privacy. They also make it clear that the right has some extension to activities relating to marriage, Loving v. Virginia, 388 U.S. 1, 12, 87 S. Ct. 1817, 1823, 18 L. Ed. 2d 1010 (1967); procreation, Skinner v. Oklahoma, 316 U.S. 535, 541-542, 62 S. Ct. 1110, 1113-1114, 86 L. Ed. 1655 (1942); contraception, Eisenstadt v. Baird, 405 U.S., at 453-454, 92 L. Ct., at 1038-1039; id., at 460, 463-465, 92 S. Ct. at 1042, 1043-1044 (White, J., concurring in result); family relationships, Prince v. Massachusetts, 321 U.S. 158, 166, 64 S. Ct. 438, 442, 88 L. Ed. 645 (1944); and child rearing and education, Pierce v. Society of Sisters, 268 U.S. 510, 535, 45 S. Ct. 571, 573, 69 L. Ed. 1070 (1925), Meyer v. Nebraska, supra.

[10] This right of privacy, whether it be founded in the Fourteenth Amendment's concept of personal liberty and restrictions upon state action, as we feel it is, or, as the District Court determined, in the Ninth Amendment's reservation of rights to the people, is broad enough to encompass a woman's decision whether or not to terminate her pregnancy. The detriment that the State would impose upon the pregnant woman by denying this choice altogether is apparent. Specific and direct harm medically diagnosable even in early pregnancy may be involved. Maternity, or additional offspring, may force upon the woman a distressful life and future. Psychological harm may be imminent. Mental and physical health may be taxed by child care. There is also the distress, for all concerned, associated with the unwanted child, and there is the problem of bringing a child into a family already unable, psychologically and otherwise, to care for it. In other cases, as in this one, the additional difficulties and continuing stigma of unwed motherhood may be involved. All these are factors the woman and her responsible physician necessarily will consider in consultation.

On the basis of elements such as these, appellant and some amici argue that the woman's right is absolute and that she is entitled to terminate her pregnancy at whatever time, in whatever way, and for whatever reason she alone chooses. With this we do not agree. Appellant's arguments that Texas either has no valid interest at all in regulating the abortion decision, or no interest strong enough to support any limitation upon the woman's sole determination, are unpersuasive. The Court's decisions recognizing a right of privacy also acknowledge that some state regulation in areas protected by that right is appropriate. As noted above, a State may properly assert important interests in safeguarding health, in maintaining medical standards, and in protecting potential life. At some point in pregnancy, these respective interests become sufficiently compelling to sustain regulation of the factors that govern the abortion decision. The privacy right involved, therefore, cannot be said to be absolute. In fact, it is not clear to us that the claim asserted by some amici that one has an unlimited right to do with one's body as one pleases bears a close relationship to the right of privacy previously articulated in the Court's decisions. The Court has refused to recognize an unlimited right of this kind in the past. Jacobson v. Massachusetts, 197 U.S. 11, 25 S. Ct. 358, 49 L. Ed. 643 (1905) (vaccination); Buck v. Bell, 274 U.S. 200, 47 S. Ct. 584, 71 L. Ed. 1000 (1927) (sterilization).

We, therefore, conclude that the right of personal privacy includes the abortion decision, but that this right is not unqualified and must be considered against important state interests in regulation.

We note that those federal and state courts that have recently considered abortion law challenges have reached the same conclusion. A majority, in addition to the District Court in the present case, have held state laws unconstitutional, at least in part, because of vagueness or because of overbreadth and abridgment of rights. Abele v. Markle, 342 F. Supp. 800 (D.C. Conn. 1972), appeal docketed, No. 72-56; Abele v. Markle, 351 F. Supp. 224 (D.C. Conn. 1972), appeal docketed, No. 72-730; Doe v. Bolton, 319 F. Supp. 1048 (N.D. Ga. 1970), appeal decided today, 410 U.S. 179, 93 S. Ct. 739, 35 L. Ed. 2d 201; Doe v. Scott, 321 F. Supp. 1385 (N.D. Ill. 1971), appeal docketed, No. 70-105; Poe v. Menghini, 339 F. Supp. 986 (D.C. Kan. 1972); YWCA v. Kugler, 342 F. Supp. 1048 (D.C.N.J. 1972); Babbitz v. McCann, 310 F. Supp. 293 (E.D. Wis. 1970), appeal dismissed, 400 U.S. 1, 91 S. Ct. 12, 27 L. Ed. 2d 1 (1970); People v. Belous, 71 Cal. 2d 954, 80 Cal. Rptr. 354, 458 P.2d 194 (1969), cert. denied, 397 U.S. 915, 90 S. Ct. 920, 25 L. Ed. 2d 96 (1970); State v. Barquet, 262 So. 2d 431 (Fla. 1972).

Others have sustained state statutes. Crossen v. Attorney General, 344 F. Supp. 587 (E.D. Ky. 1972), appeal docketed, No. 72-256; Rosen v. Louisiana State Board of Medical Examiners, 318 F. Supp. 1217 (E.D. La. 1970), appeal docketed, No. 70-42; Corkey v. Edwards, 322 F. Supp. 1248 (W.D.N.C. 1971), appeal docketed, No. 71-92; Steinberg v. Brown, 321 F. Supp. 741 (N.D. Ohio 1970); Doe v. Rampton, 366 F. Supp. 189 (Utah 1971), appeal docketed, No. 71-5666; Cheaney v. State, Ind., 285 N.E.2d 265 (1972); Spears v. State, 257 So. 2d 876 (Miss. 1972); State v. Munson, S.D., 201 N.W.2d 123 (1972), appeal docketed, No. 72-631.

Although the results are divided, most of these courts have agreed that the right of privacy, however based, is broad enough to cover the abortion decision; that the right, nonetheless, is not absolute and is subject to some limitations; and that at some point the state interests as to protection of health, medical standards, and prenatal life, become dominant. We agree with this approach.

[11] Where certain "fundamental rights" are involved, the Court has held that regulation limiting these rights may be justified only by a "compelling state interest," Kramer v. Union Free School District, 395 U.S. 621, 627, 89 S. Ct. 1886, 1890, 23 L. Ed. 2d 583 (1969); Shapiro v. Thompson, 394 U.S. 618, 634, 89 S. Ct. 1322, 1331, 22 L. Ed. 2d 600 (1969); Sherbert v. Verner, 374 U.S. 398, 406, 83 S. Ct. 1790, 1795, 10 L. Ed. 2d 965 (1963),

and that legislative enactments must be narrowly drawn to express only the legitimate state interests at stake. Griswold v. Connecticut, 381 U.S., at 485, 85 S. Ct., at 1682; Aptheker v. Secretary of State, 378 U.S. 500, 508, 84 S. Ct. 1659, 1664, 12 L. Ed. 2d 992 (1964); Cantwell v. Connecticut, 310 U.S. 296, 307-308, 60 S. Ct. 900, 904-905, 84 L. Ed. 1213 (1940); see Eisenstandt v. Baird, 405 U.S., at 460, 463-464, 92 S. Ct., at 1042, 1043-1044 (White, J., concurring in result).

In the recent abortion cases, cited above, courts have recognized these principles. Those striking down state laws have generally scrutinized the State's interests in protecting health and potential life, and have concluded that neither interest justified broad limitations on the reasons for which a physician and his pregnant patient might decide that she should have an abortion in the early stages of pregnancy. Courts sustaining state laws have held that the State's determinations to protect health or prenatal life are dominant and constitutionally justifiable.

IX

The District Court held that the appellee failed to meet his burden demonstrating that the Texas statute's infringement upon Roe's rights was necessary to support a compelling state interest, and that, although the appellee presented "several compelling justifications for state presence in the area of abortions," the statutes outstripped these justifications and swept "far beyond any areas of compelling state interest." 314 F. Supp., at 1222-1223. Appellant and appellee both contest that holding. Appellant, as has been indicated, claims an absolute right that bars any state imposition of criminal penalties in the area. Appellee argues that the State's determination to recognize and protect prenatal life from and after conception constitutes a compelling state interest. As noted above, we do not agree fully with either formulation.

A. The appellee and certain amici argue that the fetus is a "person" within the language and meaning of the Fourteenth Amendment. In support of this, they outline at length and in detail the well-known facts of fetal development. If this suggestion of personhood is established, the appellant's case, of course, collapses, for the fetus' right to life would then be guaranteed specifically by the Amendment. The appellant conceded as much on reargument.[51] On the other hand, the appellee conceded on reargument[52] that no case could be cited that holds that a fetus is a person within the meaning of the Fourteenth Amendment.

The Constitution does not define "person" in so many words. Section 1 of the Fourteenth Amendment contains three references to "person." The first, in defining "citizens," speaks of "persons born or naturalized in the United States." The word also appears both in the Due Process Clause, and

51. Tr. of Oral Rearg. 20-21.
52. Tr. of Oral Rearg. 24.

in the Equal Protection Clause. "Person" is used in other places in the Constitution: in the listing of qualifications for Representatives and Senators, Art. I, §2, cl. 2, and §3, cl. 3; in the Apportionment Clause, Art. I, §2, cl. 3;[53] in the Migration and Importation provision, Art. I, §9, cl. 1; in the Emolument Clause, Art. I, §9, cl. 8; in the Electors provisions, Art. II, §1, cl. 2, and the superseded cl. 3; in the provision outlining qualifications for the office of President, Art. II, §1, cl. 5; in the Extradition provisions, Art. IV, §2, cl. 2, and the superseded Fugitive Slave Clause 3; and in the Fifth, Twelfth, and Twenty-second Amendments, as well as in §§2 and 3 of the Fourteenth Amendment. But in nearly all these instances, the use of the word is such that it has application only postnatally. None indicates, with any assurance, that it has any possible prenatal application.[54]

[12] All this, together with our observation, supra, that throughout the major portion of the 19th century prevailing legal abortion practices were far freer than they are today, persuades us that the word "person," as used in the Fourteenth Amendment, does not include the unborn.[55] This is in accord with the results reached in those few cases where the issue has been squarely presented. McGarvey v. Magee-Womens Hospital, 340 F. Supp. 751 (W.D. Pa. 1972); Byrn v. New York City Health & Hospitals Corp., 31 N.Y. 2d 194, 335 N.Y.S.2d 390, 286 N.E.2d 887 1972), appeal docketed, No. 72-434; Abele v. Markle, 351 F. Supp. 224 (D.C. Conn. 1972), appeal docketed, No. 72-730. Cf. Cheaney v. State, Ind., 285 N.E.2d, at 270; Montana v. Rogers, 278 F.2d 68, 72 (CA7 1960), aff'd sub nom. Montana v. Kennedy, 366 U.S. 308, 81 S. Ct. 1336, 6 L. Ed. 2d 313 (1961); Keeler v. Superior Court, 2 Cal. 3d 619, 87 Cal. Rptr. 481, 470 P.2d 617 (1970); State v. Dickinson, 28 Ohio St. 2d 65, 275 N.E.2d 599 (1971). Indeed, our decision in United States v. Vuitch, 402 U.S. 62, 91 S. Ct. 1294, 28 L. Ed. 2d 601 (1971), inferentially is to the same effect, for we there would not have indulged in

53. We are not aware that in the taking of any census under this clause, a fetus has ever been counted.

54. When Texas urges that a fetus is entitled to Fourteenth Amendment protection as a person, it faces a dilemma. Neither in Texas nor in any other State are all abortions prohibited. Despite broad proscription, an exception always exists. The exception contained in Art. 1196, for an abortion procured or attempted by medical advice for the purpose of saving the life of the mother, is typical. But if the fetus is a person who is not to be deprived of life without due process of law, and if the mother's condition is the sole determinant, does not the Texas exception appear to be out of line with the Amendment's command? There are other inconsistencies between Fourteenth Amendment status and the typical abortion statute. It has already been pointed out, n. 49, supra, that in Texas the woman is not a principal or an accomplice with respect to an abortion upon her. If the fetus is a person, why is the woman not a principal or an accomplice? Further, the penalty for criminal abortion specified by Art. 1195 is significantly less than the maximum penalty for murder prescribed by Art. 1257 of the Texas Penal Code. If the fetus is a person, may the penalties be different?

55. Cf. the Wisconsin abortion statute, defining "unborn child" to mean "a human being from the time of conception until it is born alive." Wis. Stat. §940.04(6) (1969), and the new Connecticut statute, Pub. Act No. 1 (May 1972 Special Session), declaring it to be the public policy of the State and the legislative intent "to protect and preserve human life from the moment of conception."

statutory interpretation favorable to abortion in specified circumstances if the necessary consequence was the termination of life entitled to Fourteenth Amendment protection.

This conclusion, however, does not of itself fully answer the contentions raised by Texas, and we pass on to other considerations.

B. The pregnant woman cannot be isolated in her privacy. She carries an embryo and, later, a fetus, if one accepts the medical definitions of the developing young in the human uterus. See Dorland's Illustrated Medical Dictionary 478-479, 547 (24th ed. 1965). The situation therefore is inherently different from marital intimacy, or bedroom possession of obscene material, or marriage, or procreation, or education, with which *Eisenstadt* and *Griswold, Stanley, Loving, Skinner* and *Pierce* and *Meyer* were respectively concerned. As we have intimated above, it is reasonable and appropriate for a State to decide that at some point in time another interest, that of health of the mother or that of potential human life, becomes significantly involved. The woman's privacy is no longer sole and any right of privacy she possesses must be measured accordingly.

Texas urges that, apart from the Fourteenth Amendment, life begins at conception and is present throughout pregnancy, and that, therefore, the State has a compelling interest in protecting that life from and after conception. We need not resolve the difficult question of when life begins. When those trained in the respective disciplines of medicine, philosophy, and theology are unable to arrive at any consensus, the judiciary, at this point in the development of man's knowledge, is not in a position to speculate as to the answer.

It should be sufficient to note briefly the wide divergence of thinking on this most sensitive and difficult question. There has always been strong support for the view that life does not begin until live birth. This was the belief of the Stoics.[56] It appears to be the predominant, though not the unanimous, attitude of the Jewish faith.[57] It may be taken to represent also the position of a large segment of the Protestant community, insofar as that can be ascertained; organized groups that have taken a formal position on the abortion issue have generally regarded abortion as a matter for the conscience of the individual and her family.[58] As we have noted, the common law found greater significance in quickening. Physicians and their scientific colleagues have regarded that event with less interest and have tended to focus either upon conception, upon live birth, or upon the interim point at which the fetus becomes "viable," that is, potentially able to live outside the mother's womb, albeit with artificial aid.[59] Viability is usually

56. Edelstein 16.
57. Lader 97-99; D. Feldman, Birth Control in Jewish Law 251-294 (1968). For a stricter view, see I. Jakobovits, Jewish Views on Abortion, in Abortion and the Law 124 (D. Smith ed. 1967).
58. Amicus Brief for the American Ethical Union et al. For the position of the National Council of Churches and of other denominations, see Lader 99-101.
59. L. Hellman & J. Pritchard, Williams Obstetrics 493 (14th ed. 1971); Dorland's Illustrated Medical Dictionary 1689 (24th ed. 1965).

placed at about seven months (28 weeks) but may occur earlier, even at 24 weeks.[60] The Aristotelian theory of "mediate animation," that held sway throughout the Middle Ages and the Renaissance in Europe, continued to be official Roman Catholic dogma until the 19th century, despite opposition to this "ensoulment" theory from those in the Church who would recognize the existence of life from the moment of conception.[61] The latter is now, of course, the official belief of the Catholic Church. As one brief amicus discloses, this is a view strongly held by many non-Catholics as well, and by many physicians. Substantial problems for precise definition of this view are posed, however, by new embryological data that purport to indicate that conception is a "process" over time, rather than an event, and by new medical techniques such as menstrual extraction, the "morning-after" pill, implantation of embryos, artificial insemination, and even artificial wombs.[62]

In areas other than criminal abortion, the law has been reluctant to endorse any theory that life, as we recognize it, begins before live birth or to accord legal rights to the unborn except in narrowly defined situations and except when the rights are contingent upon live birth. For example, the traditional rule of tort law denied recovery for prenatal injuries even though the child was born alive.[63] That rule has been changed in almost every jurisdiction. In most States, recovery is said to be permitted only if the fetus was viable, or at least quick, when the injuries were sustained, though few courts have squarely so held.[64] In a recent development, generally opposed by the commentators, some States permit the parents of a stillborn child to maintain an action for wrongful death because of prenatal injuries.[65] Such an action, however, would appear to be one to vindicate the parents' interest and is thus consistent with the view that the fetus, at most, represents only the potentiality of life. Similarly, unborn children have been recognized as acquiring rights or interests by way of inheritance or other devolution of property, and have been represented by guardians ad litem.[66] Perfection of the interests involved, again, has

60. Hellman & Pritchard, supra, n.59, at 493.

61. For discussions of the development of the Roman Catholic position, see D. Callahan, Abortion: Law, Choice, and Morality 409-447 (1970); Noonan 1.

62. See Brodie, The New Biology and the Prenatal Child. 9 J. Family L. 391, 397 (1970); Gorney, The New Biology and the Future of Man, 15 U.C.L.A. L. Rev. 273 (1968); Note, Criminal Law — Abortion — The "Morning-After Pill" and Other Pre-Implantation Birth-Control Methods and the Law, 46 Ore. L. Rev. 211 (1967); G. Taylor, The Biological Time Bomb 32 (1968); A. Rosenfeld, The Second Genesis 138-139 (1969); Smith, Through a Test Tube Darkly: Artificial Insemination and the Law, 67 Mich. L. Rev. 127 (1968); Note, Artificial Insemination and the Law, 1968 U. Ill. L.F. 203.

63. W. Prosser, The Law of Torts 335-338 (4th ed. 1971); 2 F. Harper & F. James, The Law of Torts 1028-1031 (1956); Note, 63 Harv. L. Rev. 173 (1949).

64. See cases cited in Prosser, supra, n.63, at 336-338; Annotation, Action for Death of Unborn Child, 15 A.L.R.3d 992 (1967).

65. Prosser, supra, n.63, at 338; Note, The Law and the Unborn Child: The Legal and Logical Inconsistencies, 46 Notre Dame Law, 349, 354-360 (1971).

66. Louisell, Abortion, The Practice of Medicine and the Due Process of Law, 16 U.C.L.A. L. Rev. 233, 235-238 (1969); Note, 56 Iowa L. Rev. 994, 999-1000 (1971); Note, The Law and the Unborn Child, 46 Notre Dame Law, 349, 351-354 (1971).

generally been contingent upon live birth. In short, the unborn have never been recognized in the law as persons in the whole sense.

X

In view of all this, we do not agree that, by adopting one theory of life, Texas may override the rights of the pregnant woman that are at stake. We repeat, however, that the State does have an important and legitimate interest in preserving and protecting the health of the pregnant woman, whether she be a resident of the State or a non-resident who seeks medical consultation and treatment there, and that it has still *another* important and legitimate interest in protecting the potentiality of human life. These interests are separate and distinct. Each grows in substantiality as the woman approaches term and, at a point during pregnancy, each becomes "compelling."

[13, 14] With respect to the State's important and legitimate interest in the health of the mother, the "compelling" point, in the light of present medical knowledge, is at approximately the end of the first trimester. This is so because of the now-established medical fact, referred to above, that until the end of the first trimester mortality in abortion may be less than mortality in normal childbirth. It follows that, from and after this point, a State may regulate the abortion procedure to the extent that the regulation reasonably relates to the preservation and protection of maternal health. Examples of permissible state regulation in this area are requirements as to the qualifications of the person who is to perform the abortion; as to the licensure of that person; as to the facility in which the procedure is to be performed, that is, whether it must be a hospital or may be a clinic or some other place of less-than-hospital status; as to the licensing of the facility; and the like.

This means, on the other hand, that, for the period of pregnancy prior to this "compelling" point, the attending physician, in consultation with his patient, is free to determine, without regulation by the State, that, in his medical judgment, the patient's pregnancy should be terminated. If that decision is reached, the judgment may be effectuated by an abortion free of interference by the State.

[15] With respect to the State's important and legitimate interest in potential life, the "compelling" point is at viability. This is so because the fetus then presumably has the capability of meaningful life outside the mother's womb. State regulation protective of fetal life after viability thus has both logical and biological justifications. If the State is interested in protecting fetal life after viability, it may go so far as to proscribe abortion during that period, except when it is necessary to preserve the life or health of the mother.

[16] Measured against these standards, Art. 1196 of the Texas Penal Code, in restricting legal abortions to those "procured or attempted by medical advice for the purpose of saving the life of the mother," sweeps

too broadly. The statute makes no distinction between abortions performed early in pregnancy and those performed later, and it limits to a single reason, "saving" the mother's life, the legal justification for the procedure. The statute, therefore, cannot survive the constitutional attack made upon it here.

This conclusion makes it unnecessary for us to consider the additional challenge to the Texas statute asserted on grounds of vagueness. See United States v. Vuitch, 402 U.S., at 67-72, 91 S. Ct., at 1296-1299.

XI

To summarize and to repeat:

1. A state criminal abortion statute of the current Texas type, that excepts from criminality only a *life-saving* procedure on behalf of the mother, without regard to pregnancy stage and without recognition of the other interests involved, is violative of the Due Process Clause of the Fourteenth Amendment.

(a) For the stage prior to approximately the end of the first trimester, the abortion decision and its effectuation must be left to the medical judgment of the pregnant woman's attending physician.

(b) For the stage subsequent to approximately the end of the first trimester, the State, in promoting its interest in the health of the mother, may, if it chooses, regulate the abortion procedure in ways that are reasonably related to maternal health.

(c) For the stage subsequent to viability, the State in promoting its interest in the potentiality of human life may, if it chooses, regulate, and even proscribe, abortion except where it is necessary, in appropriate medical judgment, for the preservation of the life or health of the mother.

[17] 2. The State may define the term "physician," as it has been employed in the preceding paragraphs of this Part XI of this opinion, to mean only a physician currently licensed by the State, and may proscribe any abortion by a person who is not a physician as so defined.

In Doe v. Bolton, 410 U.S. 179, 93 S. Ct. 739, 35 L. Ed. 2d 201, procedural requirements contained in one of the modern abortion statutes are considered. That opinion and this one, of course, are to be read together.[67]

67. Neither in this opinion nor in Doe v. Bolton, 410 U.S. 179, 93 S. Ct. 739, 35 L. Ed. 2d 201, do we discuss the father's rights, if any exist in the constitutional context, in the abortion decision. No paternal right has been asserted in either of the cases, and the Texas and the Georgia statutes on their face take no cognizance of the father. We are aware that some statutes recognize the father under certain circumstances. North Carolina, for example, N.C. Gen. Stat. §14-45.1 (Supp. 1971), requires written permission for the abortion from the husband when the woman is a married minor, that is, when she is less than 18 years of age, 41 N.C.A.G. 489 (1971); if the woman is an unmarried minor, written permission from the parents is required. We need not now decide whether provisions of this kind are constitutional.

This holding, we feel, is consistent with the relative weights of the respective interests involved, with the lessons and examples of medical and legal history, with the lenity of the common law, and with the demands of the profound problems of the present day. The decision leaves the State free to place increasing restrictions on abortion as the period of pregnancy lengthens, so long as those restrictions are tailored to the recognized state interests. The decision vindicates the right of the physician to administer medical treatment according to his professional judgment up to the points where important state interests provide compelling justifications for intervention. Up to those points, the abortion decision in all its aspects is inherently, and primarily, a medical decision, and basic responsibility for it must rest with the physician. If an individual practitioner abuses the privilege of exercising proper medical judgment, the usual remedies, judicial and intra-professional, are available.

XII

[18] Our conclusion that Art. 1196 is unconstitutional means, of course, that the Texas abortion statutes, as a unit, must fall. The exception of Art. 1196 cannot be struck down separately, for then the State would be left with a statute proscribing all abortion procedures no matter how medically urgent the case.

Although the District Court granted appellant Roe declaratory relief, it stopped short of issuing an injunction against enforcement of the Texas statutes. The Court has recognized that different considerations enter into a federal court's decision as to declaratory relief, on the one hand, and injunctive relief, on the other. Zwickler v. Koota, 389 U.S. 241, 252-255, 88 S. Ct. 391, 397-399, 19 L. Ed. 2d 444 (1967); Dombrowski v. Pfister, 380 U.S. 479, 85 S. Ct. 1116, 14 L. Ed. 2d 22 (1965). We are not dealing with a statute that, on its face, appears to abridge free expression, an area of particular concern under *Dombrowski* and refined in Younger v. Harris, 401 U.S., at 50, 91 S. Ct. at 753.

We find it unnecessary to decide whether the District Court erred in withholding injunctive relief, for we assume the Texas prosecutorial authorities will give full credence to this decision that the present criminal abortion statutes of that State are unconstitutional.

The judgment of the District Court as to intervenor Hallford is reversed, and Dr. Hallford's complaint in intervention is dismissed. In all other respects, the judgment of the District Court is affirmed. Costs are allowed to the appellee.

It is so ordered.

Affirmed in part and reversed in part.

Mr. Justice STEWART, concurring.

In 1963, this Court, in Ferguson v. Skrupa, 372 U.S. 726, 83 S. Ct. 1028, 10 L. Ed. 2d 93, purported to sound the death knell for the doctrine of substantive due process, a doctrine under which many state laws had in the past been held to violate the Fourteenth Amendment. As Mr. Justice Black's opinion for the Court in *Skrupa* put it: "We have returned to the original constitutional proposition that courts do not substitute their social and economic beliefs for the judgment of legislative bodies, who are elected to pass laws." Id., at 730, 83 S. Ct., at 1031.[1]

Barely two years later, in Griswold v. Connecticut, 381 U.S. 479, 85 S. Ct. 1678, 14 L. Ed. 2d 510, the Court held a Connecticut birth control law unconstitutional. In view of what had been so recently said in *Skrupa*, the Court's opinion in *Griswold* understandably did its best to avoid reliance on the Due Process Clause of the Fourteenth Amendment as the ground for decision. Yet, the Connecticut law did not violate any provision of the Bill of Rights, nor any other specific provision of the Constitution.[2] So it was clear to me then, and it is equally clear to me now, that the *Griswold* decision can be rationally understood only as a holding that the Connecticut statute substantively invaded the "liberty" that is protected by the Due Process Clause of the Fourteenth Amendment.[3] As so understood, *Griswold* stands as one in a long line of pre-*Skrupa* cases decided under the doctrine of substantive due process, and I now accept it as such.

"In a Constitution for a free people, there can be no doubt that the meaning of 'liberty' must be broad indeed." Board of Regents v. Roth, 408 U.S. 564, 572, 92 S. Ct. 2701, 2707, 33 L. Ed. 2d 548. The Constitution nowhere mentions a specific right of personal choice in matters of marriage and family life, but the "liberty" protected by the Due Process Clause of the Fourteenth Amendment covers more than those freedoms explicitly named in the Bill of Rights. See Schware v. Board of Bar Examiners, 353 U.S. 232, 238-239, 77 S. Ct. 752, 755-756, 1 L. Ed. 2d 796; Pierce v. Society of Sisters, 268 U.S. 510, 534-535, 45 S. Ct. 571, 573-574, 69 L. Ed. 1070; Meyer v. Nebraska, 262 U.S. 390, 399-400, 43 S. Ct. 625, 626-627, 67 L. Ed. 1042. Cf. Shapiro v. Thompson, 394 U.S. 618, 629-630, 89 S. Ct. 1322, 1328-1329, 22 L. Ed. 2d 600; United States v. Guest, 383 U.S. 745, 757-758, 86 S. Ct. 1170, 1177-1178, 16 L. Ed. 2d 239; Carrington v. Rash, 380 U.S. 89, 96, 85 S. Ct. 775, 780, 13 L. Ed. 2d 675; Aptheker v. Secretary of State, 378 U.S. 500, 505, 84 S. Ct. 1659, 1663,

---

1. Only Mr. Justice Harlan failed to join the Court's opinion, 372 U.S., at 733, 83 S. Ct., at 1032.

2. There is no constitutional right of privacy, as such. "[The Fourth] Amendment protects individual privacy against certain kinds of governmental intrusion, but its protections go further, and often have nothing to do with privacy at all. Other provisions of the Constitution protect personal privacy from other forms of governmental invasion. But the protection of a person's *general* right to privacy — his right to be let alone by other people — is like the protection of his property and of his very life, left largely to the law of the individual States." Katz v. United States, 389 U.S. 347, 350-351, 88 S. Ct. 507, 510-511, 19 L. Ed. 2d 576 (footnotes omitted).

3. This was also clear to Mr. Justice Black, 381 U.S., at 307 (dissenting opinion); to Mr. Justice Harlan, 381 U.S., at 499, 85 S. Ct., at 1689 (opinion concurring in the judgment); and to Mr. Justice White, 381 U.S., at 502, 85 S. Ct., at 1691 (opinion concurring in the judgment). See also Mr. Justice Harlan's thorough and thoughtful opinion dissenting from dismissal of the appeal in Poe v. Ullman, 367 U.S. 497, 522, 81 S. Ct. 1752, 1765, 6 L. Ed. 2d 989.

12 L. Ed. 2d 992; Kent v. Dulles, 357 U.S. 118, 127, 78 S. Ct. 1113, 1118, 2 L. Ed. 2d 1204; Bolling v. Sharpe, 347 U.S. 497, 499-500, 74 S. Ct. 693, 694-695, 98 L. Ed. 884; Truax v. Raich, 239 U.S. 33, 41, 36 S. Ct. 7, 10, 60 L. Ed. 131.

As Mr. Justice Harlan once wrote: "[T]he full scope of the liberty guaranteed by the Due Process Clause cannot be found in or limited by the precise terms of the specific guarantees elsewhere provided in the Constitution. This 'liberty' is not a series of isolated points pricked out in terms of the taking of property; the freedom of speech, press, and religion; the right to keep and bear arms; the freedom from unreasonable searches and seizures; and so on. It is a rational continuum which, broadly speaking, includes a freedom from all substantial arbitrary impositions and purposeless restraints . . . and which also recognizes, what a reasonable and sensitive judgment must, that certain interests require particularly careful scrutiny of the state needs asserted to justify their abridgment." Poe v. Ullman, 367 U.S. 497, 543, 81 S. Ct. 1752, 1776, 6 L. Ed. 2d 989 (opinion dissenting from dismissal of appeal) (citations omitted). In the words of Mr. Justice Frankfurter, "Great concepts like . . . 'liberty' . . . were purposely left to gather meaning from experience. For they relate to the whole domain of social and economic fact, and the statesmen who founded this Nation knew too well that only a stagnant society remains unchanged." National Mutual Ins. Co. v. Tidewater Transfer Co., 337 U.S. 582, 646, 69 S. Ct. 1173, 1195, 93 L. Ed. 1556 (dissenting opinion).

Several decisions of this Court make clear that freedom of personal choice in matters of marriage and family life is one of the liberties protected by the Due Process Clause of the Fourteenth Amendment. Loving v. Virginia, 388 U.S. 1, 12, 87 S. Ct. 1817, 1823, 18 L. Ed. 2d 1010; Griswold v. Connecticut, supra; Pierce v. Society of Sisters, supra; Meyer v. Nebraska, supra. See also Prince v. Massachusetts, 321 U.S. 158, 166, 64 S. Ct. 438, 442, 88 L. Ed. 645; Skinner v. Oklahoma, 316 U.S. 535, 541, 62 S. Ct. 1110, 1113, 86 L. Ed. 1655. As recently as last Term, in Eisenstadt v. Baird, 405 U.S. 438, 453, 92 S. Ct. 1029, 1038, 31 L. Ed. 2d 349, we recognized "the right of the *individual*, married or single, to be free from unwarranted governmental intrusion into matters so fundamentally affecting a person as the decision whether to bear or beget a child." That right necessarily includes the right of a woman to decide whether or not to terminate her pregnancy. "Certainly the interests of a woman in giving of her physical and emotional self during pregnancy and the interests that will be affected throughout her life by the birth and raising of a child are of a far greater degree of significance and personal intimacy than the right to send a child to private school protected in Pierce v. Society of Sisters, 268 U.S. 510, 45 S. Ct. 571, 69 L. Ed. 1070 (1925), or the right to teach a foreign language protected in Meyer v. Nebraska, 262 U.S. 390, 43 S. Ct. 625, 67 L. Ed. 1042 (1923)." Abele v. Markle, 351 F. Supp. 224, 227 (D.C. Conn. 1972).

Clearly, therefore, the Court today is correct in holding that the right asserted by Jane Roe is embraced within the personal liberty protected by the Due Process Clause of the Fourteenth Amendment.

It is evident that the Texas abortion statute infringes that right directly. Indeed, it is difficult to imagine a more complete abridgment of a constitutional freedom than that worked by the inflexible criminal statute now in force in Texas. The question then becomes whether the state interests advanced to justify this abridgment can survive the "particularly careful scrutiny" that the Fourteenth Amendment here requires.

The asserted state interests are protection of the health and safety of the pregnant woman, and protection of the potential future human life within her. These are legitimate objectives, amply sufficient to permit a State to regulate abortions as it does other surgical procedures, and perhaps sufficient to permit a State to regulate abortions more stringently or even to prohibit them in the late stages of pregnancy. But such legislation is not before us, and I think the Court today has thoroughly demonstrated that these state interests cannot constitutionally support the broad abridgment of personal liberty worked by the existing Texas law. Accordingly, I join the Court's opinion holding that that law is invalid under the Due Process Clause of the Fourteenth Amendment.

Mr. Justice REHNQUIST, dissenting.

The Court's opinion brings to the decision of this troubling question both extensive historical fact and a wealth of legal scholarship. While the opinion thus commands my respect, I find myself nonetheless in fundamental disagreement with those parts of it that invalidate the Texas statute in question, and therefore dissent.

I

The Court's opinion decides that a State may impose virtually no restriction on the performance of abortions during the first trimester of pregnancy. Our previous decisions indicate that a necessary predicate for such an opinion is a plaintiff who was in her first trimester of pregnancy at some time during the pendency of her lawsuit. While a party may vindicate his own constitutional rights, he may not seek vindication for the rights of others. Moose Lodge No. 107 v. Irvis, 407 U.S. 163, 92 S. Ct. 1965, 32 L. Ed. 2d 627 (1972); Sierra Club v. Morton, 405 U.S. 727, 92 S. Ct. 1361, 31 L. Ed. 2d 636 (1972). The Court's statement of facts in this case makes clear, however, that the record in no way indicates the presence of such a plaintiff. We know only that plaintiff Roe at the time of filing her complaint was a pregnant woman; for aught that appears in this record, she may have been in her *last* trimester of pregnancy as of the date the complaint was filed.

Nothing in the Court's opinion indicates that Texas might not constitutionally apply its proscription of abortion as written to a woman in that stage of pregnancy. Nonetheless, the Court uses her complaint against the Texas statute as a fulcrum for deciding that States may impose virtually no restrictions on medical abortions performed during the *first* trimester of pregnancy. In deciding such a hypothetical lawsuit, the Court departs from the longstanding admonition that it should never "formulate a rule of constitutional law broader than is required by the precise facts to which it is to be applied." Liverpool, New York & Philadelphia S.S. Co. v. Commissioners of Emigration, 113 U.S. 33, 39, 5 S. Ct. 352, 355, 28 L. Ed. 899 (1885). See also Ashwander v. TVA, 297 U.S. 288, 345, 56 S. Ct. 466, 482, 80 L. Ed. 688 (1936) (Brandeis, J., concurring).

II

Even if there were a plaintiff in this case capable of litigating the issue which the Court decides, I would reach a conclusion opposite to that reached by the Court. I have difficulty in concluding, as the Court does, that the right of "privacy" is involved in this case. Texas, by the statute here challenged, bars the performance of a medical abortion by a licensed physician on a plaintiff such as Roe. A transaction resulting in an operation such as this is not "private" in the ordinary usage of that word. Nor is the "privacy" that the Court finds here even a distant relative of the freedom from searches and seizures protected by the Fourth Amendment to the Constitution, which the Court has referred to as embodying a right to privacy. Katz v. United States, 389 U.S. 347, 88 S. Ct. 507, 19 L. Ed. 2d 576 (1967).

If the Court means by the term "privacy" no more than that the claim of a person to be free from unwanted state regulation of consensual transactions may be a form of "liberty" protected by the Fourteenth Amendment, there is no doubt that similar claims have been upheld in our earlier decisions on the basis of that liberty. I agree with the statement of Mr. Justice Stewart in his concurring opinion that the "liberty," against deprivation of which without due process the Fourteenth Amendment protects, embraces more than the rights found in the Bill of Rights. But that liberty is not guaranteed absolutely against deprivation, only against deprivation without due process of law. The test traditionally applied in the area of social and economic legislation is whether or not a law such as that challenged has a rational relation to a valid state objective. Williamson v. Lee Optical Co., 348 U.S. 483, 491, 75 S. Ct. 461, 466, 99 L. Ed. 563 (1955). The Due Process Clause of the Fourteenth Amendment undoubtedly does place a limit, albeit a broad one, on legislative power to enact laws such as this. If the Texas statute were to prohibit an abortion even where the mother's life is in jeopardy, I have little doubt that such a statute would lack a rational relation to a valid state objective under the test stated in *Williamson*, supra. But the Court's sweeping invalidation of any restrictions on abortion during the first trimester is impossible to justify under that standard, and the conscious weighing of competing factors that the Court's opinion apparently substitutes for the established test is far more appropriate to a legislative judgment than to a judicial one.

The Court eschews the history of the Fourteenth Amendment in its reliance on the "compelling state interest" test. See Weber v. Aetna

Casualty & Surety Co., 406 U.S. 164, 179, 92 S. Ct. 1400, 1408, 31 L. Ed. 2d 768 (1972) (dissenting opinion). But the Court adds a new wrinkle to this test by transposing it from the legal considerations associated with the Equal Protection Clause of the Fourteenth Amendment to this case arising under the Due Process Clause of the Fourteenth Amendment. Unless I misapprehend the consequences of this transplanting of the "compelling state interest test," the Court's opinion will accomplish the seemingly impossible feat of leaving this area of the law more confused than it found it.

While the Court's opinion quotes from the dissent of Mr. Justice Holmes in Lochner v. New York, 198 U.S. 45, 74, 25 S. Ct. 539, 551, 49 L. Ed. 937 (1905), the result it reaches is more closely attuned to the majority opinion of Mr. Justice Peckham in that case. As in *Lochner* and similar cases applying substantive due process standards to economic and social welfare legislation, the adoption of the compelling state interest standard will inevitably require this Court to examine the legislative policies and pass on the wisdom of these policies in the very process of deciding whether a particular state interest put forward may or may not be "compelling." The decision here to break pregnancy into three distinct terms and to outline the permissible restrictions the State may impose in each one, for example, partakes more of judicial legislation than it does of a determination of the intent of the drafters of the Fourteenth Amendment.

The fact that a majority of the States reflecting, after all the majority sentiment in those States, have had restrictions on abortions for at least a century is a strong indication, it seems to me, that the asserted right to an abortion is not "so rooted in the traditions and conscience of our people as to be ranked as fundamental." Snyder v. Massachusetts, 291 U.S. 97, 105, 54 S. Ct. 330, 332, 78 L. Ed. 674 (1934). Even today, when society's views on abortion are changing, the very existence of the debate is evidence that the "right" to an abortion is not so universally accepted as the appellant would have us believe.

To reach its result, the Court necessarily has had to find within the Scope of the Fourteenth Amendment a right that was apparently completely unknown to the drafters of the Amendment. As early as 1821, the first state law dealing directly with abortion was enacted by the Connecticut Legislature. Conn. Stat., Tit. 22, §§14, 16. By the time of the adoption of the Fourteenth Amendment in 1868, there were at least 36 laws enacted by state or territorial legislatures limiting abortion.[1] While many States have

---

1. Jurisdictions having enacted abortion laws prior to the adoption of the Fourteenth Amendment in 1868:

    1. Alabama—Ala. Acts, c.6 §2 (1840).
    2. Arizona—Howell Code, c.10, §45 (1865).
    3. Arkansas—Ark. Rev. Stat., c.44, div. III, Art. II, §6 (1838).
    4. California—Cal. Sess. Laws, c.99, §45, p.233 (1849-1850).
    5. Colorado (Terr.)—Colo. Gen. Laws of Terr. of Colo., 1st Sess., §42, pp.296-297 (1861).

amended or updated their laws, 21 of the laws on the books in 1868 remain in effect today.[2] Indeed, the Texas statute struck down today was, as the

6. Connecticut—Conn. Stat. Tit. 20, §§14, 16 (1821). By 1868, this statute had been replaced by another abortion law. Conn. Pub. Acts, c.71, §§1, 2, p.65 (1860).

7. Florida—Fla. Acts 1st Sess., c.1637, subc. 3, §§10, 11, subc. 8, §§9, 10, 11 (1868), as amended, now Fla. Stat. Ann. §§782.09, 782.10, 797.01, 797.02, 782.16 (1965).

8. Georgia—Ga. Pen. Code, 4th Div., §20 (1833).

9. Kingdom of Hawaii—Hawaii Pen. Code, c.12, §§1, 2, 3 (1850).

10. Idaho (Terr.)—Idaho (Terr.) Laws, Crimes and Punishments §§33, 34, 42, pp.441, 443 (1863).

11. Illinois—111. Rev. Criminal Code §§40, 41, 46, pp.130, 131 (1827). By 1868, this statute had been replaced by a subsequent enactment. Ill. Pub. Laws §§1, 2, 3, p.89 (1867).

12. Indiana—Ind. Rev. Stat. §§1, 3, p.224 (1838). By 1868 this statute had been superseded by a subsequent enactment. Ind. Laws, c.LXXXI, §2 (1859).

13. Iowa (Terr.)—Iowa (Terr.) Stat., 1st Legis., 1st Sess., §18, p.145 (1838). By 1868, this statute had been superseded by a subsequent enactment. Iowa (Terr.) Rev. Stat., c.49, §§10, 13 (1843).

14. Kansas (Terr.)—Kan. (Terr) Stat, c.48, §§9, 10, 39 (1855). By 1868, this statute had been superseded by a subsequent enactment. Kan. (Terr.) Laws, c.28, §§9, 10, 37 (1859).

15. Louisiana—La. Rev. Stat., Crimes and Offenses §24, p.138 (1856).

16. Maine—Me. Rev. Stat., c.160, §§11, 12, 13, 14 (1840).

17. Maryland—Md. Laws, c.179, §2, p.315 (1868).

18. Massachusetts—Mass. Acts & Resolves, c.27 (1845).

19. Michigan—Mich. Rev. Stat., c.153, §§32, 33, 34, p.662 (1846).

20. Minnesota (Terr.)—Minn. (Terr.) Rev. Stat., c.100, §§10, 11, p.493 (1851).

21. Mississippi—Miss. Code, c.64, §§8, 9, p.958 (1848).

22. Missouri—Mo. Rev. Stat., Art. II, §§9, 10, 36, pp.168, 172 (1835).

23. Montana (Terr.)—Mont. (Terr.) Laws, Criminal Practice Acts §41, p.184 (1864).

24. Nevada (Terr.)—Nev. (Terr.) Laws, c.28, §42, p.63 (1861).

25. New Hampshire—N.H. Laws, c.743, §1, p.708 (1848).

26. New Jersey—N.J. Laws, p.266 (1849).

27. New York—N.Y. Rev. Stat., pt. 4, c.1, Tit. 2, §§8, 9, pp.12-13 (1828). By 1868, this statute had been superseded. N.Y. Laws, c.260, §§1, 2, 3,4, 5, 6, pp.285-286 (1845); N.Y. Laws, c.22, §1, p.19 (1846).

28. Ohio—Ohio Gen. Stat. §§111(1), 112(2), p.252 (1841).

29. Oregon—Ore. Gen. Laws, Crim. Code, c.43, §509, p.528 (1845-1964).

30. Pennsylvania—Pa. Laws No. 374, §§87, 88, 89 (1860).

31. Texas—Tex. Gen. Stat. Dig., c.VII, Arts. 531-536, p.524 (Oldham & White 1859).

32. Vermont—Vt. Acts No. 33, §1 (1846). By 1868, this statute had been amended. Vt. Acts No. 57, §§1, 3 (1867).

33. Virginia—Va. Acts, Tit. II, c.3, §9, p.96 (1848).

34. Washington (Terr.)—Wash. (Terr.) Stats., c.II, §§37, 38, p.81 (1854).

35. West Virginia—Va. Acts, Tit. II, c.3, §9, p.96 (1848).

36. Wisconsin—Wis. Rev. Stat., c.133, §§10, 11 (1849). By 1868, this statute had been superseded, Wis. Rev. Stat., c.164, §§10, 11; c.169, §§58, 59 (1858).

2. Abortion laws in effect in 1868 and still applicable as of August 1970:

1. Arizona (1865).
2. Connecticut (1860).
3. Florida (1868).
4. Idaho (1863).
5. Indiana (1838).
6. Iowa (1843).
7. Maine (1840).
8. Massachusetts (1845).

majority notes, first enacted in 1857 and "has remained substantially unchanged to the present time."

There apparently was no question concerning the validity of this provision or of any of the other state statutes when the Fourteenth Amendment was adopted. The only conclusion possible from this history is that the drafters did not intend to have the Fourteenth Amendment withdraw from the States the power to legislate with respect to this matter.

III

Even if one were to agree that the case that the Court decides were here, and that the enunciation of the substantive constitutional law in the Court's opinion were proper, the actual disposition of the case by the Court is still difficult to justify. The Texas statute is struck down in toto, even though the Court apparently concedes that at later periods of pregnancy Texas might impose these selfsame statutory limitations on abortion. My understanding of past practice is that a statute found to be invalid as applied to a particular plaintiff, but not unconstitutional as a whole, is not simply "struck down" but is, instead, declared unconstitutional as applied to the fact situation before the Court Yick Wo v. Hopkins, 118 U.S. 356, 6 S. Ct. 1064, 30 L. Ed. 220 (1886); Street v. New York, 394 U.S. 576, 89 S. Ct. 1354, 22 L. Ed. 2d 572 (1969).

For all of the foregoing reasons, I respectfully dissent.

9. Michigan (1846).
10. Minnesota (1851).
11. Missouri (1835).
12. Montana (1864).
13. Nevada (1861).

Ethics Codes

NATIONAL ASSOCIATION OF LEGAL ASSISTANTS (NALA) CODE OF ETHICS AND PROFESSIONAL RESPONSIBILITY (1988)

Preamble

A legal assistant must adhere strictly to the accepted standards of legal ethics and to the general principles of proper conduct. The performance of the duties of the legal assistant shall be governed by specific canons as defined herein so that justice will be served and goals of the profession attained.

The canons of ethics set forth hereafter are adopted by the National Association of Legal Assistants, Inc., as a general guide intended to aid legal assistants and attorneys. The enumeration of these rules does not mean there are not others of equal importance although not specifically mentioned. Court rules, agency rules and statutes must be taken into consideration when interpreting the canons.

Definition

Legal assistants, also known as paralegals, are a distinguishable group of persons who assist attorneys in the delivery of legal services. Through formal education, training, and experience, legal assistants have knowledge and expertise regarding the legal system and substantive and procedural law which qualify them to do work of a legal nature under the supervision of an attorney.

Canon 1

A legal assistant must not perform any of the duties that attorneys only may perform nor take any actions that attorneys may not take.

Canon 2

A legal assistant may perform any task which is properly delegated and supervised by an attorney, as long as the attorney is ultimately responsible to the client, maintains a direct relationship with the client, and assumes professional responsibility for the work product.

Canon 3

A legal assistant must not:

  a. engage in, encourage, or contribute to any act which could constitute the unauthorized practice of law; and
  b. establish attorney-client relationships, set fees, give legal opinions or advice or represent a client before a court or agency unless so authorized by that court or agency; and
  c. engage in conduct or take any action which would assist or involve the attorney in a violation of professional ethics or give the appearance of professional impropriety.

Canon 4

A legal assistant must use discretion and professional judgment commensurate with knowledge and experience but must not render independent legal judgment in place of an attorney. The services of an attorney are essential in the public interest whenever such legal judgment is required.

Canon 5

A legal assistant must disclose his or her status as a legal assistant at the outset of any professional relationship with a client, attorney, a court or administrative agency or personnel thereof, or a member of the general public. A legal assistant must act prudently in determining the extent to which a client may be assisted without the presence of an attorney.

Canon 6

A legal assistant must strive to maintain integrity and a high degree of competency through education and training with respect to professional responsibility, local rules and practice, and through continuing education in substantive areas of law to better assist the legal profession in fulfilling its duty to provide legal service.

Canon 7

A legal assistant must protect the confidences of a client and must not violate any rule or statute now in effect or hereafter enacted controlling the doctrine of privileged communications between a client and an attorney.

Canon 8

A legal assistant must do all other things incidental, necessary, or expedient for the attainment of the ethics and responsibilities as defined by statute or rule of court.

Canon 9

A legal assistant's conduct is guided by bar associations' codes of professional responsibility and rules of professional conduct.

ADOPTED MAY 1975
REVISED NOVEMBER 1979
REVISED SEPTEMBER 1988
REVISED AUGUST 1995

NATIONAL FEDERATION OF PARALEGAL ASSOCIATIONS (NFPA) MODEL CODE OF ETHICS AND PROFESSIONAL RESPONSIBILITY

Preamble

The National Federation of Paralegal Associations, Inc. ("NFPA") is a professional organization comprised of paralegal associations and individual paralegals throughout the United States. Members of NFPA have varying types of backgrounds, experience, education, and job responsibilities which reflect the diversity of the paralegal profession. NFPA promotes the growth, development and recognition of the paralegal profession as an integral partner in the delivery of legal services.

NFPA recognizes that the creation of guidelines and standards for professional conduct are important for the development and expansion of the paralegal profession. In May 1993, NFPA adopted this Model Code of Ethics and Professional Responsibility ("Model Code") to delineate the principles for ethics and conduct to which every paralegal should aspire.

The Model Code expresses NFPA's commitment to increasing the quality and efficiency of legal services and recognizes the profession's responsibilities to the public, the legal community, and colleagues.

Paralegals perform many different functions, and these functions differ greatly among practice areas. In addition, each jurisdiction has its own unique legal authority and practices governing ethical conduct and professional responsibilities.

It is essential that each paralegal strive for personal and professional excellence and encourage the professional development of other paralegals as well as those entering the profession. Participation in professional associations intended to advance the quality and standards of the legal profession is of particular importance. Paralegals should possess integrity, professional skill and dedication to the improvement of the legal system and should strive to expand the paralegal role in the delivery of legal services.

Canon 1. A Paralegal[1] Shall Achieve and Maintain a High Level of Competence.

EC-1.1 A paralegal shall achieve competency through education, training, and work experience.

EC-1.2 A paralegal shall participate in continuing education to keep informed of current legal, technical and general developments.

EC-1.3 A paralegal shall perform all assignments promptly and efficiently.

Canon 2. A Paralegal Shall Maintain a High Level of Personal and Professional Integrity.

EC-2.1 A paralegal shall not engage in any ex parte[2] communications involving the courts or any other adjudicatory body in an attempt to exert undue influence or to obtain advantage for the benefit of only one party.

EC-2.2 A paralegal shall not communicate, or cause another to communicate, with a party the paralegal knows to be represented by a lawyer in a pending matter without the prior consent of the lawyer representing such other party.

EC-2.3 A paralegal shall ensure that all timekeeping and billing records prepared by the paralegal are thorough, accurate, and honest.

---

1. "Paralegal" is synonymous with "Legal Assistant" and is defined as a person qualified through education, training, or work experience to perform substantive legal work that requires knowledge of legal concepts and is customarily, but not exclusively performed by a lawyer. This person may be retained or employed by a lawyer, law office, governmental agency or other entity or may be authorized by administrative, statutory or court authority to perform this work.

2. "Ex Parte" denotes actions or communications conducted at the instance and for the benefit of one party only, and without notice to, or contestation by, any person adversely interested.

EC-2.4   A paralegal shall be scrupulous, thorough and honest in the identification and maintenance of all funds, securities, and other assets of a client and shall provide accurate accountings as appropriate.

EC-2.5   A paralegal shall advise the proper authority of any dishonest or fraudulent acts by any person pertaining to the handling of the funds, securities or other assets of a client.

Canon 3. A Paralegal Shall Maintain a High Standard of Professional Conduct.

EC-3.1   A paralegal shall refrain from engaging in any conduct that offends the dignity and decorum of proceedings before a court or other adjudicatory body and shall be respectful of all rules and procedures.

EC-3.2   A paralegal shall advise the proper authority of any action of another legal professional which clearly demonstrates fraud, deceit, dishonesty, or misrepresentation.

EC-3.3   A paralegal shall avoid impropriety and the appearance of impropriety.

Canon 4. A Paralegal Shall Serve the Public Interest by Contributing to the Delivery of Quality Legal Services and the Improvement of the Legal System.

EC-4.1   A paralegal shall be sensitive to the legal needs of the public and shall promote the development and implementation of programs that address those needs.

EC-4.2   A paralegal shall support bona fide efforts to meet the need for legal services by those unable to pay reasonable or customary fees; for example, participation in pro bono projects and volunteer work.

EC-4.3   A paralegal shall support efforts to improve the legal system and shall assist in making changes.

Canon 5. A Paralegal Shall Preserve all Confidential Information[3] Provided by the Client or Acquired From Other Sources Before, During, and After the Course of the Professional Relationship.

EC-5.1   A paralegal shall be aware of and abide by all legal authority governing confidential information.

---

3. "Confidential Information" denotes information relating to a client, whatever its source, which is not public knowledge nor available to the public. ("Non-Confidential Information" would generally include the name of the client and the identity of the matter for which the paralegal provided services.)

EC-5.2   A paralegal shall not use confidential information to the disadvantage of the client.

EC-5.3   A paralegal shall not use confidential information to the advantage of the paralegal or of a third person.

EC-5.4   A paralegal may reveal confidential information only after full disclosure and with the client's written consent; or, when required by law or court order; or, when necessary to prevent the client from committing an act which could result in death or serious bodily harm.

EC-5.5   A paralegal shall keep those individuals responsible for the legal representation of a client fully informed of any confidential information the paralegal may have pertaining to that client.

EC-5.6   A paralegal shall not engage in any indiscreet communications concerning clients.

Canon 6. A Paralegal's Title Shall be Fully Disclosed.[4]

EC-6.1   A paralegal's title shall clearly indicate the individual's status and shall be disclosed in all business and professional communications to avoid misunderstandings and misconceptions about the paralegal's role and responsibilities.

EC-6.2   A paralegal's title shall be included if the paralegal's name appears on business cards, letterhead, brochures, directories, and advertisements.

Canon 7. A Paralegal Shall Not Engage in the Unauthorized Practice of Law.

EC-7.1   A paralegal shall comply with the applicable legal authority governing the unauthorized practice of law.

Canon 8. A Paralegal Shall Avoid Conflicts of Interest and Shall Disclose Any Possible Conflict to the Employer or Client, as well as to the Prospective Employers or Clients.

EC-8.1   A paralegal shall act within the bounds of the law, solely for the benefit of the client, and shall be free of compromising influences and loyalties. Neither the paralegal's personal or business interest, nor those of other clients or third persons, should compromise the paralegal's professional judgment and loyalty to the client.

---

4. "Disclose" denotes communication of information reasonably sufficient to permit identification of the significance of the matter in question.

EC-8.2 A paralegal shall avoid conflicts of interest which may arise from previous assignments whether for a present or past employer or client.

EC-8.3 A paralegal shall avoid conflicts of interest which may arise from family relationships and from personal and business interests.

EC-8.4 A paralegal shall create and maintain an effective record-keeping system that identifies clients, matters, and parties with which the paralegal has worked, to be able to determine whether an actual or potential conflict of interest exists.

EC-8.5 A paralegal shall reveal sufficient nonconfidential information about a client or former client to reasonably ascertain if an actual or potential conflict of interest exists.

EC-8.6 A paralegal shall not participate in or conduct work on any matter where a conflict of interest has been identified.

EC-8.7 In matters where a conflict of interest has been identified and the client consents to continued representation, a paralegal shall comply fully with the implementation and maintenance of an Ethical Wall.[5]

---

5. "Ethical Wall" refers to the screening method implemented in order to protect a client from a conflict of interest. An Ethical Wall generally includes, but is not limited to, the following elements: (1) prohibit the paralegal from having any connection with the matter; (2) ban discussions with or the transfer of documents to or from the paralegal; (3) restrict access to files; and (4) educate all members of the firm, corporation or entity as to the separation of the paralegal (both organizationally and physically) from the pending matter. For more information regarding the Ethical Wall, see the NFPA publication entitled "The Ethical Wall—Its Application to Paralegals."

Glossary

Acceptance: In contract law, compliance with an offer that, together with the offer, constitutes an agreement.

Actual Cause: Also known as "but for" cause, meaning "but for" the act, the harm would not have resulted.

Administrative Law: Laws created by administrative agencies.

Affirmed: A decision by a higher court which is in agreement with the decision of the lower court.

Agreement: In contract law, an offer and an acceptance.

American Bar Association (ABA): A national organization of lawyers, with divisions for nonlawyers.

Analysis: In a memorandum of law, the step that comprises a conclusion, rule of law, facts/analysis, and repeated conclusion. Also referred to as a "legal answer."

Answer: In civil procedure, a written response to a complaint.

Appeal: The act of requesting that a higher court review the decision of a lower court.

Appellant: A person who brings an appeal (also known as "petitioner").

Appellee: A person against whom an appeal is brought (also known as "respondent").

Arson: Generally, the intentional burning of the property of another person.

Assault: The act of intentionally placing a person in apprehension of an unlawful, unprivileged, imminent offensive touching. The elements of this act may be broadened or narrowed depending on jurisdiction, and on whether the act is viewed as a crime or a tort.

Attorney/Paralegal-Client Privilege: Confidential information between an attorney or paralegal and a client. Generally, such communication is protected information that may not be disclosed.

Battery: An intentional, unlawful, unprivileged, offensive touching.

Bill: A proposed law to be brought before a legislative body. The word "bill" has various other definitions in the law, usually pertaining to certain types of legal documents.

Black Letter Law: Law that is concretely clear and not subject to significant interpretation.

Brief Answers: In a memorandum of law, a statement that answers the question presented using the same language in which it was raised.

Burglary: Generally, the act of intentionally breaking and entering into a building, with the intent at the time of the break-in to commit a felony while inside.

Capacity: Legal capability (typically) to consent.

Case Brief: A summary of a case opinion.

Case Digest: Summary of case law, primarily used as a reference tool.

Case Law: Law created by the court through a case opinion.

Checks and Balances: A system of our government, designed by its Framers, whereby each branch of the government may "check" or be checked by the other two, thus "balancing" the power of government.

Citation: Information about a court case, including the jurisdiction, year of the decision, and in what legal reference source the case is located.

Civil Law: The category of law in which the plaintiff is a direct party to the action, the goal is to compensate the aggrieved party, and the method of compensation is damages (usually money).

Closing Argument: An attorney's final statements summarizing the argument presented to the court.

Code of Federal Regulations (CFR): Federal code of administrative laws, primarily used as a reference tool.

Common Law: Law incorporated from custom and usage.

Comparative Negligence: A legal doctrine whereby the plaintiff will recover damages to the extent that he or she is not negligent.

Complaint: Along with a summons, the necessary pleading to formally begin a lawsuit.

Conclusion: In a memorandum of law, a statement answering a specific question presented or an overall summary of all brief answers and specific conclusions.

Concurring Opinion: A case opinion written by a judge who agrees with all or part of the judgment, but for different reasons.

Confidentiality: The responsibility to keep information private, such as that derived from communication between a client and a legal professional.

Conflict of Interest: A legal professional's act or conduct regarding one client that is contrary to another client's best interests. Such conduct is generally considered unethical.

Congress: The U.S. legislative body, composed of the Senate and the House of Representatives.

Consent: Permission or authorization for a certain act to take place.

Consideration: In contract law, something of value offered in exchange for something else of value.

Constitutional: The legality of a particular law or act determined insofar as it is consistent with the United States Constitution.

Contract: An agreement enforceable by law.

Contributory Negligence: A legal doctrine whereby the plaintiff will not recover damages arising out of a situation in which he or she has been negligent in any way.

Counterclaim: A claim presented as a response to a claim. For example, plaintiff brings a claim against defendant, who in turn brings a counterclaim against plaintiff.

Court of Appeals: A court where appeals are brought. On the federal level, courts where district court decisions are typically appealed.

Criminal Law: The category of law in which the plaintiffs are the people of the state or country, the goal is to punish the defendant, and the means of punishment is typically fine or imprisonment.

Cross-claim: A claim brought by one party against any other party to the action.

Cross-examination: The questioning of a witness by the opposing counsel.

Defamation: A false statement made intentionally or negligently to a third person who is reasonably likely to interpret the statement in a manner that will damage a person's reputation.

Default Judgment: Judgment against a party who failed to answer or otherwise respond to a complaint brought against that party.

Defendant: A person against whom a lawsuit is brought.

Defense: An exception that may legally excuse or justify noncompliance with a law or general rule.

Deponent: A person who gives a deposition.

Deposition: Testimony of a witness under oath, taken outside of the courtroom.

Detrimental Reliance: In contract law, if one party relies on a promise to his or her detriment, that party may be compensated even where there was no contract.

Direct examination: The questioning of a witness by the counsel who calls that witness.

Directed Verdict: A verdict ordered by a judge if the judge determines that there is in fact no issue to be decided by the jury.

Discovery: In civil procedure, a process by which one party may obtain information about the other party, typically through depositions and various records.

Dissenting Opinion: A case opinion written by a judge who disagrees with all or part of the judgment.

District Attorney: A prosecuting attorney who represents the people (of a state or of the entire United States) in a criminal matter.

District Court: The lowest-level federal court.

Duress: Coercion; it occurs when a person act; against his or her will.

Ethics: A set of values about what is good, right, and just.

Executive Branch: The branch of government that carries out the law.

Facts: In a case brief, an account of what happened.

Facts/Analysis: In a legal answer, a statement that bridges the rule of law with the specific facts at hand.

Federal Government: The tier of government that is centered in Washington, D.C., and is comprised of the 50 states. Its laws apply uniformly throughout the entire nation.

Federal Reporter: A publication of certain federal appeals cases, primarily used as a reference tool.

Federal Supplement: A publication of certain federal district court cases, primarily used as a reference tool.

Felony: A crime considered more serious than a misdemeanor and generally punishable by imprisonment.

Freelance Paralegal: A paralegal whose work is, wholly or partially, conducted independently of an attorney and not monitored by an attorney.

Garnishment: An act whereby a person's assets are used to pay that person's debt, usually by court order.

Governor: The head of each state's executive branch of government.

Heading: In a memorandum of law, the opening section that indicates, among other information, the subject of the memorandum.

Headnote: A note at the beginning of a court case that summarizes the legal principles that the court concluded.

Holding: The court's decision.

Homicide: The killing of a human being by another.

Hornbook: Text that explains some principles of law by subject.

House of Representatives: The legislative body that, along with the Senate, comprises the United States Congress.

Impeachment: An official criminal proceeding against an officer of the United States, typically for misconduct while in office. For instance, a proceeding brought by the House of Representatives against the President of the United States.

Implied Warranty of Merchantability: Implied assurance that a product is fit to work for its general purpose.

Independent Paralegal: A paralegal whose work is, wholly or partially, conducted independently of an attorney and not monitored by an attorney.

Intent: A mental state of committing an act knowingly and willingly.

Intentional Torts: Torts that are committed on purpose.

Interrogatories: Written questions presented to a party in a case by an opposing party.

Involuntary Manslaughter: Homicide resulting from criminal negligence, misdemeanors, or nondangerous felonies.

Issue: In a case brief, the question brought before the court.

Judgment: The deciding opinion of a court case.

Judicial Branch: The branch of government that interprets the law.

Jurisdiction: The legal power of a court to adjudicate a case.

Jury: A group of persons selected to decide the facts of a court case.

Larceny: Generally, the act of intentionally taking and carrying away another person's property, with the intent (often at the time of the taking) to permanently deprive the rightful owner of possession.

Law Review Article: A report (usually published by a law school) about a particular case, statute, or area of the law, written by a law professor, judge, lawyer, law student, or other legal scholar. Primarily used as a reference tool.

Lease: An agreement involving the use of property, such as one between a landlord and a tenant.

Legal Answer: An organized method of answering a legal question, by listing the conclusion, rule of law, facts/analysis, and repeated conclusion. Also referred to as an analysis of a memorandum of law.

Legal Encyclopedia: An encyclopedia that explains general principles of various areas of law. Primarily used as a reference tool.

Legislative Branch: The branch of government that creates the law.

Lexis: A computerized legal research service.

Libel: Written defamation.

Litigation: The process of a case going to trial in court.

Loose Constructionist: A judge who loosely interprets the United States Constitution to justify changing a particular law.

Majority Opinion: In a court case, the opinion shared by more than half of the judges who adjudicated the case.

Malum in Se: A crime considered to be morally wrong.

Malum Prohibitum: A crime not considered to be morally wrong.

Memorandum of Law: A written document that seeks to answer legal questions presented by means of legal analysis.

Minor: A person who is under the legal age of capacity (competence).

Misdemeanor: A crime considered less serious than a felony and generally not punishable by imprisonment.

Motion: A type of pleading requesting a specific action to be authorized by the court.

Negligence: The failure to use reasonable care when such a duty of care is owed, and the breach of this duty is the actual and proximate cause of resulting harm. (The elements of this mental state will vary depending on the jurisdiction and on whether the act is considered to be a crime or a tort.)

Offer: In contract law, a proposal that, together with its acceptance, constitutes an agreement.

Opening Statement: At trial, opportunity for attorneys on both sides to introduce themselves to the jury and to briefly explain what they intend to prove.

Opinion: The decision by the judge or judges in a court case.

Paralegal: Essentially, a legal assistant. Different agencies and offices may use the term "paralegal" in different ways.

Peremptory Challenge: An attorney's right to remove a juror without stating the cause.

Petitioner: A person who brings an appeal (also known as "appellant").

Plaintiff: A person who brings a lawsuit.

Pleadings: Documents involved in a lawsuit.

Plurality Opinion: In a court case, the opinion shared by the most judges, if not more than half of the total judges, who adjudicated the case.

Precedent: A court's examination of a previous case decision in order to decide a pending decision.

President of the United States: The United States chief executive (leader of the federal executive branch of government).

Primary Source: In legal research, a firsthand source — that is, the actual law. Generally, cases, statutes, and administratives laws are primary sources.

Pro Bono Work: Legal services performed free of charge.

Procedural Law: The law that governs legal process.

Process Server: A person who serves pleadings (such as a summons and complaint) upon a party to a lawsuit (such as a defendant).

Products Liability: A product designer's or manufacturer's strict liability for products he or she places into the stream of commerce.

Proximate Cause: A test for determining whether it was reasonably foreseeable that harm would result from a particular act.

Public Defender: An attorney who represents free of charge clients who cannot afford legal services.

Questions Presented: In a memorandum of law, the legal questions that must be answered.

Reasonableness: The reasonable person standard is an objective standard whereby behavior must be deemed reasonable by the fact-finder in a particular case.

Reasoning: In a case brief, the explanation for the court's holding.

Recklessness: A mental state wherein a harmful act is not committed purposely, but where there is an extremely high degree of probability of a harmful outcome. The elements of this mental state will vary depending on the jurisdiction, and on whether the act is considered a crime or a tort.

Redirect Examination: The act of questioning a witness by the counsel who originally called that witness, after that witness has been cross-examined.

Regional Reporter: A publication of state court cases from a particular region of the United States. Primarily used as a reference tool.

Reporter: In legal research, a series of books containing a complete set of published cases from a particular jurisdiction or region of jurisdictions.

Respondent: A person against whom an appeal is brought (also known as "appellee").

Restatement: Text that explains some principles of law by subject.

Reversed: A decision by a higher court that invalidates the decision of a lower court.

Robbery: Generally, larceny by force or threat of force.

Rule of Law: In a legal answer, the reference to the law that supports the answer or conclusion to a particular issue.

Secondary Source: In legal research, an authority of law that explains or otherwise describes a primary source (i.e., the actual law).

Senate: The legislative body that, along with the House of Representatives, comprises the United States Congress.

Service of Process: The act of serving pleadings (such as a summons and complaint) upon a party to a lawsuit (such as a defendant).

Shepardizing: The act of updating the law by use of Shepard's citators.

Shepard's Citators: Publications that deal with the entire history of a particular case or statute. Used as a research tool in order to evaluate the current status of a particular source of law.

Slander: Spoken defamation.

Slander per Se: Slander where the plaintiff may automatically recover without having to prove damages.

Solicitation of Legal Services: A legal professional's act of approaching another person to offer legal services. Generally, this conduct is considered unethical.

State Government: The tier of government that presides over an individual state.

Statement of Facts: In a memorandum of law, an account of the facts that are relevant to the questions presented.

Statute: A law created by a legislative body.

Statute of Frauds: A rule of law that specifies when a contract must be in writing.

Strict Constructionist: A judge who strictly interprets the wording of the Constitution and is not likely to alter the law to fit contemporary standards.

Strict Liability: Responsibility without intent, recklessness, or negligence.

Substantive Law: The elements of the law — that is, the actual law itself.

Summons: Along with a complaint, the necessary pleading to formally begin a lawsuit.

Supremacy Clause: The U.S. Constitution's proclamation of its superiority over any state law.

Syllabus: Found at or near the beginning of a published opinion, a short summary of the case that briefly states the facts and the holding. Sometimes referred to as a "synopsis."

Tort: A civil wrong not based on a contract.

Tortfeasor: A person who has committed a tort.

Transferred Intent: Where a person intends on committing an act against one person but inadvertently commits the act against another person, the act is deemed to have been intentional against the second person as well.

Trial: The first (and, often, only) judicial phase of a lawsuit.

Unconscionable: Extremely unjust. Often used as a basis for voiding a contract.

United States Code: A text containing federal statutes.

United States Constitution: The document on which the United States government was based and continues to be the supreme law of the United States.

United States Reporter: A publication of United States Supreme Court cases.

United States Supreme Court: The highest court of the United States.

Voluntary Manslaughter: Generally, intentional homicide with mitigating circumstances.

Westlaw: A computerized legal research service.

Will: A person's declaration (usually written) regarding the disposition of his or her property after death.

Witness: In civil procedure, a person who testifies in court, usually about something he or she has seen, heard, or knows.

Index